Public Speaking in American English

A Guide for Non-Native Speakers

NANCY GRASS HEMMERT

Santa Monica College

Boston New York San Francisco
Mexico City Montreal Toronto London Madrid Munich Paris
Hong Kong Singapore Tokyo Cape Town Sydney

DEDICATION

To my mentor, my hero, my friend,
who taught me how to give my first speech,
this book is for you, Mom.

Editor-in-Chief: Karon Bowers
Assistant Editor: Jenny Lupica
Marketing Manager: Suzan Czajkowski
Production Supervisor: Beth Houston
Composition Buyer: Linda Cox
Manufacturing Buyer: JoAnne Sweeney
Editorial-Production Service, Text Design,
and Electronic Composition: Elm Street Publishing Services, Inc.
Photo Researcher: Poyee Oster

For related titles and support materials, visit our online catalog at www.ablongman.com.

Library of Congress Cataloging-in-Publication Data

Grass Hemmert, Nancy
Public speaking in American English: a guide for non-native speakers / Nancy Grass Hemmert. — 1st ed.
p. cm.
ISBN 978-0-205-43099-4 (alk. paper)
1. English language—Textbooks for foreign speakers. 2. Public speaking—Problems, exercises, etc. 3. English language—Spoken English—Problems, exercises, etc. I. Title.
PE1128.G6538 2007
808.5'1—dc22 2007016496

ISBN-13: 978-0-205-43099-4
ISBN-10: 0-205-43099-6

Printed in the United States of America

Photo credits begin on page 388, which constitutes a continuation of the copyright page.

Table of Contents

Preface

Welcome! Several years ago when I was still a young and relatively inexperienced teacher, I was asked to teach a public speaking class designed especially for non-native speakers of English. I walked in on the first day to find nervous-looking faces from Korea, India, France, Japan, and Africa. I was nervous, too. What did I, who was born and raised in Los Angeles, know about the experiences of people coming to a foreign country, speaking a complicated and confusing language, and deciphering often-contradictory nonverbal behaviors? Additionally, there was no textbook beyond the traditional public speaking textbook to rely on to help these students. So I asked them, "What are you hoping to get out of this class?" "What are you most concerned about?" "What do you think your greatest difficulty will be in passing this class?"

Luckily, they told me—slowly and timidly at first—but as some shared their thoughts and ideas, others joined in. Together, we made it through that first semester. We all learned a lot. They learned how to write and present speeches for diverse audiences using a U.S. American style of public speaking. They also learned how to gather information about their audiences and topics, how to put that information into an outline, how to practice their speeches, and how to deliver their speeches so that the audience could truly enjoy them.

They learned how to write and present speeches. I learned about some of the special challenges international and immigrant speakers face, in addition to the hardships of translating words and thoughts into a sometimes difficult and confusing language. Even worse, they had to "translate" what they knew about "proper" public address from their home culture to a very different "proper" style that is used here in the United States. For many, this second set of challenges was even more difficult than the first. Nonverbal behavior, logical arrangement, word choice, levels of formality, and audience expectations can vary greatly from one country to the next, but we often assume that everyone is aware of the cultural standards before we begin teaching the basics of public speaking. These "standards" for public speaking amount to hidden biases that must be explained, examined, and understood in order for any student to fully understand how to give "successful" presentations to English-speaking audiences. In short, public speaking in your own language is hard enough, but having to give a speech in a language other than one's own to an audience that speaks that other language can seem impossible. That is why I wrote this book.

This book is intended for college students who speak English as their nonprimary language and who are taking a standard public speaking course—that is, students newly immigrated to the United States, exchange students, and international students. This book goes beyond providing the essential elements of "good" public speaking in the United States and reveals the subtle and pronounced biases in, differences from, and similarities to public speaking standards around the globe. We will compare how various cultures and languages view public speaking to how public speaking is viewed in the United States, and give you, the student, useful, concrete, and helpful suggestions for preparing and delivering a successful speech in English to an American English-speaking audience.

How does one write a textbook that is supposed to address the particular concerns of students from all over the world who speak dozens of different languages and experience a variety of different cultural challenges? Well, that is easy—ask students who have already experienced a public speaking course to share the most challenging and confusing aspects of learning to give speeches in American English. Many of the concerns, difficulties, and challenges that you are likely to experience over the course of this semester will be similar to those of other students whose first language is not English, no matter what that first language may be.

I want to begin by talking about the terms we will use in this book. I have chosen the term *non-native English speakers*, or *non-native* for short, because I think that this term best represents the types of students drawn to this course. To me, "non-native" indicates a person who has been learning English as a second or third language, who speaks his or her other language(s) fluently and confidently, and who has a fairly good grasp of the English language—but who also might not understand some of the subtleties of the language and the nonverbal and cultural aspects of language. When we learn a new language, we often do not learn the subtle linguistic and nonverbal differences until we have inadvertently violated the rules. This can be embarrassing and can undermine our confidence.

Other terms that we often hear are *LEP* and *ESL*. I chose not to use these terms because LEP, or Limited English Proficiency, simply does not accurately reflect the difficulties you might be having in communicating in English. You might be very proficient in the formal or written forms of the English language but not yet comfortable with the formal oral uses, such as in public speaking, of the language. Similarly, ESL, or English as a Second Language, for many of you is simply not accurate because English may be your third, fourth, or fifth language. Additionally, ESL often refers to a specific department in a school or university for which this book is not designed. Finally, neither of these terms allows us to look at the hidden biases in using one language over another that are often known only by native speakers. This is the problem I hope to rectify in this book by carefully examining the various underlying or hidden biases in teaching U.S. American public speaking. Every culture has its own preferred way to communicate interpersonally, in groups, and in public. The way we communicate in the United States is just one way—not the best or the only way, just the way it is done in American English.

Like all writers, I did not write this book alone. Many people made this book possible. All too often, the dozens of people who support, review, contribute, encourage, and guide an author through the writing process receive little more than an acknowledgment at the beginning of the book, so I implore you, dear reader, to take a few minutes to quietly acknowledge those people who helped me and to read on. First, I want to thank my mentors and colleagues who contributed to this project both directly and indirectly. Thank you, Rebecca Litke, Christie Logan, Elizabeth Berry, Ben Attias, and Barbara Baird who taught me how to teach and listen, and how to account for diversity in every interaction. Thank you to Nate Brown, Deborah Kraut, Garen Baghdasarian, Gary Squier, Karen Peck, John Weaver, Brenda Antrim, and Peter Marston, who provided ideas, examples, sample speeches, and tutorials. A special thank you to Pat Lyon—I knew you were the right person for the job.

Thank you to Sergio Ortiz, who allowed me to use some of his photographs. Thank you to Paul Scott and Jimmy "Guitar" Smith, who took photographs and wrote sample speeches; even though they didn't ultimately make it into the book, the work was great and very appreciated. A big thank you goes to J. Mark Morale, who created the graphics throughout the book. He not only did a great job; he also did it with no notice, no time, and a lot of humor. Another big thank you goes to Leslie Waller, who worked months on artwork for the text and drove through Los Angeles traffic (so that I wouldn't have to) to bring it all together. And to all the models in the various photos throughout the book, thank you for being so real. A special thanks to Warren Cancilla, who carried me through the final moments of printing to make the deadline.

Thank you to my teams of student researchers and other contributors who provided content, examples, personal experiences, and sample speeches. To my dream team of Leslie Valdivia (who also contributed a sample speech), Kevin Chicas, Silverio Martinez, and Richard Morgain, who took on this challenge, who believed in the project, and who made the early stages of research possible, thank you. Thank you, Gina Cole and Lori Tyra, for getting me organized. Thank you, too, to my follow-up assistants, Joshua Holley, Harold Vancol, and Anita Sarkeesian, and their support team of Brett Bayone and Ashton Johnson, who dropped everything when I needed help and who kept me laughing through some of the rough spots. I especially would like to thank my non-native students, who tolerated surveys, discussion groups, and photo shoots and who not only test-read the book when it was done but also contributed the personal experiences, sample speeches, and examples that fill the pages of this book. The book was written not only for them but also, to a large degree, *by* them, especially those cited throughout the book in *What Others Say;* the students who contributed sample speeches, Linda Augustine, Wai Ju (Anke) Kwong, and Channelle Khoubian; and Joon Myoung Hwong, who kept word lists for me throughout the project.

Of course, huge thanks go to the Allyn & Bacon team, who made this project possible. At the top of the list, thank you to Karon Bowers, who recognized the need for this book and moved mountains to take a chance on an unknown author. Thank you to Brian Wheel, who helped me get the book started, and to Jenny Lupica and Beth Houston, who carried it through to the end with tremendous patience, support, and guidance. Thank you, too, to all the graphics, layout, design, art, editing, indexing, and other people who took the mass of computer paper and turned it into something beautiful and readable. I would also like to thank Eric Arima and his team at Elm Street Publishing Services—you guys are amazing.

Thanks, also, to the reviewers who provided thoughtful commentary on this book as it developed. These include: Virginia L. Downie, Chaffey College; Dan Flickstein, Brooklyn College; Helena Halmari, University of Florida; Elaine R. Hayden, San Antonio College; DJ Kaiser, Washington University of St. Louis; Yaping Li, College of San Mateo; Rebecca A. Litke, California State University, Northridge; Jennifer Reem, Nova Southeastern University; Carol Siri Johnson, New Jersey Institute of Technology; Shirley H. Terrell, Collin County Community College; Melinda S. Womack, Santiago Canyon College; Quentin Wright, Mountain View College.

Big thanks go to my family and friends, who have carried me through this process from start to finish. Anyone who has ever accomplished anything in life knows that we do not go it alone. Parents, siblings, cousins, and friends are the reasons any of us ever get anything done. This project is no different. Thank you to Donna Hemmert Bauman, Sandra Grass, Jodi Grass, and Ron Downie for giving me space to write, listening to me complain, and giving me ideas to get me through. To my dad, Bob Grass, thank you for telling me you are proud and for believing I could do this even when it seemed to be taking a very long time. Thank you Jennifer Solis and Rob Grass who knew I could do it. To my mom, Ginny Downie, thank you, thank you, thank you. In so many ways, we did this together. You amaze me. I always wanted to be you when I grew up.

Finally, thank you to my little family at home. To my children, Sarah and Adam Hemmert, who sacrificed dinners together and time to hang out and who patiently read, listened to, and even contributed to the book; who provided honest and constructive feedback; and who told me, "You can do it, Mom" whenever I felt like giving up, thank you. And to Deirdre Weaver, my partner, my love, my friend—where could I possibly begin to thank you? You have been and done everything for me. From start to finish of this project, you have been perfect. From setting up work space to arranging meals to scouring the library stacks to rubbing my feet, you have read, edited, contributed, researched, supported, encouraged, and more. Truly, I could not have done this without you being there at every turn. I thank you and love you.

CHAPTER 1 Introduction to Public Speaking

CHAPTER GOAL

By the end of this chapter, you will have a better understanding of the history and significance of public speaking around the world.

So, you have to take a public speaking class, eh?

Let us begin by looking at who you are and why you are here. Most likely, you are taking this class for one of two reasons: (1) The school you are attending or wish to attend requires students to take a public speaking course; (2) You believe that a public speaking course will benefit you. Additionally, you are probably in a class designed for non-native speakers of English. You speak at least one other language (and from my experience, I would guess that you probably speak two or three other languages), and you have lived much of your life outside the United States, Great Britain, or another predominately English-speaking country.

I also can predict that you are, at best, a little shy about giving presentations in English and, at worst, are ready to drop the course and run away, never to look back. Relax. Some amount of anxiety about this course is natural and healthy, even for native English speakers. Try not to worry. In this book we will address your concerns and offer many hints and suggestions on how to successfully present your thoughts, ideas, and opinions to a variety of audiences and in a variety of situations.

Rhetoric
The effective use of language in both speaking and writing; the study of persuasion and persuasive methods through speaking and writing.

In this chapter, we will look at why public speaking is so important for you to study and why in the United States we teach public speaking the way that we do. We will examine the history and biases of the "Western" style of public speaking and how this style is similar to and different from other rhetorical styles around the world. Then we will discuss the elements of communication and how culture affects the successful exchange of ideas. So, take a deep breath and let's get to work.

THE NEED FOR PUBLIC SPEAKING

No matter what country you come from, what languages you speak, what career you pursue, or where you live, public speaking is and will be an important part of your life. Although the manner in which speeches are prepared and delivered throughout the world differs, speeches are made in every language and in every country of the world. Whether proposing a toast at a wedding, giving a eulogy at a funeral, presenting research for a classroom assignment, or reporting to management on a current project, you probably have given or will give a speech as part of your personal and professional lives.

WHAT OTHERS SAY

"I have never given a speech in Farsi, but I know that it would be much different if it were given in English. For example, at the end of a speech Persians would end with a little nod with the head."

Ghazall,
Iran

You also listen to presentations frequently. As a citizen of the world, you are exposed daily to the prepared thoughts and messages of politicians, business and world leaders, advertisers, entertainers, comedians, and teachers. Additionally, many of the skills required for creating and delivering messages through public speaking are the same skills needed for effective communication in everyday life. Understanding effective presentations and speeches, then, is very important to both giving and receiving messages.

The various communication skills that you will learn in this course are the same skills business professionals look for in their employees. Recently graduated college students agree. In a 2004 study, researchers surveyed college graduates about the most important skills and competencies they felt were essential to post-college success. Communication skills, specifically oral and written communication and public speaking, were considered the most important for academic, professional, and personal success.[1] Perhaps most exciting is that the communication skills you will learn in this class can be transferred to other communication contexts, such as with family, friends, co-workers, and teachers. Successful completion of a public speaking course can offer you many benefits, both personal and professional (see Tables 1.1 and 1.2), but, as a non-native speaker of English, a course in public speaking offers *you* even more!

Communication Competence The ability to communicate appropriately and successfully.

As a non-native speaker of English, this course offers you a chance to practice speaking and listening skills in English in a controlled and safe environment. You will get to know other students with similar challenges and concerns. Like many other international and non-native students, you may feel shy about conversing in English, whether to other students or to faculty, and you may seek other students who speak your native language. Who can blame you? You listen to English all day long in school, on TV, in stores, and in restaurants. You are required to read textbooks in English for classes, ob-

TABLE 1.1 What Employers Want

1. Oral and written communication skills
2. Research/critical thinking skills
3. Interpersonal skills
4. Adaptability/flexibility
5. Teamwork/team player
6. Creative problem-solving skills
7. Leadership skills
8. Multicultural/global awareness and sensitivity
9. Organizational skills
10. Information technology/computer skills

This represents a summary of the most commonly desired skills from dozens of job search and career websites around the English-speaking world.

TABLE 1.2 Public Speaking Skills That Aid in College Success

1. Research and organizational skills
2. Pronunciation, articulation, and clarity
3. Classroom presentation skills
4. Knowing how to support an argument
5. Critical thinking and analytical skills

Students who take public speaking and/or other communication courses report higher self-confidence and greater overall college success.

serve English on highway signs, and choose meals from menus written in English. It must be exhausting! Why wouldn't you look for someone who speaks your home language? It is familiar, comfortable, and easy! The drawback is that you might get very little practice in speaking English, and, as we all know, the best way to improve speaking skills is to *speak*!

This book will also provide you with specific information on how to understand the subtle and confusing nonverbal aspects of U.S. American communication and offer you insight into U.S. cultural beliefs and values. By studying the preferred public communication patterns in the United States, you will better understand the messages you encounter from the media, from your teachers, and from others in the community. Many of the key aspects of public speaking in most cultures are simply exaggerations of the preferred styles of communication in general, so your overall ability to speak and understand U.S. American English will improve as you expand your knowledge and skills in public speaking.

CONSIDERING LANGUAGE

More countries grant "official language" status to English than to any other language in the world.

Dr. Verner Bickley, chairman of the English Speaking Union in Hong Kong, points out that "English is no longer the possession of one country or one set of countries but . . . has a vital role to play in today's world in helping people to cross communication barriers."[2] Because English is considered the "language of business" and is currently the most widely used language for business in the world, you will discover that learning the Western style, specifically the U.S. American style, of public speaking offers greater benefits in the world of business both in the United States and abroad. Indeed, other countries frequently expect to hear the U.S. American style. This is not to say that when we travel to or address audiences in other parts of the world that we should not have to adapt and tailor our messages to those cultures—we definitely should, but much of the standard in business today is borrowed from the U.S. style. Knowing this style, even only as a way to understand others, can give you an advantage in business.

HISTORY OF PUBLIC SPEAKING AROUND THE WORLD

No one country's public speaking or *rhetorical style* (i.e., the way one builds and presents an argument) is better than another's. Each culture or country develops the style that best serves the needs of its people. In fact, many cultures around the world share much of the same rhetorical history, but each country or culture has added to and/or emphasized different aspects of these rhetorical roots.

African

The earliest known text on rhetoric is from ancient Egypt, dating back to 2500 BCE. This text suggests how everyday people can structure oral arguments to defend themselves or "plead their cases" in official business. The text recommends a variety of ways to represent oneself to various audiences,

The earliest known text on rhetoric comes from ancient Egypt.

including using deference and humility with superiors, gentleness with inferiors, silence when arguing with equals, and avoidance of quarrelsome speech. In every case, the long-term development of a "good reputation" is paramount. Its underlying principle is that the good and just person seldom needs to argue because s/he is "right," and virtue will prevail.

Egyptian rhetoric also focused strongly on spirituality. Egyptians believed that when we are spiritually in tune, we can better appeal to others: "Saints, sages, seers, and poets feel connected to nature and to people, and these highly spiritual individuals often attain the highest excellence in oral and written expression."[3]

Today, the legacy of that early African rhetoric is evident in Yoruba (Nigeria). Sproule explains that in Yoruba:

> Advocacy takes place within a tribal structure of roles where there is a desire for a quick attainment of consensus to preserve communal harmony. Disputes are lodged with the appropriate official who varies from the oldest male of the family up to the King. Speakers are expected to show respect to the magistrate and to use ceremonial modes of address.[4]

Above all, the people of Yoruba value speech that maintains the integrity of the community over the success of the individual.

Western

Most scholars date the beginning of the Western rhetorical tradition to ancient Greece around 500 BCE. The need for citizens to learn effective communication skills arose from the development of democracy, which allowed

The Western rhetorical tradition can be traced back to the ancient Greeks.

people to own land, settle their own disputes in court, and participate in government. To do these things, people had to learn how to construct logical and understandable arguments, and to provide evidence for their claims.

To meet this need, a few people, known as the Sophists, began teaching communication skills, specifically oratory. Corax, Gorgias, and Protagoras were the celebrities of the time, impressing students and audiences with their persuasive and eloquent speeches. It was there that the early elements of Western public address began taking shape.

Soon Plato and Aristotle arrived on the scene. Plato challenged the ethics of rhetoric as taught by the Sophists and, after many long years of study and heartache over the best and most ethical way to discover truth, Plato developed an "ideal rhetoric" that dealt with the "proper" ethics of rhetoric as well as with issues of organization, delivery, and style.

The Western rhetorical tradition owes much to Aristotle and his work *On Rhetoric*, which offers the first systematic categorization of rhetoric. Aristotle used both the work of the Sophists and the work of Plato in developing his own comprehensive treatment of rhetoric. What emerged was a treatise on the various components of rhetoric, or the first four "canons of rhetoric": Invention, arrangement, style, and delivery (see Table 1.3).[5]

A Roman rhetorician, Cicero, added the canon *memory*. He taught a method for remembering one's presentation without the use of notes so that speakers would seem even more competent and impressive. Cicero also argued, much like teachers of public speaking argue today, that learning the ba-

TABLE 1.3 The Canons of Rhetoric

Invention: Finding and discovering the supporting material and arguments of a speech.
Arrangement: Arranging your arguments and ideas.
Style: Choosing the language.
Memory: Means for remembering a presentation without the use of notes.
Delivery: Presenting the speech.

sics of good public address is a practical way to maintain a free society. Like Aristotle, Cicero believed "the goals of teaching rhetoric, speech communication, are closely tied to two ideas—teaching individuals to speak well and teaching them the value of responsibility to society."[6]

Quintillian, another Roman rhetorician, filled out the Classical roots of rhetoric by reminding speakers that true credibility comes from truly being a good person. He stressed that one must not simply "act" good or produce a good-sounding argument; a speaker must actually be a person of good character so that his/her character will speak for him- or herself.

From these early teachers, the Western style of public address gained an emphasis on ethics, proof, logic, delivery style, and organization. You probably recognize many of these ideas and concepts because these elements of "good" rhetoric, whether written arguments or public speeches, can still be found in rhetorical styles throughout the world.

In the United States today, the preferred public speaking style of many politicians, actors, business professionals, and professional speakers uses a more personal and conversational delivery style, but still relies heavily on solid evidence and clear organization. This style combines a structured, clear, well-supported message with a conversational, warm delivery style to which audiences respond well. As researchers Morreale and Backlund tell us:

> As we advanced through the twentieth century, the communication field shifted emphasis from the individual's relation to society to the individual's relations with other individuals. . . . Many writers . . . looked at communication education and curricula as a means of achieving desirable relationships in multiple communication situations and contexts.[7]

Finally, we have to acknowledge the incredible influence global movement has had on public speaking styles here in the United States. From every speaker from around the globe who speaks to U.S. audiences, we gain a piece of his/her home style: New kinds of supporting material, different ways to organize speeches, creative language choices, and more. Every world leader, business executive, and student speaker expands the possibilities of what can and will be used by others in the United States because we all learn by observing what we like and don't like in other speakers. What we have today in the United States is the result of 2,300 years of development, and the U.S. American rhetorical style is still growing and changing today.

Although within the United States there is a wide variety of cultural variations in and a multitude of individual styles of public speaking, most handbooks, texts, and public speaking classes in the United States stress an Aristotelian approach that emphasizes statistics, examples, organization, logical arrangement, linguistic style, and clarity. Equally significant, in the United States audiences are expected to listen quietly, provide subtle feedback, and show appreciation at the end of the speech through applause; above all, U.S. American audiences appreciate originality.

Each of these elements will be discussed thoroughly in the following chapters. However, before we go on, let us look at some of the other rhetorical styles around the world and see how they are similar to and different from the rhetorical styles found here.

Asian

Rhetoric in China is not identified as a separate discipline the way it has been in the West. The closest word in Chinese to our term *rhetoric* would be *bian*. Much of what we know about Chinese rhetoric is from the "Tao Te Ching," an important Chinese historical and philosophical text. In China, rhetoric, like most aspects of Chinese society, is interconnected not only with politics and philosophy, but also with religion, ethics, social relations, and psychology.[8]

Ancient Chinese rhetoric valued sincerity, depth, and virtue. As rhetorical historians Lu and Frank tell us:

> The Taoist perspective on rhetoric is rooted in its philosophical orientation; namely *wuwei* which means to speak and act without artificiality and superficiality. . . . Taoist rhetoric condemns glib tongues, excessive talk, and flowery speech, but does not condemn speech that is appropriate to the occasion and that is aimed at achieving Te (virtue).[9]

Simple language and fewer words were honored as the better way to share ideas. Context—or the events, people, and situations surrounding the rhetorical event—was paramount: "to break truth into separable fragments is to destroy it."[10] Meaning exists only in context, and context includes everything.

Although many words emerged to describe speech behavior after Confucius, two words, *ming* and *bian*, best described the two diverging philosophies of rhetoric. For Confucius (551–479 BCE), *ming*, one form of *bian*, represented the link "between social order and proper speech behavior."[11] Thus, ming came to be used in political contexts and for social harmony. However, some began using ming to refer to a form of argument. According to Lao, they did not use politics and ethics in argumentation; instead, they "relied on reasoning, logic or metaphysical theory rather than historical and cultural evidence. . . . This school was known for its sophistry."[12] In other words, they corrupted the "pure" intent of Confucius to suit their rhetorical needs.

Although the Chinese philosophers condemned these rhetorical practices, they did not condemn bian itself, for bian still represented a good per-

Make a list of everything that you know about public speaking in your home country. Then make a list of what you understand about public speaking in the United States. Compare these two lists. What is similar? What is different? What areas do you think are going to be the most challenging for you? What areas do you think are going to be easy?

son speaking well. As Confucius wrote, "A good person should speak well; but those who speak well are not necessarily a good person."[13] Like their Greek counterparts such as Plato and Aristotle, the great Chinese philosophers denounced flamboyant and showy speeches. Today, speakers who use flowery or empty rhetoric in China are still seen as shallow, distrustful, and untrustworthy.

Similar to the Greek tradition, bian developed over many centuries and through many cultural and philosophical changes. Although Western scholars have, in the past, claimed that the Chinese do not use "logic," more recent evidence shows that the Chinese history of argument shares some fundamental similarities to that of the West, such as the uses of deductive, analogical, and inductive reasoning, among other things.

Similar to the rhetorical histories of Africa and China, the rhetorics of India and Japan also stress maintaining harmony in the community. Japanese rhetoric avoids explicit statements and arguments and instead allows the audience to draw conclusions through inferring what the speaker means as he or she talks around the topic. Japanese also value silence and withholding emotion.

India, too, according to J. Michael Sproule:

> tended to share the Chinese/Japanese interest in a speaker's invocation of cultural truths while seeking to attain harmony and consensus. The goal of the wise person in India was to gain liberation from worldly goods and desires. The effort was to gain knowledge of absolute truths through silent meditation and repetition of ritual phrases. Truthful speech was thought to be that which revealed aspects of the greater cosmic and social order of things.[14]

Again, like the rhetorical traditions of China and Japan, Indian rhetoric maintains that excessive talk and self-praise are contrary to finding truth and that sincerity, humility, and deference to social harmony are the indicators of truth being told. In all three Asian traditions, the aim is not about winning in the moment, but in slowly building trust and credibility so that in time, truth will be created along with the relationship.

South American

Central and South American countries often draw their rhetorical traditions from a variety of influences, but mostly their traditions are a combination of the Western rhetorical tradition and the individual indigenous traditions found in the various countries where the Catholic Church has a strong influence (as many as ninety-six percent of the people in some South American countries are devout Catholics). Although we will not trace the specific rhetorical history of each of these countries, here are some generalizations we can make about the South American rhetorical tradition: Most significantly, personal feelings and faith are the most accepted evidence in most discussions. Objective facts are accepted only as long as they do not interfere with subjective feelings and experiences or with the teachings of the listeners' faith. The focus on personal relationships in general as the source of true success in life makes personal relationships more important than business relationships. In presentations, this value is apparent in the way people talk less directly about specific arguments and focus more on establishing connection with the audience and finding common ground to maintain harmony within the social group or community. From a U.S. perspective, this approach may be seen as indirect, unclear, and not getting "to the point."

These represent only a sample of the various rhetorical traditions found around the world. We could write several books on each continent's, region's, or country's specific rhetorical roots. For example, other rich traditions include the Middle Eastern, European, and Russian histories of public address. To be fair, we will talk a little about some of the specifics of each of these traditions throughout the text. For now, though, it should be clear that there is not one correct history or approach to "good" public speaking or rhetoric. Each group of people has developed and refined its particular style to suit its own particular needs. In cultures where family and community are of primary importance, relationship building becomes paramount; where religion is the foundation of social life, the Bible, Torah, or Quran are the source of evidence; and where self-preservation and personal property are most valued, objective evidence and "logical" reasoning are found.

As students of the U.S. American style of public address, you can draw not only on the skills and preferences taught here, but you can also supplement and color your presentations with the styles found in your own rhetorical traditions, mixing styles to both suit and move the audience, as well as to suit you. Fortunately, the U.S. style encourages an individual, conversational style that highlights the speaker's own strengths and personality, so don't be afraid to draw from your own culture as you develop presentations to engage your U.S. American audiences.

THE ELEMENTS OF COMMUNICATION

There are five types of communication in which we participate on a daily basis: intrapersonal, interpersonal, group, organizational, and mass communication (see Table 1.4). Speeches or presentations can be given in any of these types of communication. You prepare a "speech" when you propose marriage to the love of your life. You might speak at a club meeting about your vision for the group. You may give a speech to friends and family at your graduation

TABLE 1.4 **Types of Communication**

Level	Number of People	Characteristics
Intrapersonal	1	Private and to yourself
		Your own thoughts
Interpersonal	2	One-to-one
		Private with one other person
Group	3 to 15	Usually decision-making groups (e.g., school study groups, small work groups)
Organizational	More than 15	Often mediated (bulletins, newsletters, memos, etc.)
		Large networks of people with common goals (e.g., a company, a school, etc.)
Mass	Audiences larger than those immediately present	Mediated: uses television, videotape, print, and computer
		Public communication

from college. "Public speaking," then, is not just for large audiences in traditionally public places. Public speaking can be as intimate as a dinner party with close friends or as truly public as addressing your graduating class or conducting a televised press conference announcing your company's latest cutting-edge product!

As your public speaking skills improve, so too will your overall *communication competence*. Earlier we defined communication competence as the "ability to communicate appropriately and successfully." Luckily, many of the skills you already use and the challenges you already face in your everyday conversations with friends, co-workers, and family are the same challenges you will encounter in public speaking. You will also be able to use the skills you learn here to improve your communication in other contexts.

All communication interactions have the same seven elements that affect how the message is produced, transmitted, received, and interpreted. If there is a difficulty in any one of these elements, the chances increase that the message will be altered, distorted, changed, or even not received. So what are these magical elements of communication?

Every communication interaction begins with a *sender* (also called the *speaker, presenter, source*, or *encoder*) and a *receiver* (also called the *listener, audience*, or *decoder*). The sender is the person who has an idea or thought that s/he wants to share with someone else. (See Figure 1.1.)

Because no one can directly share or experience another person's feelings or thoughts, the speaker must turn that thought into a *message*: an idea put into a form that can be actually seen, heard, or otherwise experienced by another person (e.g., a word or facial expression). The message is the third element of

FIGURE 1.1 The Communication Model

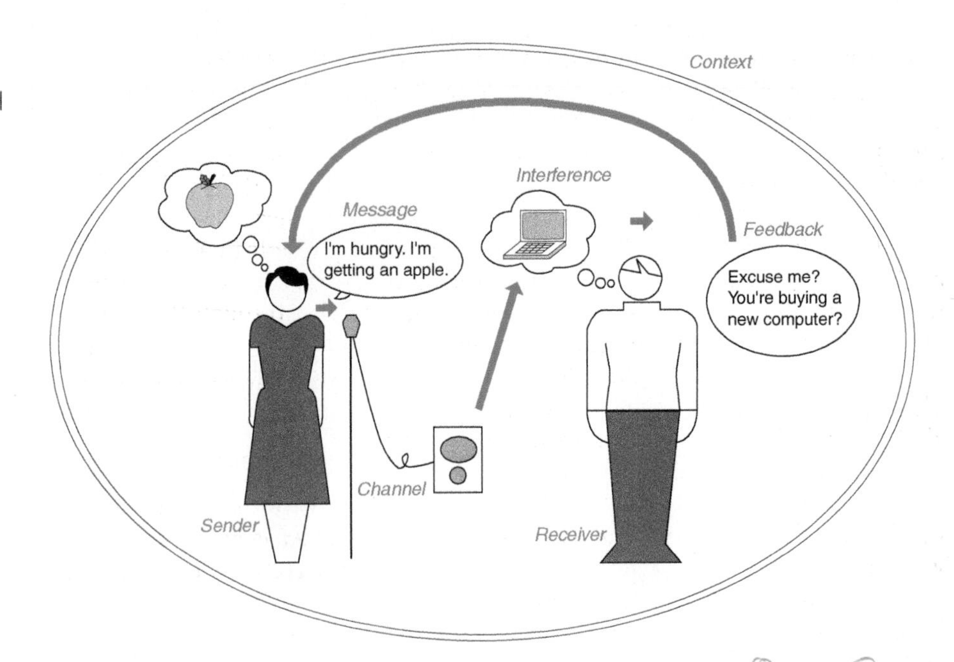

the communication process. An encoded message can be written, spoken, expressed in sign language, or shown in other ways such as wearing a favorite perfume or giving a hug. The process of turning the idea into a message is called *encoding*.

The content of the encoded message is the words: "It looks like we are going to have a storm!" Obviously, a message must be meant for someone (or many people), and that someone is the *receiver.* The receiver hears, reads, sees, smells, tastes, or feels the message and makes sense out of it by *decoding* the message (interpreting the message according to his/her own experience). (See Figure 1.1.)

The *channel*, the fourth element of communication, is the way or the mean through which the message travels from the sender to the receiver. In most public speaking situations, sound waves act as the channel carrying the speaker's voice to the audience's ears while light waves convey nonverbal elements such as facial expressions and eye contact. Sometimes the channel can be touch, such as when we give someone a hug to show support, or taste, such as when we give candy to express love. Other channels include the Internet, which carries e-mail messages; paper, which carries advertising or business messages; and television, which carries a multitude of mass media messages.

Nonverbal Communication Messages sent without the use of words, whether spoken, written, or expressed in sign language.

The fifth element of communication is called *interference*. Interference is anything that changes, distorts, or obstructs the intended message and includes the noises, thoughts, feelings, or sensations that might make it hard for the receiver to understand or decode the message accurately. Interference can come from anywhere. The speaker can create interference by using offensive language, speaking unclearly or too quietly, or by wearing inappropriate or unusual clothing. The receiver can be the source of the interference if s/he is thinking about other things, making other noises, talking to other people, or contemplating what the speaker is wearing instead of what the speaker is saying. Interference can also come from the room if the heat is too high or people are walking in and out. Anything that makes understanding the speaker's message more difficult to understand is interference.

There are three kinds of interference: physical, physiological, and psychological. *Physical interferences* come from the surrounding environment: traffic noises, rustling papers, or a pungent smell wafting through the room. *Physiological interferences* are the distractions that come from the communicators themselves. The speaker's having a particularly difficult accent to decipher, speaking too quickly, or stuttering frequently can inhibit the audience's ability to understand the message clearly. Similarly, if a receiver has a headache or is feeling chilled, s/he may not be able to concentrate effectively on the message. *Psychological interference* comes from the thoughts and feelings of the speakers and listeners themselves. If a speaker is angry, excited, worried, or scared, s/he may have trouble getting the words out coherently, or, as an audience member worrying about giving the next speech, s/he may have trouble listening at all! Think about the last time you had an argument with someone you cared about. Were you able to focus your attention on your studies immediately after? If you were like most people, the answer would be, "No." Psychological interference can be the most difficult kind of communication interference because we create it ourselves!

The sixth element in the communication process is *feedback*. Feedback includes any message, either verbal or nonverbal, that the receiver sends back to the sender in response to the message. A confused look, a question, a laugh, a frown, a nodding head, and silence are all forms of feedback. In our earlier picture of the receiver (Figure 1.1), his smile might indicate that he is happy that rain is in the forecast or that he thinks the speaker is funny.

The seventh element of communication, the *context* of the speech, includes the time, place, and occasion for the speech, as well as the cultural, psychological, and historical context of the interaction. Communication takes place all hours of the day and night, with all kinds of people, in every conceivable location and for myriad reasons. Each of these variables has an impact on the communication that occurs. Time may affect how alert we are, how hungry we are, or how much time we can devote to the interaction. Whether the communication takes place in our kitchen, at a house of worship, in school, or on the beach can determine the loudness of our voices, the casualness or formality of our language, and the style of our clothes. The purpose of the event, or the occasion, obviously influences the types of topics seen as appropriate, affects both the audience's and the speaker's expectations for what is appropriate, and determines the order in which parts of the speech might be given. For example, a speech in honor of someone's birthday is likely to include funny stories and jokes about the honoree, a casual presentation style, and the appropriate party attire. On the other hand, a eulogy for an old friend might include inspirational stories, a formal and somber presentation style, and appropriate funeral attire; but as is evident in each example, the contextual considerations are affected by the cultural context. What is "appropriate"—as in "appropriate dress"—is established by the presiding culture and the cultural expectations of the audience.

The cultural context includes all the beliefs, values, attitudes, and expectations that each of the participants has about the occasion, about communication in general, and about the proper ways in which to communicate. Throughout this book, we will discuss in depth the influence of culture on public speaking because cultural differences often cause us difficulty in constructing and interpreting messages. Our different cultures provide different rules about who should talk to whom, how it should be done, and for what outcome. If participants come from more than one culture, confusion and misunderstanding can result.

This model of communication can offer you insights into what to consider when preparing and delivering a speech. As the sender, you consider how to speak, stand, and articulate to best deliver your message. You analyze the audience to tailor the message to their personal, cultural, professional, and social circumstances. You research, plan, structure, and organize a message to be clear and interesting. You anticipate the best channel and how to manage any possible difficulties you might have with that channel. In the same way, you anticipate any possible interference that you or the audience might encounter and plan for ways to adjust to or compensate for interruptions during your presentation. You pay attention to, acknowledge, and respond to audience feedback, and consider the situational variables every step of the way. To that end, we will focus our attention for the rest of this chapter on cultural considerations that will help you better adjust messages to a diverse audience.

Rhetorical Situation
The elements (speaker, audience, topic, purpose, and context) of a communication situation that interact and influence each other and the situation.

Rhetorical Conventions
The culture-specific manner in which messages are expected to be prepared and delivered in a particular context.

CROSS-CULTURAL VIEW OF RHETORIC

When developing a speech, we consider not only ourselves and our own needs, but also the audience, the context, the topic, and the purpose of the presentation. We call these aspects of speaking the *rhetorical situation*. The rhetorical situation influences every aspect of the speech, from choosing an appropriate topic and purpose to choosing appropriate supporting materials and attire.

The rhetorical situation strongly affects how a message will be received and understood. Giving a speech during a high school orientation about the importance of earning good grades in high school seems relevant and important. Giving the same speech to a senior citizen group would seem strange. Similarly, a speech on new environmental regulations will be received differently by a group of environmental activists and a group of chemical manufacturing executives. In other words, what might be a perfectly appropriate and meaningful message in one situation might be seen as inappropriate and meaningless in another.

No matter which language you are speaking, the need to consider the rhetorical situation when developing and delivering your message remains constant. What do change are the *rhetorical conventions* associated with each rhetorical situation (i.e., the expected ways in which a message will be prepared and delivered in a particular context and to a particular audience). The level of expected formality, the appropriate dress, the types of supporting material, and the delivery method are affected by the situation. These expectations and rules associated with particular rhetorical situations are the rhetorical conventions. Rhetorical conventions in one language, culture, or country may not be the same, or even similar, in another. The expectations about how, why, when, and where brides and grooms, students and teachers, bosses and employees, politicians and constituents speak are culturally bound. The level of language formality, the terms of address, and the clothes one wears change with a change in culture.

Understanding how cultures differ, then, is crucial to appropriately adapting a presentation to a particular rhetorical situation.

Elements of Culture (Cultural Patterns)

Culture
A group of people who share the same beliefs, values, norms, and behaviors across time.

Let's look at some of the cultural influences on communication interactions. When we are talking about culture, we are not necessarily talking about a specific country or language or even area of the world. A culture is any group of people who share roughly the same beliefs, values, norms, and behaviors across time. A culture can be a group of people who share similar attitudes, ways of thinking, and rules for behaving "properly." For example, what would be the proper response in your home country if you were to overtly admire or compliment a person's necklace? In Honduras or Kuwait, the person may feel obligated to give the necklace to you, and you would be obliged to take it so that you would not offend the giver. However, in the United States or Canada, the admiration would usually be met with a "thank you" and maybe a brief explanation of where the object came from or how it was made.

In the United States, the "mainstream" culture refers to the largest, most pervasive culture recognized in this country. It is the culture most widely represented on TV, in the movies, and in literature. This is the culture that has historically been derived from the countries of Western Europe, developed largely by white European Judeo-Christian values, and driven by capitalism. Anyone who has lived in or spent time in the United States or who has been exposed to U.S. American media can identify many of the values, icons, and symbols of the mainstream U.S. culture: strong individualism, personal achievement, financial success, and consumerism; Michael Jordan, Bill Gates, Uncle Sam; Wall Street, Fifth Avenue, Rodeo Drive, and Chevy trucks; country music, rock 'n' roll, hip-hop; McDonald's cheeseburgers, apple pie, and soda pop; proms and PlayStation; Fourth of July and big parades; protests and rallies; courts and Congress; presidents and "the people." Each of these calls images of "America" to our minds. However, the United States is actually made up of many cultures within its borders. These cultures, or *co-cultures*, co-exist and influence each other as do all the cultures of the world. By understanding the basics of cultural differences when you interact with or give

Co-culture
Groups of people within a larger culture (dominant culture) who have notably different characteristics, values, beliefs, behaviors, and norms from the larger culture, while still sharing many of the characteristics, values, behaviors, and norms of the larger culture.

speeches to people from various cultures, you can better adjust your messages to them and more accurately interpret their messages to you.

Even though culture works to guide our behavior and govern our choices, it does not dictate them. Not all members of a culture will hold the same beliefs and values or act in the same ways as the majority in the culture do. That is because our families, our friends, our experiences, and our own personalities also influence us. Remember, no two people will ever be exactly alike, and it is those differences that make us individuals within our cultures.

To better understand culture, we can look at some general *cultural patterns*. Cultural patterns are "a system of beliefs and values that work in combination to provide a coherent, if not always consistent, model for perceiving the world."[15] Cultural patterns are a culture's way of seeing and behaving in the world. Although researchers have identified many cultural patterns, we will talk only about some of the most well-known and well-studied classifications.

High and Low Context

Since context sets the stage for all communication interactions, let's first look at the ways in which cultures use context. Edward T. Hall found that cultures rely on context to varying degrees in order to convey meaning in a communication interaction.[16] Contextual factors such as the location of the situation (e.g., at school, at church, in the office, or at a stadium), the relationships of the people involved (e.g., students/teacher, boss/employee, friends, or entertainer/audience), and the individual perceptions of the interactants (e.g., their attitudes about the event, knowledge of the topics being discussed, and moods) can all offer clues for decoding the message. Cultures that rely heavily on these contextual cues to convey meaning are called *high-context cultures*. Conversely, cultures that do not rely heavily on contextual cues are called *low-context cultures*.

Whereas high-context cultures such as Japan, China, Mexico, and Malaysia rely on nonverbal, implied, and subtle messages, low-context cultures such as the United States, Germany, and Sweden prefer overt, direct, and explicit messages. The U.S. preference for the direct and explicit message can be seen in such common sayings as, "Say what you mean, mean what you say" and "Tell it like it is." So when giving a speech to a low-context culture such as here in the United States, you might want to be more direct than you would be with a high-context culture. In China, on the other hand, rather than directly stating accusations or demands, you would want to be very polite and discrete.

Hofstede's Value Dimensions

The next cultural pattern we want to consider is one of the earliest taxonomies (a system of categorization), Hofstede's Value Dimensions. Hofstede identified several, dimensions of culture that "are developed in the family in early childhood and reinforced in schools and organizations, and that these mental programs contain a component of national culture."[17] These dimensions will give you a glimpse of what is valued in a culture as well as help you compare one culture to another.

The *individualism-collectivism* dimension looks at whether a culture is focused more on the individual or on the group. Notice that I said "more"; people in all cultures can and do value the needs and accomplishments of individuals and the groups around them. The individualism-collectivism dimension refers to how important each individual or group is relative to another individual or group. In individualist societies, people tend to focus more on the individual than on the group. Independence, achievement, and competitiveness are highly valued and rewarded. These cultures emphasize individual rights, privacy, and freedoms as well as praise accountability and decisiveness. Sayings such as "looking out for number one" and "I got mine" represent this loyalty to the self. In individualist countries such as Australia, the Netherlands, Belgium, the United States, and Italy, loyalty to family, community, and country can often yield to the needs of the individual. For example, in these countries, students entering college, more often than not, are expected to choose the school, major, and career that best suits them, not the school, major, or career that will best serve their families. Although many do consider their families' needs, the ultimate choice is most often dependent on the individual's desires.

In collectivist cultures, loyalty to the group is paramount. What is best for the family, the company, or the country guides decisions more certainly than "what is best for me." Collectivist cultures value cooperation and community while praising dedication, obligation, and allegiance to the group. Personal needs and concerns are often subordinated to the needs and concerns of the group. Sayings such as "All for one and one for all" and "The nail that sticks out gets hit" represent this value orientation.

Knowing whether an audience leans toward individualism (as people do in the United States) or collectivism can help you tailor your messages to better reflect the audience's values. For example, you can use "we" instead of "I" with collectivist cultures and focus on what the individual audience members gain in individualist cultures.

Cultures also vary in the amount of *power distance* with which they are comfortable. Hofstede states that power distance "defines the extent to which the less powerful person in society accepts inequality in power and considers it as normal."[18] Some cultures, such as those in Guatemala, the Philippines, Venezuela, Iraq, and Saudi Arabia, expect a large differential of power throughout society, while other cultures expect very little difference. Cultures that believe that status and power differences among people are necessary score high on the Power Distance Index (PDI), Hofstede's measurement instrument for power distance. Within these cultures, people are likely to believe that each person has a place in the social structure, that authority should be obeyed without question, and that those in power have rights and responsibilities that others in the society do not.

In terms of power distance, probably the most revealing sentence in the U.S. Declaration of Independence is, "All men are created equal." Today, just

CONSIDERING CULTURE

Students from high power distance countries who take classes in the United States often report feeling intimidated or confused by the relatively casual relationships that students have with their professors. In high power distance cultures, students and professors maintain a highly formal relationship in which the students speak to the professor only when spoken to and are expected to follow strict classroom conduct rules.

as when the document was written over two hundred years ago, not every U.S. citizen has equal access to power and status, but we still value the ideal that all people should be treated equally and be afforded the same opportunities to gain that power and status. This puts the United States relatively low on the PDI. Other low power distance countries are Norway, Costa Rica, Israel, and Yugoslavia. In these countries you may see students or children express their opinions to their teachers and parents, people with power minimizing the differences between them and their constituents, and bosses asking for input and opinions from their employees. Low power distance cultures value freedom of expression, questioning authority, and reducing hierarchies.

The "preference" for either high or low power distance is evident in public speaking situations in the degree of formality and deference the speaker shows to the audience and the audience shows to the speaker. Does the audience stand when the speaker enters the room and wait to be instructed to sit, as when the president of the United States walks into Congress? Do audience members simply begin to quiet down as the speaker approaches the podium as they do in a formal award ceremony? Or do they continue talking until they are asked several times to "quiet down so we may begin" as often happens in U.S. classrooms? These behaviors indicate a different place on the PDI. In every culture, the specific speaking context comes with its own expectations for power and authority; however, the culture's overriding value of power distance can assist you in choosing an appropriate degree of deference from which to start. Take the example of the classroom: In a high power dis-

Having difficulty with some of your reading or writing in English?

CLICK HERE http://babel.altavista.com/

Alta Vista's Babel Fish Translation site allows you to instantly translate a block of text of up to 150 words to and from eight different languages. Be sure to double-check the translations (an easy check is to have the translated text translated back into the original language to make sure it is the same). A computerized translation can make some amusing mistakes!

tance culture, students are more likely to stand when the teacher enters the room and wait for instruction to sit, whereas in the United States, we reserve such shows of deference for heads of state and clergy.

Hofstede's *uncertainty avoidance* index explains a culture's comfort level toward uncertainty and the unknown. People in every culture experience anxiety and fear when dealing with the unfamiliar, but what sparks that anxiety, the degree to which one feels anxiety when faced with uncertainty, and how much uncertainty one can tolerate are strongly influenced by culture. High uncertainty avoidance cultures such as Greece, Portugal, Uruguay, and Belgium are likely to have more rules, rituals, and regulations, and little tolerance for deviance from norms.

Low uncertainty avoidance cultures tend to be more adventurous, to minimize rules and regulations, and to welcome differing opinions and ways of living. The United States is fairly low in uncertainty avoidance, but Jamaica, Hong Kong, and Ireland are among the most tolerant of uncertainty. We will talk more about uncertainty and the anxiety it produces in public speaking in Chapter Two. For now, it is important for you to note that depending on what country you are from, you may experience a higher or lower degree of anxiety when you give a speech or even when you are an audience member.

The last of Hofstede's Value Dimensions is the *achievement-nurturance* dimension. This dimension indicates to what degree achievement or nurturing traits are valued and rewarded. Achievement traits, according to Hofstede, are those typically associated with masculinity and include assertiveness, ambition, and competitiveness, while nurturing traits are those typically associated with femininity and include empathy, equality, and interdependence. High-achievement cultures are seen in Austria, Great Britain, and Japan, while low-achievement cultures include Brazil, Canada, and Pakistan. The United States falls in the middle of the continuum, especially in the last forty years when women's rights and the self-awareness movements have increasingly encouraged people to explore alternatives to a male-centered society.

Knowing where audience members fall on this scale can help you structure your messages to have either a more competitive, ambitious tone or a more nurturing, collaborative tone. In either case, you are not expected to hold the values of the other culture. When you do not believe or value the same position, you are simply expected to adjust your rhetoric so that your audience can hear and understand your message. Think of it this way: Would you talk to a group of mothers of young children about the need to establish college funds the same way you would appeal to the fathers? In a highly masculine culture, you would not. You would appeal to the fathers' sense of responsibility as the "man of the house." You would talk about giving "children advantages to make them competitive in the job market." To the moms, you might talk about protecting their children's futures. In a more equally distributed society, you would probably use a little of both arguments to sway either set of parents.

These cultural patterns, as well as others, influence each culture's preferred communication style, which is evident in various communication interactions including public speaking. When you hear speeches in your home culture, do the speakers tend to be more direct and explicit or more indirect and implicit? Are speeches expected to be very formal and use "fancy" or highly proper language, or are they expected to be more conversational and personal? Are people at every level of society allowed or expected to participate in giving speeches throughout their lives, or do only those with the most powerful positions have that privilege? Do women give speeches?

In the United States, we tend to be direct and explicit in our speeches. We direct the audience with verbal cues that tell them not only "the way it is" but also where we are in our presentation. Public speeches are more formal than private conversations; at the same time, public speeches aim to be conversational and personal. We like to address the audience members directly and tell them how the speech is relevant to their lives. We often invite the audience to participate in our presentations, and we expect clear visual feedback to help us adjust our speech to audience needs and interests. Finally, in the United States, we expect to have at least some ability to address an audience and believe that everyone—men and women, young and old, rich and poor—should have the right to speak out (in the appropriate arenas, of course) when he or she has something to say.

No one way is the "right" way to speak. Every culture uses the style and manner that is most effective for a particular audience. Each style found around the globe is the culmination of centuries of development as each culture grows, changes, and reacts to the evolution of the world.

As you work your way through this book, try to remember not only to adjust your speaking to better fit the expectations of your audience, but also to adjust your expectations of others. If we were to judge each other using only our cultural backgrounds, understanding, values, and viewpoints, we would increase misunderstanding, confusion, and negative judgments of each other.

SUMMARY

So far we have discussed why it is so important to take a public speaking course. You have much to gain in terms of your personal, academic, and professional goals. We looked at the some of the specific skills that you can use immediately in other classes, around campus, at home, and at work such as organizing ideas, improving self-confidence, and evaluating messages. Also, a public speaking class offers you, a non-native speaker of English, practice in speaking English to a sympathetic group who can provide you with clear, honest feedback.

We also looked at the various rhetorical histories around the world and saw that in some ways, these traditions are not much different from each other. Each culture has developed its rhetorical traditions in response to societal pressures to produce effective speakers for various situations.

We examined, as well, the elements of communication and found that every communication interaction can be dissected into seven components—the sender, the receiver, the message, the channel, interference, feedback, and

HINT

Get the phone numbers and e-mail addresses of several of your speech classmates and set up a weekly study group. You can assist each other with reading the text, studying for exams, and practicing your speeches. You'll find the most sympathetic support from people who are experiencing exactly what you are experiencing.

context—and saw how each of these components can influence how the intended message is understood.

We then examined these aspects more closely and saw how culture influences and is influenced by rhetorical situations and cultural patterns in both sending and receiving messages. We learned that we construct our messages based on what our culture believes, thinks, feels, and values and that we decode the messages of others using the same filters. Where cultures fall on the continuums of high/low context, individualism/collectivism, power distance, uncertainty avoidance, and masculinity/femininity further affects who speaks, to whom they speak, what they speak about, and how they speak about it.

Above all, we learned that there is no one, universal way to give an effective presentation, but that within any culture, there are preferred ways. Our goal in this book is to expose you to and give you some insights into the preferred style used in the United States. Remember, even within the Western style there is plenty of room to include elements of your own cultural or personal style, because one strong value in the United States is individuality. Americans like to think of themselves as a great salad bowl—a mixture of flavors and textures all tossed together to make a healthy concoction. We love to see people share who they are and where they come from and what they think. So don't be afraid to flavor your speeches with your own cultural spices.

Discussion Questions and Activities

1. Think of two or three great public speakers from your culture or home country. What makes them great speakers? What sets them apart from other speakers in terms of their style and delivery?
2. How would you characterize your culture in terms of high/low context, individualism/collectivism, power distance, masculinity/femininity, and uncertainty avoidance? Do you see yourself as closely mirroring your culture in these various dimensions? Why/why not? Discuss.
3. In this chapter, we gave several examples of speaking situations you might encounter throughout your life. What speaking situations have you already encountered? In what context? How big was your audience? In what situations do you anticipate that you will have to speak? In your native language(s)? In English? In another language? How do you think the organization and delivery might be different in these various contexts and languages?
4. Hofstede and Hall are not the only researchers to develop ways of examining cultural patterns. However, both come from Western/U.S. cultural backgrounds. Try to find other classifications of cultural patterns. Who developed them? What insights can we learn from these other ways of looking at cultural differences? From what cultural/ethnic/national background were these researchers? In what way does the background of researchers affect their classification systems? What biases are revealed in the classification systems of Hofstede and Hall?

5. In this chapter we discussed various rhetorical histories from around the world. How does knowing more about these traditions—how they are similar to one another and how they differ—help you become a better public speaker?
6. Describe a recent discussion you had in which the message did not seem to reach the receiver as it was intended. In which of the seven elements of communication did the problem occur? Were there problems in more than one element? Why was it a problem? How could the sender have better constructed and delivered the message so that it was more effective?
7. In a small group (three to four people), discuss why you are taking this class, what you hope to gain from it, and what you are concerned about. Combine your lists. Then look through the textbook to see where each of your hopes and concerns is addressed. Write the chapter number next to each of the items accordingly. Make copies for everyone to refer to throughout the semester.

Chapter Quiz

Matching

Place the letter of the term on the line next to its definition.

a. Rhetoric **b.** Nonverbal communication **c.** Co-culture

d. Culture **e.** Communication competence

1. ______ The effective use of language in both speaking and writing.

2. ______ The ability to effectively use the appropriate communication in a particular context.

3. ______ A group of people who share roughly the same beliefs, values, norms, and behaviors across time.

4. ______ Messages sent without the use of words, whether spoken, written, or expressed in sign language.

5. ______ A culture within and different from a mainstream or dominant culture.

T/F, Multiple Choice, Fill-In

1. What are the five levels of communication?

______ ______ ______

______ ______

2. The degree to which a culture derives its meanings from the situation surrounding a message is referred to as:

a. Individualism/collectivism

b. Uncertainty avoidance

c. High/low context

d. Masculinity/femininity

3. Power distance is defined as:
   a. The degree to which a culture values strength.
   b. The relative strength or weakness of a country's economic health.
   c. The degree to which individuals in a culture accept unequal power.
   d. The degree to which one culture will cooperate with another culture.
4. True or false: When given a test to measure an individual's placement on the various cultural patterns developed by Hofstede, most people will score very similarly to their birth country's score.
5. Which of the following would be a channel?
   a. A hand shaking the hand of another person
   b. The smell of perfume
   c. E-mail
   d. All of the above

Chapter 1 Quiz Answers

Matching: 1. a, 2. e, 3. d, 4. b, 5. c

T/F, Multiple Choice, Fill-In: 1. Mass, Intrapersonal, Interpersonal, Group, Organizational 2. c, 3. c, 4. True, 5. d

CHAPTER 2 Public Speaking Anxiety

CHAPTER GOAL:

By the end of this chapter, you will be better able to manage your public speaking anxiety.

Welcome back. If you are feeling a little, or even very, nervous about giving speeches, I want you to know that you are not alone. Chances are that almost everyone taking public speaking at your school and at all schools in the United States today is similarly feeling apprehensive about giving a speech. This is good news . . . you are normal!

The anxiety you feel about public speaking is just one form of the more general category *communication apprehension* (CA). CA is, according to researchers, "an individual's level of fear or anxiety associated with either real or anticipated communication with another person or persons."[1] CA research covers topics such as oral communication apprehension, singing apprehension, writing apprehension, and even receiver apprehension (taking in the message).

Despite how common public speaking anxiety is, I would guess that you would still like to know how to manage your fears. Am I right? Well, that is what we are going to do in this chapter: We are going to explore some of the anxieties you might be having about giving speeches and offer suggestions on how to use that tension to your benefit. We will look first at the issues surrounding public speaking anxiety that occur regardless of the language you speak. We will talk about what anxiety is, where it comes from, how it shows itself, and how you can use the energy that anxiety produces to enhance your presentations. We will also spend a little time talking about receiver anxiety—the anxiety that comes from listening to others speak. Finally, we will look at some of the special kinds of anxiety that you might be having as a non-native English speaker in the areas of accent, pronunciation, word choice, grammar, and mechanics, as well as some of the cultural issues you might have to manage as you face your audience.

MANAGING YOUR PUBLIC SPEAKING ANXIETY

Feeling nervous about giving a speech is normal—so normal, in fact, that it is consistently listed as one of the top fears of most people, usually in the top two or three. In one often-cited and repeated survey, public speaking is listed as the biggest fear of American people—more terrifying, even, than death![2] There is an old joke that most people would rather be in the coffin than giving the eulogy at the funeral. It's a terrible thought that's nonetheless significant: People are typically uncomfortable when giving a presentation to an audience.

Nervousness about giving presentations is so common that we actually consider it *ab*normal when someone doesn't experience some amount of anxiety. Although some speaking anxiety is normal, extreme degrees of public speaking anxiety and other types of communication apprehension are not. When one's anxiety is so high that it interferes with one's ability to function normally, we call that *debilitating performance anxiety,* and it should be treated by a professional.[3] Chances are, though, that your anxiety is in the normal range. Being normal doesn't make it any less painful, of course, but as James McCroskey, one of the best-known communication apprehension researchers, tells us:

> Most people who experience stage fright are of the opinion that most other people do not experience it. They think they are among the few who do, and this makes them feel abnormal. This misperception makes an already troublesome problem even worse than it needs to be.[4]

So why is public speaking anxiety so prevalent? The anxiety comes from one of the most fundamental human responses: the fight versus flight response. When a person, as well as most other animals, is confronted with a dangerous situation, the person's body becomes flooded with the hormones adrenaline (the fear hormone) and cortisol (the stress hormone). These hormones give us a boost of energy to "stand and fight" our opponent or to flee from the danger. Today, most people are not faced with life-or-death situations, but our minds can convince us that a situation like public speaking is quite dangerous. The shaking hands, queasy stomach, sweaty palms, and racing heart are reactions to the adrenaline racing through the bloodstream. Understood this way, we can easily begin to see this extra shot of energy as a benefit and as a boost that can give us extra power to face the audience with enthusiasm and sparkle. The key is learning how to use it well.

Managing public speaking anxiety is a three-part process. We must expect that it will happen, accept the state willingly, and use it to our advantage by capitalizing on it.

Expect It

The first thing we must do to put the energy from anxiety to use is to simply *expect it*. Expect that you will have some amount of anxiety. Look forward to

Public speaking anxiety is normal, so the idea is to manage your anxiety, not to completely eliminate it.

TRY THIS

Start a public speaking journal. Begin with tracking your public speaking anxiety. Then keep track of your thoughts, feelings, experiences, successes, disappointments, and progress throughout the semester. Every once in a while, go back and read what you have written. You will be surprised at the progress you make.

it. Embrace it as part of the process of dynamic public speaking. By expecting it, you take away its power to surprise and overwhelm you, and you can then devise a plan for how to manage it when it comes.

How do you do that? First, become very aware of your individual responses to anxiety. One way to do that is to spend some time writing about your previous experiences with public speaking anxiety. Write down in detail how you felt the last time you had to speak in public. Perhaps the first day of class your instructor had you introduce yourself to the class. Did your knees shake? Did your voice quiver? Did you feel dizzy? When did the feelings start? Right before the presentation? The day before? As you were speaking? How long did those feelings last? How did you try to calm yourself? Were you successful? Did anything or anyone make you feel more comfortable or in control? When did the feelings subside? Did you calm down during the presentation as you became more involved in the presentation? Immediately after the presentation? Thirty minutes later?

Second, write down how you feel when you are just thinking about the presentations you are going to give in this class. Do you feel some of that anxiety rising? Good. Remember, that is normal. Where do you feel the tension? At the back of your neck? In your stomach? Are you having thoughts of dropping the course? Write down everything you are thinking and feeling. Recognize these feelings. Give your feelings names—fear, embarrassment, frustration, etc. Once you begin to understand your personal responses to public speaking anxiety, you are ready to prepare for and process some of that energy more effectively.

Luckily, the most important key to managing the effects of public speaking anxiety is something that you already do every minute of every day: breathing! But not just regular breathing. To manage the tension and stress associated with high-anxiety moments, you need to do some controlled breathing that will help increase your oxygen flow, a key component in relaxation.

Begin practicing proper deep breathing. Many of you may already be familiar with this type of breathing because it is commonly taught in meditation, martial arts, and yoga. The key is to do it correctly. If done incorrectly, you will not only miss the benefits of this practice, but you also risk hyperventilating and fainting, which would not be good for anyone! So read the following all the way through at least once before trying this on your own:

Hyper ver til ating

Hyperventilating
When a person breathes in and out repeatedly and very quickly. This can be dangerous and cause fainting.

1. Sit in a comfortable, upright position with your back straight and relaxed and your stomach loose. Notice where you are holding tension and try to let it go. (See photo.)
2. Roll your shoulders back and down. Many of us pull our shoulders up when we are nervous or tense. Let yours fall down and back to open your chest as much as possible.
3. Breathe gently for a few moments as you focus on your body and your breathing.
4. Breathing in from your diaphragm first and then slowly moving up through your chest, take in a long, SLOW breath through your nose (if you can't take air in through your nose, use your mouth—just remember to breathe in slowly). You should be able to take in air for a count of four.
5. Once you have taken in all the air that your lungs will hold, hold your breath for a count of three.
6. *This is very important:* Now *slowly* release your air through *pursed lips* (see photo) with as much force (from your lungs) and resistance (from your lips) as you can. As you release the air, try to let go of any residual tension from your body. You should release the air no more quickly than a count of eight. In other words, it will take you twice as long to let the air out as it took for you to breathe it in.
7. Repeat this exercise for a total of three times.

Sit straight, balanced on your sit bones. Put feet flat on the ground about shoulder distance apart. Roll your shoulders back and down.

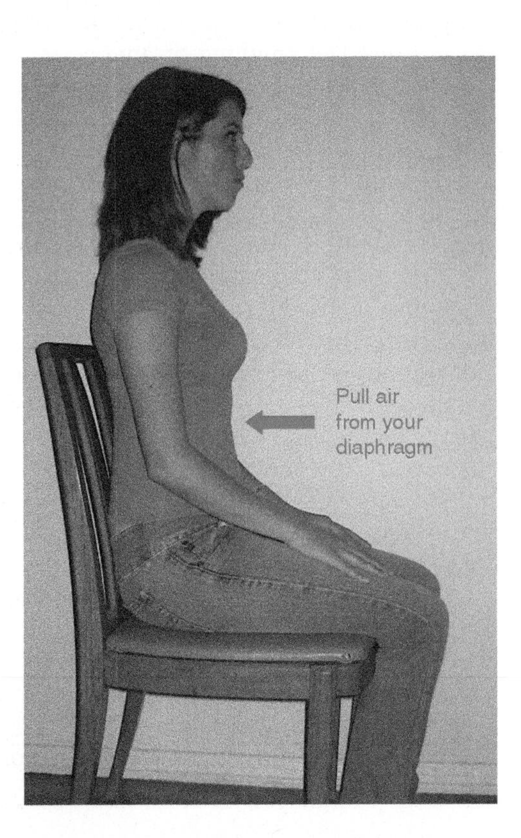

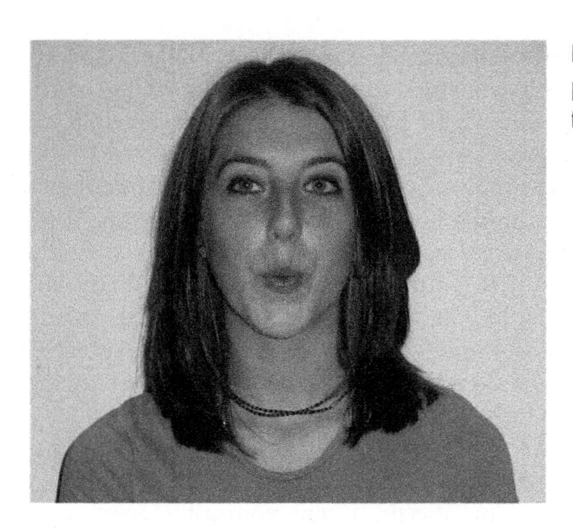

Release the air slowly through pursed lips pushing the air out with force while resisting.

Practice this breathing exercise starting today and do it at least twice a day until it becomes part of your daily routine. You can also practice using this breathing technique every time you begin to feel anxious. As this becomes part of your automatic response to anxiety, you will teach your body to immediately relax and feel calmer, giving you a sense of control over your anxiety.

Accept It

Now that you understand that there is no way to avoid becoming anxious about an upcoming presentation, you can give yourself permission to feel this way. When you feel anxiety mounting, use your breathing exercise and tell yourself, "There it is! I knew I would feel like this" and "I must be doing this correctly."

Instead of accepting public speaking anxiety as normal and predictable, some people fight it. They become critical of themselves, thinking negative thoughts like, "I am so stupid," "None of my other classmates look this nervous," "If only I could be more relaxed." You are not "stupid," and your classmates *are* nervous. Negative self-talk has been associated with poor speaking performance because negative thinking directs too much attention to the self and too little to the presentation or the audience.

Paying attention to the thoughts in your head makes it difficult to concentrate on developing the presentation before giving the speech and difficult to pay attention to the audience while giving the speech.[5] Additionally, this anxious thinking has been shown to actually increase the feelings and symptoms of anxiety.[6] So, instead of engaging in negative self-talk, replace any negative thought with a positive one like, "I am going to give the best speech I can" and "If my classmates can do this, so can I." Thomas, Tymon, and Thomas call this "envisioning success," which they define as "the tendency to have positive images about future task outcomes, that is, to build mental images of succeeding."[7] If you envision yourself successfully giving a speech, you will be channeling your energy positively, and this, in turn, will give you more control and give the appearance of being more relaxed, leaving you more mental focus for preparing and delivering your speech.

Accept your abilities for what they are. Nobody is perfect, and neither is any speech. Additionally, as a beginning English-speaking speech student, no one expects you to give a flawless presentation that rivals the greatest presentations of all time. I don't expect that, your teacher doesn't expect that, your classmates don't, and neither should you. Besides, "perfect" speeches can be boring. A few minor hesitations, an imperfectly pronounced word, or a verbal stumble can actually make the speaker seem more human and "real" to the audience.

In this course, everyone expects you to do the best you can. As long as you are able to clearly deliver your message, your audience will accept you and your presentation; therefore, you should accept yourself. Accept what you can do, identify the areas in which you need to improve, and work toward improving them.

Capitalize on It

At this point, you have anticipated your anxiety, and you have allowed yourself to experience it without beating yourself up. Now, how do you put all that extra energy to good use? Well, that part is easy. You use that energy to thoroughly research, write, and practice your speech. No, this is not a trick to get you to do more work. The more focus you put into preparing for and practicing your speech, the less anxious you will feel on speech day and the more relaxed you will appear to the audience.

First, make sure that you are truly excited about the topic that you have chosen; your enthusiasm will help you stay focused on the speech and not on your worries. We will talk about some ways to select the right speech topics in Chapter Five. For now, just know that choosing a topic that is interesting to you makes giving an interesting speech to an audience much easier.

Most students postpone writing the speech until the last minute, only to find that they have not done enough research, the writing takes longer than they had anticipated, or they don't have any time left to practice. *That* will make anyone nervous! Don't let this happen to you. Make sure that you devote enough time to preparing for the presentation well in advance of your speech day. Generally, instructors suggest one to two hours of preparation for every minute of speech time. In other words, if your instructor has assigned a five- to seven-minute speech, you should set aside six to ten hours of preparation and practice time. As a non-native speaker, you should probably plan on a minimum of two hours for every minute. You will find that the more you prepare and practice your speech, the more confident and comfortable you will become. Additionally, for those of you who are concerned about your grades, the more you prepare and practice, the better your grades will likely be.

Practice is your greatest ally for capitalizing on speech anxiety. The best plan for practicing your speech is to practice no more than three times from a full-sentence outline. (We will discuss the two types of outlines in detail in Chapter Eight.) Then practice from a key-word outline or a few note cards as many times as you can. Each time you practice, you should try to alter your words, your movements, and your vocalics slightly to make the speech seem more natural and conversational. This way, you practice the order of the points and evidence, but the exact wording remains a little more flexible.

You should also practice to a variety of "audiences." Practice in front of a mirror or a video recorder. Practice using a tape recorder. Practice out loud to yourself, and, at least once, practice your speech in front of another person. Practice for roommates, classmates, friends, family, anyone! This is very important. Practicing in front of an audience feels very different from practicing by yourself. You don't want to realize that difference for the first time when you step in front of your classmates. Also, practicing for an honest and supportive audience can provide you with valuable feedback about how you look and sound. For non-native speakers, this is especially important so that you can be assured that you are pronouncing and articulating your words correctly and clearly. Finally, you should use visualization techniques to reduce any residual CA you are feeling. There is strong evidence that visualizing, or imagining yourself giving a successful presentation, really works, not only to reduce CA, but also to actually improve your performance.[8] Successful visu-

Imagine yourself giving an energetic, enthusiastic, and entertaining presentation.

alization includes imagining every little detail of your speaking experience: waking up refreshed and energized in the morning, choosing the perfect clothing for the speech, feeling confident and excited about the presentation, being completely prepared, and giving a clear, entertaining, strong speech that the audience enjoys. Simply imagine that giving the speech is a pleasant task. Write down in vivid detail how you imagine the perfect speech day would go. Then when you are feeling relaxed (a good time is right after practicing your deep breathing exercises), read the scenario. Reread the scenario several times when you are relaxed before the speech day. This should give you that extra burst of confidence.

By expecting that you will feel anxiety before you do, accepting your anxiety as unavoidable, and capitalizing on the extra energy produced by your anxiety, you can increase your confidence and comfort when giving a speech. With more experience in public speaking, you will find that your anxiety will actually decrease and that the added energy will be a welcome part of the experience.

HINT

Before Giving a Speech

Things to do to minimize public speaking anxiety:

- Get a good night's sleep before any presentation day.
- Eat a high-protein, nutritious meal at least one hour before speaking, but avoid eating too much right before speaking as this can add to stomach upset.
- Drink plenty of water before and after your presentation (if the presentation is long, you should have water with you to sip).
- Before entering the room, walk briskly around the building to use up some of the extra energy produced by the adrenaline.
- While waiting in your seat, tighten and release your muscles.
- Avoid caffeine, alcohol, and sugar before a presentation.
- Breathe, breathe, breathe, but don't hyperventilate.

RECEIVER ANXIETY

You might also worry about listening to speeches or to lectures. We call this *receiver apprehension* or RA. Receiver apprehension is defined as "the fear of misinterpreting, inadequately processing, and/or not being able to adjust psychologically to messages sent by others."[9] Like public speaking anxiety, receiver anxiety is quite common, especially when a person is listening to someone who speaks in a language, dialect, or accent with which the receiver is not completely familiar.

What is significant about receiver apprehension is that it seems to negatively affect student academic achievement and motivation. Additionally, researchers have found that students experience high levels of apprehension when participating in foreign language classes.[10] This means that in addition to whatever difficulties you may have as a non-native student in translating or understanding a speaker's message, your anxiety about listening and understanding can actually make comprehension even more difficult![11] In other words, the more RA one experiences, the more difficult it is to comprehend and process information. Clearly, if you are having difficulty comprehending and processing what is being said, then you will likely also have a more difficult time learning the material.

For a non-native student in a public speaking class, receiver apprehension can be a significant concern, especially considering the number of accents you will be asked to listen to and comprehend. Although listening is discussed in detail in the next chapter, I want to offer you some specific suggestions here to help you reduce listening apprehension so that you can get the most out of this class and avoid the pitfalls associated with receiver apprehension's effect on academic achievement.

First of all, many of the anxiety-reduction techniques discussed earlier (i.e., deep breathing, positive self-talk, etc.) can help you relax when listening to your instructor or to your fellow students. As with reducing speaking anx-

CONSIDERING CULTURE

The University of Cincinnati offers the following advice to international students adjusting to cultural change:

Difficulties Regarding Culture Change

Many international students struggle with problems upon their entry into the US. Some of the problems identified by the international students at UC are related to language, financial situation, academic stresses, social interactions with Americans, food, and loneliness/homesickness. Other difficulties may be related to:

1. Classroom Style and the Quarter System: Classroom style is sometimes a difficult cultural difference for incoming international students. The atmosphere and expectations may be very different from the academic atmosphere of the home institutions. The quarter system may also be different since many other institutions have semester systems. The quicker quarter system may not allow the student time to get oriented to the expectations of the class.
2. Separation from Family and Friends: The move to the US often causes a separation from family and friends. The loss of this support system can be difficult, especially if they were a source of support for difficulties at home.
3. Reentry Shock: Another issue may be not only the "culture shock" of coming to the US, but also "reentry shock" when returning to their home country. Often students do not expect to be faced with changes in themselves, their country, or family.
4. Social Interactions: Sometimes expectations regarding social relationships and friendships can vary from culture to culture.
5. Academic Relationships: International students as well as their American professors are often unaware of the large impact of their cultural differences. These differences may affect the student's academic performance through their psychological health and interpersonal challenges.

Source: http://www.campusblues.com/international_students.asp

iety, try to stem the tide of anxiety by not focusing on your worries but focusing on the task instead.

Fully prepare for each class by doing all of the reading and outlining chapters whenever possible. Look up and keep a list of any unfamiliar words in the reading and bring the list with their definitions to class. In this way, you will already be familiar with many of the terms likely to be discussed during a lecture and will have the definitions of the problematic terms readily available if you forget some of the meanings.

Next, ask your instructor if you can tape-record lectures and speeches. Then be sure to relisten to the recording as soon after the class as possible. Write down any words, phrases, or concepts that are still unfamiliar or confusing to you, and ask a classmate, friend, or roommate to explain them to you. If you are still unsure about something, make an appointment with your instructor for further clarification.

While taking notes in class, try to get at least the main idea of the speaker's message. Listen for and write down repeated words so that you can look them up later. Also, write down any word that you don't know or understand readily. Keep a list of those words and learn them. Most people, including your instructors, have a preferred vocabulary of words they often use, so learning the words your instructor most often uses will help you better understand course content as well as increase your overall vocabulary.

Finally, compare your notes with those of your classmates to see how well you understand the material relative to how well the other students in the class understand it. In doing this, you will be able to fill in the gaps in your knowledge of items discussed in class that you missed or misunderstood. You will probably find that you are understanding more than you have been giving yourself credit for. In fact, studies have shown that students who are more anxious often underestimate their language competence.[12]

Although you might come from a high power distance culture that discourages asking questions during class or are shy about raising your hand, don't hesitate to ask questions during class. In the United States, teachers generally welcome questions, and some even offer participation points for those students who raise their hands, ask questions, and offer opinions. The added benefit of becoming a regular participant in class is that you will also become more comfortable speaking in front of your classmates and your teacher!

In the beginning, you may still find it difficult to understand what is being said in class, so try to remember to do all the anxiety-reducing strategies offered here. In time, you will become more comfortable with the strategies and more relaxed and confident in the classroom, which will lead to greater understanding and mastery of the material.

SPECIFIC NON-NATIVE ISSUES

As a non-native speaker of English in an English-speaking public speaking class, you are probably facing some additional worries about this course. Your overall communication apprehension is likely to be increased, and you may be concerned about such things as your accent, pronunciation, word choice, grammar, and nonverbal issues as you face your audience. Don't worry: These are common concerns and there are strategies you can use to minimize problems. In this section, we will not cover each topic in depth (much of these topics will be covered in greater detail in later chapters), but we will try to offer some quick tips to help you through your first presentations.

Accent and Pronunciation

Accent and pronunciation are among the most common areas of concern for non-native speakers. They worry that others won't understand them, that they will be made fun of, or that they will inadvertently say something embarrassing by mispronouncing or misusing a word. These are valid concerns. Even native speakers sometimes worry about this, too. For instance, they may worry that they will choose the wrong word because it sounds similar to another word.

Happily, audiences can be forgiving and will still understand what we are trying to say even if we don't say it perfectly. Additionally, audiences tend to adapt to a speaker's accent, so your classmates should become accustomed to your accent fairly quickly and be able to understand you with little trouble after only a few minutes. Still, you should make every attempt to learn the proper pronunciation of the words you want to use in your speeches. So what can you do?

First, wherever possible, choose only the words that you are comfortable using—words you know and use regularly. Choose simple, easy-to-pronounce words. Use a thesaurus to find simpler or easier-to-pronounce words, but be sure the meaning is the one you want. In addition to using words that are easier for you to pronounce, your audience will appreciate your clarity. Check the pronunciation in the dictionary to make sure that you are pronouncing the words correctly. Also, many websites now offer audio pronunciations and pronunciation guides along with word definitions so that you can hear the correct pronunciation from a native speaker (e.g., http://www.bartleby.com/61/s0.html or http://encarta.msn.com/encnet/features/dictionary/dictionaryhome.aspx).

Once you feel comfortable with the words you have chosen for your speech, practice your speech a few times, concentrating on using proper pronunciation. You can do this by recording yourself as you practice and then playing it back to see how you sound. Ask a friend, classmate, roommate, or teacher to listen to your speech and identify any words he or she had trouble

WHAT OTHERS SAY

“When I just came to America I didn't speak English very well. I often made mistakes and made others laugh. I remember I always used to confuse people by asking them "how many years they had" instead of "how old they are." I also used to always say "I don't have where to sleep?" Or "I don't have what to eat" instead of "I have nowhere to sleep or eat." . . .

The first time I came to America someone told me to "hang up the phone" and I was looking on the wall and asked "where should I hang it?"

Thankfully my English speaking skills have improved since and now I can laugh about my past mistakes.”

Marija, Croatia

Need help or extra practice with English pronunciation?

CLICK HERE These websites offer explanations, examples, exercises, and quizzes in American English pronunciation.

http://international.ouc.bc.ca/pronunciation/

http://eleaston.com/pronunciation/

http://www.manythings.org/pp/

TABLE 2.1 Easy Tricks for Problem Sounds

Sound	Trick
[t][d][l][n]	Place the tip of your tongue on your gum ridge.
[r]	Point the tip of your tongue toward the back of your throat.
[f]	Bite down on the inner edge of your lower lip, emit breath.
[v]	Bite down on the inner edge of your lower lip, emit voice.
[b]	Place your lips together, then allow an explosion of voice.
[p]	Place your lips together, then allow an explosion of breath.
[w]	Pucker your lips, slightly apart, then move them further apart. Emit voice.
[s]	Point the tip of your tongue toward your gum ridge, without touching your gum ridge or your teeth. Raise the sides of your tongue so that they touch your middle and back upper teeth. Force out a thin, pencil stream of air along the mid-line of your tongue.
[z]	Same as above. Emit voice.
[T]*	Place the tip of your tongue between your teeth and gently bite down. Emit breath.
[D]**	Place the tip of your tongue between your teeth and gently bite down. Emit voice.

*This symbol represents the "th" sound in words like "breath" or "thick."

**This symbol represents the "th" sound in words like "these" or "that."

Used by permission of Deborah Kraut of Santa Monica College.

CONSIDERING LANGUAGE

Quick Tips on Word Choice

A(n) or *the?*

- *A(n)* is indefinite, general, not particular. Use *a* before a noun that begins with a consonant to indicate "no particular" item. For example: *a* car means "any car," not a particular car. Use *an* in front of a noun that begins with a vowel. Example: *an ice cube.*
- *The* is definite, specific, particular. Use *the* before a noun to indicate one specific item. For example, *the* car means "a very specific car," perhaps the red car sitting in the driveway.

understanding easily. Ask him or her to give you feedback on pronunciation and clarity. Practice for that person until both of you feel confident that you are being very clear.

You can also use visual aids and nonverbal signals to support your meaning. For example, use a chart that outlines your main points, and point to the headings as you say them. This will help the audience become comfortable with your accent, too.

Word Choice, Grammar, Sentence Structure, and More

You may also be concerned about correct word choice. Non-native speakers often report frustration and confusion when trying to choose the right word in English to express an idea, to connect ideas, or to make a sentence flow. This is not surprising since English has approximately 750,000 words, although estimates range from 500,000 to 1,000,000![13]

When we consider that German has fewer than 200,000 words and that French has fewer than 100,000, it is no wonder that we find it difficult to choose just the right word.[14] Here I offer you the same advice as for pronunciation: Choose simpler words with which you are already comfort-

able, don't try to find the "perfect" word when a similar, simpler word will do, and test your choices (as well as your speech) on a native speaker whenever possible.

There are also some common ESL word choice and order mistakes that you should watch out for. Common ESL problem areas include the following: articles, pronouns, verb tense and subject-verb agreement, verb forms, and prepositions. We will discuss other common ESL challenges in Chapter Nine. Be sure to proofread for sentence structure, word order, and word choice using a more comprehensive grammar guide whenever possible.[15]

Remember, your instructor has experience working with students who have a wide range of English-language proficiency. S/he can probably offer you specific direction in terms of how "grammatically correct" your speech should be and recommend resources available to you on your campus. Don't hesitate to ask your instructor, counselors, and other students for assistance. You will probably find that they are happy to assist you. Additionally, there is a wealth of assistance available on the Internet for English-language learners looking for support, guidance, and clarification.

Nonverbal

You may be concerned about making nonverbal mistakes in your presentation. Again, this is to be expected. You have probably already found that many of the gestures, facial expressions, and bodily movements that you use in your native culture or country are misunderstood or ignored here. Like language, nonverbal behaviors vary from culture to culture, country to country, and sometimes even state to state within the United States! Subtle, nonverbal messages can have profound meanings to one group of people and have completely different meanings or no meaning at all to other groups of people.

In the United States, placing the thumb and index finger in the shape of the letter *o* with the other three fingers straight up means "OK," but, as you may already know, in other parts of the world this can mean "worthless" or

CONSIDERING LANGUAGE *(continued)*

Choose the correct helping verbs based on the subject:

- She/He/It: *Has, does/did, is/was, has been*
- You/They/We: *Have, do/did, are/were, have been*
- I: *Have, do/did, am/was, have been*

It is unnecessary to repeat the subject or an object in the same clause:

- Instead of *Makiko she went to the store,* say, *Makiko went to the store.*
- Instead of *The cat that had run away it came back,* say, *The cat that had run away came back.*
- Instead of *A blanket fell off the bed that we were sleeping in it,* say, *A blanket fell off the bed that we were sleeping in.*

Sometimes we can say the wrong thing without ever opening our mouths.

"money" or can be an extremely obscene gesture. To minimize misunderstandings arising from nonverbal mistakes, try to minimize using gestures that have specific meanings in your culture or language. Instead, opt for hand gestures that don't "say" anything in particular. Use your hands and arms to stress points without fixing your hands or arms into specific configurations. Specifically, avoid crossing your arms in front of your body (in the United States, this could be taken to mean that you are "closed-off" or angry); pointing (some people find this rude not only in the United States but in many other countries as well); or lifting individual fingers while keeping others down (almost any of these can get you into trouble in some part of the world—so it's better to avoid any of these finger gestures entirely).

Some other things you may want to consider: Never turn your back to the audience. This may be misconstrued as rude, and makes it harder for the audience to hear and understand you. It is also important to avoid looking down too much. Extensive eye contact is valued in the United States and indicates trustworthiness in this country. We will talk more about all aspects of good delivery, including gestures and eye contact, in Chapter Twelve. For now, you should work on looking at the audience as much as possible. Also, remember to talk in a voice that is loud enough for everyone to hear you. Again, practicing in front of others should help you become more comfortable in achieving adequate volume.

SUMMARY

All these hints, tips, and cautions may seem overwhelming at first, but if you have learned anything from this chapter, you know that PRACTICE, PRACTICE, PRACTICE is the key to becoming more comfortable with whatever challenge or anxiety you are experiencing. Practice out loud, in front of a mirror, into a tape recorder, and, most importantly, in front of other people.

Allow others to assist you in your quest to become more comfortable speaking in front of an audience and in mastering some of the quirks and inconsistencies of the English language. English is one of the most difficult—but also one of the most useful—languages in the world to learn. No one learns it overnight or without lots of practice in a variety of contexts.

Whether you call the butterflies in your stomach *anxiety, communication apprehension, nervousness,* or *excitement,* the goal is not to rid yourself of those feelings but to take control of them and direct the energy to your advantage. When you expect to feel some anxiety, accept that anxiety as normal, and capitalize on the energy it creates, you can bring life and excitement to your presentations. You might even begin to appreciate that adrenaline rush as a welcome and even enjoyable part of the experience!

Discussion Questions and Activities

1. Keep track of your self-talk. Try to catch yourself thinking thoughts that lead to self-doubt and anxiety, and replace those thoughts with coping or positive thoughts that lead to greater self-confidence. Replace "I can't do this; I am going to fail!" with "I have worked very hard on this speech; I am sure that I am going to do very well."
2. How might the various dimensions of culture (high context/low context, etc.) impact a speaker's tendency toward or away from communication and receiver apprehension?
3. Confidence in public speaking increases with practice. To increase your confidence, raise your hand and ask a question in each of your classes over the next week.
4. Get into the EGBOK (pronounced "eg-BAK") habit: Every time you start to worry about your presentation, quickly remind yourself that Everything Is Going to Be OK.
5. In addition to the hints to manage public speaking anxiety offered in this chapter, most people have their own ways of coping. Consider everything you have learned in this chapter regarding public speaking anxiety. Discuss with a classmate what you find helpful, what you do not understand, and what you think won't work. Then talk about some of the techniques each of you uses or has used in the past to deal with anxiety. How effective are they? How can you improve on your past techniques with what you have learned from this chapter?
6. Ask your instructor if you can tape-record the next lecture. During the lecture, relax and take notes as you normally would while you are recording, but leave extra lines/space on your paper. As soon as possible after class, review your notes. Then listen to the lecture. As you listen to the lecture, fill in and clarify your notes. Notice how much you actually remember and understand from your first listening. How much more were you able to understand and remember the second time you listened to the lecture? How can you use this to improve your listening in future lectures?

Chapter Quiz

Matching

Place the letter of the term on the line next to its definition.

a. Hyperventilation **b.** Communication apprehension **c.** Fight versus flight
d. Adrenaline **e.** Receiver apprehension **f.** Visualization

1. ______The hormone that is produced when a person is afraid.

2. ______A technique for managing speaking anxiety by imagining a positive outcome for a speaking situation.

3. ______The fear or anxiety related to real or imagined speaking situations.

4. ______Rapid breathing often caused by increased anxiety that can lead to fainting.

5. ______The fear or anxiety related to real or imagined listening situations.

Chapter 2 Quiz Answers

1. d, 2. f, 3. c, 4. a, 5. e

CHAPTER 3 Ethics

CHAPTER GOAL:

By the end of this chapter, you will be able to identify and avoid common ethical pitfalls as both a speaker and a listener.

What do the following scenarios have in common?

a. A speaker stands in front of the audience, mumbling and muttering to himself as he fumbles through his notes, clearly unorganized and unprepared for the presentation he is about to give. He mumbles a few ideas that seem unrelated and hard to follow and provides no evidence to support his assertions.
b. A speaker stands self-assuredly in front of an audience and proclaims her opinions about world politics as if they are fact. She manipulates her evidence to suit her arguments while leaving out large portions of relevant data that contradict her assertions.
c. A speaker presents a speech using biased and unprofessional language, calls his opponents ugly names, and plays upon the audience's emotions to coerce them into voting for an unpopular and possibly dangerous proposition.
d. An audience member is writing out her "to-do" list when she is supposed to be listening to the speaker.
e. An audience member spends his time "listening" to the speaker by critically judging the speaker's clothes, hair, and vocal patterns instead of listening to what the speaker has to say.

All of these scenarios represent unethical behaviors. Being competent at public speaking goes beyond being interesting and confident; speaking well in public also means abiding by the ethical standards of good speech preparation

The freedom to speak in the United States is one of the most highly valued rights among its citizens.

and presentation as well as the ethical standards of good listening behavior.

The United States prides itself on freedom of speech. Many believe that in the United States, you can share your opinions without repercussion. But this is not true. Freedom of speech does not mean that you can say anything you want, anytime you want to say it. Nor does it mean that anyone will or must listen to you. Freedom of speech also includes the freedom to listen and the freedom to evaluate others' opinions and presentations in terms of both content and style (referred to as *critique* or *criticism*). The freedom to speak and the freedom to listen, as with any rights or privileges, come with certain responsibilities—practical and ethical considerations that we must attend to and abide by to honor those rights and responsibilities.

This chapter examines ethical responsibilities in the public speaking context. We will define ethics, explain how ethics apply to public speaking, and explain how to avoid some common ethical pitfalls. We will pay special attention to the issue of plagiarism and some of the important cultural differences in regard to using another person's ideas in your work.

In the second part of the chapter, we will look into the fundamentals of listening, the ethical responsibilities of being a good audience member, ways to avoid some of the common listening pitfalls, and, expanding on our discussion in the last chapter, ways to improve overall listening and listening comprehension as non-native English speakers.

WHAT OTHERS SAY

"In Guatemala the candidates move from town to town instead of state to state. My parents told me that when they were younger, the entire country resembled a police state. If anyone was caught making a speech that criticized the administration of the time or the government, that person was either sent to prison or shot during their speech. Nowadays, people in Guatemala have a stronger freedom of speech, but it is the lack of an educational background that keeps them from expressing it."

Franklin,
Guatemala

ETHICS

Let's begin by looking at what we mean by *ethics*. Ethics usually refer to a system of moral principles that govern proper behavior. Our ethics tell us what is right and wrong, good and bad, just and unjust, fair and unfair. As a field of study, ethics (a branch of philosophy) are concerned with issues pertaining to morality and moral behavior.

Ethics
A system of moral principles that govern proper behavior.

Ethical considerations underlie much, if not all, human behavior, and ethical questions can be very difficult to resolve. Ethical dilemmas range from the ordinary (Do I tell my friend the truth about how awful her new haircut looks, or do I spare her feelings?) to the extreme (Is it better to let a loved one suffer a painful death or to end his/her life early?). Questions range from the simple (Do I take home paper from the office without asking?) to the complex (Do I terminate a pregnancy when the mother is certain to die if I don't?). Sometimes, as we can see by this last example, either answer leads to a terrible consequence. To make the best ethical decisions, we consider the possible consequences, both long and short term, for all affected parties, and weigh them against a pre-established ethical criterion. Not all of us will come to the same answers, because, coming from different cultures, countries, and religions, our ethical criteria or moral guidelines differ.

What does this have to do with public speaking? Well, speaking comes with power. When you are given the time and place to give a speech and you have an audience willing to listen to you, you are in a position of power. The audience gives you its attention with the understanding that you will do the best job you can, be honest, and not waste their time. You are also expected to guide them to a greater knowing or understanding or a beneficial action. If you do a sloppy job, lie, manipulate your evidence, or entice your audience to engage in an unethical, illegal, or dangerous action, you have betrayed their trust and shirked your ethical responsibilities as the speaker. In short, ethics must be considered at every stage of preparing and giving a speech. Deciding whether or not you should give a speech and choosing a topic, supporting material, and presentation style all have ethical implications. As renowned ethicist Richard Johannesen tells us:

> Potential ethical issues are inherent in any instance of communication between humans to the degree that the communication can be judged on a right-wrong dimension, involves possible significant influences on other humans, and to the degree that the communicator consciously chooses specific ends sought and communicative means to achieve those ends.[1]

Think back to the first scenario in the introduction. In that case, the speaker has clearly not thoroughly prepared his presentation. He has neither researched, organized, nor practiced his speech. This is a waste of the audience's time and energy. Many believe that wasting other people's time is akin to stealing, in essence, stealing time from their lives. They came to the speech with the expectation of trading their time for information. If the speaker fails to deliver, he has not completed his part of the transaction.

In the second scenario, the speaker essentially lies by making her evidence seem to support one idea when in reality, it supports the opposite, and she hides important contrary information. Lying is more than simply speaking untruths. Often the most serious lies include telling half-truths, knowingly omitting important facts, or manipulating statistics and facts. Clearly, dishonesty (purposefully misleading others) is unethical.

In the third example, the speaker is unethical because he uses the power of the speaking position to attack others unnecessarily. He does harm through the use of an acid tongue. The ethical argument debates issues, not people. The ethical speaker maintains civility with regard to the other people involved and attacks the ideas instead, using credible evidence and sound reasoning to support a position.

Given that each of us has differing values and beliefs, how can a public speaker expect to make ethical decisions that suit everybody? Well, the truth is that a public speaker cannot please everyone—there are few ethics that are universally accepted. Individuals, cultures, and religions vary in terms of what each considers ethical behavior, but how differences are discussed is guided by some common ethical rules or standards for all. So, then, an ethical public speaker should make sure that the *way* he or she communicates is ethical, not that everyone agrees with his or her conception of ethical behavior.

Ethical communication, according to the National Communication Associ-ation (NCA), is communication that shows respect, is honest, encourages fairness, and elevates the listeners. Sometimes we judge the beliefs, actions, behaviors, and traditions of other people as "wrong" because they seem strange or unusual. When we meet someone from a different country, culture, or even just another family, we might judge her or him as "wrong" simply because she or he does not look, act, or talk the way we do. This does not make her or his behavior unethical, just different. When we use the words *right* and *wrong* in regard to ethics, we are saying that the other person's behavior is moral or immoral. The problem is that some people's ethnocentrism leads them to believe that different *is* bad, rude, or immoral. For example, in Malaysia people speak more softly, calmly, and slowly, leaving longer spaces between words than is customary in the United States, so when a Malaysian has a conversation with a U.S. American, she might find the U.S. American pushy, rude, and impatient.

Additionally, some think that if a person disagrees with others, has a minority opinion about an issue, or expresses an unpopular opinion that is offensive to others, that person is unethical. That is not necessarily true, however. Ethics are often more about how opinions are expressed and whether or not the goals are ethical than they are about what the actual opinion or belief might be. For example, Chris believes abortion is unethical, whereas Tony believes that it is unethical to withhold from a woman the right to choose. Neither Chris nor Tony is unethical for believing as he does or by arguing for his cause. He is unethical only if he is dishonest and manipulative in his tactics to sway people to his beliefs.

Finally, a legal action is not necessarily an ethical one, nor is something unethical simply because it is illegal. For example, it is legal for a reporter to expose private details about a celebrity to the media, but that does not mean that exposing those details is ethical. The lack of privacy and constant hounding can destroy celebrity lives (consider Princess Diana). Legally, you may spend your money any way you choose. However, that doesn't mean that it is ethical to spend your rent or food money to play the lottery when others are relying on you. Similarly, peace protests in the form of sit-ins, demonstrations, and marches have long crossed the boundaries of law to fight for what is right. In many cases, it is the law that is unethical.

Common Ethical Pitfalls

So what are some of the most common ethical pitfalls that you might fall into, and how can you avoid them?

Failing to Thoroughly Prepare

Students' lives are busy. You have many demands on your time and attention. You might not spend as much time as you should preparing assignments. However, when the assignment is a speech that is to be delivered to an audience, you have an obligation to more than just yourself. You have an obligation

In 1955 Rosa Parks refused to give up her seat on a bus for a white person in defiance of an Alabama law that required black people to give up their seats to white passengers. The law was racist, unethical, and a violation of this nation's constitution. Ms. Parks' refusal to abide by the law actually represented a higher ethical standard than that represented by the law.

not to waste the audience's time. A seven-minute speech wastes only seven minutes of your life, time you are choosing to sacrifice, but seven minutes in the lives of twenty classmates is 140 minutes collectively that they did not ask to waste. Failing to prepare a well-researched, meaningful, and interesting presentation will not only garner you a poor grade; it is also unethical.

Captive Audiences
1. An audience that is in attendance because of a sense of obligation or requirement (e.g., attending traffic school).
2. An audience that is so interested in the presentation that they can't pull themselves or their attention away.

Benefiting Personally

Sometimes speakers like to take advantage of having a *captive audience* (an audience that might be there only out of obligation) to benefit themselves in some way, often without regard for what is best for the audience. It is unethical to withhold information about the ways in which you will benefit from the presentation. For example, if you are trying to persuade audience members to buy magazine subscriptions, you need to tell them that you will earn commission or prizes for selling the subscriptions.

Failing to Consider the Audience's Needs and Interests

Speeches are given for the benefit of the audience; however, they are given by a person who has a particular interest and knowledge. The trick is to match the speaker's interests to the audience's interests. Giving a speech that fails to address the concerns of the audience results in a speech that is irrelevant to and boring for the audience, again wasting the time of the audience, which is unethical.

Encouraging Unethical or Illegal Behavior

Encouraging the audience to engage in illegal or unethical behavior is most definitely unethical and can even have legal ramifications for the speaker. Students sometimes think it is amusing or "harmless" to present speeches of this nature, not realizing that there could be potentially serious consequences. In the past, students have offered speeches on such topics as:

- Growing Marijuana for Fun and Profit
- How to Avoid Paying Taxes
- How to Get a Fake ID
- Hacking Your Way to Straight A's
- Making the Perfect Martini (this is fine if your audience is of legal drinking age, but not if most of your audience is underage)
- Getting in Free to the Movies
- Pick-Up Lines That Really Work

Although these might be entertaining and interesting speeches, each is unethical because it encourages illegal and unethical behavior. Remember, if anyone (the audience members or anyone they influence as a result of your speech) can be harmed because of the speech, the speech is probably unethical.

Using Faulty Research and Supporting Material

Including sloppy research, outdated or noncredible sources, and invalid reasoning in your speech as well as citing opinion as fact and not citing sources properly are unethical. Conducting and using poor research leads to confusion and misinformation that both wastes the audience's time and could lead to damaging results.

Using Name-Calling and Other Offensive Language

Students sometimes have bad habits that translate into unethical behaviors. Criticizing others personally, name-calling, using racist and sexist language, being insensitive to differences among people and cultures, and behaving like a "know-it-all" are unethical habits that people sometimes fall into. For example:

> "He is just an idiot, so only another idiot would believe what he has to say."
>
> "Orientals should learn to speak English if they want to live in this country."
>
> "Then this lady doctor walks in to take my temperature."
>
> "Those people are sick to think it is okay to eat dog, why can't they just eat a good old-fashioned steak?"
>
> "I know because I grew up with those kinds of people, they're all alike."

Plagiarize

"to steal and pass off (the ideas or words of another) as one's own: use (a created production) without crediting the source . . . present as new and original an idea or product derived from an existing source."

Source: Merriam-Webster's Collegiate Dictionary, 10th ed., 1996, p. 888.

Plagiarizing

A serious ethical pitfall is plagiarism. Occasionally, students don't understand the expectations for original work in the United States, are too unsure of their abilities to write a good speech, or have waited too long to prepare their speeches, so they resort to using a speech they didn't write or include large portions of another's work and present it as their own. This can lead to devastating results for the student. Plagiarism is such a serious issue that we will talk at length about it later in this chapter.

Foundations of Ethical Behavior

You can be more conscientious about what you are doing and how it will affect your audience. By applying three simple words—*integrity, respect,* and *honesty*—to each step of your preparation, practice, and delivery, you can become a more ethical speaker. See Table 3.1 on page 52.

Integrity

Integrity is the unwavering commitment to adhere to high moral or ethical principles. A person with integrity, then, is someone who has decided to "do the right thing" no matter what. S/he makes decisions based on what is best for everyone and not just what is best for him- or herself. Having integrity in public speaking means committing to doing the best job possible, having a responsible goal, being fully prepared, and accepting full responsibility for one's words.

As relationship coach Virginia Downie explains,

> "Integrity" comes from the same root as the word "integration." To be in integrity, then, means that our beliefs, values, and actions all come together (integrate) to form a unified and harmonious whole.[2]

This commitment to yourself can give you the motivation and resolve to accomplish your goals even when the task seems insurmountable. Having integrity means that if you know that your speech will be due soon, you choose to do research on a Saturday afternoon instead of watching television. Integrity reminds us that it is unethical to procrastinate or cut corners.

Integrity

The commitment to abide by high moral and ethical principles and practices.

Integrity can also guide you in deciding on a topic. Ethical topics are those that are both important to you and relevant to the audience. If you are an animal rights activist, you should talk about animal rights or an endangered species by finding a way to relate the topic directly to your audience and their interests. You will find that your enthusiasm for the topic can motivate you to research the topic well and can inspire your audience.

Presentations should also benefit audiences in some way. When asked, many people say that Hitler was a great public speaker because he was able to convince the German people to follow his plan. I disagree. Hitler was effective, but that does not make him good. Hitler moved people to act through coercion, dishonesty, and manipulation, and his goals were corrupt. A good public speaker, above all, should have ethical goals. Few would argue that

Hitler's goals were ethical. It seems that even Hitler knew that his goals were unethical, as evidenced by the fact that he hid his actions from the rest of the world. If we are being completely ethical, we are not afraid to tell the world what we are attempting to do. We have nothing to hide. If you feel the need to hide your goals or the ways in which you are trying to accomplish your goals, then you are probably acting unethically.

Integrity also means that you accept responsibility for your words. If you convince your classmates to walk out in protest against a policy on campus that you don't like, your classmates may hold you accountable for their lowered grades or missed assignments. If you give incorrect or incomplete information or inappropriate advice, you could embarrass or harm your audience. For example, if a student gives a speech explaining how to stop excessive bleeding in an accident victim and suggests using a tourniquet (a tight band placed around a limb to stop uncontrollable bleeding) and a student uses this method inappropriately as a result of the speech, the speaker could be held responsible for giving incomplete information and inappropriate advice (tourniquets are not recommended in most bleeding situations due to complications that arise from their use). Integrity as a first line of defense against unethical speaking can help you draw upon your better self to make difficult choices. You will find that as you strive for integrity in public speaking, you will achieve more integrity in your daily life, and that applying integrity in your daily life improves your public speaking integrity.

Respect

Respect refers to being considerate and thoughtful toward others. To be respectful in public speaking means being sensitive to your audience's thoughts and feelings, avoiding the use of offensive language, and appreciating diversity.

Taking time to get to know your audience can help you be more ethical. Knowing your audience helps you adjust your message to their needs and feelings. This does not mean changing your opinion. Pretending to change your mind to capture your audience's attention would itself be considered unethical. Instead, tailor your message so that your audience is better able to hear and understand it. For example, you would approach a group of Catholic nuns very differently on the subject of abortion than you would approach a group of pro-choice advocates, no matter which side of the debate you are on. The types of arguments you make, the evidence you use, and the examples you cite are likely to be different for each audience at hand. Is it unethical to talk about safe sex? The answer depends on the audience. If the audience is a group of college students, probably not, but if the audience is a group of preschoolers, the answer is probably "Yes!"

Respect also means avoiding the use of offensive language. Here we focus on three categories of offensive language: obscenity, racist language, and sexist language. All languages have their taboo words. In American English these words are often referred to as "four-letter" words even though some of them have more or fewer letters than four. I am sure that most of you are familiar with some of the more offensive of these terms,

HINT

Avoiding Profanity

As a rule, when giving a speech you should strive to use more formal language and avoid more colloquial forms of speech, including profanity.

Some words are simply less offensive versions of common profanity. Other words have more than one meaning: one traditional meaning that you find in the dictionary and another, more vulgar, meaning that people use as a form of profanity. Following is a list of words that you should avoid in your speech unless you are CERTAIN that it is not offensive and that you are using the word according to its nonvulgar definition.

Ass	Fudge
Bastard	Hell
Bitch	Hooter
Boob	Idiot
Crap	Jackass
Damn	Jerk
Dang	Pissy
Darn	Retard
Dick	Shoot
Dike/Dyke	Sissy
Dummy	Stupid
Freaking	Sucks

particularly the "f-word," which is considered one of the most offensive. I will leave it up to you and your friends to discover what the rest of these words include. Other words that are not quite as obscene are often equally offensive (see the Hint).

When the occasion calls for identifying groups of people based on perceived similarities, we often turn to racial categories. Racial terms such as *black, white, Asian, Latino/a, Hispanic,* and *Native American* are overgeneralizations based on skin color, eye shape, and hair. Think about it: Would you rather be identified as Irish or white? Salvadorean or Latino? Vietnamese or Asian? Afghani or Middle Eastern? Clearly, we would all prefer our actual national or ethnic heritage to the more general term that is often inaccurate. However, it is not always practical or possible to identify every person individually. Racial categories are the only terms we have to discuss some topics, especially issues dealing with race and equality. These terms become inappropriate when they are used unnecessarily or to further marginalize, insult, or devalue a particular race, nationality, or ethnicity.

There are also terms that are commonly used but still viewed as offensive. If you use these terms, you may not realize that they are hurtful or offensive. For example, using the term *oriental* to refer to Asians, particularly of East or Southeast Asian heritage, is considered offensive. The origins of the term as both a relative term meaning "east"— describing its location relative to Europe—and as a term describing the area east of the Mediterranean as a strange and exotic land, places Europe as the "center" of humanity and marginalizes Asia as somehow outside the center compared to Europe. Of course, life in Asia is neither strange nor exotic to those living there, and Asia is not east of anything if you are in Asia! *Asian,* on the other hand, although not specific enough in most cases to describe the nationality of individuals, at least accurately describes the continent of their origin. The term is, however, still problematic because we often do not apply the term to those from India, Pakistan, Kazakhstan, and Russia, all of which are also Asian countries.

Finally, there are terms that are intended to harm, insult, or humiliate others. We call these terms *abusive language* or *name-calling*. This kind of language is unethical not only because it is hurtful, but also because the ef-

Campuses across the United States are having to ask difficult questions and make painful choices between the values of free speech and the need to control hate speech. To find out more,

http://archive.aclu.org/library/pbp16.html

http://www.scu.edu/ethics/publications/iie/v5n2/codes.html

http://www.freedomforum.org/templates/document.asp?documentID=16143

fect of this type of speech is to silence the voices of others. Abusive language is antithetical to the principle of free speech. Still, because it is a form of free speech, it is legal. Although protected under the First Amendment, name-calling and abusive language are still considered unethical. Because you are a non-native speaker, if you have encountered these terms you might not have known that they are derogatory or unacceptable. These terms are cruel, and, beyond being unethical to use them, they reduce your credibility and trustworthiness with the audience. As Stephen Lucas tells us in *The Art of Public Speaking:*

> Avoiding racist, sexist, and other kinds of abusive language is not simply a matter of "political correctness." Such language is ethically suspect because it devalues the people in question and stereotypes them in ways that assume the innate superiority of one group over another. . . . The issue is not one of politics, but of respecting the dignity of the diverse groups in contemporary society.[3]

To be ethical, you need to respect diversity. Using language that is not offensive generally and that is not racist or sexist specifically is one aspect of respecting diversity. Communities the world over have become increasingly global. This is especially true here in the United States. Indeed, you and I are examples of the rich diversity found in every city throughout this country. People come from all around the world to live, study, and work in the United States. As such, to live and work and study successfully here, many people have been learning that it is in their best interests and in the interests of others to adopt an attitude of acceptance.

To respect diversity in public speaking suggests the willingness to listen to the views of others, to learn about other ways of being and doing in the world, and to adapt to the audience's way of knowing. For example, you can greet an audience in their language, research stories from their culture to refer to in your speech, and make sure that you learn what gestures or topics they consider inappropriate or offensive.

Honesty

"I did not have sexual relations with that woman," said President Bill Clinton when confronted about his extramarital affair. This claim cost President Clinton and the country credibility. Months of investigations and millions of dollars were spent to sort out the truth of the claim because, although the U.S. American people may find it distasteful and wrong to have an affair, many find lying even more reprehensible.

In 2003, President George W. Bush convinced Congress to declare war on Iraq, claiming that he had credible evidence that Saddam Hussein was developing nuclear weapons. He claimed in his State of the Union Address:

> The British government has learned that Saddam Hussein recently sought significant quantities of uranium from Africa. Our intelligence sources tell us that he has attempted to purchase high-strength aluminum tubes suitable for nuclear weapons production. Saddam Hussein has not credibly explained these activities. He clearly has much to hide.[4]

Six months later, when sources revealed that his intelligence claims were erroneous, and evidence began to mount that not only was the intelligence information wrong, but also that officials in the White House might have known that the information was unreliable, Senator Ted Kennedy despaired:

> It's bad enough that such a glaring blunder became part of the president's case for war. It's far worse if the case for war was made by deliberate deception. . . . The American people deserve to know whether the president is making war and peace decisions based on reliable information. We cannot risk American lives because of shoddy intelligence or outright lies.[5]

Kennedy was not questioning whether or not the United States should have gone to war if Iraq had weapons of mass destruction (WMDs), but whether the government had made the decision to go to war based on information the president had not adequately verified.

To be an ethical speaker, you must, above all, be honest in what you say and how you say it. This includes making sure that your information is accurate and reliable. We expect speakers to tell us the truth, represent their facts honestly, and use only reliable information. Speakers who manipulate, eliminate, or create supporting materials and reasoning to suit their own needs can risk more than the embarrassment of having others find out: They undermine the purpose of communication, which is to share ideas and meanings. As we can see in the above examples, unethical reporting can also have expensive, far-reaching, and/or devastating results.

When selecting your supporting materials (statistics, facts, examples, etc.), be sure to use only sources that are reputable and reliable. Avoid biased sources that have their own agenda. Then verify your information with other reliable sources whenever possible, especially if the information seems unusual, surprising, or contrary to other information about the subject. Do not use rumors (also known as hearsay) as evidence. There is no way to verify the information, and more often than not, the claim turns out to be untrue.

Be sure that you are not fabricating your evidence. Making up "facts," exaggerating your findings, or manipulating them in some other way to support

TABLE 3.1 Checklist for Ethical Evidence

______	All my evidence is from reliable and credible sources.
______	My evidence is free from fabrication.
______	My evidence is free from rumors.
______	My evidence includes all relevant information (I haven't left out or omitted any important information).
______	My opinions are clearly identified as such.
______	I have credited my sources properly using an acceptable style (e.g., MLA, APA, Chicago, etc.).

your claims are all forms of fabrication. Similarly, do not leave out any relevant information. Sometimes you might be tempted to leave out a particular piece of evidence, a statistic, or a fact because it contradicts or undermines your argument. If you have to hide or adjust your evidence so that the audience will believe you, then you are being dishonest. For example, if a developer were to give a speech to local homeowners about the benefits of a proposed shopping complex without mentioning the known environmental problems the development would cause, she would be unethical.

Be sure to identify all opinions as *opinions* and not as facts. If what you are saying is a "fact," then it should be supported by independent evidence. For example, "You cannot get a job without a college education" is an opinion. You would need to support this claim with facts and statistics; otherwise you are just offering your opinion. Finally, cite all your sources properly and give proper credit for all ideas and words that are not your own.

PLAGIARISM

U.S. Senator Joseph Biden withdrew from the 1988 presidential race after plagiarizing in his campaign speeches. Novelist Alex Haley settled a plagiarism suit claiming that portions of his most famous book, *Roots,* were plagiarized from Harold Courlander's *The African.*[6] Jayson Blair of *The New York Times* was fired after revelations that he both fabricated and plagiarized several articles. Ruined careers, costly lawsuits, and personal disgrace are the results of using someone else's words and ideas as our own. In the past few years, there have been many other stories about journalists, novelists, and politicians who plagiarized portions of their work. There has also been a great deal of discussion within the educational system about the growing problem of plagiarism in schools, especially in colleges and universities.

Plagiarism occurs when a writer uses ideas or words that are not his/her own. Sometimes the violation is unintended; other times it is intentional. Unintended examples of plagiarism include not paraphrasing a passage properly, forgetting to give credit for an idea, or misunderstanding what needs to be cited and what does not. Intentional forms of plagiarism include using verbatim (word-for-word) passages without quotation marks or citing the source, buying or borrowing entire essays or speeches from friends or off the Internet and turning them in as one's own work, or piecing together a series of quotes from a variety of authors as if one has written them. All of these forms of plagiarism are viewed as unethical in the United States and in most other Western educational systems. The Western standard of authorship assumes that, unless otherwise indicated, all words and ideas are original thoughts of the author. Violation of plagiarism standards can result in failing an assignment, failing a course, and/or being expelled from school. In the case of international students, plagiarizing can lead to losing one's student visa.

Unfortunately, some very good and ethical international students sometimes commit plagiarism inadvertently because not all cultures view ownership of ideas and texts in the same way. Some cultures might see using the

Copying the words of a famous person is one obvious form of plagiarism, but copying from another student is also considered plagiarism.

© Clay Bennet / The Christian Science Monitor

ideas and words of others as a way to both honor another's work and expand on one's own ideas. As one student said, according to Carolyn Metalene:

> In our country, things are [a] little different. We may perhaps call what our teacher calls "plagiarism" as "imitation," which is sometimes encouraged, especially for a beginner.[7]

Others have been taught that good scholarship is memorizing and then reciting texts at will:

> In some Asian cultures, students are taught to memorize and copy well-respected authors and leaders in their societies to show intelligence and good judgment in their writing.[8]

However, what they are copying or quoting need not be cited simply because the works are *so* well known within the culture that "any knowledgeable reader or audience *knows* the source. Thus, since the 'acknowledgment' of the source is in the very use of it, listing them in a bibliography is at best redundant and at worst an insult to a reader's intelligence."[9]

Non-native students might also struggle with paraphrasing properly and instead simply replace words from the original source with synonyms from a thesaurus. Additionally, they may not realize that, even when they use their own words to express an idea, they must credit where the idea came from. This is often further complicated by the fact that many non-native students have not been given adequate instruction on how to avoid plagiarism.

Technology has made plagiarizing even easier for students. You can buy entire speeches and essays online. However, you should know that instructors now have technology working for them as well.

Click Here http://www.turnitin.com

http://www.plagiarism.org

http://www.canexus.com/eve/index.shtml

When an instructor suspects that a student has plagiarized all or part of his/her work, the instructor can submit the portion in question to an online plagiarism detection service to find out. Within as little as twenty minutes, the instructor can find the original source.

The best way to avoid unintentional plagiarism is to cite sources whenever you are unsure of whether you need to or not. It is better to cite too often than too seldom. More specifically, cite sources any time you use two or more of someone else's words in a row, whenever you are summarizing or paraphrasing the words or ideas from a source, and any time you think your audience might not know a piece of information even if some other people view it as "common knowledge." You should also note that the need to cite sources is not limited to paper sources such as books, journals, magazines, and newspapers. You must cite all sources, including interviews, class lectures, television and radio programs, brochures, and websites. Anytime you are using the words or thoughts of another person, you must cite that person! Also see Table 3.2 on page 56.

CONSIDERING CULTURE

Plagiarism, Legends, and Myths

Lise Buranen, in her article "But I *Wasn't* Cheating: Plagiarism and Cross-Cultural Mythology," investigated the claim that Middle Eastern and Asian cultures may view plagiarism differently than do Western cultures. She found that while there is some truth to the rumor, much of the world teaches similar practices with regard to properly citing sources. In China, a very high-context culture, the tradition is to imply the credit, whereas in the Western world (consistent with a low-context cultural pattern), the standard is for very explicit, formal citations following a consistent style (MLA, APA, Chicago, etc.). However, in recent decades the move throughout the world has been toward a more Western model.

Source: Lise Buranen, "But I *Wasn't* Cheating: Plagiarism and Cross-Cultural Mythology," in *Perspectives on Plagiarism and Intellectual Property in a Postmodern World,* Lise Buranen and Alice M. Roy, ed. (New York: State University of New York Press, 1999), 69.

TABLE 3.2 **Dartmouth College Offers the Following Advice to Avoid Plagiarizing**

Cite sources for all verbatim quotations of two or more consecutive words.

Readers expect to know the original source of any quotation, whether for the purpose of checking its accuracy or using it in their own work. Exact wording, or even a single distinctive word, taken from a source should be placed in quotation marks.

Cite sources from which you paraphrase or summarize facts or ideas.

Whenever you rely on another's information or ideas, you should cite your source, even if you do not use a verbatim quotation. When you paraphrase a source in your work, be sure to organize this summary or paraphrase in your own distinctive manner, mold it into the flow of your argument and use your own words and sentences. If you do make use of even part of a sentence, be sure to use quotation marks. Seeming to paraphrase when you are in fact quoting is considered plagiarism.

Cite sources for ideas or information that could be regarded as common knowledge but which you think your reader might still find unfamiliar.

This case addresses those situations where no definitive boundary exists between an idea that has not originated with you but which seems generally well-known . . . and a well-known idea you intend to interrogate pointedly or to treat as a distinctive or seldom well-understood concept (Freud's notion of the Oedipus complex, for example). . . . In general you need not cite the source of information that seems part of our common stock of knowledge. For example, you can assume that your readers know that the atomic structure of water is H_2O; that Jane Austen wrote *Pride and Prejudice*; that Martin Luther King, Jr. was a leading figure in the U.S. civil rights movement; or that Charles Darwin claimed that new species of plants and animals evolve over long periods of time. Citing references for such facts is unnecessary.

Cite sources for materials that you might not normally consider as "texts" because they are not written.

Your sources might include materials such as public lectures, architecture, laboratory procedures, musical compositions, films, audio or visual tapes, works of art, maps, Web pages, statistical tables, or electronic databases. If used as in the cases listed above, any non-written source also must be cited.

Source: "Sources: Their Use and Acknowledgment," The Dartmouth College Sources Website http://www.dartmouth.edu/~sources/, (copyright 1998) <http://www.dartmouth.edu/~sources/about/when.html>.

You do not have to cite a source when you are providing the results of a survey or experiment that you conducted; sharing personal experiences, opinions, or ideas; and referring to facts and cultural references understood to be "common knowledge." (Be careful here! What is common knowledge in one culture may not be common knowledge in another.) However, if you are unsure, it is better to cite the source.

In Chapter Six we will discuss how to cite sources in your outline and bibliography, but you need to do more than include source information for your instructor; you must also provide it for your audience. To cite sources in speeches or "out loud," simply state whom you are quoting or paraphrasing, what his or her expertise is, and/or where you got the information. For example:

As a direct quote:

> According to Virginia L. Downie, in her book *Together: A Relationship Survival Kit*, "if the power to mold your life is in your hands, . . . you are free to shape your life in new and beautiful ways."[10]

As a paraphrase:

> Virgina L. Downie reminds us in her book *Together: A Relationship Survival Kit* that we are able to create our lives any way we wish to because we hold all the power to make decisions for ourselves.[11]

Citing a statistic:

> The 2002–2003 academic year welcomed over 586,000 international students to U.S. universities and colleges, according to the Institute of International Education's annual report.[12]

Students are sometimes tempted to purposefully plagiarize or even fabricate (create "facts" and "stats") in their speeches. Every instructor can tell stories about students buying papers off the Internet, cutting and pasting large portions of text from a source into their speech, using A speeches from former speech students, or simply making up information for a speech. All I can say about this is *don't!* Intentionally attempting to pass off someone else's work as your own or blatantly lying about your facts can lead to serious trouble.

ETHICS AND RESPONSIBILITIES OF LISTENING

Maurice walked up to the front of the class, trying to look confident in his traditional Scottish kilt. "Why did I think that wearing a kilt would be a good idea for my speech?" he wondered. "Everyone is laughing at me." Indeed, several of his classmates were snickering and whispering to each other about Maurice's "dress." During the speech, all Maurice could think about were the smirks on the faces of some of his classmates and the looks of pity on the others. He stumbled through what had been a beautifully written, thoroughly researched, and carefully practiced presentation.

Jamie had a different problem. No one laughed, no one giggled, no one even bothered to smile encouragement. Instead, as Jamie looked out across the sea of her classmates, she noticed two students passing notes to each other, another student sleeping soundly behind sunglasses and a baseball cap, and one student reading for another class. The few people who were paying attention did not make up for the fact that the others were clearly uninterested in what she had to say. She finished her presentation abruptly and returned to her seat, embarrassed and vowing that she would never speak in public again.

As an audience member, sometimes it is difficult to give your full attention to what the speaker is saying because his/her visual aids, mannerisms, or mistakes distract you. You may let your mind wander to other classes, your to-do list, a date that you have tomorrow, or even your upcoming speech. You might decide to catch up on reading, socializing, or some much-needed sleep. You may even think that you are listening when you are actually only passively hearing words float across the room. In fact, it is often easier to ignore another person's presentation than to pay attention to it. Listening takes time, effort, and often a great deal of patience and understanding. Who has the time or energy for all that? *You* do! You ethically made that commitment when you signed up for this class. In addition to your ethical responsibilities as a speaker, you have ethical responsibilities as an audience member.

Hearing versus Listening

First, let's make a distinction between *hearing* and *listening*. In English, we often use these words interchangeably:

> Did you hear/listen to the report on the radio yesterday?
>
> Are you listening to/hearing me?

However, these two words refer to different, but related, things. *Hearing* refers to the passive, physiological process of receiving sound waves. Sound waves enter the ear canal and vibrate the eardrum, which sends a signal to the brain that sound is occurring. However, we can hear sounds without actually paying attention to them. Think about it. What can you hear right now? (See Try This.)

Listening is actively paying attention or attending to the sounds around you. When we listen, we not only hear sounds; we also try to grasp the meaning of what we hear. When we are listening to another person, we are actively trying to understand his or her message.

Listening Mistakes

Most people are not very good listeners, which is ironic considering that we spend more time listening than doing any other communication activity! Every day we spend at least fifty percent of our awake time listening, and students spend up to ninety percent of their time at school listening![13] Unfortunately, most people have received more training in how to drive a car or how to make a sandwich than in how to listen effectively. As a current or former ESL student, you have an advantage over many native English speakers in that you have probably received at least some training in how to listen in English for understanding, and you have, no doubt, been practicing the art of listening concentration in a variety of communication contexts. Still, in this section, we will look at some of the most common mistakes people make when listening to others and offer some tips on how to further improve your listening and listening-comprehension abilities.

Listening

Close your eyes and listen to every sound you can hear right now. Can you hear traffic noise? Dogs barking in the distance? Birds outside your window? A faraway airplane or siren? Are there other people in the room eating, breathing loudly, flipping pages, clearing their throats, tapping, writing, talking? Is the heating/cooling system droning quietly in the background? What other sounds can you hear? Before we asked you to actively pay attention to these other noises around you, you probably did not notice most of these sounds, but your ears and brain were hearing them. This is the difference between hearing and listening. When we listen, we actively choose to give attention to the sounds we are hearing.

Listening Mistake #1: Allowing Yourself to Be Distracted

Listeners sometimes make the mistake of allowing themselves to become distracted by things the speaker does, the environment, or personal concerns. A speaker who has hair in an unusual style or color, a multitude of facial piercings or tattoos, and a strong, unfamiliar accent or who thumps the podium repeatedly may unintentionally be directing your attention away from the message. Allowing your mind to wander away from the message to the speaker's appearance or delivery is a mistake that will lead you to miss the message.

Loud cars outside, cell phones ringing, commotion in the hallway, a hot or cold classroom, or strong smells can also lead your attention to the environment instead of the speaker's message. The urge to catch a glimpse of the rare sports car, to see whose phone is ringing, or to figure out where those wonderful barbeque smells are coming from can be a strong enticement to forget about the speaker and his/her message.

Personal concerns can also become distracting. If you are tired, hungry, angry, in love, excited, nervous, or bored, you may find it difficult to keep your focus on what the speaker is saying. Instead, you may be compelled to take a nap, plan your lunch date, or plot your revenge. You may even be nervous about your own upcoming speech. The tendency to let your mind wander for personal reasons can be the most difficult distraction to ignore.

Listening Mistake #2: Prejudging

Another mistake that listeners make is prejudging the speaker and the message before they have even heard what the speaker has to say. You might think that the speaker "looks" boring. You might have heard a rumor that s/he is not believable or honest. You might assume, based on earlier experiences with the speaker, that you and the speaker do not agree on any issue, so no matter what s/he has to say, you already "know" that you won't agree.

If you already know the speaker's topic, you might think that you know what s/he is going to say or what kind of arguments s/he will present. You might think you know all there is to know about the topic, or, conversely, you might think that the topic is too complicated or difficult for you to understand. In any of these situations, deciding that you already know all about the speaker and his/her message will make listening to and understanding the message more difficult. Remember, we often hear only what we want to hear. Like blocking out the sounds of traffic and the birds outside, we can block out messages that we don't want to hear.

Listening Mistake #3: Concentrating Too Hard

Unlike the listeners who ignore the speaker or do not bother to concentrate on what he or she is saying, some listeners make the mistake of concentrating too hard. This is a common problem for people who are afraid they won't understand the message or who want to try and remember everything the speaker says. You might try to write down everything the speaker says, only to find that you cannot write fast enough to keep up and start missing words and sentences and whole sections of the speech. You might try to keep a list in your mind of every point the speaker makes along with all the details, even the irrelevant ones, only to find that you can't keep that much detail in your mind at one time. Additionally, listeners can make themselves more nervous by trying to concentrate too hard, which further complicates the listening process. When we are nervous, we become distracted by our own state of mind.

Listening Mistake #4: Pretending to Listen

Another mistake listeners make is pretending to listen when they are actually paying attention to something else. This mistake, called *pseudo-listening,* is often used as a cover-up. When your mind wanders, you might still nod and smile at the speaker in all the right places. You might jot down a few words to appear to be taking notes, when in actuality you are making a to-do or grocery list.

Listening Mistake #5: Reacting Emotionally to "Triggers"

Sometimes listeners start listening carefully to a speaker but then become distracted by something the speaker says. Some words can shock, upset, or startle us so much that we find it difficult to continue listening. We call these words *trigger words* or *red flag words* because they trigger, or elicit, a strong emotional response. Profanity; racist, sexist, or hateful speech; or slang can create unnecessarily strong emotional reactions in the audience. When we hear these words, we tend to "shut down" and stop paying attention to what the speaker is saying and start listening to our own concerns.

Tips for Improving Listening

Ethically, you have a responsibility to listen to other speakers, not just to show respect but also to improve your understanding of issues, your critical thinking, and your public speaking skills. Fortunately, there are several strategies you can use to avoid the common listening mistakes and to improve your listening skills and comprehension.

Tip #1: Prepare to Listen

Preparing and planning to listen will help you focus your attention on the speaker and limit the number of unexpected distractions. Be sure to get enough sleep the night before so that you are not sleepy during the presentation. Eat before getting to class so that you do not become hungry during the presentation. Even a small snack before class can help reduce distracting hunger pains. Dress in layers (wear a sweater over a lightweight shirt and bring a jacket) so that if the temperature becomes uncomfortable, you can easily adjust your own comfort level.

Before the presentation begins, anticipate what the speaker might talk about. Generate a list of questions you would like the speaker to answer. If you are listening to a class lecture, be sure to do all the relevant reading in advance so that you have a clear idea of the topics to be covered. Anticipating the topics can help you be a better-informed audience member and make understanding much easier.

When you arrive at the class or presentation, turn off your cell phone or pager and remind those around you to do the same. Choose a seat that is comfortable and allows you to easily see and hear the speaker and any visual aids and audiovisual equipment. Sit up straight, get out any note-taking materials that you need (paper, pens, tape recorder, etc.), and put away any of your belongings that might draw your attention away from the speaker. On the top of your paper before the speaker begins, date and specify the event, the name of the speaker, and the topic.

Tip #2: Listen with Respect

Resolve to listen openly and with respect for the speaker. Tell yourself that you will acknowledge and then suspend any judgments you hold about the speaker or topic so that you can hear the speaker's entire message without the influence of your predisposed ideas. Also, actively prevent yourself from attending to the speaker's physical appearance, vocal patterns, and bodily actions. If you find yourself being distracted by the speaker, refocus your attention back to the topic.

Tip #3: Listen for Content/Meaning

As you begin listening to the presentation, jot down the main points of the speech. Listen for words that indicate significant points. Signposts (words or phrases that indicate where in a speech a speaker is, such as *first, second, next, finally*) and transitional statements (statements that move a speaker smoothly from one key idea to the next) can indicate important ideas in the speech. Write down any repeated words or phrases and any idea or word the speaker defines or describes in detail. Do not try to write down everything the speaker says, only the larger, more important points.

Relate what the speaker discusses to your own understanding, knowledge, and experience. Think of your own examples. This will help you integrate the information into your own knowledge.

Most speakers will summarize their speech with a brief conclusion that reviews the main points and key ideas of the speech. Listen carefully to the conclusion to be sure that you did not miss any key points and to verify that you understood the speaker's message.

Tip #4: Attend to Nonverbal Messages

Pay attention to the nonverbal messages the speaker sends that support the verbal message. Often, speakers will reinforce important ideas with hand gestures (indicating the point number with fingers) and vocalics (speaking louder to stress important points). Carefully examine the visual aid for additional support for the speaker's message, but do not become distracted by the visual aid. Pay attention to why the speaker has chosen the visual aid and how it supports the verbal message. Look for the logical connection between the visual aid and the verbal message.

Tip #5: Review the Message

As soon as you can after the presentation or class, review your notes and fill in any additional information you can recall. We begin to forget what we heard very quickly. After forty-eight hours, we remember only about twenty-five percent of what we heard. Reviewing immediately after a presentation aids our ability to remember more and for a longer period of time.

If you have questions for the speaker that he or she did not answer during the presentation and you have an opportunity before leaving, approach the speaker and ask for clarification. You can also talk to other audience members and ask them what they understood or learned from the presentation. They might be able to provide you with additional information, understanding, and perspectives on the presentation. If they cannot, investigate the topic further as soon as possible following the presentation. In the Internet age, you have the advantage of being able to do a quick search of the topic. This review process will help you remember, reinforce, and clarify the information presented.

ADDITIONAL TIPS FOR NON-NATIVE LISTENERS

As a non-native listener, you may also have additional challenges when listening to lectures or fellow students' speeches. Researchers have found that even second-language learners who have high sentence comprehension sometimes have difficulty identifying key ideas in conversations, lectures, or speeches. In spoken English, speakers often offer clues to the listener regarding the organization of ideas, which ideas are most important, and how the ideas relate to one another. Speakers also offer cues such as previews of upcoming main ideas, summaries of important ideas already discussed, emphasis to highlight key ideas, and connectives to signal the beginnings of, end-

TABLE 3.3 **Examples of Discourse Cues**

Previews: "Let's look at the three steps involved in applying for a scholarship."
Summaries: "To review," "To summarize," "In conclusion"
Emphasizers: "This is important," "Above all," "Most importantly"
Signaling connectives: "first," "in addition," "also," "finally," "however"

ings of, and transitions between ideas.[14] Listen for these cues from the speaker to help you understand how the speech is organized and distinguish the importance of ideas (see Table 3.3).

Researchers have also found that second-language learners sometimes have trouble understanding spoken words that they understand easily in written form. My mother used to tell me a story about when she taught ESL classes. She and the other instructor took the students to a restaurant to practice ordering from a menu in English. The server asked the first student if she wanted "soup or salad," and the student responded, "Yes, I will have the super salad!"

This story emphasizes what you already know: English does not always sound the way it is written. You might, as in the soup example, not be able to discern where one word ends and another begins. You might give an alternate meaning to a word that has more than one meaning (*to, too, two; here, hear; they're, their, there; bear, bare; no, know*). You might not recognize an alternative pronunciation of words that you are otherwise familiar with (*often* pronounced "OF-ten" or "O-fen"; *tomato* pronounced "toe-MA-toe" or "toe-MAW-toe"; *conflict* pronounced "KÄN-flict" or "ken-FLICT"; *cement* pronounced "si-MENT" or "SE-ment"; *formidable* pronounced "FOR-me-de-bel" or "fer-MI-de-bel"). You might be familiar with the written word but not with its (often unpredictable) pronunciation (*ought* is pronounced "ôt"; *ghetto* is pronounced "GE-toe"; *knowledge* is pronounced "NÄ-lij"). You may also have difficulty dividing words or discerning the boundaries between one word and the next in free-flowing speech.[15]

There are ways to improve your overall comprehension. First, take notes. Write down the words that the speaker stresses and/or repeats. Writing down what you hear will not only help you translate what is being said, but it can also let you know when you have misunderstood a word or its pronunciation. Further, notes give you a chance to go back after a lecture or speech and look up confusing words or ask others for clarification. Finally, writing down the stressed and repeated words can help you discern the key ideas of the presentation.

Whenever possible, tape-record presentations. Listening more than once to a presentation can familiarize you to the various accents, pronunciations, and rhythms of a variety of speakers. As you know, over the course of a semester you tend to become more comfortable with the speech patterns of in-

Syllabic and Stressed Languages

Unlike "syllabic languages" (languages that give equal importance to each syllable in a word) such as Italian or French, English is a "stressed language" (a language that stresses certain words while de-emphasizing others). Distinguishing among the various words in a sentence can be problematic for non-native speakers. The stressed words in sentences are usually the *content words* (the nouns, verbs, adjectives, and adverbs), and the non-stressed words are the *function words* (determiners, auxiliary verbs, prepositions, conjunctions, and pronouns). Additionally, most content words in English put stress on the first syllable of the word or the word itself if it is a single syllable, thus helping you find the boundaries of the individual words as well. If you listen for the stressed words, you will be better able to understand the intended meaning while at the same time becoming familiar with the rhythm and flow of spoken English.

Source: Kenneth Beare, "How to Improve Your Pronunciation," *English as 2nd Language*, About.com, http://esl.about.com/library/howto/htpronounce.htm.

dividual professors. In a speech class, you need to also become comfortable with the speech patterns of your classmates, who are likely to have accents from all corners of the Earth. The more you focus your concentration on listening, the more comfortable you will become listening to and understanding all kinds of English speakers.

SUMMARY

Ethics in public speaking and listening follow the same general rule of ethics in everyday life: When in doubt about whether or not to do something, don't do it. Speakers sometimes simply do not realize that they are engaging in unethical behavior. They write a speech that sounds good to them and fulfills a personal need, but they haven't examined whether or not the speech is relevant to the audience, or they haven't considered the legal or ethical implications of their presentation to the audience.

To avoid these common ethical pitfalls, carefully consider what you choose to discuss, research carefully and thoughtfully, include all relevant information, and present it openly and fairly. Review the Checklist for Ethical Evidence (Table 3.1) as you research and choose your supporting materials, and cite your sources accurately to avoid plagiarizing. By maintaining integrity, respect, and honesty throughout the speech's writing and delivery process, you are sure to fulfill your ethical obligations while you avoid plagiarizing.

When listening to others, give them your full attention and respect. Don't allow your attention to wander. Keep focused and save your judgments until you have heard everything the speaker has to say. At first, it may seem that being an ethical speaker and listener is too difficult to achieve, but in reality, it is simply a matter of being sincere, honest, and careful.

Discussion Questions and Activities

1. During the next round of classroom speeches, practice being a good audience member by listening attentively to each speaker (looking directly at the speaker, taking notes on the key ideas, providing encouraging feedback) and by applauding enthusiastically at the end. Remember, good audiences make good speakers.

For questions 2–5: In each of the following scenarios, identify the specific ethical pitfall the student has fallen into and offer suggestions for how the student could have avoided being unethical in his/her speech.

2. A student gives a stand-up comedy routine about college life instead of giving a speech—it's entertaining and the audience loves it.
3. A student needs to make some more sales at her part-time job selling cell phones, so she gives a speech to persuade her classmates to sign up with her cell phone company but leaves out some of the advantages of the competition's service plans.

4. Senior citizen discounts are very helpful to senior citizens, so a student decides to give an informative speech telling his classmates about some of the best senior discounts available locally.
5. A student defends her choice to teach her classmates how to obtain a fake identification card by saying, "Everybody uses a fake ID, right? What's wrong with telling fellow students about a better way to get one and not get caught?"

Chapter Quiz

1. True or False: Speaking well in public means abiding by the ethical standards of good speech preparation and presentation.
2. True or False: Researchers have found that second-language learners sometimes have trouble understanding spoken words that they understand easily in written form.
3. Unintended examples of plagiarism include:
   - **a.** Not paraphrasing a passage properly.
   - **b.** Forgetting to give credit for an idea.
   - **c.** Misunderstanding what needs to be cited and what does not.
   - **d.** All of the above
4. All of the following are common ethical pitfalls EXCEPT:
   - **a.** Failing to thoroughly prepare
   - **b.** Citing sources
   - **c.** Benefiting personally
   - **d.** Failing to consider the audience's needs and interests
5. List three of the most common mistakes people make when listening to others.

   ____

   ____

   ____

6. List three ways to improve listening comprehension.

   ____

   ____

   ____

Chapter 3 Quiz Answers

1. True, **2.** True, **3.** d, **4.** b, **5.** Allowing oneself to become distracted; Prejudging the speaker and message before listening; Concentrating too hard. **6.** Prepare to listen; Listen with respect; Listen for content/meaning.

CHAPTER 4 Analyzing the Speaking Situation

CHAPTER GOAL

By the end of this chapter you will be able to conduct a three-level audience analysis.

Let's talk about sex. Imagine that you have been asked to give a presentation next week to a group of people in your community. The only thing you know about the presentation is that the topic is *sex*. Because you know there is not enough time to talk about EVERY aspect of sex in one presentation, you will have to narrow down the topic; so what will you talk about specifically? I have asked this question of my students many times. Here are some of the actual topic suggestions they've given:

Abstinence	Safe sex
Alternatives to intercourse	Sexual assault
Birth control	Sexual harassment
Dating	Sexual orientation
Different attitudes of men and women	Sexually transmitted diseases
Handling rejection	Understanding your body
Looking "sexy"	Viagra
Religious considerations	

Each of these could make a very interesting speech. However, you still have a big challenge. I forgot to tell you something very important about your presentation; luckily, you did not forget to ask me: "To whom am I speaking and for what occasion?" These are two of the most important questions a speaker can ask before giving a speech. As a matter of fact, the audience and the circumstances of the presentation do not influence only what you will talk about and how you will talk about it, but also whether or not you should even agree to give the speech! Why? Because a speech is given for the benefit of the audience, not the speaker. Unfortunately, asking questions about the audience and the event is often the most overlooked step in developing a speech.[1]

Like a gift, speeches are given to an audience for their enjoyment, enhancement, and enlightenment. For an audience to fully appreciate your presentation, you need to adapt your speech to the audience and occasion while making the presentation fit you. In other words, you need to consider the complete speaking situation: Who is your audience? What is important to them and what are their attitudes toward you, your topic, and the occasion? We call this *analyzing* the speaking situation. Given the importance of analyzing the speaking situation, some other questions you might want to ask are:

- How many people will be in the audience?
- What is the sex/gender make-up of the audience?
- What is the age range of most members of the audience?
- Do they belong to an organization?
- Is the presentation a requirement or is the audience there by choice?
- What time of day will the presentation be?
- Will the audience be fed before, during, or after the presentation?
- How long are they expecting me to speak?

Giving a speech is like giving a gift. You select a gift for a particular person (a necktie is not a good present for a little girl) and wrap it up for a specific occasion (Santa Claus wrap is not appropriate for birthday gifts). The gift must suit the person and the occasion!

- Why have they asked me to speak?
- Are they expecting me to talk from personal experience, or will I need to do extensive research?

There are three levels in analyzing the speaking situation: (1) Analysis of the speaking context, (2) demographic audience analysis, and (3) dispositional audience analysis. Your analysis of the speaking situation will guide your speech preparation process from start to finish: from choosing a topic to selecting supporting materials to designing visual aids to crafting the perfect conclusion. Let's begin by examining some features you may know that are common to U.S. American audiences.

STARTING ASSUMPTIONS: ADAPTING TO THE HOST CULTURE'S MORES

As a non-native speaker of English, you have both advantages and disadvantages when it comes to understanding and adapting to an English-speaking audience. As a non-native speaker, we can assume that you have direct experience with at least one other culture and language. This means that you are already acutely aware that there is not only one way to view the world. You have been exposed to other values, attitudes, and beliefs that many English-only speaking people have not.

Self-Analysis

Before conducting an analysis of your audience, conduct an analysis of yourself. As you read this chapter, jot down how you would "measure up" as an audience member. Chart your demographic profile and your core values, attitudes, and assumptions. Keep and use this profile to identify the ways in which you are similar to or different from the members of your audience.

Ethnocentrism, as we discussed in Chapter One, is the belief or attitude that one's own culture or ethnic group is somehow superior to all others. People behave sometimes as if their culture's ways of behaving are the "right" ways. As we grow older and are exposed to alternative ways of being and behaving in the world, we learn that our culture is not the only "right" one, although sometimes we still act as if it were. People who have lived in more than one culture learn that there are differences in the ways cultures approach everyday challenges.

When preparing and delivering a speech, it is important to continually keep in mind that every person has a different set of beliefs about right and wrong, better and worse, and true and false. To help audiences receive the intended message, good speakers adapt to the audience's way of knowing, seeing, and understanding the world. As a non-native speaker, your experiences in more than one culture can be a true asset.

On the other hand, you might not be familiar with some of the common, more subtle behaviors, attitudes, values, and beliefs of U.S. American audiences. Depending on what culture(s) you most closely identify with, you might find the behaviors of an American audience surprising, unpredictable, or even rude. Therefore, before we begin our discussion on analyzing the speaking situation, I want to give you some background into U.S. American ways of thinking that might help you better understand the audiences you are likely to encounter when speaking in the United States. Of course, I say this with the full understanding and acknowledgment that most audiences in the United States today are made up of people from around the world.

The list in Table 4.1 should give you a good idea about some of the less obvious aspects of audiences in the United States. Now, let's look at how we can analyze a speaking situation in *any* country

CONTEXTUAL AUDIENCE ANALYSIS

When you are first asked to give a speech, you are likely to ask some of the following questions before you even accept the invitation:

- What is the event about?
- Is it part of a larger series of events?

TABLE 4.1 Characteristics of U.S. American Audiences

U.S. Americans:

- Are often comfortable using first names even with people they have just met. Typically, they reserve titles for particular professions such as political officials, teachers and professors, and medical professionals. Don't be surprised if an audience member addresses you by your first name. (U.S. Americans are typically unfamiliar with cultural norms that use middle or surnames.)
- Expect people to look them directly in the eye. If someone avoids eye contact, they tend to view the person as untrustworthy or dishonest.
- Expect speakers to be energetic and personal, but to use a professional speaking style. Slang, colloquial language, and sloppy grammar are not appreciated.
- Have grown up on mediated messages, especially on television, so they appreciate presentations with a variety of visual aids that reiterate the message through pictures.
- Tend to speak loudly and quickly and often find it difficult to listen to very soft speech, but they appreciate speakers who speak clearly and slowly.
- Are cooperative audience members. When you ask them to participate, they will usually comply enthusiastically, but be careful not to embarrass individuals.
- Are likely to listen attentively and give a great deal of feedback in the form of head nodding and smiles.
- Usually participate enthusiastically during question-and-answer sessions. Many audience members will go beyond asking you questions and will try to offer their own opinions and insights.
- Like to have a personal interaction with the speaker, so be prepared to have several people approach you after your presentation to further discuss your ideas.

- How big will the audience be?
- What date, day, and time will the event take place?
- Am I the only speaker or the keynote speaker?
- Where will it be held?

All of these questions are part of the first level of analysis. You are trying to find out the context in which you are expected to present. You might be asking some of these questions simply to determine if you are available during that time and day. You might be asking other questions to develop a picture of the event and what might be expected of you. In either case, the answers offer important clues about how you should choose your topic and prepare your presentation. There are two areas to consider when examining the context of a speaking situation: the *purpose* and the *logistics*.

Purpose

When examining the purpose of the event, you want to discover who is sponsoring the event, why they are having the event, what other activities are taking place around the event, and what the organizers expect from you before, during, and after the event. The first question to ask is, "*Who is sponsoring this event?*"

Organizations are established to promote and support particular goals. Knowing who is putting on an event can offer valuable insights into the attitudes and expectations of the organizers in asking you to speak. For example, imagine you have been asked to give a speech about college life in the United States. You were referred to the group by one of your professors because you are a serious student who has excelled in both the academic and the social aspects of college life at your school. Think for a minute about what you might want to talk about or how you might approach such a speech. Then ask, "*Who is sponsoring the event?*" How might you start clarifying your approach to the speech based on the following answers?

Keynote Speaker
(also, *keynoter*)
The main speaker at an event or the person who delivers the most important speech at an event (especially at a conference, convention, or political event).

A job placement center

A local high school

The college's board of trustees

You might imagine that the job placement center is looking for someone to inspire out-of-work adults to go back to school. The high school is probably trying to prepare students for the transition to college, and the board of trustees might be promoting the college to the local community. You don't yet have all the information you need to create your presentation, but you have some preliminary information to help you start to formulate your ideas.

The next question to ask is, "*What is the purpose of the event?*" Once, I was asked to speak to a group about interpersonal relationships. The initial invitation simply said, "You will need to talk to a group of men and women about something related to relationships for about an hour." On further inquiry, I discovered that the sponsor of the event was a shelter for homeless families and that the parents in each of the families were required to attend a one-hour workshop each week to improve their skills as parents, as workers, and as citizens. This information certainly helped me further clarify my topic selection and plan strategies to relate to the audience.

In general, classroom speeches are meant to exhibit your learning. Usually, the instructor assigns the general topic and purpose of your presentation. However, when asked to speak outside the classroom, it is important to discover the specific purpose of the event so that your speech fits into the goals of the event. Are the organizers hoping that you will persuade the audience to vote for or against a particular measure? Do they want you to teach the audience how to do something? Is it an award ceremony? If so, you should strive to create excitement. Is it a funeral? In that case, you will want to honor and move the audience. Is it a protest? Your job there is to motivate and energize supporters. Are you being asked to give a commencement or graduation speech? In that speech, you will want to inspire and create hope.

The next question to ask is, "*Is this part of a larger event or am I the 'main attraction'?*" This is an important question. Are you one in a series of speakers, part of a panel discussion, the warm-up for the main speaker, or the actual keynote speaker? Is this one event in a series of events lasting all day or for several days, like during a conference or festival? Is this a recurring event? Does it take place every week or month or year? Is there a vote taking place? Will there be entertainment? Will people be eating or drinking before or during the event? The answers to these questions will influence how you engage the audience and what you hope to accomplish in your presentation.

If you are one of many speakers, learn about the other speakers and their topics so that your speech does not inadvertently overlap or contradict theirs. If you are on a panel, find out how your expertise complements the expertise of others on the panel and focus your attention on the areas for which you were picked. If you are speaking before the keynote speaker, adjust and adapt to his/her topic as much as possible (that is not to say that you have to change your attitudes or beliefs in any way; you simply want to avoid inadvertently "stealing the thunder" of or "overshadowing" the main event).

If you are the keynote speaker, find out if others will speak before or after you, and if and how you will be introduced. Do you need to provide a brief biography, or will you be introducing yourself? If you are speaking at a conference, you should find out what the theme of the conference is and what the other speakers will be talking about (it is also a good idea to attend other conference presentations).

Awards, food, cocktails, votes, or announcements can also affect the audience members' ability to focus on your presentation. Such distractions affect their mood and can make them even more enthusiastic. Weigh these factors when preparing your speech. Planning for potential distractions can greatly reduce surprises during your presentation.

Finally, ask, "*What is expected of me before and after my presentation?*" Do the organizers want you to participate in some or all of the other events? They may invite you to attend tours or other presentations, or go out with VIPs after the presentation. Are they expecting you to arrive right before your speech and leave immediately after? After I gave a luncheon speech to a community service organization last year, the attendees started fidgeting and looking around nervously. The president apologized as she asked me to leave, saying they always had a closed business meeting immediately after the speaker was finished. Unfortunately, I had not been told about this prior to the engagement, nor had I asked. Luckily, we have both learned our lesson from this slightly embarrassing moment.

Logistics

Now that you have some general information about the event, let's find out something about the details of the event and the audience.

Size of Audience

The number of people in the audience has a significant impact on how you should plan and deliver your speech. Generally, the smaller the audience, the less formal and more personal a presentation can be. For a larger audience, the presentation should be more formal and generic. With a small audience (i.e., fewer than ten to fifteen people), you can likely tailor the message to specific concerns of audience members, adapt easily to feedback you receive during the presentation, include activities for the audience to try, and ask for audience comments and questions throughout the presentation. As the size of the audience increases, you will know less and less about each individual person. In turn, you have less of a chance to respond and adapt to feedback from individuals and might be able to take a few questions only at the end.

Imagine giving a speech on how to use the Internet to conduct academic research. Imagine speaking to a group of two, three, or four people. How about a group of twenty or thirty people? How about two or three hundred people? With a small group you can probably have participants gather around while you demonstrate on your computer and then give them an opportunity to find information on their own. You can also answer any questions that the individual participants have, adapting your presentation moment by moment to their needs and concerns.

With a medium-sized audience, you might give the presentation in a computer lab where each participant or every two participants have access to a computer to follow along with your tutorial. You can take questions from the audience to clarify any confusion, but overall, you will follow your planned outline.

A very large audience requires a more formal language and delivery style as well as requires the use of a public address system.

For a large audience, you are likely to use an overhead computer-projection system that is easily visible to the audience. The lights over the audience will likely be dimmed, so acknowledging feedback and questions will be difficult. You might provide a brief flyer that highlights some of the key points of the presentation, since audience members will not get a chance to practice your suggestions during the presentation.

From these examples, you can see that the size of the audience influences not only the formality of the language and delivery of the presentation, but the supporting materials, visual aids, and audience interaction as well.

Timing

The timing of the event includes the time of day and the amount of time for the speech. Early in the morning, late in the evening, before a meal when everyone is hungry, or after a big meal when everyone is full and sleepy all affect an audience's attention span. Although people's preferences vary, many teachers and professional speakers avoid having to speak from about 1:30 p.m. to about 4:00 p.m. Why? Because this is the "sleepy" time of day for many people. Typically, people have just eaten lunch or they have become overly hungry. Most have already put in half a day of work or school.

If you know that you have to give a speech during this time of day, be sure to plan an interesting attention getter that gets your audience members excited, out of their seats, or actively participating in the presentation. To increase classroom energy, students have had their classmates stand up and stretch as part of a relaxation speech, do simple yoga poses for a yoga speech, and stand up instead of raise their hands for an opening audience poll.

The amount of time you are allotted for your speech is also an important consideration. Shorter time limits of five to ten minutes indicate that you should cover your points concisely and directly. Longer time limits allow for more extended examples, stories, and extensive background information and supporting material.

You should develop your presentation to fit easily into the time limits set forth for the event. Going significantly over or under the allotted time can irritate audience members and cause them to lose interest and you to lose credibility.

Venue

You will also need to know about the venue where you will be speaking. What kind of room is it? Is it inside or outside? How many people does it accommodate? Will the audience be sitting in auditorium-style chairs, rented fold-up chairs, at tables, behind desks, or standing? Are there decorations in and around the room that might detract from your presentation? Will there be noises from inside or outside the room that might make it difficult for the audience to hear you? Is there anything special or historic about the location that you can comment on or relate to your topic? Is the room typically too hot or cold? Can the temperature be controlled? Knowing the answers to all of these questions will help you prepare for and adjust to any potential disruptions or difficulties presented by the physical setting itself.

You should also become familiar with any equipment available for your use. Is there a working overhead projector, television, VCR/DVD player, audio equipment, chalk- or whiteboards, and/or flip charts with pens? Will you have an easel to display any posters you have prepared? Does the organization offer computer-projection equipment? And, most importantly, do you know how to use it? The best plan for handling equipment issues is to ask what is available, whether you need keys or help to access the equipment, and how to work the equipment once you are there. Then, if at all possible, arrange to visit the venue in advance of your presentation so that you can see the room and the equipment for yourself. It is a good idea to run through your presentation with visuals if you can at that time. If you cannot do this before the day of your speech, then arrive at least an hour early to check and test the equipment.

Now that you are comfortable with the what, where, when, and how of your presentation, let's look more closely at the *who:* your audience!

DEMOGRAPHIC AUDIENCE ANALYSIS

Not all audiences are alike, nor are all the people within an audience alike. How can you discover what is likely to be important to your particular audi-

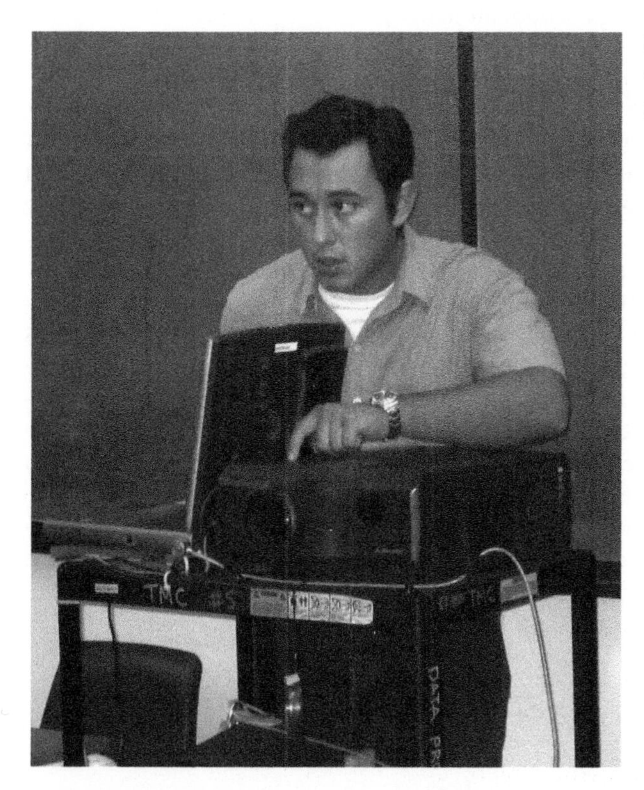

Becoming familiar with the venue and how your audio-visual equipment works in advance will save you time and difficulty on speech day.

Audience Analysis
Examining a potential audience to better understand their experiences and emotions in order to adapt a message to them.

ence? You have to examine the audience and make some predictions about what they are likely to find interesting and to what they are likely to respond. Examining the audience to better understand their motivations and experiences is called *audience analysis.*

How important is audience analysis to topic selection? Well, for the speech in the introduction about sex, audience analysis would have revealed that the audience is a group of kindergartners—boys and girls in a public school, ages five to six years old. Hmmm. . . . This should change everything. One hopes that you would not discuss any of the previously suggested topics with this audience. Instead, you might focus on simple physiological differences between men and women. You might discuss the roles of "mommies" and "daddies," or social roles (that it is OK for boys to play with dolls because one day they may be daddies and for girls to play with cars because one day they, too, will drive).

What if I told you that you were to speak to a group of seventy-year-old men? What would you talk about then? How about a group of widowed forty- to fifty-five-year-old women? A group of teenage boys from an inner-city school? A group of girls from a Catholic high school? How about a group of young women from a rape crisis center? Men in prison? A group of college students who all have different backgrounds? Surely, for each of these audiences you would adjust the topic almost instantaneously to something more appropriate for each: Viagra for the elderly men, dating tips for the women, and abstinence for the high school audiences.

Homogenous versus Heterogeneous Audiences

Demographics
A list of general characteristics of a particular group of people, audience, or segment of the population.

Demographics are the general characteristics of a particular audience or segment of the population. Demographic information is often information that you can "check off" in a box. You provide demographic information any time you fill out a form asking for your age, sex, income, ethnicity, religion, education level, etc. In the above examples, the audiences were relatively *homogenous audiences* (audiences made up of people with similar backgrounds, attitudes, and experiences) relative to age and/or sex. *Heterogeneous audiences* are more complex and represent a wide diversity of origins, backgrounds, experiences, and attitudes. The degrees of heterogeneity and homogeneity will vary for each of the demographic characteristics. Which characteristics are most relevant for your topic will determine whether you approach your audience as homogenous or heterogeneous.

Demographic information can be very useful for making some general assumptions about an audience. For example, what can we assume about the following person?

Age: 17

Sex: Male

Education: 11th grade; public school

Income: $10,000 a year

Religion: Catholic

Race/ethnicity: White/U.S. American

Language(s) spoken: English

We can probably assume that he is familiar with most references to current U.S. pop culture because he goes to a public high school, is white, and was born in the United States. He has most likely been exposed to the U.S. mass media for at least three to six hours every day of his entire life. He is familiar with Janet Jackson, Arnold Schwarzenegger, McDonald's, Reese's Peanut Butter Cups, Nike, and *The Simpsons*. He seems to have a lot of expendable income for a young man his age. He has had some religious training in the Judeo-Christian tradition, so he is probably familiar with major biblical references such as Adam and Eve, Moses, and Jesus Christ. He understands, and probably celebrates, the religious significance of Christmas and Easter.

If you were a marketer, you would probably try to sell him car accessories, music, snack foods, sodas, and fast food. You might try to lure him into sports like skateboarding or snowboarding. You might use beautiful young women, high adventure, and images of "manliness" to sell your products. Do you have a clear picture in your mind of this person and what he is like? This is how demographic information works. By gathering a few bits of information about a person or an audience, the speaker or marketer creates a profile. Often, the profile can be quite useful if it is used to make some general assumptions about likely common experiences of others in the same demographic profile. Demographics do not prove or provide evidence for common life experiences, nor do they necessarily predict behaviors or attitudes. Demographics do, however, give us insights into potentially common experiences and statistically likely possible outcomes.

Age

As you saw from the example at the beginning of this chapter, the age of an audience can have a powerful impact on your choice of topic, supporting materials, delivery style, and visual aids. As we pass through various stages in our lives, what is important and interesting to us changes. Our values change, our outlooks on the future and past change, our daily challenges change, and our fears change.

The age of your audience might also affect the types of supporting material you choose. If you have a group of senior citizens, you can refer to the dramatic political, social, and technological changes they have witnessed in their lifetimes, which include commercial air travel, computers, nuclear proliferation, the end of the Cold War, interracial marriage, and television. Although the names Mahatma Gandhi, Adolph Hitler, Marie Sklodowska Curie, Chairman Mao Zedong, John and Robert Kennedy, Maria Montessori, Shah Mohammed Reza Pahlavi, Salvadore Allende, Pablo Picasso, and Albert Schweitzer are probably significant to most people throughout the world who have a high school education, they are merely names from the past to many people under thirty. They do not have a personal connection to those names

Consider what topics you might choose for a group of 12- to 14-year-olds. What kinds of topics might you choose to discuss with them? Video games, goal setting, extracurricular opportunities, community youth programs, avoiding drugs and alcohol, and peer pressure are topics that would be interesting to this age group. Would these same topics work for most 30-year-olds? Probably not.

or the historical events connected to them. However, many older generations can still remember personally the contributions and crimes associated with each of these names.

For most of your college classroom speeches and presentations, your audience is likely to contain many young people between the ages of eighteen and twenty-three since the majority of college students fall in this age range. People in this age group from around the world have some similar life experiences. Students studying in the United States in this age group are likely to have common experiences with technology, popular culture, and education even if they come from a country other than the United States. Most will be adept at using computers but unable to use a card catalog. Most own CDs, but will never have owned vinyl record albums. They own or have used a cell phone, know how to download interesting ring tones and games onto the cell phone, and know how to text-message through a cell phone, but have never used a rotary phone. They have probably been to the movies, seen a concert, and eaten fast food in the past six months, but never had to wait months or years to be able to purchase the movie they saw or the music they heard. They have probably seen at least one reality TV show but not a variety show. They probably own at least one pair of jeans, but have never owned a pair of culottes; have or have had a pair of Nike shoes, but not saddle shoes; and know what a VW Bug looks like, but not a Ford Edsel. They can most likely associate a face to the names Snoop Dog, Britney Spears, and Michael Jackson, but probably not to names like Dionne Warwick, Annette Funicello, or Shawn

Cassidy. They understand the difficulties of meeting assignment deadlines, reading boring textbooks, and "cramming" for exams, but not the difficulties of attending board meetings or writing quarterly reports.

If you can better identify with the first set of references than with the second set in each example, then you are probably a "twentysomething" instead of a "thirty-, forty-, or fiftysomething." Clearly, age does make a difference in terms of life experiences, knowledge, and interests.

Sex/Gender

The sex of the audience can also play a significant role in what you talk about and how you choose to talk about it. If you have a mixed-sex group (approximately equal numbers of men and women), you will want to focus your discussion on issues that resonate with both men and women.

Both women and men are concerned with being successful in their lives. However, what success means to a woman may be different from what success means to a man. For example, women often place more emphasis on their success in relationships such as with a partner or spouse and with their current or future children. Men often focus more on career and financial success. This is evident in the amount of time and energy each is likely to spend reaching these goals.

You will also want to avoid using masculine terms to refer to all people. Using only masculine terms can be irritating to people in your audience who find the terms outdated and imprecise. Use terms such as *humanity* instead of *mankind;* say *we* or *they* instead of *he;* and use gender-neutral alternatives to formerly gender-specific job descriptions (*police officer* instead of *policeman, chair* instead of *chairman, flight attendant* instead of *stewardess,* etc.). By using gender-neutral terms, you will avoid offending people in your audience and be more accurate in your references, keeping the women in the audience from having to guess whether or not you're including them in the discussion. As Stephen Lucas warns,

> An astute speaker will also take care to avoid using sexist language. Almost any audience you address will contain people—men and women alike—who will take offense at words and phrases that convey stereotyped or demeaning views of women.[2]

In single-sex audiences (audiences that consist entirely or primarily of one sex), you can tailor your

WHAT OTHERS SAY

A culturally diverse audience really affects your speech because you don't really know how your audience would respond to your speech. On the other hand, homogenous audience means that the group of people that formed your audience comes from the same beliefs or culture. To prepare a speech for a homogenous group is easier since you know what reaction to expect from the audience. You can actually prepare your ideas or message by the culture atmosphere that your audience is part of. A diverse audience would make you to be more careful with your presentation.

Alma De Jesus, Mexico

The great thing about speaking to a diverse audience is that it is more exciting for both sides. I am more aware about the people's reactions and I would assume the audience is interested in my delivery as well since I am culturally different to them too. Thus, more attention is given on both sides. In addition, an unfamiliar audience may inspire me. When making an effort to adjust my speech accordingly, I may abandon rigid ways of doing speeches or get new ideas deriving from my attempt to see the other perspective.

Julia Kaeufler, Germany

message even more precisely for the experiences of the group in front of you. Men's interests are often sparked by references to power, speed, performance, and competition. They often appreciate sports, automobile-, and object-related metaphors. Women often respond well to references to empowerment, safety, understanding, and connection. You should not, however, assume that men will not care about or respond to the latter or that women will not enjoy the former. Remember, these are generalizations, not rules.

Race and Ethnicity

Race and *ethnicity* are terms that are used interchangeably but are not the same thing. Race, the more general of the two terms, refers to physical or biological similarities that distinguish groups of people as different or separate from one another. Race does not indicate a common culture or national origin. In the United States most races are distinguished by skin color and eye shape. When we refer to black, African-American, Hispanic, Latino/a, white, Caucasian, Anglo, Middle Eastern, or Asian, we are referring to racial categories.

Ethnicity, according to Lustig and Koester, refers to a "wide variety of groups who might share a language, historical origins, religion, identification with a common nation-state, or cultural system."[3] This means that just because two people are categorized as members of the same race, they do not necessarily share the same ethnicity or culture. You probably already know this to be true. I have heard many international students object to being called "Asian" or "Latino" or "black" because they identify themselves as Korean, Japanese, Indian, Spanish, Mexican, Salvadorian, Jamaican, or Kenyan.

The problem with racial categories is that they do not consider the individual. They lump very diverse cultures and ethnicities into broad categories that do not accurately reflect common experiences or a common culture. However, because people do not always know a person's country of origin, they respond to him or her according to racial categories. Because race is such a big issue in the United States, it would be remiss not to consider the racial composition of your audience when preparing a speech. Additionally, keep in mind that people associated with a racial category often have some common experiences based on race. For example, as Lustig and Koester tell us,

> Although race may have been used initially to set African Americans apart from Caucasian U.S. Americans, African American culture provides a strong and unique source of identity to members of the black race in the United States. Scholars now acknowledge that African American culture, with its roots in traditional African cultures, is separate and unique and has developed its own set of cultural patterns. Although a person from Nigeria and an African American are both from the same race, they are from distinct cultures.[4]

As a non-native speaker of English, you no doubt have had firsthand experience with the frustrations of being misidentified, mislabeled, or stereotyped due to the race/ethnicity distinction. You know how different the attitudes, beliefs, and values can be within a racial category or even within an ethnicity or nationality. Having said this, it can be helpful to know the ethnic or racial characteristics of your audience. Imagine that you are going to give a speech to several different clubs on campus, trying to persuade them to participate in a "day of activism." How would you adapt your speech to the Asian-American Student Club? The Black Collegians? The Latino/a Student Union? The Middle Eastern Student Association? Each group represents different concerns and priorities based on the common ethnicity or race of its members. Knowing those concerns and priorities might assist you in securing the club's participation.

Religion

Although a person's religion is often closely associated with his/her ethnicity and culture, you should make a special effort to discover the religions of your audience members in instances where the topic matter has strong moral implications. Speakers sometimes make the mistake of assuming that the texts, attitudes, and beliefs of their own religion should be evidence enough for all audiences. They aren't! Every religion has its own beliefs, values, attitudes, and texts that it finds most compelling. For example, if you were giving a

CONSIDERING CULTURE

Crossing Cultural Lines

Organizations and clubs can create a sense of purpose and belonging that crosses traditional cultural divides. Common values, beliefs, attitudes, and norms that are associated with the various groups can create a mini-culture of their own. This is often referred to as *organizational culture.* Some organizations explicitly state their independence from any particular country or government culture in order to honor their organization's values. As an official NGO (non-governmental organization), the International Committee of the Red Cross is one such organization.

On their website they state that:

> The International Committee of the Red Cross (ICRC) works around the world on a strictly neutral and impartial basis to protect and assist people affected by armed conflicts and internal disturbances. It is a humanitarian organization with its headquarters in Geneva, mandated by the international community to be the guardian of international humanitarian law, and is the founding body of the International Red Cross and Red Crescent Movement.
>
> While the ICRC maintains a constant dialogue with States, it insists at all times on its independence. Only if it is free to act independently of any government or other authority can the ICRC serve the interests of victims of conflict, which lie at the heart of its humanitarian mission.

Source: Copyright © 2004 International Committee of the Red Cross, http://www.icrc.org/web/eng/siteeng0.nsf/iwpList2/About_the_ICRC:Discover_the_ICRC.

speech on same-sex marriages, quoting biblical scripture might fall on deaf ears to an audience of Hindus, Muslims, and atheists. Instead, you might want to veer away from moral or religion-based arguments and focus on legal or human rights arguments. However, if you were going to give a speech on abortion to an audience of Catholic teenagers, you very likely would incorporate church doctrine and biblical references.

Again, a person's religious affiliation does not guarantee that s/he agrees with or abides by all of her/his religion's doctrines; knowing that affiliation simply provides clues into that person's likely orientation toward various values and beliefs.

Group

Think about all the groups and organizations to which you belong. You might belong to a club on campus, a research or study group, a fraternity or sorority, or a church social club. Work groups, schools, fraternities and sororities, clubs, and political parties can influence the attitudes of the people who belong to them. People are often very proud of being members of particular groups. Knowing about the groups with which your audience is affiliated can offer you ample opportunities to make personal connections with the audience and to build your credibility.

There are scores of associations, unions, societies, organizations, and clubs throughout the United States and the world, such as the American Civil Liberties Union, the Screen Actors Guild, Amnesty International, Young Republicans, the American Cancer Society, the International Association of Business Communicators, the International Association of Athletics Federations, the International Society for Environmental Ethics, Rotary International, Kiwanis Club, and many more. There is a club or organization that caters to the interests and concerns of people with almost any hobby, job, issue, or disease you can think of. What brings people together in these groups is a common interest. It is that common interest that is of interest to you in your audience analysis.

To find, research, investigate, or discover various organizations from around the world, check out this website.

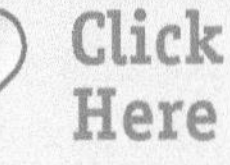

http://www.contact.org

The website of Action Without Borders allows you to search for organizations from 154 countries by name, interest, opportunities, and more. Results will include a description of the organization, contact information, and web links (if available).

How to Use Demographic Information

Now that you understand some of the individual demographic characteristics, let's look at how to use that information in developing your speech. First, remember that you collect and use demographics to better understand your listeners, not to manipulate and control them. Every person in your audience is an individual. The information about common patterns will simply help you better predict what will resonate with a particular audience and how they are likely to respond to your message.

Second, remember that no single characteristic or combination of characteristics can give you a true understanding of a group or any individual in that group. Like most people, you have probably been unfairly or inaccurately judged by others who have stereotyped you based on one or two demographic characteristics. Indeed, much discrimination is due to this kind of overgeneralization. Just remember, the differences within any group are

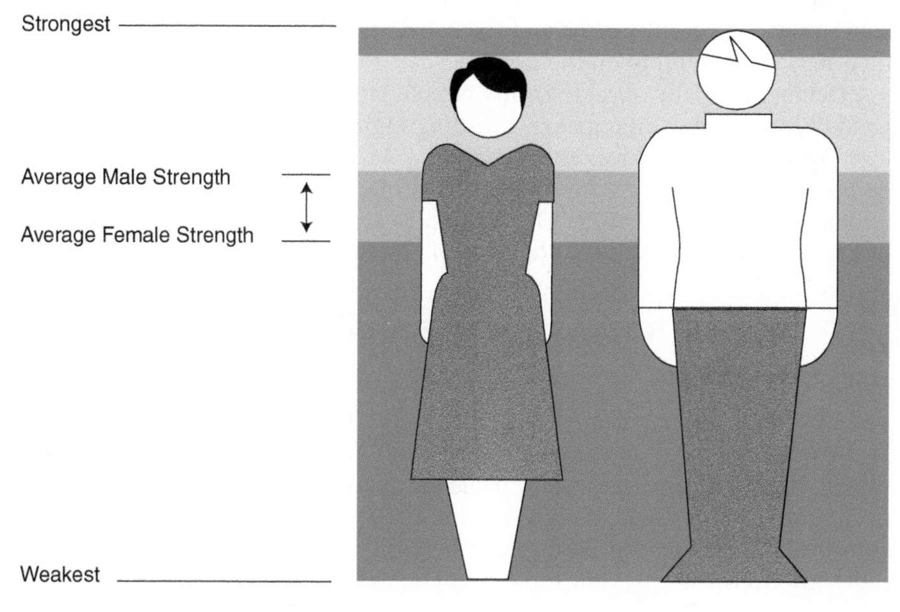

FIGURE 4.1 If each of these continua represent the range of physical strength of *all* men and women, we can see that men are about 25% stronger than women on average. We also see that there are many men who have less physical strength than women. In other words, just because, *on average*, men are stronger than women, does not mean that all men are stronger than all women.

Notice that the difference between the strongest man and the weakest man is greater than the difference between the average man and the average women. In other words, the difference between individuals within a group is greater than the average difference among groups of people. However, people tend to overexaggerate those differences, making it seem that all people in one group are more or less of something than all people in another group. This is simply not the case.

greater than the differences between the averages of two groups. For example, even though men are, on average, physically stronger than women, we cannot assume that all women are weaker than all men (see Figure 4.1). There are many women who are physically stronger than the average man, and there are many men who are physically weaker than the average woman. People often make the mistake of exaggerating the differences among various groups of people when, in reality, the average differences might be quite small.

Now, let's return to our seventeen-year-old white male (eleventh-grade education, $10,000/year income, Catholic) from earlier. I neglected to give you one important piece of demographic information: He has one child whom he is supporting. This, of course, changes our picture of him. As marketers, we might now be inclined to sell him things like inexpensive diapers and baby formula instead of new jeans and power drinks. Our image of him has gone from a young man with expendable income to a young man who is at or below the poverty line. We no longer see him "hanging out" with his friends and driving fast cars (although he very well could be). We might picture him quitting school and working a second job or living with his or the baby's mother's parents, or he and the baby's mother may be trying to handle their new responsibility on their own.

Demographically speaking, this couple is not predicted to have a very good chance of staying together, finishing high school, or ever going to college. Again, demographics can be deceiving: Many teen couples with children do not break up or quit school, so it's important to remember the limitations of demographic information. Demographics are not indicative of a situation or lifestyle; they are simply a predictor of more or less *likely* outcomes.

DISPOSITIONAL AUDIENCE ANALYSIS: ATTITUDES!

The next step in analyzing the speaking situation is to analyze the specific factors affecting your audience's attitudes and abilities to hear your message, called *situational* or *dispositional audience analysis*. In examining the situation, start with what you know about the audience in terms of demographics, and then build upon that knowledge by looking at particular audience attitudes toward the event, your topic, and you as the speaker.

Attitudes Toward the Event

First, ask yourself about audience members' feelings and expectations for the speaking event itself. Are they willingly in the audience, or are they required to be there for an assignment, for their job, or by the department of corrections? Do they get something for being there, or are they attending for their own interest? Students are generally required to attend the speeches of their fellow classmates. Therefore, a classroom audience is not always a willing audience. How audience members feel about attending the event can influence your ability to engage them. When an audience is unwilling, you need to spend more time finding ways to connect the material to their needs and interests than you will with an audience that has chosen to attend the event.

You should also be sensitive to the audience's expectations for the event. Audiences come to events with clear ideas about what to expect in terms of content, formality, length, and tone of the speaker's message. To capture interest, tailor your message to fit the theme of the event; meet the audience's expectations about how long or short your presentation should be; and match your tone and language to fit the mood and formality of the event.

Expectations about events are highly culturally bound. Remember, each country, religion, and culture has varying expectations about celebrations, rituals, political events, and presentations. Knowing the demographic information of your audience, you can investigate the particular expectations that your audience will likely have for the specific event. For example, if you want to speak at a good friend's wedding, it would be helpful to know that in the United Arab Emirates[5] and Saudi Arabia,[6] alcohol is not consumed, which means that toasting does not exist; and in China, usually it is the host who toasts the guests.[7] Were you to offer a toast in these contexts, your good intentions might not be well received.

Attitudes Toward the Topic

The next questions you should ask are, "*What does my audience know and what are their opinions about my topic?*" Has your audience heard about your topic? Is it a topic that most people have learned about in school? Is it a topic that is featured in big headlines in the news lately? Is it a famous historical event? Is it part of pop culture? Is it a new invention? A new perspective on an old concept or argument? Is it a revolutionary new treatment for a deadly disease? What are audience members likely to already know about your topic, and what might be confusing, troublesome, or bizarre to them? Not everyone has the same knowledge base, and this is especially important to keep in mind when you are dealing with an audience that has been educated in different countries and raised with different religions. It is important to accurately predict what your audience is likely to already know about the subject so that you can provide adequate explanations, definitions, and examples. At the same time, you do not want to inadvertently underestimate what the audience knows about your topic and bore or insult them by telling them what they already know.

Generally, the more the audience knows about your subject, the greater the amount of detail and complexity you can add to your speech; the less the audience knows, the more simplified your handling of the topic should be. The best choice is a topic with which the audience has some familiarity and is one about which the audience is interested in expanding their knowledge (see Table 4.2). For example, most people are familiar with the AIDS epi-

TABLE 4.2 Consider the Following

Which of the following would be more appropriate for your speech class on the topic of Buckminsterfullerenes?

1. "Buckminsterfullerene, C60, the third allotrope of Carbon, was discovered in 1985 by Robert Curl, Harold Kroto, and Richard Smalley. Using laser evaporation of graphite they found Cn clusters (where $n > 20$ and even) of which the most common were found to be C60 and C70. For this discovery they were awarded the 1996 Nobel Prize in Chemistry.

   "Since the discovery of fullerenes over a decade ago, much research has gone into these promising molecules. In 1990 an inexpensive and efficient method to produce fullerenes by the gram (or even kilogram) was discovered by W. Krätchmer and D. R. Huffman. This paved the way for more research into practical applications of the molecules."[1]

2. "In 1985, a group of scientists discovered a 60-carbon atom molecule, only the third known form of pure carbon (after diamond and graphite). These molecules, which are formed by vaporizing graphite, may be used in the future to manufacture protective coatings and even treat cancer."[2]

Unless your classmates are studying advanced chemistry, you would probably choose the second example because it provides a brief explanation and focuses on usage.

[1]Andy Hungerford, "Buckminsterfullerenes," *Student's Nonotechnology Home Page, Michigan State University website,* http://www.msu.edu/~hungerf9/bucky1.html (retrieved April 12, 2004).

[2]"Buckminsterfullerenes (Buckyballs)," *Science Kit and Boreal Laboratories,* http://Sciencekit.com/category.asp?c=429359 (retrieved April 12, 2004).

demic throughout the world, so you might want to talk about recent discoveries or new treatments.

Now, let's consider the audience's interest in your subject matter. People are motivated to listen to things that are of interest to them. People tend to follow the WIIFM (pronounced "WIF-um") principle: What's in it for me? People want to know how your topic affects their lives, makes their lives easier, or is a threat to their health, safety, or happiness. One challenge you have throughout the speech-making process is identifying and addressing the WIIFM of your audience. If your topic is not of immediate interest to them, you need to make it interesting. For example, when discussing cancer, you can relate it to the audience's or their families' risks for the disease, personal experiences, or the hope for a cure.

Knowing where your audience stands on an issue can be vital to preparing the right argument. We call an audience who mostly agrees with our position or the topic *a sympathetic audience*, an audience who is indifferent to the topic *a neutral audience*, and an audience who is opposed to our topic or position *a hostile audience*. We can often anticipate an audience's disposition toward a topic simply by knowing a little about their demographics. Like in the example of Catholic nuns and the issue of abortion, we can make fairly accurate guesses about where groups of people stand on issues. However, sometimes we need to investigate further. How would your audience feel about an increase in tuition to build a new football stadium for the college or about increasing the entrance requirements for your school? These questions are complicated and require further inquiry. Do not make the mistake of assuming that because your audience is like you in some significant ways, they will agree with you on most issues. Many factors influence each person's attitudes and beliefs.

Sympathetic Audience
An audience who is favorable to both the speaker and the topic or position of the speech.

Neutral Audience
An audience who is neither favorable nor unfavorable toward the speaker and/or the topic or position of the speech.

Hostile Audience
An audience who is not favorable to the speaker and/or the topic or position of the speech.

If you are facing a hostile audience, you will need to spend time establishing common ground with the audience and creating goodwill (i.e., a trusting and open climate between you and the audience that shows that you are not trying to take advantage of or manipulate them). For example, since the 9/11 attacks in the United States, the American Civil Liberties Union, a nonprofit "organization devoted to protecting"[8] individual rights and freedoms in the United States, is often at odds with the Federal Bureau of Investigation, "the investigative arm of the U.S. Department of Justice,"[9] as to how far the Bureau should and can go to investigate potential terrorists or terrorist activity. So on June 13, 2003, when Robert S. Mueller, III, director of the FBI, addressed members of the ACLU at their first membership conference, he was facing a very hostile audience. They may have not disliked him, but they were hostile to the FBI's counterterrorism work.

Mr. Mueller, knowing how unpopular he and his organization were, immediately began by complimenting the group on their work:

> I welcome the opportunity to speak to you today, and I want to recognize the ACLU for its commitment to protecting our civil liberties. You have a long and proud history of standing up to defend the freedoms guaranteed to us by the Bill of Rights and the Constitution.

He established common ground by pointing out common values: "The FBI and the ACLU share these values, as well as concern for the safety of all Americans." Then he acknowledged their differences while reinforcing their similarities:

> However, since 9/11, many complex law enforcement issues have arisen, and on some of those issues, we disagree. In meetings with Anthony and other ACLU members, we have discussed some of these differences. I think that this exchange of ideas is important—especially with those who disagree. Because as a citizen of this country, I believe, like you, that our freedoms—including the right to disagree—are sacred.[10]

The audience listened and even smiled during his presentation. At the end, his listeners applauded and many admitted being impressed by what the director had to say.[11]

With a neutral audience, you want to create a sense of energy or urgency to convince them of the importance of your subject before moving them to

Robert Mueller of the FBI talks about the reorganization of the FBI during a news conference.

action. With a sympathetic audience, you don't need to convince them to agree with you (they already do) about the importance or significance of the topic but should encourage them to become more active in the cause or to spread the word. Always be aware that you are not likely to encounter a uniformly hostile or sympathetic audience. Audiences are made up of individuals with individual opinions and tastes. Your goal is to discern the likely attitudes or dispositions of the majority of your audience.

Attitudes Toward the Speaker

Classmates in your speech class are likely to be very supportive of you, yet there are times when audiences do not like or support the speaker. Again, we call these *hostile audiences,* while we call those audiences who do like us *sympathetic* and those in between or who know nothing about us *neutral.* Similar to the three types of audience dispositions in terms of your topic, you should handle audiences who are hostile, sympathetic, and neutral to you by adapting your message to their attitudes about you. If they are hostile, establish common ground and goodwill; if they are sympathetic, build on those positive feelings; and if they are neutral, give them reasons to believe and trust you.

Classroom audiences are rarely hostile toward an individual; instead, any hostility is likely against the topics or opinions about those topics, as in Robert Mueller's situation. For the most part, if you do ample research and present your findings and opinions fairly and with confidence, most audiences will give you a fair hearing. Ask yourself if there is anything about you or your position in the class that might cause your classmates to become suspicious or untrusting of what you say. If the answer is "yes," then you need to address the problem in your speech.

CONDUCTING AUDIENCE ANALYSIS

So far we have talked about what you need to know about your audience and the situation in which you will speak, but how do you find this information? Well, there are many ways to gather information about an audience. You can conduct interviews, hand out questionnaires, observe your audience, and ask questions from the organizer of the speaking event.

Asking Event Organizers

As discussed earlier, your speaking situation analysis should begin as soon as you are asked to give a speech. Use the checklist below (Table 4.3) to guide you. Keep this information easily available for follow-up questions that might arise. Call or e-mail the organizer when you have a few questions to ask at one time. That way you avoid questioning the organizer more often than necessary.

Surveys/Questionnaires

A survey is a method of gathering information from people through the use of questionnaires. You can gather both demographic and dispositional informa-

TABLE 4.3 **Questions to Ask the Event Organizer**

Organizer's Name: _____ Phone: _____ E-mail: _____

Other Contact: _____ Phone: _____ E-mail: _____

1. Who is sponsoring the event? How many people will attend?
2. When will the event be (date and time)? How long is the event? How long am I to speak?
3. What is the purpose of the event? What is my role in the event? Am I the main attraction?
4. What are you expecting of me before and after my presentation?
5. Where will the event take place? Indoors or outside? What kind of venue is it?
6. What equipment is available in the room? Will I have technical support?

tion through a well-crafted questionnaire. For demographic information, you can simply create a form, much like a credit application, that audience members fill out by checking the appropriate boxes.

For more specific information about the audience's attitudes and experiences, you can ask fixed-alternative, scaled, or open-ended questions. *Fixed-alternative questions* ask the person filling out the questionnaire to choose between one or two choices, usually *yes, no,* and *maybe* (or *unsure*) (see Table 4.4). These types of questions can be useful to discover general attitudes, but they do not allow the questioner to learn the degree to which people agree or disagree or how much they know about the topic.

Scaled questions allow you to learn not only what the audience knows or whether they agree, but also how much they know or to what extent they agree/disagree. Like the fixed-alternative questions, the answer possibilities are limited, but with scaled questions, the answers are on a continuum (see Table 4.4).

TABLE 4.4 **Fixed-Alternative Questions, Scaled Questions, and Open-Ended Questions**

Examples of Fixed-Alternative Questions

Are you in favor of legalizing marijuana for medicinal uses?
Yes_____ No _____ Unsure_____

Are you familiar with the Einstein's Theory of Relativity?
Yes_____ No _____ Unsure_____

Examples of Scaled Questions

How often do you eat at fast food restaurants?

Seldom	Often

How important is having children to you?

Not Important	Very Important

Senior citizens should be required to take a driving test every two years.

Strongly Disagree	Strongly Agree

Examples of Open-Ended Questions (note that on the questionnaire, you need to leave ample room for answers to get the most information)

Describe your most embarrassing moment: _____

Describe your typical school day: _____

What do you plan to do after you graduate from college? _____

Open-ended questions provide the greatest flexibility because they allow respondents to answer freely. They allow for detailed responses and provide insight into topics that you might not have anticipated. Open-ended questions can, however, be difficult and time consuming to read and interpret. Additionally, respondents can offer information you were not looking for and omit information you need (see Table 4.4).

Interviews

Interviewing members of your audience can provide you with valuable information about individuals within your audience and can give you insight into attitudes held by similar individuals. However, interviews are time consuming and do not offer the broadest understanding of a particular audience.

Observations

You can learn by observing your audience. When planning a presentation for class, you might take time to talk with your fellow classmates before and after class. Pay attention to the topics they discuss. Are they focused on politics?

HINT

Once You Start, It Is Too Late to Find Out!

Avoid the temptation to conduct audience analysis at the beginning of or during your speech. It is too late to ask polling questions (e.g., "How many of you eat fast food at least once a week?") once you have already begun. You might get unexpected answers or answers that do not support or even contradict the point you are trying to make in your speech. Find out *in advance* the opinions or habits of your audience in order to avoid embarrassment.

CONSIDERING CULTURE

Nonverbal Feedback Is Culturally Bound

A U.S. American chemist working for a major multinational technology developer was sent to India to introduce a highly complicated piece of instrumentation he had developed. His audience was a group of scientists at an engineering conference. He conducted a thorough analysis of the speaking situation and felt confident that he had adapted his speech properly to his audience.

Unfortunately, throughout most of the presentation, he noticed people tossing their heads side to side, not dissimilar to the way people in the United States indicate "no," but in a more elliptical fashion. Also, many in the audience were blinking and closing their eyes. In the United States, this would indicate confusion, disbelief, or a lack of understanding. The chemist interpreted the behavior as "no, we don't agree" or "we don't understand." He explained again, slowed down, and repeated the message, but the more he did this, the more pronounced the head shaking and blinking became.

During the break, he asked the organizer of the event why audience members were shaking their heads "no." The organizer instantly understood the confusion and explained, "Here, in India, shaking the head and blinking are signs of understanding and encouragement. They were signaling to you, 'Yes, keep going; we understand.'" As the lecture resumed, the scientist felt a renewed sense of confidence, knowing that his message was being clearly received.

School issues? Pop culture? This might lead you to understand what is interesting and important to them.

Observation of your audience does not stop there. You should observe your audience throughout the actual speech, looking for signs of agreement, boredom, confusion, and frustration. This will help you adapt your presentation to your audience's needs throughout your presentation. The more information you can gain about your audience before or during your presentation, the more likely you will be to create a presentation that will be meaningful, interesting, and understandable to your audience.

USING YOUR ANALYSIS

Once you have gathered all this information about your speaking situation, you need to put it to good use. Keep the picture of your audience in your mind as you choose and refine your topic. Ask yourself what supporting material is likely to inspire, move, or influence them the most based on their common experiences, attitudes, and interests. Even when you are choosing what to wear for your presentation, use what you know about the context, the people, the time of day, and the purpose of the event. Choose something that increases your credibility (we will talk about appearance and dress in Chapter Twelve). A suit for a classroom speech might be too much, but jeans might make the audience think you don't take your speech or the audience members seriously.

When practicing your speech, imagine your audience in front of you. Hear your words as if you are the audience. Audio or video record your practice sessions so that you can hear what you sound like to your imagined audience and make adjustments accordingly.

Pay attention to what happens the day of your presentation and what the other speakers are talking about. Quickly think of ways to incorporate what they have said into your presentation. Nothing endears a speaker to an audience faster than when he or she makes a reference to something that they have all just experienced together. For example, minutes before Olga was to give her speech, a small earthquake shook the classroom. When she began her speech, Olga and her classmates were still rather distracted. Olga said, "I expected to move mountains with my speech, but I meant it figuratively!" Her classmates gratefully laughed, breaking the tension, and then enthusiastically turned their attention to what she had to say.

When you are in front of the audience, be sure to continue observing them and adapting to feedback they offer. This might be difficult if you are unfamiliar with U.S. American nonverbal signals. Look for signs of confusion: furled eyebrows, wide eyes, and a cocked head.[12] If they seem lost, go back and explain again. Audiences in the United States show understanding by nodding their heads and maintaining focused eye contact and relaxed or pleasant facial expressions. Shaking the head from side to side, frowning, and avoiding eye contact show disagreement or displeasure with a point.

Finally, be ready for unforeseen interruptions. If someone walks in, stop talking for a moment, acknowledge the person, and continue when everyone has refocused on you.

SUMMARY

Speeches are made for audiences, not speakers. Keeping this simple principle in mind should help guide you as you thoroughly analyze each speaking situation. The more similar you are to your audience in terms of demographic profiles, the easier it should be for you to adapt your presentation. There are several steps in analyzing the speaking situation, beginning with looking at your own starting assumptions about speaking and audience behavior. You should then conduct a thorough analysis of the context of the speaking situation. Find out about the *who, what, when, where, why,* and *how* of the situation by asking the event organizer and, when possible, visiting the venue in advance.

Then conduct a thorough audience analysis, looking closely at both the demographics of the audience and their particular attitudes regarding your topic, you, and the event. By observing, surveying, and researching your audience, you should be able to get to know some of their likes and dislikes, common experiences, and ways to tailor your speech.

You want to create the best possible situation for sending your message and having it received loud and clear. By taking the time to thoroughly analyze your speaking situation, you can better adapt your entire presentation, from topic choice and parting words to the needs, attitudes, interests, and experiences of the audience whether they are sympathetic, hostile, or neutral to your topic, your position, or you.

Discussion Questions and Activities

1. Attend a public lecture or presentation (your school newspaper should offer a listing of events on campus). Position yourself so that you can observe both the audience and the speaker. Take notes on what you observe. Identify the type of presentation and venue for the event and what your expectations were about the event (level of formality, purpose, etc.). How did the audience greet the speaker (i.e., stand, applaud, sit quietly)? Did the audience applaud or provide vocal feedback during the presentation? After the presentation? Note the expressions on audience members' faces. What nonverbal feedback did they provide the speaker? How can you use this information to make predictions about your audience?
2. Get into a small group with three or four of your classmates. Discuss how audiences differ in the various countries with which you have familiarity. How would you behave differently if you were in an audience in another country? Discuss the similarities and differences among the various countries you and your classmates represent as well as the United States.

3. Develop an audience questionnaire to analyze your classroom audience for your next speech. Include questions that seek demographic, attitude, and experiential information that will help you adapt your speech.
4. Make a list of all the ways you think you might be similar to or have common experiences with each of the following audiences:

U.S. American teenagers	People thirty-five to fifty years old
International students	Sports enthusiasts
Married women	Former members of the military
Single men	Mechanical engineering majors
Recovering alcoholics	Tourists
Cancer survivors	Five- to ten-year-old children

Chapter Quiz

1. What are some of the first questions you need to ask when analyzing the context of a speaking situation?
2. True or False: A speech is given for the audience.
3. Which of the following represent demographic characteristics:
   a. Age, religion, attitudes, and income
   b. Religion, attitudes, income, and group membership
   c. Age, attitudes, group membership, and religion
   d. Age, religion, group membership, and income
4. True or False: Audience analysis is less important to topic selection than to other aspects of speech preparation and delivery.
5. List the three levels of analyzing the speaking situation.
6. Name three demographic characteristics and three dispositional characteristics. Include an example of each.
7. A neutral audience is one where the audience is:
   a. Sympathetic to the speaker and the topic.
   b. Hostile to the speaker and the topic.
   c. Indifferent to the speaker and the topic.
   d. Predisposed to the speaker and the topic.

Chapter 4 Quiz Answers

1. What is the event about?; Is it part of a larger series of events?; How big will the audience be?; What date, day, and time will the event take place?; Am I the only speaker or the keynote speaker?; Where will it be held? 2. True, 3. d, 4. False, 5. Contextual, demographic, dispositional, 6. (A variety of answers could be here.), 7. c.

CHAPTER 5 From Topic to Purpose to Thesis

CHAPTER GOAL

By the end of this chapter you will be able to write a clear thesis based on an appropriate speech topic and purpose for a given audience.

Students often complain that they don't know what to talk about in their speeches. They think that all the "good topics" have already been chosen by other students, that the topic they are interested in would be boring to the other students, that the instructor has already heard every topic they might want to discuss, or that all the topics seem "boring." Yet, when pushed to carefully consider their hobbies, interests, concerns, and experiences, students eventually come up with a topic that is interesting to them, their classmates, and their teacher. As a matter of fact, my favorite part of teaching speech is the opportunity to hear about people, ceremonies, events, and ideas from all around the world. Most teachers get to hear only themselves share what they know with their students, but speech teachers get to hear students' stories, too. It is truly a gift. Here are just a few subjects I have learned about from my students:

Animal testing
Bermuda Triangle
Blood donation
Capoeira
Cesar Chavez
Cloning
Communism
Dangers of cell phones
Diabetes
Dreams
Emigration/immigration
Frida Kahlo
Gay rights
Global warming
The Hanbok: Traditional Korean dress
Human rights
Islam
Judaism
Machu Pichu
Moroccan food
NASCAR racing
Obesity
Organ donation
Quinceñeras
Samburu marriage ceremonies
Tai chi
Tempura egg painting
Teotihuacán
Turkish baths
Yoga

The number of possible topics is as endless as the number of people, places, and ideas in the universe. This richness is one of the reasons it can be difficult to choose just the right topic for your speech.

In this chapter you will learn how to choose and narrow speech topics, adapt your topic to fit the speaking situation, develop a general and a specific purpose statement, and further refine your topic with a thesis statement. (See Figure 5.1.)

CHOOSING A TOPIC

Imagine that each molecule in the room you are in represents one possible speech topic. Now, imagine that for each of those molecules (topics) there are one hundred different possible variations of the topic or the way in which you discuss the topic. For instance, consider some of the topics you could discuss about flowers:

Types of flowers
Life span of flowers
Biology of flowers
Seeds versus bulbs
Meanings of flowers
History of horticulture
Flower farming
Buying wholesale flowers
Choosing wedding flowers

Reproduction of flowers
Uses of flowers
Flower arranging
Flower planting
How to draw flowers
Crossbreeding of flowers
Rare flowers
Process of cross-pollination
Making paper flowers
Decorating with flowers
Medicinal uses of flowers
The floral industry

And this is only a partial list of possibilities! Take a moment and jot down some of the topic ideas that came to your mind as you read this list. The possibilities should seem limitless. To begin narrowing down your topic, you need to start with a general subject (e.g., *flowers*) that you can narrow down to fit the needs of your speaking situation.

Choosing a General Subject

Sometimes the process of choosing the subject of your speech is as easy as reviewing the assignment instructions. Does the assignment ask you to do a biography? To critique a book? Are you being asked to motivate the audience to volunteer in the community? If so, then your topic choices are already considerably narrowed. Now you simply have to choose a famous person, book, or organization on which to focus.

If you are given minimal guidance in terms of the specific topic or subject, what do you do then? In this case, you should be sure to select a subject that you already know something about or one that you can reasonably investigate in the time you have. Make sure you choose a topic that is interesting to you and the audience as well. Remember, enthusiasm is contagious, and you will be working with your topic quite extensively in researching, writing,

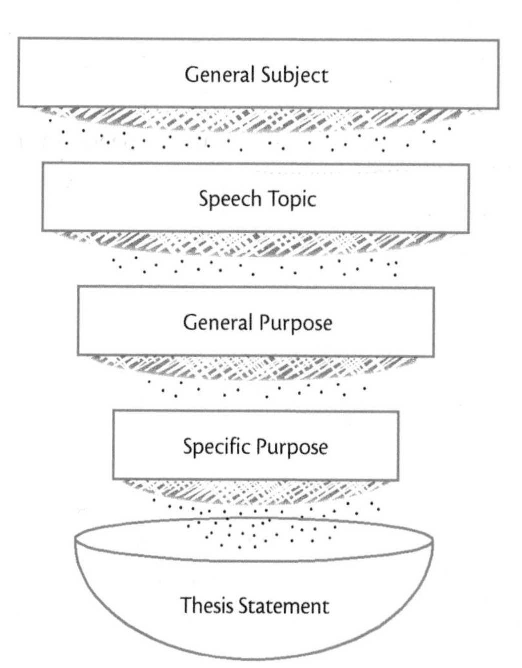

FIGURE 5.1 Think of developing your speech from topic selection to thesis like a filter that continually refines your ideas until you end up with only the substance that you need to write your speech.

editing, and presenting it. Choose a topic that you will be excited to share with your audience. Don't spend too much time choosing a topic, however. Indecision can cost you valuable research and preparation time. Once you have a few good choices, pick one and start working.

After spending some time generating topic ideas for your speech, you will likely reach one of four conditions: (1) You have several good speech topics in mind and think you know which one you would like to work on; (2) you are flooded with too many ideas and can't decide on the right one; (3) you have a general subject in mind, but don't know how to narrow it down to a specific topic; or (4) you can't think of any "good" topics—the few you have considered all seem too simple, too complicated, or too boring. If you are in the first category, evaluate your topic against the "Rules for Selecting a Topic" (Table 5.1) and then move on to the "Specific Purpose" section of this chapter. But if you are in one of the latter categories, like most students will be, continue reading.

How to Choose a Subject

As a non-native speaker, you might be additionally concerned because your knowledge base and interests may be considerably different from those of your audience. However, your experiences and background can actually be a terrific asset when choosing a topic. Your culture and language offer a wealth of interesting and unique topics that your audience is not likely to have encountered before. To generate a list of interesting and workable ideas for your presentation, start with a list of general subjects that can be subdivided into topic areas that, in turn, offer a variety of specific topics (e.g., *music* is a general subject, *rap music* is a topic area of music, and the *origins of rap music* is a specific topic). See Table 5.1.

"Organic" Subject/Selection

The first technique for finding a workable subject for your presentation is to consider yourself, your audience, and the occasion at which you will be speaking to see if any subjects emerge naturally. In Chapter Four we talked about analyzing the speaking situation and adapting presentations to fit the speaker, the audience, and the speaking occasion. Well, here is your first chance to put that analysis to use.

Consider Yourself

Ask yourself, "What is interesting to me?" What kinds of music do you listen to? Who is your favorite artist? What kinds of movies do you like? What are your hobbies? What do you want to do when you graduate? What are the biggest changes you have ex-

WHAT OTHERS SAY

Selecting a topic has caused me the most difficulty when preparing for this speech. There were so many different topics that it was very hard to narrow it down to just one. Also, I didn't know how specific my topic should be because I didn't want to be too vague and general but instead I wanted to really teach my classmates about something that would interest them. I also tried to choose a topic that I am personally excited about so that I could support my speech with personal examples, experience, and genuine enthusiasm.

I tried to pick a topic that will be appropriate for the class and that would be original and interesting because as diverse as this class is, there are always some universally interesting topics that everyone can enjoy and relate to no matter what country they came from, what major in college they chose, or what their interests are.

Puskovic, Hungary

TABLE 5.1 **Rules for Selecting a Topic**

No matter what topic you choose, it should fit the following criteria:

- It is a topic about which you already have knowledge, but can find out more.
- It is a topic that is of interest to you.
- It is a topic that is of interest to your audience.
- It is a topic that neither underestimates nor overestimates the audience's knowledge or intellectual capacity.
- It is a topic that can be sufficiently discussed in the time allotted.

Source: Adapted from Alan H. Monroe, *Principles and Types of Speech,* 4th ed. (Chicago: Scott Foresman and Company, 1955), 164–166.

perienced in your travels from home? Students like you have generated a long list of interesting topics when asked these questions—for example: "the nightlife of Hong Kong," "the art of Frida Kahlo," "the mind of Alfred Hitchcock," "the architecture of Mexico," "car safety innovations, compliments of NASCAR," "how to choose the right graduate school," and "Portuguese tea houses (*casas de cha*)." You do not have to know everything about the subject you choose, just enough to guide you in your research.

You should also note that research has shown that choosing a topic that is familiar and of interest to you can actually reduce your speaking anxiety. Speakers who choose topics less familiar or interesting to them have more anxiety and less comfort when giving the speech.[1] See Table 5.2.

Consider the Audience

Put yourself in the culture of your audience and ask yourself, "What is likely to be interesting to this particular group? What topics are relevant and important to their lives?" A student a few semesters ago gave a speech on "The process of donating blood." She explained how a donor fills out a form, has a brief exam, lies on a table, and then enjoys juice and cookies. This was not an

TABLE 5.2 **Generating Speaker-Related Subjects**

- Look at subjects that you have firsthand or special knowledge about: hobbies, interests, your major, experiences.
- Look at subjects related to organizations, clubs, and companies to which you belong: student clubs, employers, volunteer organizations, foundations, unions.
- Look at the issues that are important to you: child-related issues, human or civil rights, hunger, environment.
- Look at culture-related issues: language, rituals, customs, history, environment, architecture.

Source: Adapted from William Norwood Brigance, *Speech: Its Techniques and Disciplines in a Free Society,* 2nd ed. (New York: Appleton-Century-Crofts, Inc., 1961), 183–185.

Adam is interested in music and has recently learned how to play guitar, so he chose "How to Choose the Right Guitar" as his speech topic.

interesting speech to the audience because most students had at least a general understanding of what it is like to give blood. In addition, most of the information was irrelevant to the students who had no intention of giving blood. Discussing the blood shortage crisis, how it can affect everyone, and what can be done about it would have been more compelling, interesting, and meaningful. The student might have better used the time if she had encouraged her classmates to donate blood and had included a brief overview of the process to make it seem less frightening. See Table 5.3.

TABLE 5.3 **Generating Audience-Related Subjects**

- Current interests and knowledge of the audience might suggest topics: Students might be interested in effective study techniques or word processing shortcuts; parents might be interested in disciplining practices or academic-enrichment opportunities for their children; doctors might be interested in new treatments or medical equipment.
- The social, economic, or religious beliefs of the audience might suggest a topic: Environmentalists are concerned with the health of the oceans; corporate and business leaders are interested in the stock markets; religious groups enjoy having their tenets reaffirmed.
- The local community of the audience might suggest a topic: Does the local town suffer from overcrowding, traffic congestion, poor schools? Does the town enjoy unique recreational opportunities like skiing, fly-fishing, hiking, surfing, polo, midnight basketball?

Source: Adapted from William Norwood Brigance, *Speech: Its Techniques and Disciplines in a Free Society*, 2nd ed. (New York: Appleton-Century-Crofts, Inc., 1961), 182–183.

Consider the Occasion

Audiences and event organizers have expectations about which subjects and topics are appropriate and which are taboo. In choosing a subject based on the speaking occasion, ask, "What types of topics are appropriate for this occasion?" Bachelor party speeches are quite different in tone and content from wedding toasts. Eulogies offer comfort and condolence; baptism blessings offer hope for the future. Sales meetings motivate, and award ceremonies congratulate. Be sure that your topic fits the mood and expectations for the event. For example, imagine that you have been asked to give a speech at your town's "Diversity Day," in which the residents are celebrating various ethnic and cultural backgrounds. Assume that they have asked you to speak because you are an international student. What would you talk about? You could talk about your experiences with diversity, either in your country of origin or as an international student. You wouldn't talk about the political climate on your campus, vegetarianism, or rain forests, because your knowledge of those topics is not why they have asked you to speak.

Brainstorming

Brainstorming
An idea-generating technique used by groups or individuals to develop creative solutions to a problem.

Brainstorming is the process of coming up with as many ideas as possible in a short amount of time without critique. In other words, when you brainstorm you write down all the ideas that come to mind, no matter how silly, irrelevant, boring, or challenging they may seem. You simply write everything that comes to mind without editing, refining, or judging.

Brainstorming sessions are effective for developing a list of potential speech subjects. Use the guidelines in Table 5.4 on page 109 to generate a list of possible subjects for your next speaking assignment. Here is an example of subjects generated in a two-minute brainstorming session:

Adoption	Volunteering	Greenhouse effect
Animal care	Donating blood platelets	Music
Dolphin communication	Recycling	Forensic science
Conspiracy theories	Herbal supplements	Left-handedness
Breast cancer	Essential oils	Genetics

If you are still having trouble coming up with a topic, go to the "Librarian's Index to the Internet."

http://lii.org/

This site offers a wealth of topic ideas and links to credible librarian-selected Internet resources.

Dangers of cell phones	Medical careers	Alzheimer's disease
Car maintenance	Gun-control environment	NASCAR racing
Sleep deprivation	Financial aid	Dairy products
Vegetarianism	Latest discoveries in biology	

Narrowing Your Choices

At this point, you should have a fairly long list of potential subjects. More than six or seven good choices are still too many, so now you need to narrow down your choices to just a few. First, eliminate any topics that you are not that excited about or interested in. Of the remaining topics, clarify which topics are the most interesting to you. Eliminate the topics that are on the bottom of your list.

Next, choose which ones you think would be the five most relevant, interesting, and meaningful subjects to your audience. Eliminate those that are too complicated, boring, or simplistic. Can each of the remaining topics be narrowed down and refined to fit in the time allotted without compromising the quality of the presentation? If not, eliminate them. Of the remaining, choose two or three with which to work. Rank them from the most to the least promising topics. Use the top-ranked subject to begin narrowing your subject to a topic in the next section. If it turns out not to work, choose the next one, and so on, until you have settled on your topic.

Use these words to inspire you when you can't think of more subjects during your brainstorming session.

Animals	Hobbies	Personal interests	Science
Careers	Issues	Places	Sports
Current events	Music	Processes	Transportation
Entertainment	People	Rituals/ceremonies	

From Subject to Topic

If you had unlimited time, say, weeks or years, and a willing, interested audience, you could take the general subject you have chosen and tell the audience all there is to know about it. However, time and audience interest are limited to maybe five or ten minutes. Therefore, you will need to narrow your subject down into one specific topic to discuss in your speech. For instance, if you chose *music* as your subject, you might discuss your favorite band, Mozart's influence, the growing popularity of drum circles, how to strum a guitar, the history of jazz, the origins of country music, Romanian dance music, the native instruments of China, or music therapy. You would choose one aspect that fits the speaking situation, which includes the audience and the time available.

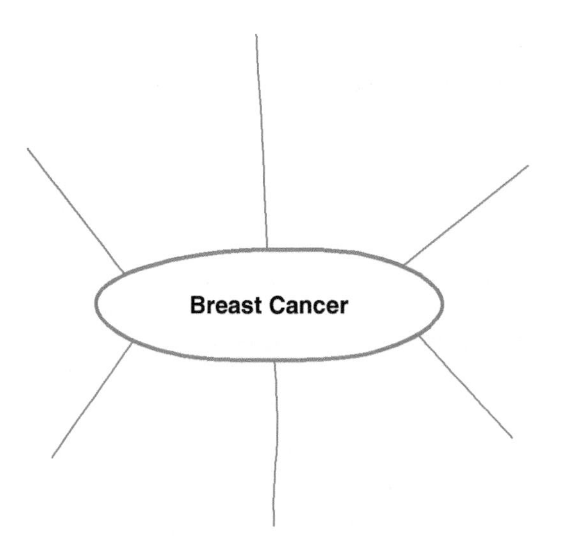

FIGURE 5.2 Mind Mapping

Mind Mapping

Mind mapping is a second brainstorming technique that is used to clarify and simplify complicated topics.[2] When you mind-map, you start with a general subject, such as breast cancer. You write the subject in the middle of a blank sheet of paper, draw a circle around it, and then give it some "legs" (see Figure 5.2). Now brainstorm all the possible specific topics you can think of related to the general subject (Figure 5.3). As you free-associate, draw legs from each of the specific topics as needed to follow the associations you make.

What other topics can you think of that relate to breast cancer? In the past, students have done informative speeches on breast cancer in minority populations, male breast cancer, the disease's growth and development, effects of breast cancer on the partners and families of patients, and performing self-exams. Students' persuasive speeches have focused on donating to various breast cancer foundations, volunteering for breast cancer fund-raising events, and walking in breast cancer walk-a-thons. The possible topics are limited only by your imagination.

Unlike simple brainstorming, mind mapping goes beyond idea generation and actually starts to group together related ideas that may later become your main points and support. Notice in Figure 5.3 how treatments, new discoveries, symptoms, prevention, causes, and support are various aspects of breast cancer that one might choose as a speech topic.

Radiating from each of these are further *subdivisions* (individual sections of a larger item, idea, or topic) of those aspects. Mind mapping gives you a visual representation of your ideas and shows how they are related. Once you have sufficiently narrowed your subject to a specific topic for your speech, you are ready to refine it even further by developing your specific purpose statement.

Subdivide
The breaking down of an item, idea, or object into smaller parts.

Subdivision
The individual parts of a larger item that, when combined with the other individual parts, make up the whole.

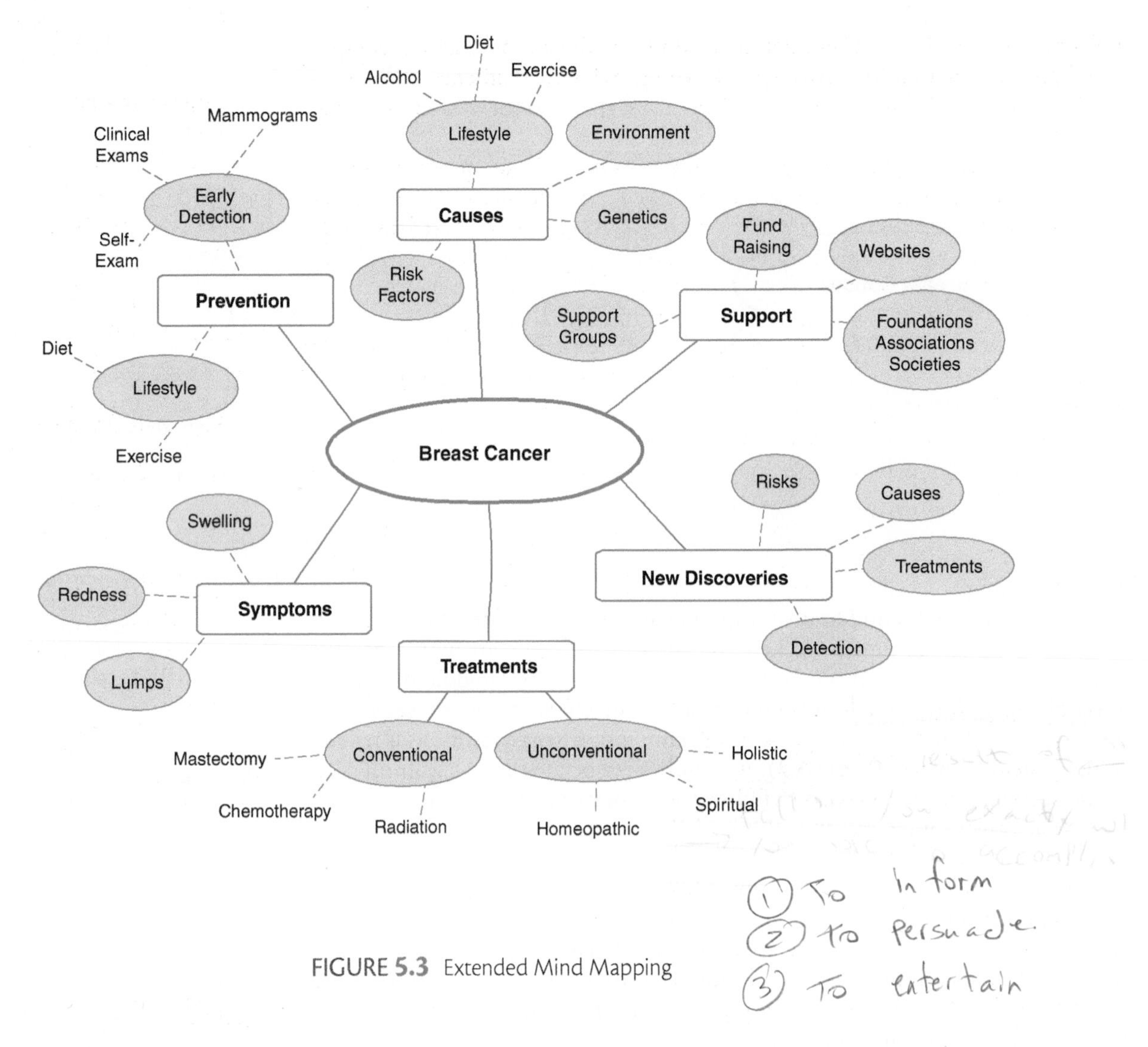

FIGURE 5.3 Extended Mind Mapping

GENERAL PURPOSE

General Purpose
The overriding goal of the speech expressed in the infinitive verb form that guides the development of the topic. A general purpose can be to inform, to persuade, or to entertain.

You might be surprised to learn that every time you speak, you are doing so for one of three reasons: offering or requesting information, trying to persuade or asking to be persuaded, or simply wanting to connect with others. Not surprisingly, your general purpose for a speech will be to inform, to persuade, or to entertain. We call this level of topic refinement "identifying the *general purpose.*"

Usually for classroom speeches, your instructor will assign the general purpose of the speech. For example, if the assignment calls for informing your audience, the general purpose would be *to inform.* Informative speeches are those that teach, explain, define, clarify, and demonstrate. You might teach the class how to make a dish from your native country, explain the significance of a wedding ritual, define an unusual theory, or clarify a complicated process. In an informative speech, you provide the audience with information and knowledge they are not likely to have or extend and clarify what they already know.

If the assignment instructs you to ask the audience to do or believe something, then the general purpose would be *to persuade*. Persuasive speeches include those that convince, advocate, motivate, and consider. Persuasion goes beyond providing information to the audience members; it asks them to think, do, or believe something that they may or may not initially want to think, do, or believe. You might advocate changing the laws prohibiting euthanasia, ask for volunteers for a blood drive, or argue that *Shrek* is the best children's movie ever made. Persuasion is necessary whenever disagreement is present. If everyone agreed, we would not need persuasion!

If your purpose is to inspire, excite, welcome, commemorate, or memorialize, your general purpose is *to entertain*. Speeches to entertain (these are also referred to as "special occasion speeches") are those that give special meaning to occasions in our lives. They may present information the audience does not already have or move audiences to a new belief or even to action, but their overriding purpose is to make an event more meaningful and worthwhile to the audience. Special occasion speeches hold the audience's at-

An MC (master of ceremonies) gives speeches to entertain in between the event's other speeches.

HINT

Improving Your Mind Maps

The following suggestions can improve the effectiveness of your mind maps:

- *Use single words or simple phrases:* Too many words clutter the mind map, making it hard to read and understand (e.g., write "cause," rather than "most common causes of breast cancer").
- *Print words:* Use clear writing that you will be able to read easily when you are done.
- *Use color to separate the subdivisions:* Color can help separate ideas more easily and distinguish between the various levels or subdivisions.
- *Use symbols:* Choose a consistent symbol system that helps you quickly identify the various levels and connections (e.g., circles for main points, squares for first-level subdivisions, triangles for third-level subdivisions).
- *Show linked ideas:* Sometimes ideas in one area of the map relate to other areas as well; be sure to show those connections using cross-linkages (i.e., draw a line from one idea to related ideas).

Source: Adapted from *Mind Maps—A Powerful Approach to Note Taking* on *Mind Tools: Essential Skills for an Excellent Career*, http://www.mindtools.com/pages/article/newISS_01.htm (retrieved July 7, 2004).

tention by giving them words to savor and enjoy. Eulogies, after-dinner speeches, presentation and acceptance speeches, commemorative speeches, and graduation speeches are all examples of special occasion speeches. We will discuss each of these types of speeches in detail in Chapters Thirteen and Fourteen. For now, just remember that all speeches fall into one of the three general categories. If you have been given the general purpose statement, simply write it at the top of your paper (see the speech outline template in Table 8.1) and move on to choosing and refining your topic. If you have not, read on.

If your instructor or the event organizers have not given you the general purpose of the speech, you can determine the likely purpose by analyzing the speaking situation. Ask for the expectations of the audience and the organizers of the event, and ask yourself what you personally want to achieve as a result of giving the speech. Are you hoping to change or move the audience to action in some way (persuade)? Do you want to inspire or amuse them (entertain)? Are you looking to teach or enlighten them (inform)? Once you have decided your general purpose, write it at the top of your page using the infinitive form of the appropriate verb:

General purpose: To inform

Or General purpose: To persuade

Or General purpose: To entertain

Now that you have your general purpose and speech topic, you are ready to develop your specific purpose statement!

Specific Purpose
A single infinitive phrase that identifies the audience and specific goal of a speech.

SPECIFIC PURPOSE

So far, you have identified a subject, selected a topic, and determined a general purpose for your speech. Now you can use that information to create a specific purpose statement. The specific purpose statement is the backbone for developing, writing, and delivering your speech because the specific purpose statement tells you exactly what you hope to accomplish as a result of giving your speech. You can also think of it as the desired response you want to receive from the audience at the end of your speech. Like the general purpose statement, the specific purpose statement is not part of your actual speech—you won't actually say it, but it will guide your research and writing throughout the speech-development process. The specific purpose brings your audience analysis, general purpose, and speech topic together into one statement that identifies your goal. These examples show the relationship among the subject, topic, general purpose, and specific purpose:

Subject: Cigarette smoking

Topic: Smoking as an addiction

General purpose: To inform

CONSIDERING CULTURE

What Topics to Avoid

What topics are considered appropriate or taboo is sometimes culture-specific. What is acceptable to discuss in public in one country might not be appropriate in another. To avoid inadvertently offending your audience or embarrassing yourself, you must handle some topics very carefully or avoid them entirely with some audiences. Such topics may include finances, sex, religion, or politics. Consider the following:

- Brazilian audiences can be offended by references to Argentina (a long-time rival).[1]
- Political topics, particularly local politics or politics relating to the country of origin of audience members, are often off-limits to those from South and Central America and many Asian countries, but are enjoyed in Spain.
- Audiences around the world respond negatively to being criticized by the speaker, so avoid topics that criticize the audience.
- Personal topics such as hygiene, health, money, family, and business can be taboo in India, France, Spain, and Norway, but are welcome in Fiji, Hong Kong, and the Philippines.
- The Swiss avoid discussions about weight and diet.[2]

Offending others is not the only thing to consider when you are trying to eliminate possible topics from your list. In general, avoid topics that:

- Describe complicated processes that require extensive visualization, imagination, or memorization (e.g., "how to fix an automatic transmission" or "how a computer creates images on a monitor").
- Require the use of highly specialized vocabulary or depend on extensive background knowledge that you are not certain your audience already possesses (e.g., "identifying and alleviating the problem of differential gain").
- Are overly complex and will overwhelm the audience with statistics and complicated reasoning (e.g., "the postulates of quantum theory").
- Are excessively personal subjects that people would feel more comfortable reading about in privacy (e.g., "unusual sexual practices" or "how to cope with embarrassing gas").
- Are too commonplace, obvious, ridiculous, or superficial. For example, most adults already know how to make a peanut butter sandwich, the importance of exercise, and the dangers of drug abuse. To explain these would insult the audience's intelligence.

[1] Roger E. Axtell, *Do's and Taboos Around the World*, 3rd ed. (New York: John Wiley & Son, Inc., 1993), 70.

[2] Ibid.

The end goal of your speech determines your general and specific purpose.

Specific purpose: To inform a group of high school students how cigarette smoking becomes addictive.

Compared to:

Subject: Cigarette smoking

Topic: Banning cigarette smoking

General purpose: To persuade

Specific purpose: To persuade the student council to vote in favor of a ban on cigarette smoking on campus.

Compared to:

Subject: Cigarette smoking

Topic: Quitting cigarettes

General purpose: To entertain

Specific purpose: To entertain a group of former smokers about the often-amusing difficulties of quitting smoking.

Notice that the specific purpose statement restates the general purpose, includes a brief description of the audience, and states the speaker's goal. You

TABLE 5.4 **Brainstorming Guidelines**

1. Find a comfortable place to sit where you will not be distracted or interrupted.
2. Provide yourself with plenty of clean paper and a pen or pencil.
3. Give yourself a time limit. Ten minutes is usually sufficient.
4. Start writing. Write down every possible subject or specific topic that comes to mind.
5. Do not evaluate, criticize, change, or edit any of your ideas. Just write them down as they come to you.
6. Use free association: Allow one idea to lead to other ideas naturally without censoring them (e.g., "light-sun-moon-stars-celebrities-Johnny Depp").
7. If ideas stop coming, use a "seed" word (a word, phrase, or category to reignite your thinking).
8. Do not stop writing new ideas until you have reached your time limit.
9. When time runs out, stop writing.

should also note that the specific purpose is written as a statement, not as a question.

Instead of: *How are crayons made?*

Use: *To inform my classmates about the process of manufacturing crayons.*

Also, be sure to use clear and precise language when writing your specific purpose statement. Avoid colloquial, figurative, and vague language.

Instead of: *To inform my classmates about some really cool new clubs at school.*

Use: *To inform my classmates about the three new clubs on campus.*

Instead of: *To inform my buds about the free stuff they can get online.*

Use: *To inform my fraternity brothers about online promotional programs that offer free gifts.*

Because the specific purpose statement should be targeted, representing one clear goal of the speaker, it should contain only one idea or goal. See Table 5.5.

Instead of: *To inform my classmates about the dangers of using a cell phone and the new law prohibiting cell phone use while driving.*

Use: *To inform my classmates about the dangers of using a cell phone.*

Or: *To inform my classmates about the new state law prohibiting cell phone use while driving.*

As you develop your specific purpose statement, consider each of the following:

HINT

Specific Purpose Statement

When you are having difficulty developing your specific purpose statement, ask and answer this question out loud: "What *one* thing do I want my audience to do, know, feel, or understand as a result of hearing my speech?" Sometimes talking about your goal out loud can help you clarify your ideas before committing them to paper.

- *The authority and ability of the audience:* Can the audience actually accomplish or do what you are asking of them? Choose a specific purpose that they can attain.
- *The attitude of the audience toward your topic:* If you are dealing with a hostile audience, you will need to be realistic about what you are hoping to accomplish in one speech. Sometimes just asking them to listen to your concerns openly is the best you can do.
- *The spirit of the occasion:* Your specific purpose should be in-line with the mood, tone, and reason for the event or occasion.
- *The time constraints of the speech:* Choose a specific purpose that you can reasonably accomplish in the time allotted.
- *The needs of the speaker:* Are the goals consistent with your beliefs, values, and attitudes, and do they promote your larger goals or interfere with them? Choose a specific purpose that not only meets your goals for the speech, but is also consistent with the goals for your life.

Now that you have your specific purpose statement, you are ready to craft your thesis statement.

THESIS STATEMENT

If you went to a college success seminar and your roommate later wanted to know what the main speaker had discussed, you could tell him, "She gave tips on how students can manage their time by prioritizing activities, making a study schedule, and combining activities." What you told your roommate was the thesis or central idea of the presentation. A thesis statement (also called a *central idea*) encapsulates the entire speech into a single declarative sentence. The thesis explains the topic of the speech (time management tips for students) and previews the main points (prioritizing activities, making a study schedule, and combining activities).

The thesis must match the goals of the specific purpose statement and must preview the main points in the same order and manner in which you will cover them in the speech. For example:

Instead of:

Specific Purpose: To inform my classmates about how to avoid sleep deprivation.

TABLE 5.5 **The Specific Purpose Statement:**

- Begins with your general purpose: To inform, to persuade, or to entertain.
- Includes a reference to the audience—either "my audience" or a brief description of the audience, "my speech classmates."
- Is written as an infinitive phrase (not a question or fragment).
- Includes only one goal or idea (avoiding *and, or, but, so,* etc., will help).

CONSIDERING LANGUAGE

***Thesis* in Many Different Languages**

The use of thesis statements is not exclusive to English. Each language uses thesis statements, although how they are written and used can be different. The following are translations of *thesis* in several different languages:

Dutch: *thesis*
Japanese: 説
Spanish: *tesis*
Chinese: 論題
Italian: *tesi*
Korean: 논제
French: *thèse*
Russian: **тезис**
German: *these*
Greek: διατριβη

For more advice on creating effective thesis statements,

Click Here http://owl.english.purdue.edu/handouts/print/general/gl_thesis.html

Purdue University's online writing lab offers a printable handout on developing thesis statements.

Thesis: Sleep deprivation can create many emotional, physical, and personal problems.

Use:

Specific Purpose: To inform my classmates about how to avoid sleep deprivation.

Thesis: You can avoid sleep deprivation through time management, avoiding alcohol, and using relaxation techniques.

Or:

Specific Purpose: To inform my classmates about the dangers of sleep deprivation.

Thesis: Sleep deprivation can create many emotional, physical, and personal problems.

If your thesis is:

Route 66 had a powerful impact on the culture, transportation, and economics of the United States.

Your main points would *not* be:

I. The route of Route 66
II. The best landmarks on Route 66
III. The best restaurants on Route 66

Instead, they would probably be:

I. Route 66 influenced the culture of the United States.
II. Route 66 shaped transportation in the United States.
III. Route 66 had an effect on economics in the United States.

At this point, it is important to recognize that your thesis is only a *working* thesis statement. In other words, if you feel the need to change the direction of your speech, adjust your purpose, switch a main point, or rearrange the organization of your main points, you will need to make the necessary corrections to the purpose, thesis, or main points as needed.

TABLE 5.6 Rules for Writing Thesis Statements

Thesis statements should:
• Contain a single idea that is divided into main points.
• Be consistent with the specific purpose statement and main points of the body.
• Be written as a full sentence, not a fragment.
• Be written as a declarative sentence, not a question.
• Be specific, not vague.

To write your thesis statement, you will need to decide on your main points. For now, pick what you think your main points will most likely be. For some speeches, it is as simple as saying: *There are three factors to consider when choosing a graduate school.* The *three factors* represent the three main points.

Check to see if your topic has natural subdivisions. Some topics reveal their main points in the specific purpose: *To inform my audience about the causes and effects of global warming.* The main points are (1) the causes of global warming and (2) the effects of global warming. Speeches that explain how to do something (a process speech) are easily divisible into the steps of the process. Speeches that focus on the history or development of something can be divided into time periods such as *past, present,* and *future* or *beginning, middle,* and *end.* For more help on choosing and developing main points see Chapters Six and Eight.

Finally, to ensure a clear and logical thesis statement, follow these simple rules:

- The thesis statement must be written as a full sentence, not a fragment.

Instead of: *The four steps to a healthier lifestyle.*
Use: *There are four simple steps to having a healthier lifestyle.*

- The thesis statement should be written as a declarative statement, not a question.

Instead of: *Why should you wear shoes that fit?*
Use: *Wearing well-fitting shoes makes walking easier, leads to better skeletal health, and improves your mood.*

- The thesis statement should be written in specific language, not in vague or figurative language.

Instead of: *Making hip holiday frames is super easy and fun.*
Use: *The simple three-step process of making holiday frames can be fun for the whole family.*

The thesis statement is the road map for your speech. Follow it! As you research, focus on only the materials directly related to your thesis and main points. See Table 5.6.

SPECIAL BENEFITS AND OPPORTUNITIES FOR NON-NATIVE SPEAKERS

As a non-native speaker of English, you have some special opportunities because you have most likely been exposed to more than one way of thinking and knowing and to different cultural traditions, rituals, customs, languages, and ceremonies. You have undoubtedly learned the works of authors, poets, and artists that may not be well known in the United States or even translated into English. You can use this knowledge base to your benefit.

Do not be afraid to incorporate other cultures' or languages' ways of thinking and knowing into the U.S. style of communication. As we have discussed, some cultures enjoy using more storytelling and quotes than is common in the United States. Some languages use more metaphor and stylistic devices. As you develop your topic and purpose for your speech, spend some time trying to think of a topic specific to your native language. This will help you think more creatively. Additionally, use your knowledge of the different cultural traditions, rituals, customs, and ceremonies and of the authors, artists, and poets you have encountered in your native language and culture to create a speech topic that your audience is not likely to have encountered before.

Finally, as a non-native student (especially if you haven't been in the United States for very long), you might enjoy hearing topics that are often all-too-common for native English speakers but new and interesting to you. Because you are most likely in a class with students from countries throughout the world, you will have many opportunities to hear about life in countries from around the globe.

CROSS-CULTURAL VIEW OF RHETORIC

Rhetorical Situation
The elements (speaker, audience, topic, purpose, and context) of a communication that interact and influence each other and the communication.

Rhetorical Conventions
The culture-specific manner in which messages are expected to be prepared and delivered in a particular context.

When developing a speech, consider not only yourself (your goals, style, abilities, and expertise) but also the audience, the context (the culture, occasion, venue, time, etc.), the topic, and the purpose of the presentation. You will recall from Chapter One that we call these aspects of speaking the *rhetorical situation.* The rhetorical situation influences every aspect of the speech, from choosing an appropriate topic, purpose, and supporting materials to choosing how you dress. The rhetorical situation also strongly affects how a message will be received and understood. What might be a perfectly appropriate and meaningful message in one situation might be inappropriate and meaningless in another.

In Chapter Four we looked closely at analyzing the audience and the speaking situation, and at the influence these factors have on your speech. In this chapter we've continued our look at the rhetorical situation by examining the speech topic and purpose. We have also explored the roles of audience and context in making topic and purpose selections and learned how to adapt our personal style and expertise to the topic and purpose. However, we have not yet discussed how understanding these aspects helps us adapt our communication from situation to situation and from one culture, country, or language to another.

Rhetorical situations exist in every culture and country around the world. No matter which language you are speaking, it is always important to consider the rhetorical situation when developing and delivering your message. What do change are the *rhetorical conventions* associated with each rhetorical situation.

Rhetorical situations come with a set of rhetorical conventions (i.e., the expected ways in which a message will be prepared and delivered in a particular context and to a particular audience). The level of expected formality, appropriate dress, types of supporting material, and delivery method is affected by the situation (i.e., the audience, the occasion, the venue, and the purpose). These expectations and rules associated with particular rhetorical situations are the rhetorical conventions.

Rhetorical conventions in one language, culture, or country may not be the same, or even similar, in another. The expectations about how, why, when, and where brides and grooms, students and teachers, bosses and employees, politicians and constituents speak are culturally bound. The level of language formality, terms of address, and clothing changes with a change in culture. Even the ways time is used in storytelling have to follow certain rules to meet audience expectations.[3]

Cultural differences in rhetorical conventions can lead to misunderstandings between audiences and speakers. Although it would be impossible to teach every rhetorical convention associated with every culture, we can become sensitive to the significance of these conventions and become aware of the potential impact they may have on our communication with others from different cultures.[4]

To appropriately give a speech in a language or culture different from one you are completely familiar and comfortable with, be sure to find out the specific rhetorical conventions of that culture for that situation. Otherwise, one day you could find yourself giving a hilarious acceptance speech for a well-deserved award, only to find out later that your hosts expected solemnity and humility.

SUMMARY

Starting with the universe of possible speech topics, you reduced, eliminated, narrowed, and refined your speech topic using an inventory of your personal knowledge, background, and experience. You investigated your activities and interests and also considered current events, audience interests, and recent events in your community. You brainstormed. When you were finished, you had lots of potential subjects to choose from that seemed relevant, interesting, and meaningful.

Next, you began sorting through and eliminating subjects from the list. You crossed off subjects that seemed too complicated, insignificant, or boring for you and your audience. You erased subjects that could not be adequately discussed in the time allotted. You prioritized and you picked. Using mind mapping, you narrowed down your subject even further until you had a specific topic and even some ideas for main points.

After you found a specific topic you could work with, you developed your purpose. Based on your previous analysis of the speaking situation, you decided on a general purpose—to inform, to persuade, or to entertain. Then you further used that analysis to combine your subject and general purpose into a specific purpose. You made the specific purpose into a single statement that included your general purpose, a description of your audience, and a statement of your goal for the speech. Then you went one step further and developed a thesis statement—a single declarative sentence that summarizes your speech, including your main points. Wow! You have been busy!

All of this work centered around each aspect of the rhetorical situation—speaker, audience, context, topic, and purpose. You learned that the rhetorical situation guides the development and delivery of a speech through a set of rhetorical conventions—the rules, expectations, and customs relevant to a particular situation. We discussed how rhetorical conventions are bound not only by the situation but by the culture as well. You learned to investigate not only the rhetorical conventions of a unique or unusual situation but also the unique cultural conventions associated with common rhetorical situations. Even though the speaking occasion (graduation, wedding, funeral) is identified the same way in different cultures, it may not be handled in the same manner.

Happily for you, now that you have your road map, also known as your *thesis*, the road to researching and developing your speech will be much easier.

Discussion Questions and Activities

1. Get into a group with three of your classmates. First, for about fifteen minutes ask each other about your various interests, hobbies, and experiences. Then take out a piece of paper and designate one person to be the recorder. Have everyone in the group generate topic ideas. The recorder should write down all the ideas without editing or adding commentary. When the idea generation has slowed down (after at least ten minutes), narrow the list to the best ten ideas.
2. Flip through a variety of newspapers (local and national) and magazines. Jot down the subjects covered in each. From those subjects, brainstorm as many topics as you can think of that would be interesting to your classmates. Organize the topics into two categories: those topics that are persuasive and those that are informative.
3. Come up with an informative and a persuasive specific purpose statement for each of the following general subjects:

Smoking	Tattoos	Cultural differences
Diabetes	Wedding rituals	Auto racing
Immigration	Islam	Health care

4. Choose three of the specific purpose statements you created in question #3, and develop a thesis statement for each. Remember, you will first need to generate some main points.
5. Identify what is wrong with the following specific purpose statements and rewrite them correctly.
   - To teach my classmates about the hottest new cell phones.
   - To show the audience that they should vote in the school elections.
   - To inform my classmates about why they need to donate blood today.
   - To persuade my classmates about the importance of a healthy diet.
6. Identify what is wrong with the following thesis statements and rewrite them.
   - Believe it or not, these three cell phones are hot.
   - The four reasons it is so important to vote in school elections.
   - Donating blood today is important.
   - Why should you eat a healthy diet?
7. Consider everything you have learned in this chapter. In what ways are the ideas and concepts similar to how you have been taught in the past to develop ideas, write papers, or create speeches? In what ways are they different? Do you feel that there are cultural differences that influence the way in which people create texts? Why? Why not? What other factors influence the manner in which one develops ideas into texts (whether written or spoken)?

Chapter Quiz

Matching

Place the letter of the term on the line next to the proper example.

a. Rhetorical situation **b.** General purpose **c.** Rhetorical conventions
d. Thesis **e.** Subdivision **f.** Mind mapping

1. ______ The expected ways in which a speaker will develop and present a speech to an audience based on the context.
2. ______ The central idea of a speech.
3. ______ An individual component of a larger item or idea that when combined with other components create the whole.
4. ______ The speaker, the audience, the context, the topic, and the purpose..
5. ______ A way to develop a subject into a specific topic.
6. ______ To inform, to persuade, to entertain.
7. True or false: Persuasive speeches never contain information, only claims.

8. True or false: "To inform my classmates about the process of donating blood" is an effective specific purpose statement.

9. Which of the following is the most effective thesis statement?

a. Why don't you donate blood today?

b. Donating blood will save lives.

c. Donating blood is safe, fast, and easy.

d. I want you to donate blood.

10. Which of the following is true about creating a thesis statement?

a. A thesis statement should be in the form of a question.

b. A thesis statement should include the main points.

c. A thesis statement needs to make a reference to the audience.

d. A thesis statement does not need to be a full sentence.

Chapter 5 Quiz Answers

1. c, 2. d, 3. e, 4. a, 5. f, 6. b, 7. False, 8. True, 9. c, 10. b.

CHAPTER 6 Research

CHAPTER GOAL

By the end of this chapter you will be able to create and follow a research plan that employs credible Internet and non-Internet sources.

If you were introducing yourself to the class, describing your most embarrassing moment, or explaining why you are taking this class, you would not have to look very far to find material for your speech. All you need is in your head. To introduce yourself, you could list your hobbies and interests, describe your talents or fears, or tell a story about some important moment in your life. To describe your most embarrassing moment, you would describe the scene, explain what happened, and relate how you felt. To explain your reasons for taking the class, you would describe the requirements for your major, your personal or career goals, or your desire to increase your confidence. In each of these scenarios, you might include an object to show to the audience—a favorite book, a picture of a place or a person, or an enlarged copy of your acceptance letter to your favorite university. All the supporting material (see Chapter Seven for a full discussion of supporting materials) could come from you because the topic *is* you. You are the foremost expert on *you*. In other words, you wouldn't have to do any research. You wouldn't need to interview experts or leaf through encyclopedias, journals, and books. For most other speeches, however, you need to conduct research to find the right examples, statistics, facts, and quotes to support the thesis and main points.

Supporting Material
Anything that clarifies, amplifies, proves, describes, explains, or makes a speech more interesting.

Imagine that you are going to give a speech about becoming a naturalized citizen of the United States. Your thesis is:

There are five steps to becoming a naturalized citizen of the United States.

Your main points are:

I. Preparation
II. Application
III. Fingerprinting
IV. The interview
V. The oath

What kinds of information will you need to explain each step of this process clearly to your classmates? Where will you look for the information? Where will you even begin?

If you are unfamiliar with researching in the United States, you may have additional concerns, such as, "Is the library set up the same way as in my country?" "How do I include information from non-English sources?" "How do I use quotes from another language?" "Where do I find academically acceptable research?" "When is it OK to use the Internet?" This chapter will answer these questions.

First, we will clarify what we mean by *research*. Then we will address particular concerns you might have as a non-native English speaker. Next, you will learn how to conduct efficient and effective research by examining the resources available in the library, on the Internet, through interviews, and from your own knowledge base. From there you will learn how to make a research plan and discover how to manage the information you find.

TABLE 6.1 **What Is Research?**

The word *research* is commonly used to describe two types of researching activity and the results of that research. This can cause confusion when discussing "how to do research."

Research (verb): To review relevant and available information about a topic in order to increase one's knowledge and understanding.

Research (verb): To conduct experiments and/or analyze data to create new understanding about a particular topic; to add to the collective knowledge base about a topic through experimentation, survey, and analysis.

Research (noun): The information collected through researching.

For example, if you were doing research on dolphin communication, you might be simply trying to discover what dolphin communication is. You might look in a general subject encyclopedia or do a quick online search for new or recent discoveries in the field of dolphin communication. You might look at the related research in the fields of marine biology, zoology, veterinary medicine, communication, and oceanography to see what research has been conducted on dolphins and their communication.

On the other hand, you might be trying to develop the argument that dolphins do more than communicate; they actually use language. In that case, you would analyze arguments that both agree and disagree with your position, and compare the research in the field of dolphin communication as well as the research in linguistics and communication about the requirements for communication to be considered language. If you were a researcher in one of these fields, you might even conduct your own original research to test your theory that dolphin communication constitutes language. In each of these research scenarios, the information you find to answer your inquiries is also called *research*.

WHAT IS RESEARCH?

Research is the process of systematically searching for facts, principles, and opinions about a particular subject or topic. Many think of research as simply looking through encyclopedias and books for relevant facts and figures about a topic, but research can take many forms (see Table 6.1). For some, doing research can seem very intimidating, confusing, difficult, or boring. For others, it is the most interesting part of speechmaking and speechwriting.

Personally, I love to research, and I suggest that you think of research as an adventure into a world you may have never known before, an exploration that piques and satisfies curiosity and leads you into unexpected places. During your research you will meet people both in person and on paper, discover new ways of seeing the world, and learn new and interesting facts. You will also build confidence as a student. Doing research takes knowledge, skill, and practice. In this section, we will address some of the concerns you may have about doing research, review how to use the library, and discuss how to make a research plan.

STRANGE NEW WORLDS

If you are not from the United States, you might not be familiar with how to conduct library research here, the expectations for doing research, or how to use the information once you find it. Luckily, the reasons for, uses of, and processes of doing research are strikingly similar throughout the world. Whether for speechwriting or speechmaking, people conduct research to find information, to gain greater understanding, to develop opinions, or to extend their knowledge base in a particular subject or topic. However, there are some important differences in library research among various countries and some specific challenges you might face that need to be addressed.

If you have had some experience researching and using libraries in the United States, you may be quite comfortable doing research for your speech already. If so, great! In the next section you will find information that will help you make the most of your research. However, if your only research experience is what you've done in another country or some limited research here in the United States, you might find the system a bit intimidating and confusing because, although there are many similarities, there are some differences in library organization, available resources, and lending practices throughout the world.

For many students, non-native or not, one of the greatest obstacles in learning to conduct library research is a lack of confidence. You might feel unsure of how to begin, and your uncertainty may feel so overwhelming that you avoid the library altogether and attempt to do all your research online. This is a common feeling of most people when they are faced with something new, in a strange place, and with little knowledge about what to expect and how to proceed. Fortunately, these feelings will quickly subside as you become familiar with the library. Experience is the best way to build confidence. In the meantime, here are some steps you can take to build your experience and confidence quickly:

WHAT OTHERS SAY

"*I feel confident about what I need to do and what I shouldn't do because that is what I have learned throughout this whole semester. Since I chose a topic that I am really interested in, I enjoyed doing the research. New information was all interesting to me and helped me brainstorm my ideas.*"

Hiroko Sugano,
Japan

- **Take an online tour** of the library before going there. Many libraries now offer online tutorials about how to use the library, where to find relevant materials, where to find the online catalogs and how to use them, which databases are available, what the lending and copying rules are, when the library is open, and how and when you can best use the research librarians to assist you.

The library classification identification number can be found taped to the spine of each book in the library. Can you tell which classification system these books are using?

- **Take a library tour.** Most libraries, especially those of colleges and universities, offer tours at the beginning of, and sometimes throughout, the semester.
- **Go with a friend or classmate** to the library the first few times. You can help each other become comfortable using the library.

Library Classification System
The manner in which a library collection is organized, allowing people to find materials quickly and easily.

Children in the United States are taught the Dewey Decimal library classification system in grade school when they learn how to use the library and, chances are, you did, too, because the Dewey Decimal Classification (DDC) system is the most widely used library classification system in the world. However, many libraries around the world and in the United States use other systems for organizing their collections. For example, in the United States most college and university libraries use the Library of Congress classification system (LC), and Japan uses a system called the National Diet Library System (NDLC).[1]

Luckily, all classification systems have a clear, learnable logic that a librarian would be happy to explain to you, but for now, take a moment to review the fundamentals of the Library of Congress system since this is the system that you are most likely to encounter at your school library (see Table 6.2).

Another challenge you might encounter is that not all libraries offer the same access to online databases. Not only do the databases differ from one country to another, but they also differ from one library to another, so as you approach each new database, it might seem strange and unfamiliar, and the interface might look different. However, you should know that even though

TABLE 6.2 Locating Materials in the Library Using the Library of Congress Classification System

The LCC system divides all information into twenty-one categories of knowledge that correspond to a letter of the alphabet (*I, O, W, X,* and *Y* are not used).

These twenty-one categories are divided further by adding additional letters.

- *B* refers to Philosophy, Psychology, and Religion in general.
- While *BC* refers to Logic, *BQ* refers to Buddhism, and *BJ* refers to Ethics specifically.

The categories are subdivided again by adding numbers:

- BJ 71-1185 refers to History and Systems of Ethics.
- BJ 1518-1697 refers to Individual Ethics, Character, and Virtue.

The *stacks* (the bookcases in the library where materials are kept) are arranged alphabetically, then numerically, by call numbers (the specific LCC number of the library material). So, when you find the call number of a particular work, you can go to the stack that has the letter and numbers that correspond to the work you are seeking.

For example, if you searched for a book using the keywords *social interaction* and *communication*, one of the books you might find is:

The Individual, Communication & Society, edited by Robert W. Rieber (1989).

If you chose that book, you would see that its call number is:

BF
637
C45I52

This tells you that this book is on Psychology (BF), specifically, Applied Psychology (637). For now, don't worry too much about the meaning of the letters and numbers; they simply further identify the book title and author. What is important is that they help you locate it alphabetically and numerically on the shelf. Look for the shelves marked BF and then search numerically on the shelves.

Rieber's book would be between:

BF		BF
637	and	637
C45H236		N66

they may look quite different, all databases actually work in quite similar ways.

Everyone has her or his favorite resources. If you are using a library that's new to you, you might wonder if you can access some of the newspapers, databases, dictionaries, or encyclopedias with which you are most comfortable and familiar. If your library doesn't offer access to your favorites, don't worry; you can access many, if not most, newspapers and publications online, and many are available in print through the mail and sometimes at larger newsstands (especially in large metropolitan areas). Many libraries now offer

To access many newspapers from countries around the world via the web,

Click Here www.world-newspapers.com/

Here are a few examples of the links you will find:

The Hindu (India) www.hinduonnet.com/

Kantipur Daily (Nepal) www.kantipuronline.com/kantipur.php

Mmegi (Botswana) www.mmegi.bw/

Granma International (Cuba) www.granma.cu/

The Japan Times www.japantimes.co.jp/

The Jerusalem Post www.jpost.com/

Antara Indonesian News Provider www.antaranews.net/

Chechen Press (Chechnya) www.chechenpress.info/

525-ci gazet (Azerbaijan) www.525ci.com/

Online Public Access Catalogs (OPAC), which might allow you to access information through the Internet or through home delivery. These services are usually fee-based and often require registering on the website. However, the fees are usually very reasonable and the registration is usually confidential.

Additionally, you may be able to obtain remote library privileges from your home country in some instances, especially if you are still legally a resident. Some libraries allow remote access to nonpublic databases if you have an account there. You can find out if you are qualified for an account or if you can purchase one by visiting the library's website.

Beyond being more familiar and easier to use, these sources can offer information that might not be readily available in the United States. However, do not rely solely on these sources for your research. Although these sources are familiar and credible to you, your instructor and your audience will expect you to have also done research using standard, credible sources from the United States.

Keywords
The words you use to find the information in a database. Keywords are usually drawn from the terminology used in the field of study in question.

Terminology
The set of words and expressions used in a particular field or topic of study.

Another problem you might have is that the words, or terminology, you are using might not translate as you expect. When you do a search, you use *keywords* (sometimes called *subject terms*) relevant to the topic you are researching. Once you begin researching, you might find that the keywords you are using are not giving you the results you want. The problem might be one of translation. Some words do not translate from one language to another as you think they would. If you have this problem, you should try other keywords. You can:

- **Use a thesaurus** to find other, similar words. Maybe the word you are looking for has several similar translations in English.
- **Note the keywords** of a relevant article, and then use them to do additional searches. Articles and book citations found in the library are

FIGURE **6.1** Sample of Research Results

Here is an example of another book you might find by using the search terms "communication" and "social interaction."

Title: Handbook of communication and social interaction skills
Author(s): Edited by John O. Greene and Brant R. Burleson.
Publisher: Mahwah, N.J.: L. Erlbaum Associates, 2003.
Keywords/Subjects:
Social Interaction
Interpersonal Communication
Interpersonal Relations
ISBN: 0805834176
Call Number: HM1111. H36 2003

shown with the appropriate keywords listed near the top (see Figure 6.1).

- **Ask** your instructor, the librarian, or classmates for keyword suggestions.
- **Do an Internet search** on your topic and find the common words used to discuss the topic. These represent the terminology of the subject.

Another concern you might have is that you will not understand the information once you find it. Most research is written in more formal language than what most students (even native students) are used to using. As a nonnative speaker, understanding such dense and sophisticated language can prove difficult. If that is the case, try researching complicated subjects in your native language first and then either translate the information into English or find the English equivalent to the article, book, or database information. Many university libraries, especially those that serve diverse student populations or those that offer degrees in ethnic studies or languages, offer newspapers, books, and other printed material in a variety of languages. Check with your school's librarian.

Additionally, books, journals, and newspapers are often printed in many popular languages. Find the book or article in both English and a language with which you are more comfortable. (Note: Once you find the book in one language, you should be able to simply use the author's name or title to find it in a second language.) Read the information first in your native language so that you can better understand the information. Then reread it in English to find the exact information you hope to quote, reference, or use. This saves you time and mistakes in translating the information yourself.

HINT
You can purchase books, CDs, videos, and more from a variety of countries and in a variety of languages by going to:
http://www.amazon.com
Click on "International" in the menu.

As a student you have borrowing privileges at your school and probably with a few others with which your school is affiliated. For example, community colleges sometimes have partnerships with nearby universities. Additionally, many colleges and universities have *interlibrary loan programs* that allow students from one college in the system to order articles and books from other colleges in the system. This allows you to search for materials in several libraries (sometimes simultaneously), each of which specializes in the topics reflecting its particular academic programs. The drawback is that research takes more time because you have to wait for the materials to be delivered to your campus. Either your library's website or the librarian will know what libraries you can access and how to order materials from them.

Do not hesitate to ask the librarian for help. If you are concerned about wasting his or her time, jot down your questions ahead of time and write down the answers you receive so that you do not have to ask again later. As you become comfortable with your surroundings, you will find that researching can be easy and fun.

TYPES OF RESEARCH MATERIAL

Before you begin developing a research plan, you need to know the difference between primary and secondary resources, what resources are available to you, and how to access them. You should also be aware that not all research is conducted in a library. The Internet, interviews, and your own knowledge and experience can provide a wealth of material as well.

Primary and Secondary Sources

Primary sources are information from actual events or individuals you are studying. For example, if you wanted to find out what life was like on the battlefields of World War II, you could search for letters written by a soldier describing his battlefield experience. Artistic works (paintings, movies, novels, poems, music, etc.), original documents (birth and death certificates, letters,

CONSIDERING CULTURE

Ethnographic Research

Sociological research into cultures is called *ethnography.* Ethnography began with Western researchers studying non-Western and native cultures. However, due to the damaging effects of colonization and missionary work on these cultures, researchers have begun to focus attention on other developed countries and on their own cultures. Three kinds of ethnography have emerged:

Microethnography: The study of very small subgroups within a larger culture.

Macroethnography: The study of a larger cultural group, such as a tribe or community.

Autoethnography: The study of self as it relates to one's cultural phenomena.

Source: Meredith D. Gall, Joyce P. Gall, and Walter R. Borg, *Educational Research: An introduction* (Boston: Allyn & Bacon, 2003).

videotape of an event, government documents, etc.), and interviews with firsthand sources are examples of primary sources.

Secondary sources are removed from the actual events or people. A history book describing life on the battlefield would be a secondary source. Textbooks, documentaries, reviews, articles, and most lectures (unless the lecturer is sharing a personal experience) are secondary sources. Secondary sources summarize, critique, and interpret events.

Knowing whether the information is a primary or secondary source is important because primary sources offer firsthand or eyewitness testimony, whereas secondary sources offer a summary or an interpretation of an event sometimes years, decades, or centuries after the event. Even when they are reporting recent events, statistics, or test results, secondary sources are sometimes not very reliable because they occasionally overgeneralize, misrepresent, or misinterpret the information. For that reason, wherever possible, use primary sources and check a variety of secondary sources to verify any factual or statistical information you might find in the primary sources. A good place to begin finding both primary and secondary sources is the library.

Library Resources

Libraries contain material arranged in three sections: books, reference materials, and periodicals; but you can also find multimedia materials (videotapes, audiocassettes, and slides) and electronic resources (CD-ROMs and Internet-based databases) at the library (see Table 6.3).

Books

Books offer comprehensive views and greater detail of topics than articles, websites, or newspapers do. However, while they offer great breadth and depth of information, they often lack timeliness. Be sure to check the copyright date in books to be sure that they are not outdated. The importance of timeliness is largely dependent on the topic. For example, if you were to discuss the history of tea ceremonies in Asia, a book from ten or fifteen years ago would probably be OK since their history stays the same. However, if you were doing a speech on the treatments of Alzheimer's disease, a book older than five years ago would be too old. The knowledge about and treatment of Alzheimer's have increased and changed dramatically in the past few years.

Not long ago, to find a book in the library, you would search through the *card catalog*. The card catalog consisted of a series of cabinets with little drawers that were filled with cards organized by subject, title, and author. Each book could be found by looking under one of these categories and locating the appropriate card. The card provided a call number that indicated where in the stacks and on the shelves the book was located. This was a good system, but computers have made it better and faster.

Today, almost all libraries have computerized or database card catalogs. Usually, near the main entrance and on every floor of a library you will find computers that are reserved for searching the catalog database. These com-

The library's computerized catalog can direct you to the relevant books you need in just a few key strokes.

puters are often separate from the computers used to access a library's other electronic databases or the Internet. Additionally, most libraries now offer access to the catalog online, so you can locate materials before actually going to the library.

Database
A computerized collection of related information organized for rapid search and retrieval.

You can search the library's catalog using a combination of author, subject, and title words. For instance, in our example about dolphin communication, you might enter "communication" as a *subject word* search and "dolphins" as a *title word* search. Using this combination, I came up with three titles from a local university's online catalog. (See Figure 6.2 for a sample computerized card catalog entry.) The ability to sort and refine your search using a variety of terms will save you from having to sort through each title individually to determine which titles suit your research.

Reference Materials

When was the Bolshevik Revolution? What countries border Tunisia? Who is Corazon Aquino? What is the root and history of the word *sincere?* How many new U.S. citizens were naturalized in 1957 and in 2007? The answers to these questions can be found in your library's reference section. The reference section of a library contains dictionaries, encyclopedias, directories, biographical sources, quotation books, atlases, almanacs, and yearbooks, all of which provide specific factual and statistical information.

- **Dictionaries** come in several types. General dictionaries, such as *Merriam-Webster's Collegiate Dictionary* and the *Cambridge Dictionary,* identify parts of speech, provide pronunciation assistance, and offer the most common definitions of words in a particular language (many academic libraries offer dictionaries in a variety of languages). Some dic-

FIGURE 6.2 Computerized Card Catalog Result

Record 1 of 1 for search "**DOLPHINS BEHAVIOR**"

Author:	Connor, Richard C.
Title:	The lives of whales and dolphins/Richard C. Connor and Dawn Micklethwaite Peterson
Edition:	1st Owl Book ed.
Publication information:	New York: H. Holt, 1996.
Physical Description:	xiii, 233 p. [16] p. of plates: ill.(some col.), maps; 24 cm.
General Note:	At head of title: From the American Museum of Natural History.
General Note:	Includes index.
Held by:	MAIN
Subject term:	Whales—Behavior.
Subject term:	Dolphins—Behavior.
Added author:	Peterson, Dawn Micklethwaite.
Added Author:	American Museum of Natural History.

Holdings
Main

Call Number	Copy	Location
QL737.C4 C595 1996	**1**	**Stacks**

tionaries, such as the *Oxford English Dictionary* (*OED*), also offer the etymology of a word or saying. Specialized dictionaries, such as the *Cambridge Dictionary of Philosophy,* offer more detailed definitions and explanations of subject-specific terminology not normally found in a general dictionary.

Etymology
The origin, history, and development of a word.

- **Encyclopedias** provide a general introduction to a subject along with a bibliography for further study. General encyclopedias, such as *Encyclopedia Brittanica* and *The World Book Encyclopedia,* offer brief introductions in every subject imaginable. Specific encyclopedias, such as the *Encyclopedia of Science,* offer more detailed explanations of subjects relating to a particular field.
- **Directories** provide brief information, including contact information, about individuals and organizations associated with particular professions, interests, or geographical areas. The most familiar directory is the phone book, but at the library you can find *Dun and Bradstreet's Million Dollar Directory,* the *International Directory of Company Histories,* the *Foundation Directory,* the *Encyclopedia of Associations,* and even the *Directory of Unique Museums.*
- **Biographical sources** contain information about well-known people from around the world. The *Who's Who* series, the *Dictionary of*

In most libraries you can find a copy of the Oxford English Dictionary *that has been compacted to hold several volumes of information in one or two large books. The* OED *is a great resource for researching the etymology or origins of a word.*

American Biography, and the *International Dictionary of 20th-Century Biography* are among the more commonly held collections.

- **Quotation books** are collections of famous, meaningful, and funny quotes arranged alphabetically by either subject or author. Commonly used quotation books are *Bartlett's Familiar Quotations* and the *Oxford Dictionary of Quotations.*
- **Atlases** provide maps, pictures, facts, and tables that illustrate geographic locations (such as the *Rand McNally College World Atlas*) or a particular subject (such as *Gray's Anatomy of the Human Body*).
- **Almanacs and yearbooks** are published annually and provide information and statistics relating to a particular activity, geographical area, field, or organization in a specific year. They include:
  - The *Statistical Abstract of the United States,* a collection of statistics from the U.S. Census Bureau on the economic and social conditions of life in the United States. You can find information on births, income, religion, diversity, and crime from this resource, which is also called the *National Data Book.*
  - The *World Almanac,* which provides photos, statistics, and information on such things as countries, economies, celebrities, world leaders, religions, history, sports, education, presidents, and science. From precipitation extremes in Antarctica to gold production in the

TABLE **6.3 Library Resources**

Here is a partial list of locations of particular types of information. Remember, this is a partial list just to get you started. Let your imagination and curiosity help you find interesting, unusual, or hard-to-find information as you progress.

If you need:	Try:
Definitions, alternative words, specialized terms, word origins	Dictionaries, glossaries, thesauruses
General or background information	General and specialized encyclopedias, books
Biographical information	Biographies, *Who's Who,* biographical dictionaries, *Biography Index*
Statistics	Statistical abstracts, almanacs, yearbooks
Current events	Newspapers, magazines, full-text databases (Lexis-Nexis)
Information on scholarly research	General or subject-specific periodical indexes, such as the *Reader's Guide to Periodical Literature,* InfoTrac, ERIC, or *Periodical Abstracts.*

Congo to commercial fishing in Chile, you will find it in this book, along with photos of your favorite celebrities, an endangered species list, and a list of the top-selling computer software.

- The *Farmer's Almanac,* which provides farming and gardening information, long-range weather forecasts, astronomical information (tables, schedules, etc.), and an interesting mix of trivia, tips, recipes, and stories.

Periodicals

Periodicals are published at regular intervals (e.g., daily, weekly, monthly, or quarterly); common examples are newspapers, magazines, and academic, trade, and professional journals. Although topics may not be discussed as broadly in periodicals as they are in books, periodicals offer the most up-to-date news, information, and research available in print (live news coverage and the Internet are often up-to-the-minute).

Newspapers and magazines cover general interest topics designed for a broad audience (e.g., *Newsweek,* the *New York Times,* the *Washington Post, Time, Cosmopolitan,* and *Sports Illustrated*) and specialized topics for specific audiences (e.g., *Today's Bride,* the *Wall Street Journal, Backstage, Computer Gaming World,* and *Yachting*). Additionally, you can find newspapers and magazines in many languages other than English that address the needs of particular cultural groups. In periodicals you will find the latest information on current events, research, tips, stories, and more.

To find information on your topic in newspapers, do a subject search using the *National Newspaper Index,* ProQuest, or other newspaper database. A search will give you the newspaper titles, dates, and page numbers of the articles along with a brief abstract of the articles. Use the abstract to decide if the article is right for your project. Some databases now offer full-text versions of articles that you can either print out or have e-mailed to you.

For magazines use the *Reader's Guide to Periodical Literature,* the most popular resource for searching magazines and some journals. The *Reader's Guide* is organized by subject, author, and title, but I suggest using a subject search with keywords. This will save you time and frustration because sometimes titles do not clearly reveal the topics discussed and you don't want to limit your results to only the authors with which you are familiar.

Peer Review
A system of review used to evaluate academic and professional research and writing before it is accepted for publication.

Academic, trade, and professional journals offer special interest information on specific fields of study, occupations, or professional organizations. Journals contain the latest research findings in a field. They are highly credible as a source because they are extensively *peer reviewed* for accuracy. However, because journals are written for scholars and professionals in the field, journals can be very technical, hard to understand, and filled with details that may be of no interest to you. To find material for classroom speeches, read the abstract to see if the article contains the information you seek, and pay special attention to the discussion and conclusion because this is where you will find a summary of the significant findings.

Full-text Database
A resource that offers access to entire articles online or through a database, not just a reference to where the article can be located.

There are a number of indexes available for searching for journal articles. Here are some that students use most frequently:

- **Lexis-Nexis:** Covers legal, business, tax, and regulatory documents and publications.
- **JSTOR:** Subscription-based collection that offers multidisciplinary and discipline-specific collections. Not all libraries have access to all collections. Individual collections include business, language and literature, music, mathematics and statistics, and ecology and botany. Ask your librarian which collections your library offers.
- **ERIC:** The Educational Resource Information Center database funded by the U.S. Department of Education offers citations, abstracts, and information from journals, dissertations, conference papers, and education-related resources.
- **Ethnic NewsWatch:** Newspapers, magazines, and journals relating to news, culture, and history in the ethnic press.

Using the Internet

As a citizen of the modern world, it is important that you become comfortable with accessing information on the Internet. If you don't have access to the Internet at home, you can access it from a local public library or at your school's library.

The Internet, a worldwide system of networks that interconnects computers, can be a wonderful source for up-to-the-minute information on every topic conceivable (see Table 6.4). Many websites offer not only reliable and timely information but also links to other related sites, images, sound bites, and more. As of the writing of this book, according to Search Engine Watch, the number of web pages on the Internet is well into the billions![2] As such, there are tremendous opportunities for accessing diverse opinions, research, stories, and ideas by "surfing the Net." However, because the Net is so large and is open to anyone with a computer, there are drawbacks to using the Net as well.

One mistake people make when doing research is typing one or two words into a search engine and pulling up thousands, if not millions, of websites. Unfortunately, most of these websites do not contain credible, useful, or relevant information. For example, by typing "dolphins" into Google, I came up with 2,750,000 hits. By adding "communication," I reduced the number to 155,000 hits. By adding quotation marks around the words *dolphin communication,* I was able to reduce the number even further to 2,860—a much smaller number, but still too many sites to sort through to find which ones offer the information I need.

Another problem with using the Internet for scholarly research is that much of web content is unregulated. In other words, no one has to prove that what s/he says is accurate or true; the sources might not be credible, opinions are not always identified as such, and the information might be outdated. Without a careful review of the information and its sources, you may find yourself inadvertently perpetuating misinformation to your audience. For these reasons, it is important to learn how to research efficiently and effectively on the Net.

More is not necessarily better when researching on the Internet. The goal is to find the most relevant, useful, credible, and timely sites in the least amount of time. To search efficiently on the Net, reduce to a reasonable number the number of *hits* you get. You can do this by using more than one or two search terms to locate information. The more specific you can be, the fewer sites you will be shown and the more likely they will contain just the information you want. For example, library research on dolphin communication reveals that dolphin communication differs above and below water and that

TRY THIS

When entering search terms into a search engine, **use quotation marks** around phrases and **use more than one phrase at a time.** This will limit your search by finding only web pages that have both complete phrases instead of pages that include each of the individual words throughout the page.

For example, by typing "dolphin communication" and "burst pulse sounds" into Google, I received only eight hits, all of which had useful, relevant information.

CONSIDERING LANGUAGE

Cite, Site, Sight

A homophone is a word that is pronounced the same way as another word (e.g., *blue* and *blew*), but has more than one meaning and/or spelling. Homophones can be very confusing because, in speech, we do not see the spellings of words. This can be particularly confusing when two words are being used in the same context. For example, "You must cite the site properly." In this chapter, we use the homophones *cite* and *site.* To make matters more complicated, there is also a third word in this homophone, *sight.* You will find quick definitions of the three below.

Cite: To document or give credit to a source of information; to quote a person or to mention an example as proof or support. *How do I cite a lecture in a bibliography?*

Site: Short for *website*—a specific location found on the Internet—*Visit our site at www.sumadek.com*; a place or area where something is located or something occurred—*England was the site of the first World's Fair.*

Sight: The object of what you see—*an amazing sight to see*; the ability to see—*eyesight.*

Hit
The web page or source retrieved that matches your search criteria when searching for information on a database or on the Internet.

TABLE 6.4 **Where to Look for Information on the Internet**

Search engines: Programs found on the Internet that are designed to search for particular keywords on the Net and to provide links to the websites, pages, and documents that contain them. *Benefit*: Can search billions of sites quickly and can use exact phrase searching. *Drawback*: Unedited, all sites with term revealed without regard to relevance and credibility. Examples include:

- Google—www.google.com
- Lycos—www.lycos.com
- Webcrawler—www.webcrawler.com
- AltaVista—http://altavista.com

Directories (also called *subject directories*): Can search programs that are human edited (a trained professional reviews sites for quality) and organized by subject categories and subcategories. Examples include:

- Librarians' Index—www.lii.org
- Infomine—infomine.ucr.edu
- Academic Info—www.academicinfo.net
- Yahoo!—www.yahoo.com

Metasearch engines (also called *metacrawlers*): A search tool that searches several search engines simultaneously and provides the results of all the searches on one page. Examples include:

- Dogpile—www.dogpile.com
- Vivisimo—http://vivisimo.com
- Hotbot—www.hotbot.com
- Metacrawler—www.metacrawler.com

there are three types of sounds: echolocation/click trains, whistles, and burst pulse sounds. By entering "recent discoveries in dolphin communication, echolocation, whistles, burst pulse sounds," a search revealed only twenty-two hits. A quick review of the individual articles and sites revealed that most are university, research, government, and nonprofit related sites that provide recent, relevant, and credible information.

Interviewing

Another excellent source of information is directly from experts, professionals, and other individuals who have special knowledge about a subject. Whether it is a marine biologist, an ocean preservation activist, a surfer, or a lifeguard, you might be able to obtain unusual, interesting, or hard-to-find information about dolphin communication through conversations with people who have had firsthand experiences with dolphins.

Interviewing is a special kind of communication interaction that might feel intimidating or overwhelming to you. However, with a little preparation,

Interviewing an expert on your topic is a great way to get unusual and interesting supporting material that you won't find in books!

you may begin to feel that interviewing is not only an excellent source of information but also an enjoyable way to meet people and to practice using English in new contexts. The key is to prepare ahead of time, take clear and useful notes during the interview, and write up your results accurately after the interview.

Before the interview:

- **Identify what you hope to accomplish in the interview:** *To obtain stories about surfers' interactions with dolphins.*
- **Choose a person to interview,** an interviewee, who is most likely to be able to provide the information you seek: *Amy Cobb, world-class surfer.*
- **Contact the person.** Identify yourself and the purpose of your call: *Hi, my name is _____. I am a student at _____ and I am doing research for a speech on dolphin communication. I was hoping that you might be willing to give me an interview.* (Don't expect to conduct the interview over the phone during the first call.)
- **Agree on a quiet place and time** for the interview that is convenient for the interviewee.
- **Decide how you are going to record the interviewee's answers:** Notes? Audiotape? Videotape? You must obtain your interviewee's permission in advance if you plan to either tape- or videorecord the interview.
- **Prepare several interview questions** (review types of questions in Chapter Four): *When was the first time you had an interaction with a dolphin? How often do dolphins swim close to surfers? Have you ever heard dolphins communicate with each other? Have you ever sensed that a dol-*

phin was trying to communicate with you? What is the best interaction you have ever had with a dolphin?

During the interview:

- **Explain the interview process** to the interviewee: *I have several prepared questions that I am going to ask you. Then you can share with me any additional thoughts you might have that would be helpful. We should be done in about twenty minutes.*
- **Look at the interviewee** as s/he answers your questions and listen carefully to the answers.
- **Don't try to write down every word.** Take brief notes, except for exact quotes you want to use later. If needed, ask for clarification on anything that is not absolutely clear.
- **Thank the interviewee** after the interview.

Immediately after the interview:

- **Go over your notes** as soon as possible. Fill in any information you might have forgotten to write down, clarify anything that is unclear, and add your own observations.
- **Send a thank you note** to the interviewee.

Remember to be polite and courteous to the interviewee; he or she is doing you a favor.

Drawing on Your Own Knowledge and Abilities

Although I have saved this section for last, in actuality, you will be drawing on your own knowledge and abilities from the start of the research process. After all, it was probably your interest in and knowledge of the subject that drew you to your topic. Your own stories, opinions, experiences, and education count as part of your research base.

Wherever you look in the library, be sure to look at the materials around the item you were looking for. You may find other relevant and useful information you hadn't expected to find.

To access and organize your personal knowledge, make a list of what you know about the subject and examples, stories, or ideas you have about how to handle the topic. Writing the information down will ensure that you don't forget any of your ideas and will give you a good foundation for developing a research plan.

DEVELOPING A RESEARCH PLAN

If you were about to set out on a trip, you would plan where to go, how to get there, and what to see and do on the way. Without a clear plan, you would spend a lot of time and energy not getting very far. The same is true with research. To find the greatest amount of relevant and useful information, you need to start with a plan. A research plan will help you stay on track. A plan will also tell you when you have arrived at your destination so that you avoid the temptation to keep researching endlessly.

A good research plan begins with you, a pen, and some paper (you can also do this on your computer). Write your topic at the top of a blank sheet of paper (see Figure 6.3). Then, along the left-hand margin, write the general purpose, specific purpose, and thesis you developed in Chapter Five. Next, develop sentences for each of your main points and write them under your thesis statement.

Remember, your specific purpose, thesis, or main points may change as you progress through your researching and writing, so don't make the mistake of trying to force the speech to follow the original plan if that plan is not working. Think of it this way: If you were on a car trip and your car broke down, you would have to take an alternative means of transportation.

Next, create two columns under the first section. Label the first column "Wish List"; you call it a wish list because it is everything you hope you will find during your research. Label the second column "Where to Find." Put Main Point #1 under the Wish List column. Then brainstorm questions about Main Point #1 that you and your audience might have about that main point. Staying with our dolphin communication example, our first main point is *Dolphins communicate by using echolocation.* What kinds of information would you want to have to prove this point? Here are some possible questions:

What is the definition of echolocation?

How does echolocation work?

Can a dolphin ever lose the ability to use echolocation?

For what reasons do dolphins use echolocation?

Do all dolphins use echolocation?

Are dolphins born knowing how to do this or is it taught?

Are there different sounds created for different meanings in echolocation?

What is the latest research in echolocation?

FIGURE 6.3 An example of a research plan for a speech on dolphin communication

Dolphin Communication

General Purpose: To inform
Specific Purpose: To inform my classmates about three types of dolphin communication.

Thesis: Dolphins communicate by using echolocation, whistles, and burst pulse sounds.
Main Points:
I. Dolphins communicate by using echolocation.
II. Dolphins communicate by using whistles.
III. Dolphins communicate by using burst pulse sounds.

Wish List	Where to Find
Echolocation:	
What is the definition of echolocation?	Dictionary, encyclopedia, aquarium website
How does echolocation work?	Encyclopedia, aquarium website, marine biology text
Can a dolphin ever lose the ability to use echolocation?	Interview with Marine Biologist (IMB), Marine Biology Journal (MBJ)
For what reasons do dolphins use echolocation?	Aquarium website, IMB, book on dolphins
Do all dolphins use echolocation?	MBJ, book on dolphin communication
Are dolphins born knowing how to do this or is it taught?	Books on dolphins and dolphin communication
Are there different sounds created for different meanings in echolocation?	MBJ, IMB, books on dolphins and dolphin communication
What is the latest research in echolocation?	Scientific journals and newspapers, MBJ, IMB, scientific
aquarium publications	
Whistles:	
(Repeat the same procedure as above)	
Burst Pulse Sounds:	
(Repeat the same procedure as above)	
Additional Information:	
Find a story about a dolphin using communication to save a person or another animal.	Mainstream newspapers, animal websites, Discovery website, Animal Planet

Write down as many questions as you can think of for Main Point #1. Then repeat the process for each point. Do this until you have ten to twenty questions for each main point. Finally, go back to your question for Main Point #1 and jot down where you think you might find the information. Review the types of sources that are available to you in the library, on the Internet, through interviews, and from your own knowledge base. Repeat this process for every question you have.

As you create your research plan, allow yourself to adjust your main points, thesis, or research questions as you see fit. Your research plan will be finished when you have a clear idea of what you are looking for and a good idea of where you might find it. This entire process should take you no more than one hour, but the time it will save you when you get to the library is immeasurable.

Using this research plan, begin searching your library's databases to locate the information. Often you can do this from home. Jot down the call numbers of books or have the articles sent to your e-mail account. That way, when you get to the library, you have to retrieve only a few items from the shelves. If you get lost or are unsuccessful, you can show your plan to the librarian, who can give you further direction. Many librarians have told me that they are thrilled to see a student with a clear research plan. It gives them a concise picture of what the student needs, what the student has tried, and where the student may have become lost or confused.

EVALUATING RESOURCES

Although most books, magazines, and journals go through extensive reviews to ensure that the information is accurate, honest, and up-to-date, you need to critically evaluate each and every source you find to be sure that it is credible, current, and appropriate for your speech.

Credibility

- Who is the author?
- What credentials or expertise does s/he have that s/he can provide this information?
- Who is sponsoring or publishing the information?
- Does the author or any institution the author is affiliated with stand to gain something based on the information?
- Does the information emphasize one viewpoint more so than an opposing viewpoint?
- Is this information consistent with other published works on this subject? If not, is there a good reason for the discrepancy?
- Is there documentation to support the claims the author makes?

Currency

- When was the information discovered, published, created, or updated?
- Is there likely to be newer information available about this topic?
- Is the subject in a field that is new, evolving, or changing?
- Is this the most recent information available on the subject?

Purpose

- What is the purpose of this information: to inform, to entertain, or to persuade?
- Who is the intended audience for this information?
- What is the author, publisher, or sponsor hoping to accomplish by providing this information?

HINT

The Seven Steps of Research[1]

Create a checklist using these seven steps of research as your research guide.

STEP 1: _____ Create a research plan by stating your topic as a question; identifying the keywords, concepts, and ideas; developing a set of research questions; and brainstorming possible resources for the information you seek.

STEP 2: _____ Do a preliminary background search of your topic using encyclopedias, textbooks, and lecture notes. Make note of keywords and relevant bibliographic information.

STEP 3: _____ Find books and audiovisual materials using the online card catalog.

STEP 4: _____ Find periodical articles using both print and electronic indexes.

STEP 5: _____ Search the Internet to find up-to-the-minute updates and information on you topic.

STEP 6: _____ Evaluate your sources in terms of credibility, currency, and purpose.

STEP 7: _____ Cite your sources using a standard formatting style such as MLA or APA.

1. Adapted from the Santa Monica College website www.library.smc.edu/research/researchguide/skill1.htm. Retrieved 7/20/04.

- Does this information clearly support your specific purpose and thesis?
- Is the information relevant to and appropriate for your audience and purpose?

Based on your answers to the above questions, ask yourself, "Is the information appropriate to use in my presentation?" If the answer is "no" or "I'm not sure," then find another source. The strength of your presentation is only as strong as your weakest source.

MANAGING INFORMATION

As you research, you will quickly realize that you cannot check out every book, journal, newspaper, and magazine you find, nor will you be able to remember everything you read or where you found it. Therefore, you need to have a system for managing the information you gather as you find it.

Even if you borrow books and make photocopies of articles, take notes on the information found in each of your sources. One way to do this is to photocopy every source you want to use, including the specific pages of a book you intend to use. This way you can take notes in the margins and highlight useful quotes, facts, and statistics. The advantages of photocopying are that you reduce the bulk of sources, maintain the integrity of the information until you are ready to use it (if you take notes instead, you may misquote, take the material out of context, or forget the significance of the information), and can write notes next to the relevant information.

The drawbacks of photocopying are that it can be expensive, you may find it hard to organize the information (some parts of a source may be useful in one part of a speech while others may be useful in another part), and you may inadvertently not copy all the information you need (this is especially true of bibliographic information). To avoid the drawbacks, copy what you are sure to need. Choose a color to identify each of the main points of your speech and then use sticky notes in matching colors to mark the sections relevant to each main point. When copying from books, be sure to copy all the relevant pages, especially the title page and the copyright pages. When copying journal or magazine articles, copy the entire article, including the endnotes and bibliography as well as the title/front page of the publication.

Another good technique for managing your research is to use note cards. Note cards give you a compact way to summarize, categorize, and organize the information you find and make writing your speech easier when the time comes.

You will need at least two note cards (3 × 5 or 4 × 6 work best) for each source you want to use. First, make one *bibliography card* for each source you have gathered. Include all the necessary bibliographic information using a standard formatting style (see Table 6.5). Include the author's name, the date of the publication, the name of the book (or article and journal title), publisher information, and the page numbers. If it is a website, include the URL (website address) and the date you retrieved it from the Internet. Finally, provide a brief summary, an *annotation*, of the book or article (see Figure 6.4).

Annotation
A brief summary, note, comment, or explanation about a text.

FIGURE **6.4** Bibliography Card
Collecting bibliographic information as you research will save you time and frustration when it is time to create your bibliography sheet.

Downie, Virginia L. (2002). *Together: A Relationship Survival Kit.* Upland, CA: Downie Publications.

A guide to improving interpersonal relationships by changing attitudes and individual communication behaviors. Good for specific tips on improving relationships.

Second, make *information cards* for every individual piece of information (i.e., each fact, quote, statistic, story, and example you might want to use) that you find in each source. Begin by creating categories of information; usually you will have at least one category for each main point, the introduction, the conclusion, and miscellaneous information. At the top of each card, write down which category this piece of information falls into. Then list what kind of information it is, a brief reference to the source from which it came, and the information itself (see Figure 6.5).

As you write down the actual information, be very clear about whether or not you are quoting the source directly or paraphrasing. If you are unsure later, you run the risk of plagiarizing the original source inadvertently.

You will find that note cards are particularly helpful later when you begin writing your speech because you can group the cards according to where they are likely to be used in the speech. Some students have told me that they make cards for each of the main points and then lay out the cards on the floor in the form of the outline to give themselves a clear visual indicating how the pieces of information fit together before they sit down to write the outline. Where one point or piece of information does not fit, they can easily move it or remove it.

FIGURE **6.5** Information Card
Information cards help keep your important facts and quotes easy-to-find.

Problem: Definition

Downie, (2002). *Together.*

Quote from page 19: "The ego, like a loyal guard, seeks to protect you from self doubt."

 CITING SOURCES

As discussed in Chapter Three, giving proper credit to your sources is essential to avoiding plagiarism. This type of giving credit is called *citing sources*. In giving speeches, you are expected to cite your sources by stating the sources out loud *and* by citing them properly at the end of your outline in a bibliography sheet.

There are several citation styles commonly used in academic work, such as MLA and APA. Before choosing a style for your presentation, ask your instructor which style s/he prefers. Most styles require author's name, date of publication, name of the book or article (and name of the journal or publication the article came from), the name of the publisher, and the page numbers. How these are arranged varies by style (see Table 6.5).

When citing sources in your speech, include the name of the author or sponsor of the research and the title of the publication where you found the information. Not only is this important for avoiding plagiarism; it also actu-

TABLE 6.5 **Using MLA and APA Documentation Styles**

(For comprehensive coverage of the MLA and APA documentation styles, refer to the *MLA Handbook for Writers of Research Papers,* 6th edition, and the *Publication Manual of the American Psychological Association,* 5th edition.

	MLA	APA
Books	Hall, Bradford J. Among Cultures: The Challenge of Communication. Fort Worth, TX: Harcourt, 2002.	Hall, B. J. (2002). *Among cultures: The challenge of communication.* Fort Worth, TX: Harcourt College Publishers.
Periodicals	Lindsley, Sheryl L. "A Layered Model of Problematic Intercultural Communication in U.S.-Owned Maquiladoras in Mexico." Communication Monographs 66 (1999): 145–66.	Lindsley, S. L. (1999). A layered model of problematic intercultural communication in U.S.-owned maquiladoras in Mexico. *Communication Monographs, 66,* 145–166.
Websites	Shapiro, Irving D. "The Parables of the Castaways, the Caveman and Dr. Smith, and the Incarcerated Serf." A Treasure Trove of Worldly Wisdom. 2003. Mans Sana Foundation. 26 July 2004 <http://www.menssana.org/books/treasure.html>.	Shapiro, I. D. (2003). The parables of the castaways, the caveman and Dr. Smith, and the incarcerated serf. *A treasure trove of worldly wisdom.* Retrieved July 26, 2004, from http://www.menssana.org/books/treasure.html

ally increases your credibility. Audiences like to know that you are going beyond your personal knowledge and backing your claims with credible sources. Citing the source out loud shows that you have done your research and that you are not afraid to reveal your sources.

Instead of: *Property crime rates have been declining for more than twenty years.*
Use: *According to the National Crime Victimization Survey conducted by the Bureau of Justice Statistics (BJS), property crime rates have been declining for more than twenty years.*[3]

Instead of: *Overweight pre-adolescent children have about a fifty percent chance of still being overweight as adults.*
Use: *The American Cancer Society tells us in the 2004* Cancer Prevention and Early Detection Facts & Figures *that overweight pre-adolescent children have about a fifty percent chance of still being overweight as adults.*[4]

Instead of: *It has been said that "All great achievements require time."*
Use: *Poet Maya Angelou once said, "All great achievements require time."*

Instead of: *I read an article that said NASA prepares astronauts and tests technology using an underwater marine laboratory.*
Use: *A July 2004 CNN article by Michael Coren claims that NASA uses an underwater marine laboratory to test technology and to prepare astronauts for space.*[5]

The first time you reference a particular source, use the complete reference. If you refer to the same source again, use a shorter reference:

> BJS tells us that violent crimes have decreased dramatically since 1994 as well.
>
> According to the same Cancer Society report, overweight adolescents have a seventy percent chance of remaining overweight as adults.

After referencing your sources as you speak, provide a bibliography page at the end of your outline that includes a complete bibliographic reference for every source you used in writing your speech.

Managing your information takes a little more time in the beginning of your speech-writing process, but it will save you enormous time and endless frustration in the long run.

SUMMARY

This chapter has provided some guidance on doing research. You should feel confident about going into a library and finding your way around the computerized card catalog and the online databases. You know where to find the reference librarian for assistance; you know how to find out about borrowing privileges from various libraries and how to benefit from a library even without borrowing privileges.

The research plan forms the foundation of your research and your speech. If you follow the guidelines for preparing a research plan, you will have a clear idea of what you are looking for, where you are likely to find that information, and when you have found it. Later, the research plan and the works you found as a result of the plan will help you begin writing your speech.

Remember that in the library, you will find materials organized into three major sections: reference materials, books, and periodicals. The reference section is where you find facts, quotes, statistics, and resources that can lead you to other sources in the library. Reference materials, including dictionaries, encyclopedias, directories, and almanacs, are generally up-to-date and credible but provide only raw numbers or cursory information.

Books provide more comprehensive coverage of topics and offer commentary or explanation, but they become quickly outdated, especially in rapidly changing subject areas such as health care and politics. Periodicals, including newspapers, magazines, and academic and professional journals, offer up-to-date research, discoveries, and commentary on both general interest subjects (fashion, sports, health, and finance) and more narrow professional academic subjects (engineering, law, human sexuality, archeology, communication, and biology). These library sections are the first place to go to develop a broad-based understanding of your topic.

The Internet and computer databases offer computer access to some periodical and journal articles as well as up-to-the-minute research findings, statistics, facts, and opinions that you may not find anywhere else. However, because the Internet is largely unregulated, you must carefully consider the quality of the sources.

As with all resources, you must evaluate the information based on its currency, credibility, and purpose, but you must be especially careful when evaluating the usefulness and credibility of Internet sources. Your sources are only as good as they are believable to your audience. Skeptical audiences will question the motives, honesty, and believability of your sources. Your job is to ensure that each of your sources is trustworthy.

Each of these resources can provide you with a wealth of useful information, but the information is useful to you only if you have it arranged and organized. Use the tips for managing your information and create two note cards for each source and record the information carefully and accurately. This will save you time and frustration later if you can't remember who said what. You will be especially grateful for having taken the time to record the bibliographic information when you are ready to create your bibliography sheet. Whether your instructor requires APA, MLA, or some other documentation style, you will have all the information you need at your fingertips.

Research can seem like an overwhelming or intimidating process, but by following the guidelines set forth in this chapter and by gaining research experience, you will find that researching becomes easier and easier. Who knows? Maybe one day you will even begin to view it as the most enjoyable part of preparing a speech or writing a paper!

Discussion Questions and Activities

1. Create a research plan using the guidelines provided in this chapter. Include your specific purpose, thesis, and main points. Try to generate at least ten questions for each main point and three possible sources for each question.
2. Find the following information in your school's library:
   - A quote by Aung San Suu Kyi, Burma (Myanmar).
   - The number of international students in U.S. colleges and universities in 2004.
   - A newspaper article on crime trends in a local city.
   - The biography sections and write down titles of three books you would be interested in reading.
   - How much a photocopy costs and whether or not you need to purchase a copy card.
   - Yesterday's *New York Times, Wall Street Journal,* and at least one international paper.
   - Whether your library carries *TESOL Quarterly, Nation's Business, World Communication,* or the *American Journal of Psychiatry.*
   - The word *sincere* in the *Oxford English Dictionary.* What is the origin of the word?
3. Create a bibliography card and an information card for each source you found in question 2. Be sure to include an annotation on each bibliography card and at least one piece of usable information on the information cards.
4. Again using the sources you found above, create two bibliography pages: one using MLA format and one using APA format.
5. Investigate three libraries in your local area: your school's library, the public library, and another one. Find out if their websites include a virtual tour of or introduction to the library. Plan a visit to each library. If possible, take an actual tour.
6. Freewrite for ten minutes about your concerns about researching. What areas of research give you the most trouble? Why? Brainstorm possible ways to overcome each of your concerns. Make a list of your top five research goals.

Chapter Quiz

Matching

Place the letter of the term on the line next to the proper example.

a. OPAC **b.** Keywords **c.** Peer review
d. Annotation **e.** Etymology **f.** Call number

1. ______ This article reviews the current state of blood supplies in the United States, with particular attention given to the areas of greatest need.

2. ______ Another name for subject terms.
3. ______ Hobby (noun): A pastime or activity used for enjoyment or relaxation. Originally from "small horse," then "mock horse," and finally, "toy riding horse." Transferred to pastime as an activity that does not go anywhere.
4. ______ Smith, Betty. *A Tree Grows in Brooklyn*. PS3537.M2895 T7 2002.
5. ______ Library service that allows users to access library databases remotely.
6. ______ A process of analyzing and critiquing professional and academic texts.
7. True or false: The MLA documentation style is always preferable to the APA style.
8. True or false: The Dewey Decimal System is the most widely used library classification system in the world, but is not the system preferred by colleges and universities.
9. Which of the following is NOT a recommendation for building confidence and experience in using the library?
   - a. Do all your research from home using the Internet.
   - b. Go to the library with a friend or classmate the first few times.
   - c. Take an online tour of the library before going there.
   - d. Take a library tour in person whenever possible.
10. Which of the following is a primary source?
    - a. An article in a national newspaper about an event.
    - b. An interview with a survivor of a major disaster.
    - c. A textbook description of a historical event.
    - d. A lecture from a world-renowned historian.

Chapter 6 Quiz Answers

1. d, 2. b, 3. e, 4. f, 5. a, 6. c, 7. False, 8. True, 9. a, 10. b

CHAPTER 7 Supporting Material

CHAPTER GOAL

By the end of this chapter you will be able to choose the most effective supporting material for a given speaking situation.

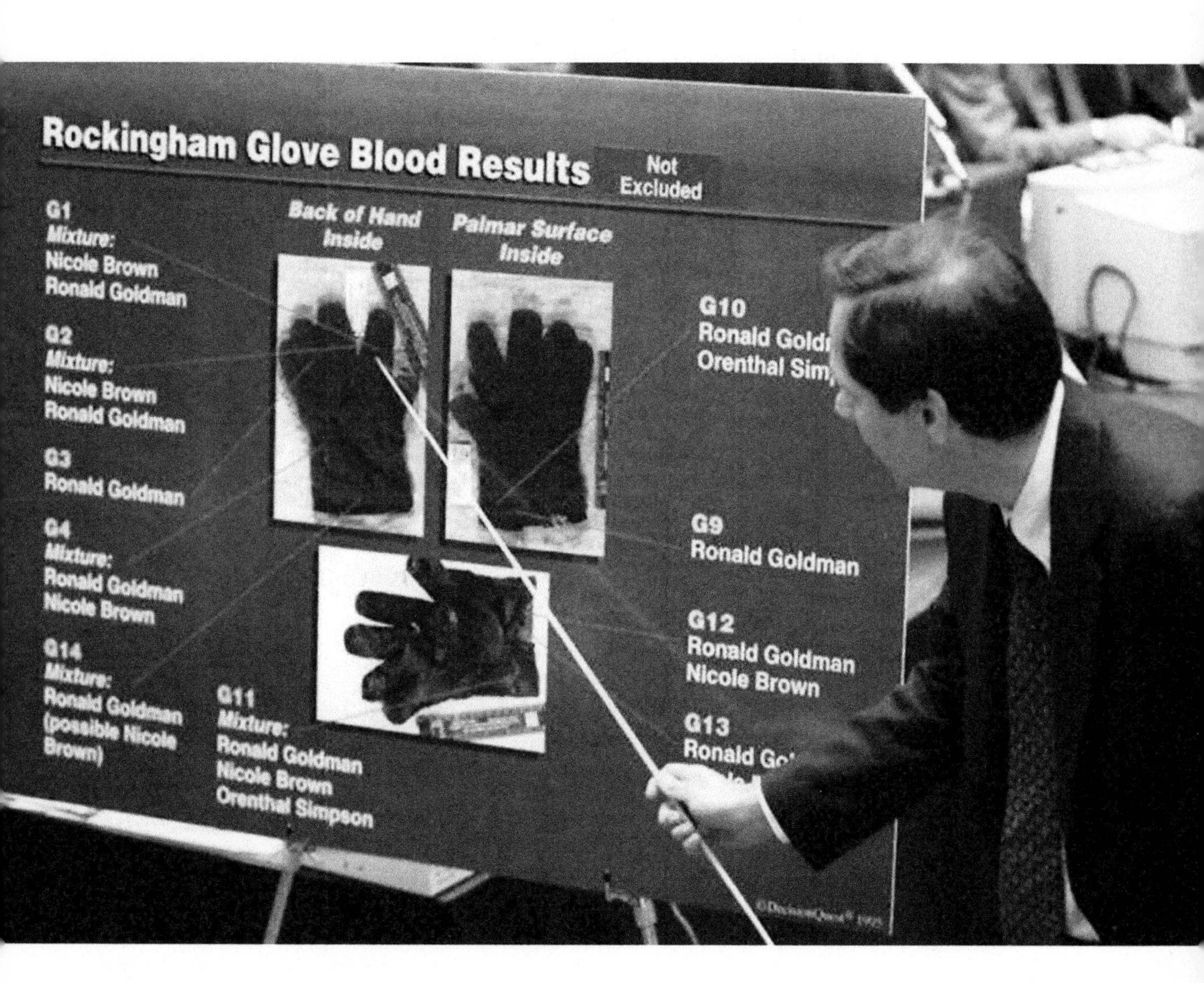

What is wrong with the following speech?

> The most common misconceptions about alcoholism are that it is a moral weakness, that alcoholism affects only the alcoholic, and that the only alcoholics are skid row bums. Many people believe that alcoholism is a sign of moral weakness and have a hard time accepting it as a disease. That alcoholism affects only the alcoholic is another common misconception. The stereotype of the alcoholic as a destitute and homeless old man or woman is also quite common. Whether it's the belligerent homeless person, a family member, or a close friend, please be more compassionate and understanding of the alcoholic.

Well, the speech has a clear thesis statement, right? The main points are clear, and a summary is provided at the end, so what is wrong with it? The problem is that there is no content to this speech. The speaker fails to give any evidence or examples to support her claims. A speech without supporting material is hardly a speech. Indeed, it is a mere repetition of the thesis. Supporting material brings a speech to life, provides additional information, makes an argument compelling, and makes an audience laugh, cry, and cheer.

The information used to support our ideas and claims is called *supporting material*. Supporting material ranges from stories and examples to facts and statistics and to graphs and photographs. Anything that supports, proves, or illustrates a statement or claim is supporting material. In this chapter we will discuss the various types of supporting material, starting with the types of support you will use to write your speech. We will end by discussing the cultural implications of choosing supporting materials and how you can best adapt your cultural preference to that of the audience. In Chapter Eleven we will discuss presentation aids such as graphs, models, audio clips, and videotape that you can use to further support your speech.

WHAT OTHERS SAY

If there is a language difference between the speaker and the audience, avoid any words or phrases that might cause misunderstanding. And when researching the speech, pay attention to some examples, comparisons, and other supporting materials that will relate to a wide range of listeners. I think it is better for the speaker using visual aids to bridge gaps in language or cultural background.

Yin Wai Lo, Hong Kong, China

TYPES OF SUPPORTING MATERIAL

If you were to tell a friend about an exciting concert you attended, you would likely go beyond saying, "I went to a concert that was very exciting." You would tell where the concert was held, how many people were there, how long it lasted, what unique special effects the band used, or what the people you met there were like. You might describe the stage in detail, quote a funny joke the singer told, or explain how hard it was to get the tickets. You might show the T-shirt you bought, the ticket stub, or autographed picture of the band.

When we speak in everyday conversation, either in English or in any other language, we use examples, stories, and facts to bring the conversation to life. We naturally provide evidence to back up our claims and make our conversations more interesting. Without the supporting material, there is little reason for your friend to believe that the concert was "very exciting." Supporting material proves claims, clarifies statements, explains the subject, defines difficult terms, and relates the topic to the audience.

Supporting material can be divided into six categories. The first five categories represent the information you use in the text of your presentation, that is, what you plan to say or write. They include facts, examples, statistics, quotes, and comparisons. The sixth category, which we will discuss in detail in Chapter Eleven, is made up of the "extras" you include to help your audience understand what you tell them and to make the presentation more interesting. These extras include visual aids, audio material, videotape, aromas, and samples for your audience to taste, touch, or take home. We call this category *presentation aids*.

Facts

Detectives, scientists, and juries are concerned with facts. They need to know the who, what, where, when, how, and why. Facts can be proved through direct observation, have been repeatedly verified by credible observers, or are generally accepted as true by members of a society (i.e., information that has been proved, verified, or repeated so many times that it is considered common knowledge). For example:

- Water boils at 212°F or 100°C.
- John F. Kennedy was president of the United States in 1962.
- The earth rotates at a speed of 1,670 kilometers/hour (1,070 miles/hr).[1]
- Diet and exercise can reduce a person's risk of heart disease.

Each of these facts can be tested or verified through observation or research. Factual information is necessary in almost all speeches to provide background information, context, and reasons for the claims in a speech. Along with simple statements of fact, you can present factual information in your speech through definition, description, and explanation.

Definitions

Definitions provide the meanings of words and phrases that are likely to be unfamiliar to an audience. Sometimes a term will be entirely new to an audience, such as *nanotechnology*. Other times familiar words are arranged to make new or different meanings, like *above the fold*. Definitions can come from:

- **A dictionary:**
  - *Nanotechnology,* according to *Merriam-Webster's Collegiate Dictionary*, is "the art of manipulating materials on an atomic or molecular scale esp[ecially] to build microscopic devices."
  - *Above the fold*, according to *The Electronic Commerce Dictionary*, is the "top portion of a Web page which can be seen without scrolling."

Fact, Inference, or Opinion

Sometimes we have a difficult time distinguishing among facts, inferences, and opinions. Facts are verifiable and unquestionable. Inferences are conclusions drawn from the available evidence. Opinions are subjective views or assessments based on an individual's personal tastes.

Read the following paragraph and then identify the numbered statements as either fact (F), inference (I), or opinion (O):

A tall and handsome scientist entered the laboratory and walked past the assistant sitting at the desk. The scientist said, "Good morning, Anne." Just then the phone rang. Anne whispered a few words into the receiver and then hung up. "I have to go," the assistant said and hurried out of the room. The scientist, confused, said, "What was that all about?"

1. ______ The scientist was tall and handsome.
2. ______ The scientist who entered the room said good morning to his assistant.
3. ______ Anne answered the phone.
4. ______ Anne left the room in a hurry.
5. ______ The tall and handsome scientist was confused.

Answers can be found at the end of the chapter.

- **An expert in the field:**
  - The National Nanotechnology Initiative says that for something to be defined as *nanotechnology*, it must include all of the following:
    1. Research and technology development at the atomic, molecular, or macromolecular levels, in the length scale of approximately 1–100 nanometer range.
    2. Creating and using structures, devices, and systems that have novel properties and functions because of their small and/or intermediate size.
    3. Ability to control or manipulate on the atomic scale.[2]
  - According to Donna Baumann, executive of Inter.Net of Canada, "Above the fold is the amount of a web page that you can see on a web page without having to scroll down. Advertisers prefer having their ads placed above the fold."[3]
- **Your own definition:**
  - When my biology teacher first explained *nanotechnology* to me three years ago, it sounded like something out of a science fiction movie—microscopic robots and submarines used in the human bloodstream. I was more afraid than excited about what new frontiers this miniscule monster might discover. However, I have come to better under-

stand this tiny technology as the art and science of building and using structures as small or smaller than atoms and molecules.

- Having a coffee and checking my e-mail at an Internet café last week, I overheard another patron tell his friend to, "Place the larger text above the fold." Since I usually consider myself in-the-know when it comes to new lingo, I did a little investigating to find out what *above the fold* means. I discovered that above the fold is an old newspaper term that refers to the top half of a newspaper's front page, the part still visible when the newspaper is folded in half. Today, website designers and web marketers use the term to refer to the top part of a web page that is immediately visible to viewers without their having to scroll down or across.

If a word has multiple meanings, controversial and conflicting definitions, or a definition that reflects an opinion on the subject, or if you are using a special or unique definition of a word, you will need to clarify which meaning of the word you are using. For example, in Chapter One we defined *rhetoric* as "the effective use of language in both speaking and writing; the study of persuasion and persuasive methods through speaking and writing." In actuality, this represents two definitions: One perceives rhetoric as the technique of using language effectively for many purposes. The other perceives rhetoric specifically as a means to persuade. The former definition is in-line with the majority of this book with regard to speaking, but when we talk about persuasion in Chapter Fourteen, the latter definition will apply.

Sometimes a speaker might want to use a very narrow or unique definition of a word that is not commonly used. This is called an *operational definition*, a unique definition that is tailored specifically by the speaker to clarify how the term is to be understood in that discussion.

Definitions are helpful only if they help the audience to better understand a message. To do that, use definitions only when they are necessary, use the word only as defined, and be sure that it is understandable to your audience. If you define too many terms that the audience doesn't need to know, they will become bored. If you change the meaning or use the word to represent multiple meanings or use other words in place of the term defined, you will confuse the audience. If your definition is complicated or confusing, you will not only have defeated the purpose of defining the term, but also possibly frustrated and further confused your audience.

Descriptions

A description is similar to a definition in that it serves to clarify and explain, but instead of describing words and phrases, descriptions describe people, processes, and things. Like a well-written novel, vivid descriptions allow the audience to see, hear, taste, smell, and touch the scene. Let's say Maria described the following scene as the opener for her speech:

> Imagine a young woman flying down the highway, the crashing waves of the Pacific on her left shoulder, dramatic bluffs on her right. She drinks

CONSIDERING LANGUAGE

Acronyms and Abbreviations

U.S. Americans love acronyms and abbreviations. We have CEOs, the CIA, the FBI, and HUD. We send a FAX, review P&Ls, and earn PhDs, and this would be OK if everyone always understood what we mean by our abbreviations and acronyms. Unfortunately, too often speakers neglect to provide definitions or explanations when they use them. This creates a SNAFU of understanding between speaker and audience. So if you feel compelled to start using acronyms and abbreviations, be sure to first clearly identify what they mean, and then use them sparingly.

Key:

CEO: Chief Executive Officer
CIA: Central Intelligence Agency
FBI: Federal Bureau of Investigation
HUD: Housing and Urban Development
FAX: Facsimile
P&L: Profit and Loss statement
PhD: Doctor of Philosophy
OK: Okay
SNAFU: Situation Normal All Fouled Up

Describing a scene in detail can help the audience "see" what you are saying in their heads. This improves understanding and retention.

> in the clean ocean air and warm sunshine flooding the interior of her new red convertible. Her favorite song comes on the radio. As she reaches down to turn up the volume to full blast, her car crosses the double yellow line headfirst into the 18-wheeler speeding toward her. . . . Every day thousands of accidents occur when otherwise good drivers take their eyes off the road for just a few seconds.

Had Maria simply stated, "Every day thousands of accidents occur when otherwise good drivers take their eyes off the road for just a few seconds," the audience might not have fully understood the implications of her statement.

Remember to use descriptions sparingly, include specific details wherever possible and relevant, and keep descriptions brief. Although descriptions create images, they are meant to support the larger message of the speech and not to be the entire focus of the speech. Include a few descriptions to keep the audience members interested and to help them understand the impact of your points. Do not include descriptions simply to have them; include them only when they serve the purpose of your speech.

Explanations

Whereas a description describes who, what, where, and when, explanation tells how and why something happened or operates. When giving a talk on the dangers of teen smoking, you might want to explain how nicotine affects normal brain functioning, or you might explain why teenagers are the most likely age group to begin smoking. Explanation walks the audience through the process so that they can make the connections or follow the steps themselves.

Be careful to be accurate and to include all relevant steps or connections in your explanations. Neglecting to mention even one small, but relevant, piece of information can cause confusion and misunderstanding. As with descriptions, use explanations sparingly, be specific in your details, and keep them brief. A mixture of well-placed facts, clear definitions, vivid descriptions, and careful explanations will add substance and credibility to your presentation.

Examples

Examples illustrate, clarify, and illuminate concepts, skills, theories, opinions, and ideas. Examples bring a speech to life by linking the material discussed and the "real world." Examples can be factual or hypothetical and brief or extended.

Factual examples are those derived from "real life." They are examples of persons, places, or things that actually exist or events that have happened. Factual examples can be drawn from your own experiences, the experiences of friends and family, current or historical events, and pop culture. *Hypothetical examples* are imagined—things that have not yet happened. Usually, they are a compilation of typical instances or experiences people might have, but not necessarily a reference to a specific instance. For example, if the story Maria told about the young woman's car accident was based on a true story, that would be a factual example, but if Maria made up the story, it would be hypothetical. Looking at Maria's example, would you say that it is a factual or a hypothetical example? In either case, you should always let your audience know whether your example is factual or hypothetical (see the "Hint").

Brief examples are examples that are sometimes only a word or two long. Often speakers provide a brief list of examples to clarify what they mean or use several brief examples in a row to make a point. By offering more than one quick example, you give the audience many opportunities to connect to the information.

- There are many types of name-brand sugar-free sweeteners available today, such as NutraSweet, Stevia, Sweet-n-Low, and Splenda.
- The notion of preserving people after death is age-old. Ancient Egyptian rulers were mummified to preserve their bodies for the afterlife. In the 1770s Ben Franklin wrote that he wanted to be "immersed in a cask of Madeira wine, 'til that time when he could be recalled to life." In the last century all manner of cryonics has been featured in science fiction novels, movies, and magazines.

Extended examples are more detailed than brief examples, although they vary in length. Extended examples can range from several sentences, called an *illustration*, to a longer story that is used throughout the speech, called a

Examples
Specific references or stories that illustrate and clarify a point, idea, theory, skill, or opinion.
Brief examples: Relatively short examples designed to clarify a small point or a single word or idea, often ranging from one word to a sentence.
Extended examples: Longer examples that offer greater detail and support a larger point.
Factual examples: Examples taken from actual events, people, or things; based in reality.
Hypothetical examples: Examples that are invented by the speaker; not based in reality.

HINT

Using Examples

Unless you are referring to something the audience is certain to recognize as factual, you should identify whether your example is hypothetical or factual. The following words and phrases can help.

Factual

You might remember when . . .
Last week (yesterday, last year, etc.) I had a similar experience . . .
This actually happened to my mother . . .
The following actually happened on (date).

Hypothetical

Imagine that . . .
What if you were to . . .
If I were to design the perfect . . .
Let's say . . .
Suppose a person . . .

narrative. Extended examples draw in audience members personally because extended examples tend to be emotional and compelling. One student used this story to show the origin of her fear of death:

> When I was six years old my grandfather died. I remember clinging tightly to my mother's hand in terror, lost in the wails, moans, screams, and the slow, dragging sound of the song "Swing Low, Sweet Chariot" being sung by the choir. I cringed behind my mother's skirt when I saw my grandfather's face looking up through the glass window on his huge black-lacquered coffin. I was terrified when a man threw himself in anguish on the coffin as it was being lowered in the ground. That was my first experience with death.

We can identify with the child's fear and confusion because the student paints a picture from her experience that helps the audience visualize the scene and imagine what it must have felt like to be that six-year-old child.

Leslie laced the following story throughout her speech on alcoholism:

> My friend Paula killed a man while driving drunk. She told me that she never thought that would happen to her. She also said that she never meant to hurt anybody and that she was only trying to have a good time. . . .
>
> She destroyed that man's family and ripped her own family apart. The family of the man she killed will never see him again. Her parents were devastated when she went off to jail. Paula's mother told me that being a mother herself, her heart goes out to the mother of that man. . . .
>
> Paula was only twenty years old when she killed that man. She was not even of legal drinking age.[4]

The first paragraph supported her point that drunk driving accidents are common and can happen to anyone who drinks and drives. The second paragraph supported her point that the damage done by alcohol goes beyond what it does to the alcoholic. The third paragraph supported her point that alcoholism does not discriminate because of age or experience with drinking. Maintaining one story that is threaded throughout the speech can pique the audience's interest because they are waiting to hear "what happens next."

Statistics

Addressing the International trade and technology summit in Calgary, Canada, Jacques Duchesneau made the following point:

> In 2003, over 570 billion Canadian dollars' worth of trade crossed the Canada–U.S. border. Or as *Globe and Mail* columnist Jeffrey Simpson put it recently, that's more than 1 million dollars in merchandise trade between our two countries each minute of every hour throughout the entire year. This is a preoccupation for all of us. On May 27, the headlines in all the papers said "White House Fears Attacks / FBI on High Alert." . . . In fact, a survey conducted in the

CONSIDERING CULTURE

Supporting Material in Kenya

Cultures differ in terms of the supporting material they prefer. Kenya, which has more than forty distinct cultural and linguistic groups, places great value on public speaking, but the types of supporting materials Kenyans prefer is markedly different from that of the United States and Canada.

As members of a collectivist, high-context culture, Kenyans historically have not done extensive formal research (although that is beginning to change) because they are less moved by statistics and facts than by relationships. Therefore, narratives, especially personal stories, are highly valued. "In the West an overuse of personal stories might make the speaker appear not to be objective, but not with us. We believe you only really know about something if you've experienced it."*

Other supporting materials include proverbs, songs, and audience response—a technique whereby the speaker does not finish a sentence but waits, instead, for the audience to fill in the blank.

*Anne Neville Miller, "An Exploration of Kenyan Public Speaking Patterns with Implications for the American Introductory Public Speaking Course." *Communication Education* 51(2) April 2002.

> U.S. in April and May 2004 revealed that 89 percent of affluent Americans cited the potential impact of terrorism on the economy as their number 1 concern.
>
> A year ago, one single cow in Alberta tested positive for BSE, also known as mad cow disease.
>
> And this one cow meant that Canadian beef exports—the third highest in the world in 2002, valued at over 4 billion dollars—dropped virtually to zero.
>
> About 90 percent of all Canadian beef exports had gone to the United States, but all this was lost when the U.S. chose the security of its own industry over continued trade. . . .
>
> I mention this in order to establish that trade is very much at the mercy of crisis events.[5]

Using statistics, Duchesneau shows precisely how crisis events negatively impact trade. Numbers in the form of percents, averages, and tallies provide specific, concrete, and compelling evidence to support claims. Statistics show that a problem exists, how big the problem is, or how fast it is growing. They also show relationships, the effectiveness of a solution, or trends.

There are several ways to use numerical data in a speech including tallies and values. A *tally* is simply a number indicating how many there are of something. Speakers use tallies to explain such things as how many car accidents are attributed to drunk driving in a year, how many people attended a peace rally, and how many children are born deaf in a decade. A tally can be simply an expression in actual numbers, such as "Approximately one hun-

Statistics
Numerical values used to describe or characterize a defined grouping, population, or occurrence.

dred students attended today's lecture" or "CNN reported that over 250,000 people marched for peace in San Francisco last weekend."

Tallies can also be expressed in *percentages* and *ratios*. Percentages indicate how many there are of something out of every 100 (e.g., 75%). Ratios show a relationship between numbers (e.g., 3 of 4). Often, percentages are expressed as ratios (75% = 3 out of 4). Both are excellent ways to show significance and frequency, especially when relating a very large number (ketchup can be found in 97% of all U.S. homes) or a very small number (you have a 1 in 250,000,000 chance of winning the lottery) in a way that shows how relevant the number is to the audience members' daily lives. For instance, instead of telling the audience that "204.3 million U.S. Americans have Internet access at home," you can say, "Three out of four people in the United States now have Internet access at home." The ratio allows the audience to consider four people they know, thus relating the information directly to their lives.

Values are a way to express numbers in terms of their significance to a larger set of numbers. There are three values: mean, median, and mode. The *mean* is the average of a set of numbers. Finding the average can be useful when you want to get a sense of what is happening with a large amount of information. Averages are often used to indicate what is "normal." For example, averages are used to determine grade-level expectancies for children in the United States. However, averages can be deceiving because one extreme sample will skew the results. Looking at the average price of homes in an area might be misleading if the houses that were sold cost $165,000, $200,000, $220,000, $165,000, and $2,000,000. Even though $1,150,000 is the average, it is certainly not typical.

The *median* is the middle number in a set of numbers that have been arranged in ascending or descending order. The median shows a more realistic picture of what one might expect from a set of numbers. In the price of homes example, the median would be $200,000. This is a closer approximation to what a new home buyer might expect to pay.

The *mode* is the number that is found most frequently in a set of numbers. (See Table 7.1.) Which is the mode in our home example? Right, $165,000.

Be careful when using statistics: Too many numbers can be confusing or overwhelming to an audience. Here are a few simple guidelines you can follow:

- *Explain the meaning of your statistics and how they relate to the point you are making*. Don't assume that your audience will understand the significance of the numbers and how they relate to the point you are trying to make. Instead of saying only that "thirty-three percent of all women will be sexually assaulted in their lifetimes," add, "That means that one out of every three women you know will be victims."
- *Round numbers up or down to a simpler number*. Large numbers are complicated and confusing to remember. Rounding or simplifying numbers makes it easier for the audience to retain and understand them. Which of the following has the greatest impact and is easiest to understand and remember?

TABLE 7.1 **Mean, Median, and Mode**

What are the mean, median, and mode of these student ages?
18, 28, 31, 21, 17, 18, 19, 22, 20, 18, 23, 22, 18, 20, 32, 26, 18, 21, 23, 22, 24
First, arrange the numbers in either ascending (from lowest to highest) or descending (highest to lowest) order:
17, 18, 18, 18, 18, 18, 19, 20, 20, 21, 21, 22, 22, 22, 23, 23, 24, 26, 28, 31, 32
To find the mean, add up all twenty-one numbers (461). Then divide by the number of numbers added (21). 461/21 = 21.95 (round it to 22). The mean or average age in this class is 22.
To find the median, look for the number that is in the middle of all these numbers (21).
The mode is the number that occurs most frequently; in this case, it is 18.

- Thousands of people died in 2002 from alcohol-related accidents.
- In 2002, 17,419 people died from alcohol-related accidents.
- Over 17,000 people died in 2002 from alcohol-related accidents.[6]

- *Relate numbers to something that is familiar to the audience.* Numbers sometimes have little meaning to people. By relating them to something that is familiar, the numbers will have more meaning and impact. To impress upon the audience how much ketchup is consumed per year, Joyce said, "About 190,000,000 gallons of ketchup are produced in the United States each year. That is enough ketchup to fill 190 Olympic-sized swimming pools!"
- *Use statistics sparingly.* Use numbers only when they make your point best. Too many numbers will overwhelm the audience. Consider the following:

  > The five countries with the highest homicide rates that do not impose the death penalty average 21.6 murders per every 100,000 people, whereas the five countries with the highest homicide rate that do impose the death penalty average 41.6 murders every 100,000 people.
  >
  > The average murder rate per 100,000 people in U.S. states with capital punishment is about 8, while it is only 4.4 in abolitionist states.[7]

  Can you determine the significance of all these numbers? The point the author is trying to make is lost in the numbers. His argument would have been clearer had he said:

  > In states and countries that still use capital punishment, the homicide rate is almost double what it is in states and countries that have abolished the death penalty.

- *Use visual aids to present statistical information.* It is often a good idea to summarize and organize your statistical information into a visual aid.

To find statistics on international demographics, populations, economics, trade, education, health, crime, and more, go to:

Click Here

http://lib.mansfield.edu/intstat.html

Mansfield University of Pennsylvania hosts this website, which provides links to statistical information from around the world.

Quotations

Quotations, also called *testimony*, add credibility to a speech as long as the audience considers the source to be credible—the right person to make the point. Each person you quote should be an authority on the subject either through experience, vocation, or education.

Experts

Who is an expert? Well, to some degree, we are all experts on something. You might be an expert at being a student, a musician, or an athlete. You may have special training related to your job. Others are experts in law, medicine, finance, trade, education, environment, and many other fields. When you want to reinforce a point, you can add authority to your claim by quoting an appropriate expert. If you are discussing diabetes, quote an expert not only in medicine but also one in diabetes. If you are discussing hip-hop music, quote a hip-hop producer or a well-respected artist. In this way, you borrow credibility from the experts.

If you are quoting someone the audience is unlikely to know, be sure to provide both the name and the credentials of the expert. For example:

- According to D. Weaver, inventor and owner of Laurel Music, "The hardest part about starting a business is overcoming the fear."
- In a recent *Scientific American* article, Dr. Hunter G. Hoffman, director of the Virtual Reality Analgesia Research Center at the University of Washington, claims that "Pain has a strong psychological component. The same incoming pain signal can be interpreted as more or less painful depending on what the patient is thinking."[8]

Laypeople

The term *laypeople* refers to people who have no particular expertise in terms of education or work experience with regard to a particular topic but who can tell us about their personal experiences, reactions, and emotions. Again, we are all experts in our own lives. Firsthand or eyewitness accounts of events

Sometimes we need to include the opinions and views of experts or witnesses to add additional credibility to our evidence.

can be powerful evidence. Newspapers and news programs rely heavily on the testimonies of everyday people to express the human side of important events. You can use individual perspectives as well to build your evidence.

- Rob lost his home in two earthquakes separated by twenty-three years. He told me, "I was ten during the 1971 Sylmar earthquake. I remember the house groaning and creaking as my dad and I tried to force the door open. The house was so damaged we couldn't afford to make the repairs, so we lived in a camper for a couple of months until we could find a new place to live. The second time, in 2004, I was the father trying to get my kids to safety. That house was a total loss."
- After years of debate, thousands of dollars, and months of confusion, the school's online registration program is finally running smoothly. The attitude on campus seems to have changed from one of aggravation to one of relief, as Tonya, a graduating senior, says, "I just registered last night and this was the easiest and fastest registration I have ever had here. I can't believe everyone made such a big deal about it; it wasn't hard at all."

As you can see, laypeople's testimony can be especially useful for conveying the emotional side of a story.

Literature

Quotations from books, classic novels, proverbs, and famous speeches also make terrific supporting material for speeches. Frequently, speakers open or close speeches with famous quotes because they can convey an idea eloquently and succinctly.

- *A discovery is said to be an accident meeting a prepared mind.* Albert von Szent-Gyorgyi (1893–1986)
- *To accomplish great things, we must dream as well as act.* Anatole France (1844–1924)
- *A person reveals his character by nothing so clearly as the joke he resents.* Georg Christoph Lichtenberg (1742–1799)

There are many books and websites dedicated to providing excellent quotations arranged by subject and author. As with any other supporting material, cite the source of your quote properly and do not overuse quotes. As a non-native speaker of English you have additional resources for finding suitable quotes for your speech because you can quote from another language and then translate the meaning for the audience.

Comparisons

Sometimes it is hard to describe, define, or prove a point by using an explanation or description. The words are hard to find, the idea is too complicated or obscure, or the product is so new that the language to describe it does not yet exist. In these cases, you can use comparisons to connect the person, object, idea, or event to something familiar, well known, and understood. *Comparison* is the process of examining two or more people, places, or things to discover the ways in which they are similar or different.

Comparisons that refer strictly to areas of similarity are called *analogies*. Analogies can be either literal or figurative. Literal analogies make comparisons between events, times, places, and people that are actually very similar. Comparing one war to another or comparing the symptoms of one disease to another would be making a literal comparison.

Figurative analogies point out similarities between seemingly unrelated things. This type of analogy is creative and often relies on metaphor and simile (see Chapter Ten) to make the comparison. Figurative analogies also ask more from the audience since audience members are required to use their imaginations to make the connections. Many great speakers from around the world have artfully used analogy to make powerful statements. Here is one example from Dr. Martin Luther King, Jr.'s famous "I Have a Dream" speech that mobilized the Civil Rights Movement in the United States:

> In a sense we have come to our nation's capital to cash a check. When the architects of our republic wrote the magnificent words of the Constitution and the Declaration of Independence, they were signing a promissory note to which every American was to fall heir. This note was a promise that all men—yes, black men as well as white men—would be guaranteed the unalienable rights of life, liberty, and the pursuit of happiness.

> It is obvious today that America has defaulted on this promissory note insofar as her citizens of color are concerned. Instead of honoring this sacred obligation, America has given the Negro people a bad check, a check which has come back marked "insufficient funds." But we refuse to believe that the bank of justice is bankrupt. We refuse to believe that there are insufficient funds in the great vaults of opportunity of this nation. So we have come to cash this check—a check that will give us upon demand the riches of freedom and the security of justice.[9]

Most people can identify with the embarrassment and shame of a "bad check" (whether on the writing or receiving end of the transaction). By connecting white Americans to the writing side of the check and African-Americans to the receiving side, Dr. King gave both the opportunity to see their positions in the race structure of the United States at that time.

Both literal and figurative analogies can be problematic for non-native speakers because the comparisons do not always translate between cultures or languages. Many analogies make references to the common historical, cultural, and popular knowledge of a society. If the audience has a different background than the speaker, the references may not be recognized or understood. For example, I recently used an analogy with the term *valley girl*. Valley girl was a derisive 1970s and '80s term for a wealthy teenage girl from the San Fernando Valley in Los Angeles who used an energetic, overly dramatized talking style. The blank stare I received told me that the analogy was not a good one.

Additionally, cultures find similarities between unrelated things in different ways. This is apparent in the many terms, sayings, and proverbs that fail to translate from one language to the next. In Mexico, the Spanish word for *elbow*, *codo*, is also a disparaging term for someone who is cheap—what is known as a *cheapskate* in English. The relationship between a cheap person and an elbow escapes most U.S. Americans.

For these reasons, when using analogies, be certain that your references are familiar to your audience. Use references that most people in the world can understand, such as major world events, international figures, common environmental phenomena (rain, snow, volcanoes, etc.), and similar life experiences (births, deaths, hunger, pain, love, hope, etc.):

> My sorrow fell upon me like a cold, misty rain, settling slowly and softly until I was shivering and my body heavy from the weight of sadness.

CULTURAL IMPLICATIONS OF SUPPORTING MATERIALS

Like everything else in life, a person's culture influences which types of supporting material he or she finds the most convincing. Each culture has preferences for types, frequency, and use of supporting materials. Some cultures prefer numbers and graphs; others prefer stories and examples. Many cultures like a combination of supporting materials. No matter what country or culture you come from, you can learn to appreciate and use many forms of supporting material.

Cultures vary in terms of how they process information and what they consider to be believable supporting material. Therefore, you should choose supporting materials based on your audience in terms of how they are likely to perceive, process, and accept the information. The two dimensions referred to here are associative and abstractive thinking, and the faith, feeling, and fact dimensions. To a greater or lesser degree, cultures tend to fall on one end of these dimensions, but most cultures employ a variety of styles to some degree. Understanding the tendencies in your culture and those in the United States or any culture will help you better adapt your supporting materials to your audience.

The associative and abstractive thinking dimension refers to how people process information. *Associative thinkers* tend to process information by relating new ideas and concepts to past personal experiences. In other words, they associate the new information with prior experience, information, or understanding. Cultures higher on the associative thinking scale tend to use an educational style grounded in memorization that encourages mechanical recall without deep understanding of underlying meaning. When dealing with cultures high in associative thinking, give plenty of examples from the audience's everyday lives, relate new ideas to their cultural values and ideals, and explain places, events, and people in terms of significant and well-known landmarks, historical or cultural events, or national heroes. Countries that prefer associative thinking include Bolivia, China, Egypt, Hungary, Italy, Kenya, Paraguay, and Russia.

Abstractive thinkers tend to come from cultures that have a problem-solving orientation to education. Abstractive thinkers enjoy dealing with new ideas when they can use information from a variety of sources and imagine or visualize the new ideas or concepts—in other words, when they can go beyond what they know and have experienced and relate a new idea to general principles. Abstractive thinking has been viewed as a more intellectual way of processing information; hence, it is often found in highly educated people in all cultures regardless of the culture's overall preference for information processing. Countries that prefer abstractive thinking include Canada, Germany, Israel, the Netherlands, New Zealand, and Poland. It is important to note that with the spread of Western education (and students studying abroad), many countries are moving away from associative toward more abstractive thinking.

As a student in the United States, you have undoubtedly become familiar with the preference for abstractive thinking here regardless of the style you might have been accustomed to originally. Again, all people are capable of and can use either style; what we are talking about here is a preference for absorbing new information. Knowing that the preferred style is abstractive in the United States but that many people in the United States hail from other cultures, you may want to aim for a mixture of both styles. Definitions, explanations, and statistics are more in-line with the abstractive style. Concrete examples, appeals to the audience's experiences, and detailed visual aids—particularly pictures and objects—are more associative.

The faith, feeling, and fact dimension refers to the types of evidence people feel are the most credible, relevant, and meaningful. This dimension answers the question, "What do these people/does this culture accept as *truth*?" Some cultures prefer evidence that is based on faith. They rely on the tenets and teachings of a belief system such as a religion or a political ideology. These people are moved most by quotes from the Bible, the Torah, the Quran, or another religious text, and they respond to appeals to nationalism, a constitution, or strong political allegiance. Countries and cultures that prefer evidence based on faith include Denmark, Finland, Hong Kong, Nicaragua, Pakistan, Saudi Arabia, and Sri Lanka.

Some cultures rely more heavily on evidence that is based on feelings, also called *subjective evidence*. These people look at relationships with other people and rely on their instincts and emotions to guide their decision making. References to loyalty to, love for, and responsibility to family, friends, and community carry a lot of force for these people. The preference for evidence based on feelings is the most prevalent style in the world. Some of the countries that prefer subjective evidence include Belarus, Costa Rica, El Salvador, Japan, Mexico, South Korea, and Venezuela.

Other cultures rely more on objective or factual information for evidence. People in these cultures look for provable statistics and facts. Much of the Western world relies heavily on factual evidence, in some cases almost to the exclusion of faith- or subjective-based evidence. Countries that prefer factual or objective supporting material include Australia, Canada, England, France, Poland, and Switzerland.

Again, you have probably already guessed that the United States prefers factual information over evidence that is based in subjective feelings or faith. This is apparent in common sayings such as "just the facts, ma'am," as well as in the First Amendment of the U.S. Constitution's separation of Church and State. However, you will remember from Chapter One that U.S. Americans are also individualistic, so they also enjoy references to how the information affects them personally or professionally. Most U.S. Americans are proud of this country and this country's values of freedom, equality, and fairness; thus, appeals to these values can be very effective. However, U.S. Americans are also human and have feelings, so facts alone may not be effective. Facts with a well-placed appeal to feelings can be very persuasive.

When dealing with a U.S. American audience, you do not have to forego appeals to feelings or greater values, but you might want to use them as additional support to your factual evidence. Statistics, dates, names, times, and facts can be very effective when combined with references to personal benefit or a higher good.

The key is learning what to use with which audience, but remember, there is no "foolproof" formula for convincing an audience or for maintaining their interest. The best strategy is to thoroughly analyze your audience and to choose materials that are best suited to their interests, needs, and concerns. When in doubt about a particular audience, use a mix of materials that draws upon the various styles.

SUMMARY

From explanations to examples, from descriptions to definitions, from facts to stats, you are now familiar with the various types of supporting materials you can use to explain, defend, clarify, support, and prove your points. When writing your speech, remember to choose each of your supporting materials based on the needs of the audience, the credibility of your sources, and the relevance and help the supporting material gives to your point. You won't be able to use all the information you found during your research, so be selective and choose the most compelling statistics, the most colorful examples, and the clearest definitions. This will not only keep your speech to a reasonable size, but it will also ensure that only the most interesting information gets included in your presentation. Giving too much information to the audience will overwhelm and bore them, and bored audiences stop listening.

Finally, as you choose your supporting materials, remember to consider your audience's likely preference for types of information. If they are primarily a U.S. or Canadian audience, they are likely to prefer at least some factual information for each point, they will want to know why the information is of particular interest to them, and they will probably appreciate being asked to think beyond their own personal existence and experience. Combining the various styles of evidence with an emphasis on the factual and at least a touch of the abstract is most likely to engage your audience.

Answers to *Try This: Fact, Opinion, or Inference*: None of the statements is a fact!

1. O: Tall and handsome are subjective judgments.
2. I: We can only infer that the assistant is the same person as Anne. Also, we don't know if there are actually two scientists in the story: one already in the laboratory and one who entered. Anne might also be the second scientist or another person altogether.
3. I: We don't know for sure if the receiver referred to is the receiver of the phone that rang or if Anne was on another phone or other transmitting and receiving device.
4. I: We don't know if the assistant is Anne or not.
5. I: Again, if more than one scientist is in the room, we don't know which one was confused.

Discussion Questions and Activities

1. Identify each of the following statements as a fact, inference, or opinion:

   ______ On August 9, 2004, Ryan Matthews became the 115th death row inmate to be freed in the United States.[10]

   ______ Capital punishment should be abolished because it is a cruel and unusual punishment.

   ______ The comprehensive trials and appeals ensure that few death row inmates are wrongfully convicted.

   ______ The recent increase in overturned convictions due to improved DNA evidence shows that many more death row inmates are likely to have been wrongfully convicted.

   ______ Capital punishment should be maintained because it is a reasonable punishment for a terrible crime.

   ______ From 1976 to July 2004, there have been 916 executions in the United States.[11]

2. In groups of three to four students, discuss your next speaking assignments. Share your topics and main points and then brainstorm possible supporting material for each student's speech. Come up with as many specific suggestions as you can using as many types of supporting material as possible. Supporting material examples: the formal definition of capital punishment, an explanation of the rules for using capital punishment, statistics on the number of inmates currently on death row, expert testimony from a prosecutor and a public defender, a graph showing the relative increase or decrease of capital punishment convictions over the last ten years, etc.

3. Using a book of quotations from your school library, find two quotes for each of the following themes:

   Education Jealousy

   Diversity Success

   Freedom Grief

4. Find the mean, median, and mode for the following set of numbers:

   62, 59, 48, 75, 92, 55, 75, 85, 62, 94, 69, 62, 97, 88, 79

5. Think about the last time you were moved by an article, a speech, or a story. What kind of supporting material did the author use? What did you find the most compelling? Why? What other information might the author have included that would have made the story or argument even more powerful? What kinds of evidence do you generally find to be the most persuasive or convincing? Is this a personal preference? Does your preference match your culture(s)' preferences for evidence? Why? Why not?

6. Develop two literal and figurative analogies that you can use to describe an event or phenomenon in your upcoming speech.

7. A sample narrative speech that uses description, explanation, definition, brief examples, quotes, and statistics appears later. Identify the various supporting material included and evaluate the effectiveness of each.

Chapter Quiz

Matching

Place the letter of the term on the line next to the proper example.

a. Metaphor **b.** Literal analogy **c.** Factual example
d. Ratio **e.** Definition **f.** Tally

1. ______ Four out of five students surveyed claimed that they receive some sort of financial assistance from their families.
2. ______ The parking problem on our campus is similar to what colleges in other major cities face when they have increased enrollment and more commuter students: too few parking spaces for too many cars.
3. ______ Enrollment in distance-education courses among college students rose from 1.7 million in the 1997–98 school year to 3.1 million in the 2000–01 school year.[12]
4. ______ A peaceful island in a sea of confusion, he sat quietly amid the chaos.
5. ______ One such incident occurred right here on Main Street last week, when a police car chasing a suspect ran a red light, slamming into the side of a delivery van. Thankfully, no one was hurt this time.
6. ______ In other words, arrangement has to do with how you organize your speech effectively.
7. True or false: It is always preferable to use facts and statistics instead of examples.
8. Which of the following experts would be the most credible in a speech that is arguing to legalize medical marijuana?
   - **a.** A friend who smokes pot and works for a local marijuana legalization campaign
   - **b.** An oncologist (a doctor specializing in the treatment of cancer)
   - **c.** A sick patient who uses medical marijuana
   - **d.** The executive director of NORML, the National Organization to Reform Marijuana Laws

Speech for Analysis

Sample Speech: Analyze the following speech in terms of the types of supporting material the author used. Were these the most effective and appropriate choices to help the audience understand the speech topic? What other supporting material might the author have used to better explain, clarify, or illustrate the topic? Was the material appropriately cited?

The Autobahn
by Angela Bittleroff

Imagine yourself on a stretch of road. A perfect road with a Porsche and you can go as fast as you want to. How fast would you go? 70 mph? 100? Faster? And how would you feel? Would you feel some fear? Maybe freedom? In this class we can learn so much about each other's culture. And I want to teach you about the German culture through the medium of the Autobahn, which you might not know a lot about. I am familiar with it of course since I am from Germany, I have driven on the Autobahn, and I have experienced the culture all of my life. The Autobahn reflects cultural values through the way it is built, the traffic rules that are attached to it, and the way we use it.

Let's start with how technological and engineering advances represent German culture. We know we are famous for building things for our engineering. Hyde Flippo in his book *The German Way: Aspects of Behaviors, Attitudes, and Customs in a German-Speaking World* says that the "Autobahn is an extensive network of limited access freeways much like the American one." The main German automobile club, APAC, said that in 2004 there were 7,500 miles of Autobahn and it continues to grow.

On the Autobahn there are only varying speed limits—no fixed one. It depends on how fast the traffic goes at a certain time. However, it is illegal to go below 40 miles per hour. According to an A&E home video production, *The Modern Marvels: The Autobahn*, 50% of the Autobahn has no speed limit at all. You can even pass police cars.

The road itself is designed for speed. In *Modern Marvels* it is said that the Autobahn has a surface of 27 inches of thickness. That is twice as thick as American freeway surfaces and it lasts twice as long. All curves are designed in wide angles and the street never rises or falls over 4%, so you can go as fast as you want all the time. Here you can find some examples of the Autobahn. Here we have a big Autobahn cross and this is the largest bridge in Germany.

The Autobahn has specific traffic and driving, which represent German structure in its life. Of course you need to get a driver's license, and for that you need to go through driving school and that's a law. There are 12 hours of theory where you learn the laws and 25 to 45 hours of driving. That means driving on city roads, at night, and of course on the Autobahn. So everyone with a license has driven on the Autobahn. It's very important. So there is some dedication and discipline involved in this, and in my own experiences it takes three to four months to get a driver's license. It will cost between $1,500 and $2,000. According to Mark Rask, a racing enthusiast who is in *Modern*

Marvels, there is a rule called ektfond, that means you have to drive on the right. Passing is only allowed on the left. It's illegal if you pass on the right. That causes all slow traffic to drive on the right and fast people can go on the left because of no slow drivers, no Sunday drivers. So you have to be focused and aware of your surroundings because if you are not, you will have a BMW in your back honking at you to get out of the way.

The Autobahn is also safer than the American interstates. According to James Clash in his article "The Joy of the Autobahn" in *Forbes* magazine, the Autobahn death rate in 2001 was 6 billion per passenger miles versus 8 billion on American interstates. This is partly due to the maintenance that is performed on the Autobahn. Seven billion dollars are spent every year to fix the Autobahn and that doesn't mean just filling up potholes. If there is a crack, the whole section is torn out and replaced. So the driving experience is great.

We love the Autobahn so much and it is so famous for how we use it with our cars. It has been said, "Germans take driving very seriously," and that is true. In driving school we learn how to drive a stick shift so we know how to handle our cars. Germany is also Europe's largest carmaker. And you know our cars, BMW, Mercedes, Porsche, they are designed for the Auto and tested on the Auto.

Phillip Patton in *Modern Marvels* says, "Driving is an activity in itself in Germany." That means you don't drink, you don't eat; you are driving. You are experiencing the feeling of driving, the freedom, going as fast as you want to go, and just letting go. It is just great. So great, in fact, that a lot of people from other countries come to Germany just to drive on the Autobahn. If you look at tour guides, you will always see something about the Autobahn and the rules on it because it is very special.

On your handout there are some pictures that just reflect the popularity of the Autobahn itself and the whole driving experience. We love driving. We love cars. That's a big part of our culture.

In conclusion, the Autobahn reflects our cultural values through the way it is built, through the traffic laws assigned to it, and the way we use it with our great cars. I hope you are curious about it, and the next time you are in Germany you should definitely rent a fast car and drive on it and you will experience a feeling that my uncle describes as exhilarating, intimidating, and liberating all at the same time. And you can only enjoy this in Germany, nowhere else in the world.

Works Cited

Clash, James. "The Joy of the Autobahn." *Forbes*, September 2003.

Flippo, Hyde. *The German Way: Aspects of Behaviors, Attitudes, and Customs in a German-Speaking World*. McGraw-Hill, 1996.

Modern Marvels: The Autobahn. The History Channel. April 2006.

Chapter 7 Quiz Answers

1. f, 2. b, 3. d, 4. a, 5. c, 6. e, 7. False, 8. b

CHAPTER 8 Organizing the Speech

CHAPTER GOAL

By the end of this chapter you will be able to effectively, clearly, and logically outline a speech's introduction, body, and conclusion.

When I was an undergraduate, I disliked writing, not because I didn't have anything to say or because I wasn't skilled at creating good sentences and paragraphs or even because I had difficulty with the grammar or spelling, although occasionally these things did prove challenging. I didn't like to write because I seemed to have tremendous difficulty organizing my ideas. I would start with one idea and begin writing at the top of the page, and somewhere near the bottom of that page or halfway through the second, I would realize that I had completely lost my point. I had research materials galore (I love to research), and I had plenty of ideas; what I did not have was organization. I did not know how to group my ideas into main points or how to outline. I didn't even know how to write a thesis statement. What was worse, I was sure that I should be able to write a good essay or speech without them. Luckily for me, my mother is also a professor and she taught me how to develop a thesis, organize my ideas, and create an outline from which I can either write an essay or give a speech. Thanks, Mom.

In this chapter, you, too, will learn how to organize your ideas and put them into an outline. In Chapter Five, you learned how to write a thesis statement based on some quickly developed main points, and now that you have done your research, you can refine your main points and update your thesis. First, we'll look at the various logics cultures prefer to organize presentations and arguments and how they compare to the preferred organizational patterns in the United States. Then we'll move on to outlining your speech.

Since speeches are outlined from the inside out—starting with the body and moving to the introduction and conclusion—let's begin by discussing how to order or organize your speech, when to add support, and where to use connectives. Then we will discuss what goes into strong introductions and conclusions. Throughout this process you will learn how these elements are placed into your full-sentence, or preparation, outline. Finally, you will learn how to create and use a speaking outline to deliver your speech.

DIFFERENT LOGICS

Not everyone organizes information in the same way. Some people employ a direct, step-by-step manner to explain and clarify a topic. Others like to explore several dimensions of a subject simultaneously by invoking both the minds and hearts of listeners. Still others like to share information the way they share a good story, using vivid details, solid character development, and implied morals or lessons. These preferences are often culturally bound. Some researchers believe that "Rhetorical action is not a strictly psychological, rational, or even sociological question; it is a historical one"[1] because we are the products of our cultures. In other words, how we say something as well as what we say are partly due to culture and not just personal choice. Therefore, to learn how to write or speak in another language, you have to learn not only that language but also the logic preferred by speakers of that language.

Even if you speak English with little or no accent and use grammar and syntax like a native speaker, you may find that writing and formal speaking in

English causes you difficulties. Maybe your instructors have told you to be more direct, to avoid digressions, or to avoid repeating yourself. You might have been told that you tend to provide ample details and examples, but do not directly relate your point to the supporting material. These difficulties are not uncommon, nor do they reflect some sort of inability on your part. Instead, these differences reflect rhetorical differences among cultures.

The creation of a piece of rhetoric, whether written or spoken, is a process of making choices.[2] The choices we make are often culturally driven. Language, history, and social structure influence the rhetorical choices preferred within a particular culture. Usually, we do not formally learn these rhetorical preferences until fairly late in our academic careers, but by then, we have passively learned the flow and rhythm of what is considered *good rhetoric* in our culture. This can be problematic when we learn a new language and create speeches and essays in that language.

Rhetorical Structure
The manner in which a piece of writing or a speech is presented, developed, organized, and supported.

Much ESL research over the past forty years has found that beyond learning the grammar, lexicon, and syntax of a language, a non-native speaker also needs to learn the rhetorical structures of the new language, whether that language is English, French, Tagalog, or Hindi. Each culture has preferences for the ways in which the people of that culture construct, organize, and support their arguments and ideas in formal speech and writing. In other words, how you write an academic essay or prepare a political speech in one culture will vary, sometimes significantly, from how you would write an essay or speech in another culture.

Contrastive Rhetoric
The study of writing styles across cultures to identify varying rhetorical structures; originally developed as a method to teach ESL students to write effectively in English.

Robert Kaplan, one of the most influential researchers in linguistics and the teaching of ESL, referred to this as the *logic* of a language.[3] His research

World leaders have learned to be effective in meetings with other world leaders by adapting their rhetorical structure to suit the speaking situation.

led to an area of study known as *contrastive rhetoric,* which examines the similarities and differences in writing logic across cultures. Critics of contrastive rhetoric complain that the differences outlined between and among languages are often too simplistic, overly generalized, and biased toward English preferences. Additionally, when discussing cultural preferences, we can sometimes come to the wrong conclusion: that there is only one preferred style within a language or culture.[4]

Although much controversy has surrounded these ideas, one thing has become clear: There is no one right way to construct an argument, present an idea, or organize information; there are only preferred ways based on the culture and expectations of the audience. As we discussed in Chapter One, all aspects of speechmaking, including organization and rhetorical style, are based on the rhetorical situation. Each culture uses many forms and styles, depending on the purpose of the communication.

For your purposes, it may be helpful to get a sense of the rhetorical preferences in your culture compared to the dominant U.S. American preferences so that when necessary, you can adapt your preferred style to the preferred style of your audience.

The structure of American English writing begins from an audience-centered perspective. English-speaking Americans, both U.S. and Canadian, place the responsibility for understanding on the writer. Hence, there is a strong preference for a direct, clear, and coherent structure that is free from digressions (departures from the main idea or thesis).

Speeches and essays in American English focus on a single idea or thesis that is developed methodically by previewing the thesis and main points in an introduction, developing each of the main points in order, and then reviewing the thesis and main points in the conclusion. This linear format allows the author to lead the listener or reader to the conclusion in a step-by-step process.

Individual points are organized to show the relationship and relative importance of one idea to another. In essays, the main idea usually begins a paragraph, and the support for that idea follows. Paragraphs are made up of concise sentences that explicitly state the relevance and importance of the idea. Paragraphs and main points are carefully and explicitly connected to each other through a series of connectives (connectives are discussed later in this chapter).

Because the United States and Canada are individualistic countries, American English values originality and personal expression of opinions.[5] However, the tone tends to be more formal, creating a distance between the author (speaker) and the reader (audience) and placing the author in an *expert* position.

Conversely, Arab writing is characterized by circular reasoning, wherein the author revisits an idea from several different perspectives. The ideas are not subordinated one to another as they are in American English, but are coordinated through a series of *ands* (wa) as sentence connectors. Arab writing

CONSIDERING LANGUAGE

Bilingual Functional Shifts

Using a word from one part of speech (e.g., a noun) from one's native language as a different part of speech (e.g., a verb) in a new language is called a *bilingual functional shift.* These shifts introduce words to the new language.

Language learners do this because sometimes the idea they are trying to share does not exist in the new language or because it is easier than to use a complicated, longer version in the new language. Following are some examples from Pakistani English:

Verbs in English
To gherao = to blockade, picket
To challan = to be charged a fine, or given a traffic ticket

From Urdu nouns
gherao = a blockade
challan = invoice, remittance, citation*

*Robert J. Baumgardner. " 'To Shariat or Not to Shariat?': Bilingual Functional Shifts in Pakistani English," *World Englishes* 11(2/3) pp. 129–140, 1992.

CONSIDERING CULTURE

Rhetorical Strategies

Think about your native language and culture. What are the characteristics of a good essay or speech? Is there a preference for linearity or circularity? Does your culture's rhetorical preference allow for digressions or extra information? Does it stress short, clear, explicit sentences or long, expressive, emotional constructions? Compare this with your audience's preferences. If your audience is primarily American, you may want to adapt your style to be more direct, concise, and clear. As Alexandra Rowe Henry so eloquently put it in her book *Second Language Rhetorics in Process:*

> To communicate, the cross-cultural rhetor must sometimes reject preferred rhetorical strategies and, instead, choose strategies appropriate to the contextually defined and culturally biased audience.

is marked by repetition, an informal style, and highly expressive language. Arabic rhetoric aims to create an insider relationship between the author and the reader that fosters solidarity, intimacy, and warmth.[6]

Asian writing tends to be more indirect. Often, writers and speakers do not reveal their main points until the end of the text. Implication leads the reader to discover the thesis indirectly. Asian rhetoric stresses aesthetics; as such, Asian writers use language that is more figurative. Because Asian cultures tend to be more collectivist and high in uncertainty avoidance, Asian writing values homogeneity. Imitation of respected writers and extensive use of quotation are common.[7]

German writing, along with the writing of other Romance and Slavic languages, is characterized by frequent digressions and extraneous information within main points that are otherwise organized linearly, giving the impression of being less linear but providing greater depth of information. Germans sometimes find English linearity, with its restrictions on digressions, to "lead to a conclusion based on a more limited perspective."[8]

As discussed earlier, do not be afraid to incorporate your own style within the new style. As English has spread throughout the world, cultures have adapted it to their particular cultural needs and preferences, thus increasing the range of acceptable styles and logics used in English writing and speech.[9] Remember, among American preferences are individuality and creativity. By incorporating your style into the American style, you will accomplish a more interesting presentation that will still be easy for the audience to follow and understand.

> **HINT**
> **Using Microsoft Word**
> If you are using Microsoft Word, you can create an outline template in your computer by typing in the form in Table 8.1 and then saving the document by selecting *document template* under the *Format* drop-down menu. Now, each time you have to write a speech, open the outline template and do a *Save as* for that speech. You will never have to type in the outline format again!

PREPARATION OUTLINES

When builders set out to construct a house, they do not begin with the front door. Instead, they begin with the foundation, then frame the structure, then add the walls and roof, and, finally, add the doors and windows. Speechwriting is also the process of building a structure. Extemporaneous speeches are not written out as an essay; they are outlined. The outline is the structure of your speech. In constructing speeches you do not begin with your opening words. You begin with the foundation. Recall that in Chapter Five you began with your general purpose, specific purpose, and thesis statement. These represent the foundation of your speech. From there, you can build the rest of your speech using the speech outline template (see Table 8.1).

The preparation outline is the structure of your speech. The outline provides a visual representation of how the various points and subpoints relate to

TABLE 8.1 **Outline Format**

Title
General Purpose:
Specific Purpose:
Thesis:
Introduction
I.
II.
III.
IV.
(Transition:)
Body
I.
(Transition:)
II.
III.
(Transition:)
Conclusion
I.
II.
III.
______________ *Separate Sheet* ______________
Bibliography

each other and to the overall thesis. Unlike an essay, where you must actually read every word to follow the argument, an outline gives you an instantaneous overview of how the speech fits together. Subpoints are breakdowns or subdivisions of main ideas. They provide the proof for or explanation of the main points. Sub-subpoints provide detail and explanation for the subpoints, and so on. The preparation outline includes all the important information you will need in your speech, including:

- The general purpose, specific purpose, thesis, and main points
- All your evidence, examples, stories, and explanations for your main points
- An introduction that gains the attention of your audience, establishes your credibility, and previews the speech
- A conclusion that summarizes your main points and leaves the audience with something to think about
- Connectives that help you move smoothly from one point to the next
- A works cited sheet at the end to show where you found your supporting materials.

Since you have already developed the general and specific purposes and the thesis, you can begin building the body of your speech. As you begin filling in the outline, here are a few simple outlining rules you should know:

- **Identify each component of the outline clearly:** As shown in the template, label the general purpose, specific purpose, thesis, introduction, body, conclusion, connectives, and works cited sheet. You do not need to bold, highlight, underline, center, or italicize these items.
- **Use full sentences for the first two to three subdivisions:** A preparation outline is also called a *full-sentence outline.* As such, use full sentences for each main point, subpoint, and, when needed, sub-subpoint.
- **Do not use questions for main points, propositions, or claims:** Main points, propositions, and claims are what you are teaching or proving; state them as assertions, not questions.
- **Use consistent symbolization:** Alternate between Roman and Arabic numbers and upper- and lowercase letters like so:
  I. Main point
    A. Subpoint
      1. Sub-subpoint
      2. Sub-subpoint
    B. Subpoint
    C. Subpoint
      1. Sub-subpoint
      2. Sub-subpoint
      3. Sub-subpoint
  II. Main point
- **Use only one sentence for each number or letter:** Do not include more than one sentence per point. If you have more than one sentence to explain in a point, you need to subdivide the point into subpoints.

- **Make sure that every subdivision has between two and five points:** Subdivisions indicate that you have divided a higher-level point into parts. Logic tells us that when we divide something, even once, we will have at least two pieces (think of breaking a single pencil in half; you cannot have fewer than two pieces). On the other hand, more than five subdivisions are hard for the audience to follow or for the speaker to remember, so limit the number of main points and subpoints to no more than five at each subdivision.
- **Do not include connectives in the symbolization system:** Connectives do not provide any claims, new information, or supporting material; they are included only to help the speaker move from one idea to the next smoothly; therefore, do not include them in your numbering system.

Organizing the Body

Clear organization helps the audience understand and retain your message, increases your perceived competence, and shows a clear relationship among your ideas. As a non-native speaker, using a clear, predictable organizational pattern can relieve some of your linguistic worries because the organization makes following the discussion much easier for the audience. That is, the organization gives a clearer context for the speech and increases predictability.

Organizational Patterns

Organizational Patterns
The systematic ways of grouping information together so that one point naturally leads or relates to the next.

In Chapter Five, you developed some preliminary main points to guide your research. You chose those main points because they seemed to "fit" logically. However, as you researched, you may have found that those main points didn't quite work or there may have been a better way to organize your speech. The following represent some of the most common and easy-to-use organizational patterns taught in American English.

Chronological

Chronological organization refers to organizing the main points according to time or sequence—what happens first, second, and so on. Speeches about events and processes are often organized chronologically. The main points in these speeches are often marked by words such as *first, second, third* or by specific references to time such as, "In the 1950s. . . . Then in the 1960s. . . ." Chronological order is helpful for explaining how to complete a process because the main points walk the audience through the steps in the same order they occur. For example:

Thesis: By gathering, combining, and baking the right ingredients, a gourmet dinner can be as quick and easy as 1-2-3!

Main Points:
I. First, you need to gather and measure fresh ingredients.
II. Next, combine the ingredients carefully and in the right order.
III. Finally, bake your mixture thoroughly.

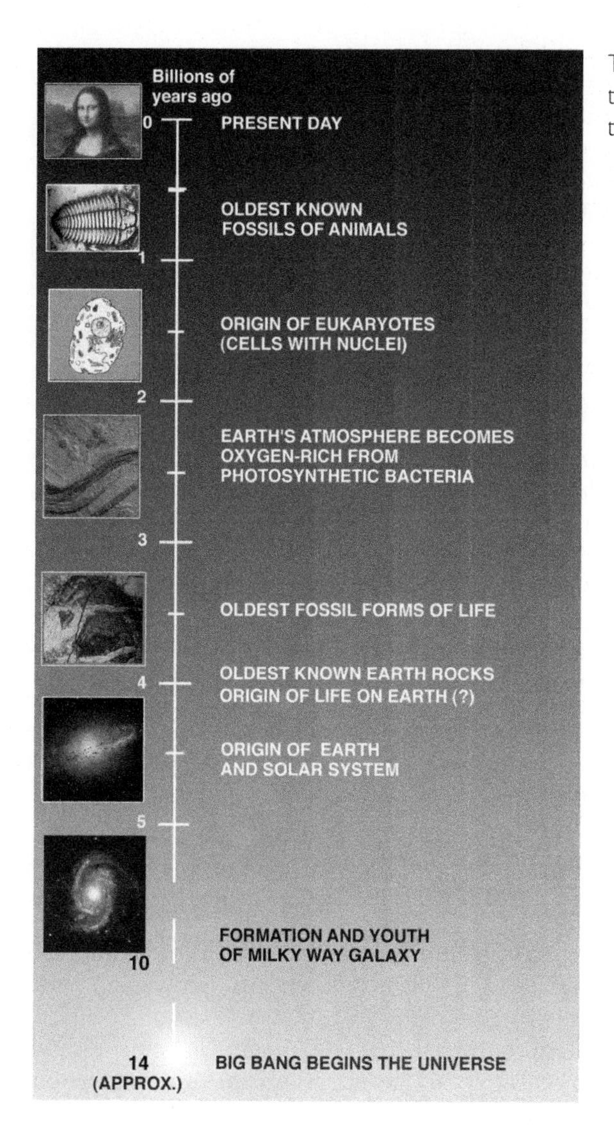

Timelines are a visual representation of chronological order, the organizational pattern that organizes the main points in time order.

Thesis: Starting with a need, developing into an idea, and ending with a sellable product, the history of the SumaDek Listening Display represents the true spirit of the American Dream.

Main Points:

I. In 2000, Deirdre had a CD to sell and no good way to promote it.

II. By 2001, Deirdre came up with an idea for selling her CD that sold not only the CD but also the display in which she sold it.

III. In 2002, Deirdre created a marketable version of her CD display stand to sell to other musicians, and it is selling today.

Want more information on organizing and outlining your speech?

Click Here http://www.speechtips.com/

SpeechTips.com is a "free guide to speech writing and delivery" that offers a ssistance in planning, writing, and delivering speeches.

Spatial

When you give directions to your house, you give them spatially: "Go north on Main Street for two miles. When you come to the fork in the road, stay right. At the traffic signal on Second Avenue, make another right. You will be heading east. The house will be on the south side of the street." Spatial organization orders main points according to position or direction: in other words, *where* something exists in space. Words like *up, down; front, back; top, bottom;* and *east, west* are common in spatially organized speeches. Speeches that describe places or objects frequently use spatial organization. For example:

Thesis: The Inland Empire, the Westside, the Valley, and Downtown each offer different treasures that combine to make Los Angeles one of the richest metropolitan areas in the world.

Main Points:

I. The Inland Empire to the east of Los Angeles offers easy access to the city while only minutes away are world-class mountain and desert resorts.
II. The Westside of Los Angeles is home to some of the most famous Los Angeles hallmarks, including its beautiful beaches, Hollywood landmarks, and fabulous restaurants.
III. The San Fernando Valley, to the north of Los Angeles, is home to some of the world's most famous movie studies and quaint suburban neighborhoods.
IV. In the center of this golden metropolis is Downtown Los Angeles, home to the city's vibrant concert halls, civic center, sports arenas, and financial district.

Thesis: Since the tragedy of 9/11, access to the Statue of Liberty has been limited to three areas: the lobby, the promenade, and the pedestal.

Main Points:

I. The lobby of the Statue of Liberty houses an exhibit on the original torch.
II. The promenade around the Statue of Liberty provides fantastic views of the statue and New York Harbor.
III. The pedestal of the Statue of Liberty houses an exhibit on the history and symbolism of the statue.

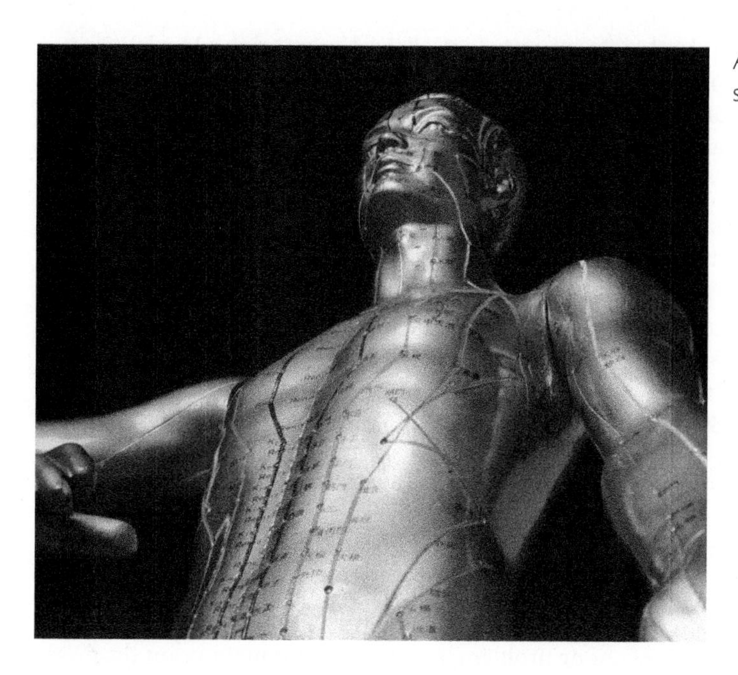

Acupuncturists learn where to place the needles spatially—they learn the zones of the body.

Problem-Solution (Problem-Cause-Solution)

Problem-solution order shows the existence of a problem and then presents a solution to the problem. As such, problem-solution format organizes a speech into two main points: Main Point I identifies a problem and Main Point II identifies a solution. Problem-solution is used in both informative and persuasive speeches. In informative speeches it is used to show how a problem was resolved. Speeches about diseases and historical events are sometimes presented in problem-solution order. In persuasive speeches, problem-solution order establishes a problem and the speaker proposes a possible solution. For example:

Thesis: Because car accidents related to cell phone use are on the rise, using a cell phone while driving should be made illegal.

Main Points:

I. Car accidents attributed to cell phone use are on the rise throughout the country.
II. Congress should pass a bill outlawing cell phone use while driving.

Thesis: After repeated outbreaks in the first half of the twentieth century, polio has almost disappeared in the United States due to the Salk vaccine.

Main Points:

I. Polio epidemics in the first half of the twentieth century led to millions of deaths and disability.
II. The discovery of the polio vaccine in 1955 by Jonas Salk halted the spread of the disease in developed countries worldwide.

Occasionally a third main point is included when using problem-solution: the cause of the problem. A speaker may add a main point on the cause of the problem if, and only if, the solution addresses the cause of the problem. Then the organizational pattern is referred to as problem-cause-solution. Here is an example:

Thesis: Teenagers are starting to smoke cigarettes in alarming numbers due to the aggressive advertising tactics of the tobacco industry; therefore tobacco advertising accessible to minors must be banned.

Main Points:

I. Teenagers are the fastest-growing group of new smokers.
II. Despite tobacco company claims, cigarette advertising is still aggressively targeted to minors through billboards, posters, and sponsorship programs.
III. Tobacco advertising that will likely be viewed by minors should be banned.

Causal

Causal organization shows a cause-and-effect relationship. This organizational pattern also contains only two main points: The first main point discusses the cause of an event or problem, and the second main point discusses the effects of that event or problem. Speeches about the causes and effects of certain diseases or of a particular historical event can be very effective and easy to organize. For example:

Thesis: Frequently attributed to a poor diet and exercise, adult-onset diabetes leads to many serious secondary health problems.

Main Points:

I. Adult-onset diabetes is caused, at least in part, by poor diet and exercise.
II. Adult-onset diabetes, when left untreated, can lead to heart attack, stroke, blindness, and kidney disease.

Thesis: The Civil Rights Movement of the 1950s and '60s began with the Montgomery bus boycott in 1955 and resulted in many social, political, and legal changes in the United States.

Main Points:

I. The Civil Rights Movement of the 1950s and '60s began with the Montgomery bus boycott in 1955.
II. The Civil Rights Movement provided greater opportunities and ensured voting rights for, and ended legal segregation of, people of color in the United States.

Topical

Topical organization divides a topic into logically related categories. Use topical order when there is an obvious and consistent way to divide the topic into parts. Dividing a person's life into *the joys*, *the challenges*, and *the accomplishments* or into *career*, *family*, and *hobbies* would be examples of topical divisions. Words such as *reasons, types,* or *aspects* indicate a topical organization. For example:

Thesis: I have learned about the wonders of love through my family, my friends, and my pets.

Main Points:

I. My family has taught me that love is about support.
II. My friends have taught me that love is kindness.
III. My pets have taught me that love is unconditional.

Thesis: Indian gaming should be expanded because it benefits the state, the tribes, and children.

Main Points:

I. Indian gaming benefits the state by providing increased revenue and decreased public assistance.
II. Indian gaming benefits the individual tribes by providing jobs, money, and tourism.
III. Indian gaming benefits children by providing money to improve educational facilities both on and off reservations.

Persuasion-Specific Organizational Patterns

In Chapter Fourteen, we will discuss the various types of persuasive speeches in detail. For now, just be aware that there are some organizational patterns that are used specifically when giving persuasive speeches, including Monroe's Motivated Sequence, criteria-satisfaction, and comparative advantages.

Choosing an Organizational Pattern

When deciding which pattern to choose for your speech, focus on what best suits the purpose of your speech and which pattern seems to be most appropriate for that purpose. Avoid trying to use one pattern with an extra point or two because you didn't know where else to put them. Settle on a pattern, and then fit your main points to that pattern. This will help you stay focused on your purpose and avoid diverging, including irrelevant information, or getting lost.

Adding Subpoints and Sub-subpoints (Filling in with Supporting Material)

Once you have your main points, you are ready to begin filling in the outline with your subpoints and sub-subpoints. Your subpoints and sub-subpoints

TABLE 8.2 Tips for Developing Main Points

• Limit the number of main points to no fewer than two and no more than five.
• Be sure each main point discusses only one idea.
• Word main points similarly so that they are easily distinguishable as main points from one point to the next (use parallel wording whenever possible—see Chapter Ten).
• Balance the main points to be roughly the same size. If one main point is four sentences long and the others are fifteen sentences long, you have a balance problem.

are your supporting materials. They are the explanations, examples, statistics, stories, and quotes you gathered to write your speech.

Make certain that each subpoint directly addresses the main point it follows and that each sub-subpoint addresses the subpoint it follows. Do not include irrelevant or tangential information, no matter how interesting it may be. If it does not relate to the point being discussed, do not include it. You may find a more appropriate place for the information later, or you might want to include it in your introduction or conclusion.

Within your main points you will need to follow a logical organizational pattern as well. Often, within main points, the pattern used is topical. The patterns do not have to be the same from one main point to the next, just logical and consistent within each main point. However, sometimes repeating the pattern from one main point to the next can make creating the outline much easier. For example:

Thesis: Social problems surrounding drug use occur in every generation, but how the issue is addressed changes with the times.

I. (*Chronological*) In the 1920s, prohibition against alcohol was instituted to fight poverty, poor health, and poor hygiene.
    A. (*Problem*) In the early 1900s alcohol was thought to be the reason behind much poverty, poor health, and poor hygiene.
    B. (*Solution*) To solve these social ills, the production and consumption of alcohol was made illegal nationwide.

II. (*Chronological*) In the 1930s, Prohibition was repealed to fight the corruption and crime surrounding the illegal production and consumption of alcohol.
    A. (*Problem*) Prohibition led to dangerous homemade alcohol, increased use of more dangerous drugs, organized crime, and rampant corruption among public officials by the 1930s.
    B. (*Solution*) To solve these social and political ills, Prohibition was repealed in 1933.

At each subdivision, remember to indent one full tab. This shows that the new subdivision is a breaking up of the point immediately above it, which gives a visual representation of how the various points fit together.

Finally, the United States is a time-centered society. Time limits, on time, and overtime are very important concepts to U.S. Americans. If you exceed or go under the allotted time of your speech, your credibility, and, in the case of a speech class, your grade will likely suffer. Therefore, be sure the amount of information you include is consistent with the time limits allowed for your presentation. You can do this by timing yourself while you read the body of your speech out loud at a normal conversational pace. Your reading should take about seventy-five percent of the total time allotted for the speech. (When your speech is completely finished, the body should take up about ninety percent of your speech time; the introduction and conclusion will make up the other ten percent.)

Connectives

After you feel comfortable with each of your main points and their supporting material, add connectives to help you move smoothly from one main point to the next. Connectives provide clues as to where in the speech a speaker is. They can be as short as a word or phrase or as long as a compound sentence. They are used at the beginning of main points, between main points, and in the introduction and conclusion. There are three major types of connectives: signposts, previews/summaries, and transitions.

Signposts are single words or small phrases that point to where you are in the speech or focus on key ideas—for example, words such as *first, second, third, to begin, to conclude, in conclusion, in summary, therefore, however, yet,* and *in closing*. Signposts act as signs for the audience.

Previews let the audience know what you will be talking about next. The most important preview in a speech is the thesis statement because it previews all the main points; but main points themselves are also a form of preview because they indicate what you are about to talk about in depth. *Summaries* are the opposite of previews in that they let the audience know what you have already discussed. The most important summary is the conclusion, where you review the main points of the speech.

Transitions wrap up one point and introduce the next in one sentence: *Now that we have seen how family and friends represent love in my life, let's look at the furry side of love.* Transitions give the speaker a smooth way to lead the audience out of one main point and into the next. You will notice that a transition is a mini-summary connected to a mini-preview in one sentence.

Signposts, previews, and summaries are part of the overall outline structure because they provide relevant information without which the speech would not be complete. Transitions, on the other hand, are not part of the numbered/lettered outline structure because they simply repeat and preview to move the speech along. As such, transitions are separated by being placed inside brackets or parentheses and labeled as transitions (see outline template):

> (Transition: In addition to the physical effects of smoking, we need to look at the social effects of this dangerous habit.)

Carefully chosen and placed connectives can make a speech smooth and easy to follow.

Introductions and Conclusions

Even though introductions and conclusions do not contain the content of your message like the body does, they do play important roles in getting your message across. Like the front door of a house, an introduction goes on last, but it is the first place through which the audience enters a speech. The introduction is your first chance to gain your audience's attention, secure their interest, and establish your credibility. The conclusion, the back door of your speech, is your last chance to make sure that the audience understands your message before they exit.

Primacy
The first message received in a communication.

Recency
The last, or most recently, received message in a communication.

The importance of introductions and conclusions for solidifying a speaker's message can be understood through the *principle of primacy-recency.* Primacy refers to the first thing an audience hears, and recency refers to the last thing an audience hears.

Although research has been inconclusive about which is actually more effective in reinforcing a message, one thing is clear: Both work to reinforce, clarify, and convey the message. This means that even if your audience doesn't listen attentively to the body of your speech, they can still receive and retain much of your message from the introduction and conclusion. People listen most closely to the beginning and the end of a speech. Furthermore, when an audience becomes engaged at the beginning of a speech, they are more likely to maintain their interest in the message.

Additionally, if you are concerned because of your accent or pronunciation about the audience's understanding you, well-planned introductions and conclusions give you an opportunity to start strongly and can help the audience adjust more quickly to your speaking style.

Introductions

Dan marched to the front of the room in full military fatigues. He turned sharply to face the audience. The audience members began to giggle nervously as he just stood there standing at attention for five seconds . . . ten seconds . . . fifteen seconds. As people started looking to each other for an explanation, suddenly the soldier pulled a ruler from behind his back and crashed it down onto the desk in front of him. The audience members jumped. A few gasped. Dan simply said, "*Stress: Trembling hands, nervous giggles, and pounding heart. How do you deal with stress?*"

Dan effectively grabbed the full and undivided attention of his classmates. He went on to discuss how his job as a drill sergeant in the Army had trained him to both induce and manage stress in recruits. His speech, as he explained, would teach the audience about how they could manage stress in their lives as students. As Tad Simons tells us:

> Most public speaking experts would probably agree that the first two minutes of any presentation are the most critical. That's because . . . the presenter must somehow snare listeners' attention, prove that he/she is a worthwhile distraction from the shuffle and swirl of their day, smile, breathe and naturally move with grace and purpose . . . and lay the critical groundwork . . . of the presentation.[10]

As such, an effective introduction fulfills four objectives aimed at the audience:

I. Gain the attention of the audience.
II. Relate the topic directly to the audience.
III. Establish the speaker's credibility.
IV. Preview the body of the speech (thesis).

You will remember that the introduction of the outline template has four main points. These four goals represent those four main points. You place

Fake It Until It Is True

Your speech does not begin when you start speaking. It begins the moment you arrive on speech day. The audience may notice nervous, unconfident behavior as you are waiting to give your speech and as you walk up to the podium. Therefore, you should not give in to expressing anxiety, nervousness, or a lack of confidence. When you allow yourself to express your hesitations, you give yourself permission to fail. Instead, pretend to yourself and the world that you are completely relaxed, confident, and comfortable. You will find that you will not only appear more confident and relaxed but will also actually feel more confident and relaxed.

- Focus your attention on the other speakers and activities, not on yourself.
- Sit quietly and try to look relaxed.
- Walk up to the podium confidently and with purpose.
- DO NOT say, "I'm so nervous."
- Begin with your planned opening words in a clear, loud voice.

each of these main points in your outline in the same order shown here. If any main point in the introduction exceeds one sentence, remember to subdivide the main point into subpoints. However, note that you will never have subpoints for Main Point IV because that is the thesis statement, and the thesis statement is only one sentence long!

Gaining the Audience's Attention

As the famous lawyer Clarence Darrow said, "Unless a speaker can interest his audience at once, his effort will be a failure."[11] The first words you speak or actions you take at the lectern can set the mood for the rest of your speech. There are several attention-gaining strategies you can use to start your speech off right (see Table 8.3). Remember, it is not only important that your attention getter gets the audience's attention, but also that it is related to your topic and purpose.

Attention-Gaining Techniques

Table 8.3 on page 186 offers a few of the techniques you can use to gain your audience's attention, but don't let these suggestions limit your creativity. Other attention-gaining techniques include referring to recent happenings, thanking the audience for the opportunity to speak to them, engaging the audience in an activity, or including audiovisual elements. Speakers have made audiences stand up, exercise, and practice deep breathing. Speakers have also played musical instruments, shown scenes from movies, and read poetry. The only limit to creating an ear-catching attention getter is that it needs to be relevant and appropriate to the speaking situation—the audience, context, purpose, and speaker.

TABLE 8.3 **Attention-Gaining Strategies**

Strategy	Explanation	Example
State the importance of the topic	Some topics are so important that a speaker needs to do little more than simply state the topic. Telling the audience that a serious problem exists or that something important is about to happen can often be enough to gain the audience's attention.	I. Tonight, 840 million people will go to bed hungry worldwide, according to James Morris, head of the United Nations World Food Program. A. "About 18,000 kids died today because of hunger. That's one every five seconds," he said.* B. World hunger is quickly becoming the biggest social, economic, and political problem in the world today.
Startle the audience	An intriguing statement or some shocking or unusual act is a great way to arouse interest quickly. This can be done simply with a statement such as, "Who would like to confess their sins?" You can also gradually build up to the statement. Actions can also be used to startle the audience—pounding on the podium, giving a Tarzan yell, or acting in some other creative way can be very effective, but be cautious to not overdo it.	I. Take a moment and think of the three women closest to you. A. Who comes to mind? 1. Your mother? 2. Your friend? 3. Your sister? B. Now, guess which one will be sexually assaulted in her lifetime. C. Washington State University's Women's Resource Center says that one in every three women will be sexually assaulted at some point in her life.
Arouse the curiosity of the audience	By not immediately revealing the topic but teasing the audience with hints or questions, you can engage their curiosity and interest, or as Elie Wiesel did in his speech about "The Perils of Indifference," you can wait to reveal the subject until the end of the story.	"Fifty-four years ago to the day, a young Jewish boy from a small town in the Carpathian Mountains woke up, not far from Goethe's beloved Weimar, in a place of eternal infamy called Buchenwald. He was finally free, but there was no joy in his heart. He thought there never would be again. Liberated a day earlier by American soldiers, he remembers their rage at what they saw. And even if he lives to be a very old man, he will always be grateful to them for that rage, and also for their compassion. Though he did not understand their language, their eyes told him what he needed to know—that they, too, would remember, and bear witness. "And now, I stand before you, Mr. President—Commander-in-Chief of the army that freed me, and tens of thousands of others—and I am filled with a profound and abiding gratitude to the American people."†
Use quotations	Beginning a speech with a short quotation that introduces the topic can add meaning, depth, and/or humor to the opening of a speech.	Used to introduce a speech on NASA's mission: "Space the final frontier. . . . To explore new worlds. To seek out new life and new civilizations, to boldly go where no man has gone before."‡

Tell stories	Most of us love to hear stories because we can visualize the scene and relate to the characters. Brief stories as attention getters must be clearly related to your topic and thesis and delivered well to be effective. Stories that are too long, unfocused, or not obviously connected to the speaker's thesis can confuse and frustrate an audience. When outlining a story, include the details and complete sentences up to the third subdivision. After that, use keywords to remind yourself of the necessary details to include.	A young woman told the following story while discussing the dangers of undiagnosed heart disease: I. A seven-year-old girl and her grandmother speed down the highway toward a home the little girl has never seen. A. The girl asks dozens of questions about the home of her heritage. 1. What does it look like? 2. Do I look like my cousins? B. Suddenly the smile on her grandmother's face fades and the color drains from her face. 1. Before the child can ask a frightened, "What's wrong?" the grandmother collapses behind the wheel. 2. The little girl, terrified and confused, does the only thing she can think to do. a. She grabs the wheel. b. She stops the car. C. The little girl saved the car and herself. 1. Unfortunately, there was nothing she could do to save her grandmother. 2. Undiagnosed heart disease had taken her life prematurely.
Ask questions	Questions can be an excellent way to engage the audience and get them to become active in the presentation. Ask either polling questions or rhetorical questions. Polling questions require the audience to actually answer the question posed. After they answer, acknowledge their answers and let them know when you are finished polling: "You can put your hands down" or "You can be seated." Rhetorical questions are questions that do not require an answer. Ask them to point out the obvious or to stress a truth.	Polling Questions • How many of you speak more than two languages? • Raise your hand if you have visited one of the Seven Wonders of the World. • If you have ever been a victim of a crime, please stand up. Rhetorical Questions • Do you want to live a happy life? • A world of famine, war, poverty, and chaos, is that what we want to leave for our children? • You go to school and work, you study, you suffer through boring lectures, tedious readings, you show up to work on time, and you don't complain, but for what reason? What do you have to show for it?

* James Morris in Stephen Dunphy, "World Hunger also an Economic Problem" Business and Technology, The Seattle Times 14 July 2004. Retrieved on Aug 24, 2004 from http://seattletimes.nwsource.com/html/businesstechnology/2001978904_dunphy14.html

† Elie Wiesel, "The Perils of Indifference" Speech on April 12, 1999 in Washington D.C. Social Justice Speeches Retrieved on Aug 24 2004 from http//www.edchange.org/multicultural/speeches/elie_wiesel_perils.html

‡ Gene Roddenberry "Space the Final Frontier" Copyright 1996 & 1970 Bruin Music Company.

TABLE 8.4 **Guidelines for Developing an Effective Attention Getter**

Attention getters should be:
• Brief, usually no more than three or four sentences in standard classroom speeches
• Creative and interesting
• Relevant to the topic and purpose of the speech
• Appropriate to the speaking situation
• Thoroughly practiced

Another effective technique is, later in the speech or in the conclusion, to revisit or recall the introduction. This gives psychological unity to a speech. The audience feels that they have traveled all the way through the message and have ended up back where they began.

Relating to the Audience

The second goal of the introduction is to relate the topic directly to the needs and interests of the audience. This means that you need to relate the topic explicitly to the audience and briefly explain why this speech is important to them in their lives. We refer to this as addressing the WIIFM (pronounced "WIF-em"): What's in It for Me?

When you watch the news or read the paper, what stories do you find the most interesting? What is it about those stories that grabs your attention? Why those stories and not the others? The answer is that those are the stories that are the most relevant to your life, your concerns, and your interests. People pay attention to things that affect them directly. For instance, would you be more interested in a speech about the rising costs of books in general or one about the high cost of college textbooks? Would you be more likely to listen to the statistics regarding the prevalence of rape in the United States or the statistics of sexual assaults on your campus?

No matter what other interest-arousing techniques you use, you still need to relate the topic directly to your audience. Tell them how the information in your speech affects them. Use your audience analysis to show them how this information specifically touches their lives. Imagine after the 9/11 tragedy in New York City, a fire captain gave a presentation on professionalism to newly graduating firefighters. After showing a brief tribute film to the NYC firefighters, he said:

> In the wake of September 11th, fire-fighters and fire departments around the country have exhibited their true characters through their dedication to professionalism in the midst of heartrending tragedy and personal loss. You are now a part of this honorable team. We expect, the public expects, that you will faithfully follow in this Department's tradition of professionalism.

For most speeches, you can relate the topic to your audience in a single sentence at the start (e.g., "Learning about the warning signs of hypertension can help you protect yourself from this silent killer" or "As parents of small children, you need to know about the hidden safety dangers lurking in your home"), but remember that you must continue relating the topic throughout your speech to maintain the audience's interest and attention.

Credibility

Throughout this book, we have talked about the importance of establishing and maintaining your credibility. Again, credibility is the degree to which the audience finds you believable and trustworthy. If the audience does not find you to be credible, they will not listen to or hear your message. Credibility is developed throughout the speech-making and giving process. You gain credibility by thoroughly researching and preparing your speech, giving credit to your sources, handling yourself with confidence, and showing the audience that you know what you are talking about.

In the fire captain's speech, he established his credibility by saying, "I have been a firefighter for 22 years and have witnessed first hand the strength that our professional code can give you when your fear and sadness want to creep in." He shows that he has a long history as a firefighter and that he truly believes in the code. Furthermore, he continues expressing his connection to the new firefighters by acknowledging common fears and concerns.

For some non-native speakers, this last part is the hardest to accomplish because you might have come from a culture that discourages explicit references to one's accomplishments or expertise. In the United States, asserting one's expertise and experience is considered appropriate, even necessary. Although less obvious statements of expertise have begun to emerge in public speaking, there is still a strong expectation that you, as the speaker, will let the audience know why they should trust and listen to you. Luckily, this can be a brief statement and can be adapted to your comfort level quite easily: "As a fellow commuter student, I too have experienced the frustration of being late to class due to a lack of parking spaces, and I decided to do something about it."

Thesis

This part is easy. Simply copy your thesis statement from the top of your outline and paste it into Main Point IV of the introduction. Your introduction is done! It should be clear to you now that the introduction invites the audience into the speech, tells them why the speech is important for them to hear, provides a statement that stresses your expertise or interest in the topic, and previews the body of the speech in the thesis.

Clearly, the introduction is crucial for helping the audience become interested in your presentation, but a strong introduction is also beneficial to you as the speaker. When an audience is motivated to listen and feels a connection to the speaker, the speaker can draw energy and confidence from the audience that can carry him or her through the rest of the presentation. A well-planned and thoroughly rehearsed introduction gives you the power and confidence to start your speech enthusiastically; it also motivates your audience to listen more carefully and immediately establishes a rapport between you and the audience.

TABLE 8.5 **Fire Department Professionalism Introduction**

If we were to outline the complete introduction of the fire captain's speech, it would look like this:

Fire Department Professionalism

General Purpose: To inform

Specific Purpose: To inform the newly graduated firefighters about the professionalism in the Los Angeles County Fire Department.

Thesis: The Los Angeles County Fire Department's professionalism can be attributed to its integrity and its dedication to good service.

Introduction

I. I would like to share something with you (show video clip dedication to the New York City Fire Department).

II. In the wake of September 11th, firefighters and fire departments around the country have exhibited their true characters through their dedication to professionalism in the midst of heartrending tragedy and personal loss.

   A. You are now a part of this honorable team.

   B. We expect, the public expects, that you will faithfully follow in this Department's tradition of professionalism.

III. I have been a firefighter for 22 years and have witnessed first hand the strength that our professional code can give you when your fear and sadness want to creep in.

IV. The Los Angeles County Fire Department's professionalism can be attributed to its commitment to integrity and its dedication to good service.

Now that you have prepared an outstanding introduction, refine it by practicing with as few notes as possible until you feel comfortable giving your introduction with energy and power.

Conclusions

Conclusions are, in some ways, the opposite of introductions. Whereas the introduction draws the audience into the speech, the conclusion leads them out. Whereas the introduction previews, the conclusion summarizes; and whereas the introduction gains attention, the conclusion sends them away with something to think about. As Aristotle said, "The introduction sets the mood or tone for the speech. The conclusion brings everything together in one final point or appeal." Conclusions do the following:

I. Signal the end of the speech.
II. Briefly summarize the body of the speech.
III. Leave the audience with a memorable impression.

The main points in the conclusion do not have to come in this exact order, in contrast to the main points in the introduction, as long as all three goals are met.

TABLE **8.6 Outline of a Conclusion**

Conclusion
I. In conclusion, Kahlil Gibran wrote, "When you love you should not say, 'God is in my heart,' but rather, 'I am in the heart of God,'" so too, I believe.
II. From cuddling with my rabbit, to holding a sick friend's hand, to caressing the faces of my children, love has delivered me into the heart of God.
III. In your travels through life, I hope to find each of you in the heart of God as well.

WHAT OTHERS SAY

My knowledge on how to organize papers, arguments and speeches in my country is actually a lot similar to the way it's done here in the U.S. You're not encouraged to begin with an "attention getter" but you definitely need them somewhere in the speech. The good attention getter in my country would be an "illustration or dramatic story," "little known facts or statistics," and "complimenting the audience." A usual conclusion would be restating the purpose of your speech and a good conclusion would involve making your audience go a certain direction. The only difference that I could find was that of the "attention getter" where in my home country of Chile you rarely use the one where you ask the audience a question when introducing the topic.

Daniel Oleas, Chile

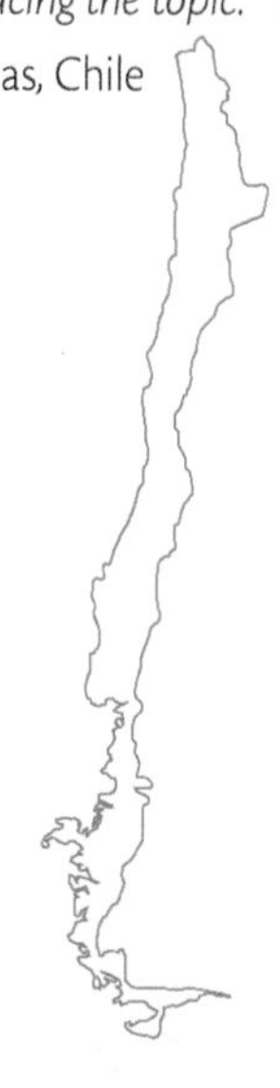

Signaling the End

The first objective of the conclusion is to smoothly move the audience out of the body of the speech and toward the end of the speech. No one likes to hear a speech end unexpectedly with, "That's it" or "I'm done." To move the audience toward the conclusion you can say, "In conclusion," "Before I end," "On a final note," or "To conclude." Say something that clearly tells the audience that you are done with the body of the speech and are almost done speaking. This often helps the audience refocus their attention and listen carefully for your concluding remarks.

Briefly Summarize

Before your final words, you should summarize your speech for the audience. This should go beyond restating your thesis statement; you should also include the additional information that you revealed in the body of the speech. Summaries are typically no longer than three sentences and are often only one sentence long. Your goal is to review the information one last time to reinforce your thesis and main points:

> As we can see from the stories of Allison, Emily, and Ashley, the challenges of being a teenage girl range from the fear of social ostracism to a lack of self-esteem to the everyday challenges of managing school, work, and family.

End with Impact

The final words of your speech should leave the audience with something to think about, do, or consider. This is your last chance to impress upon them the importance of your topic or to ask them to take action. You can use many of the same techniques that you use to develop an attention getter. You can use quotations, refer back to the introduction, ask a question, or provide a

A powerful and clear ending lets the audience know when to applaud and with what degree of enthusiasm.

dramatic statement. For example, Nelson Mandela concluded his acceptance speech for the Nobel Peace Prize in 1993 by saying:

> Let the strivings of us all prove Martin Luther King Jr. to have been correct, when he said that humanity can no longer be tragically bound to the starless midnight of racism and war.
>
> Let the efforts of us all prove that he was not a mere dreamer when he spoke of the beauty of genuine brotherhood and peace being more precious than diamonds or silver or gold.
>
> Let a new age dawn![12]

THE SPEAKING OUTLINE

Now that you have created a thoughtful, well-researched, and organized preparation outline, you need to know that this is *not* the outline you will be using when you actually give your speech. The preparation outline is for *preparation*. It prepared you to give your speech, to organize your ideas, and to include all the supporting material and references you worked so hard to gather. However, if you were to use that outline to actually give your speech, you would find yourself reading instead of talking to the audience. That is not fun for anyone. If you can read your speech, so can the audience. Why not just make copies and hand them out instead of standing up in front of your audience and talking to them?

When I tell my students that they must speak using only one side of one page for notes, most of them panic. They think they can't do it. They plan to memorize the speech or think that they can "sneak" extra notes up to the lectern. If these thoughts are running through your head, relax. You *can* do this. A speaking outline is your friend. More often than not, students report being amazed at how easy the speaking outline actually made giving the speech. After the initial insecurity, they find that not being tied to specific words and not having to remember everything word for word actually made giving the speech easier because they could focus on what they wanted the audience to know and not on saying it "exactly right." Think of it this way: If you were going to call your parents to ask to borrow money, you would probably plan what you wanted to say before picking up the phone. You might even rehearse a dozen times what you plan to say, each time a little different from the time before. When you finally call, you adapt and adjust your message to the moment. You say it differently from how you practiced it, but you still cover all the important points. Giving a speech using a speaking outline is surprisingly similar to that.

The speaking outline is a shorthand version of your speech: It includes the same lettering and numbering but not all the words. A speaking outline is also called a *keyword outline* because it contains only keywords or trigger words to help you remember what you want to say and when you want to say it. The keyword or speaking outline is what makes extemporaneous speaking so powerful. By eliminating most of the words and phrases, the speaker is forced to come up with the exact wording of the speech the moment he or she is speaking the words—just like in natural, spontaneous conversation. Additionally, because there are only a few words to focus on, the speaker can engage in more eye contact, respond to audience feedback, and include new information as needed.

Don't worry: In making the speaking outline, you won't lose everything you planned to say, just the words you don't need! You will be allowed to keep your thesis statement and your quotes, statistics, and cues to help you stay focused.

Creating a speaking outline is easier if you have been using a computer for your preparation outline. If you have been using a computer, do a *Save as* and work from the new document (I usually name the document "title.speaking.doc"). If you are not using a computer, be sure to re-create the same format for your new outline as you had for the original. Keep the original preparation outline because you will need it later. Keep the title at the top of the page, but erase your name and class information, the general and specific purpose statements, and the thesis at the top of the page. Keep the identifiers *Introduction, Body,* and *Conclusion.* Delete the works cited page.

Beginning in the introduction, eliminate all but one to three words of each main point and subdivision. Occasionally you will need a few more words, especially if you are condensing the subpoints into a main point. The idea is to use as few words as possible to remind yourself of what you need to say without giving yourself all the words to say it. Remember to keep quotations complete (you need to quote others accurately). DO NOT change the numbering or lettering or how any of the speech is aligned. You want to maintain the visual representation you built to help yourself remember your ideas and how they fit together. You may keep your first sentence, thesis, transitions, and last sentence if necessary. You will find an example of a speaking (keyword) outline at the end of this chapter.

A speaking outline is most useful if it is formatted to look the same as the original outline, but feel free to enlarge the font to make it easier to read from a distance. Add in any "stage cues" you think might help you, such as "slow down," "pause here," "make eye contact," "show visual," etc. Ideally, the speaking outline for a five- to seven-minute speech should fit on one side of one sheet of paper. However, different instructors have different expectations regarding the length of a speaking outline. Ask your instructor what your outline's length should be.

USING NOTE CARDS

Some instructors prefer that students use note cards instead of a speaking outline. If that is the case, think of each note card as representing a main point. You can have one note card for the introduction, one for each main point, and one for the conclusion. That is, if your speech has three main points, you should have no more than five note cards.

When writing the note cards, follow the same guidelines as you did to create a speaking outline. Maintain the outline structure, but reduce each line to three words or fewer, keeping the important quotes and statistics. Number and label each card clearly in case they become mixed up (see Figure 8.1). That way, you can easily find your place.

When you begin your speech, hold the note cards low and in one hand. Lift them just enough to see them (waist level is best) and do not hold them up in front of your face. As with the speaking outline, you should practice using your note cards until you feel comfortable enough to be able to talk naturally and maintain eye contact while giving your speech.

TABLE 8.7 **Guidelines for Creating a Speaking (Keyword) Outline**

- If possible, create the speaking outline from a *Save as* of the preparation outline.
- Maintain the same visual format as the preparation outline (keep all the same numbering and lettering).
- Eliminate unnecessary components (i.e., student information, general purpose and specific purpose, works cited page).
- Reduce the number of words to fewer than three per point.
- Make the speaking outline clear and legible.
- Include delivery/stage cues.
- Practice, practice, practice using the speaking outline.

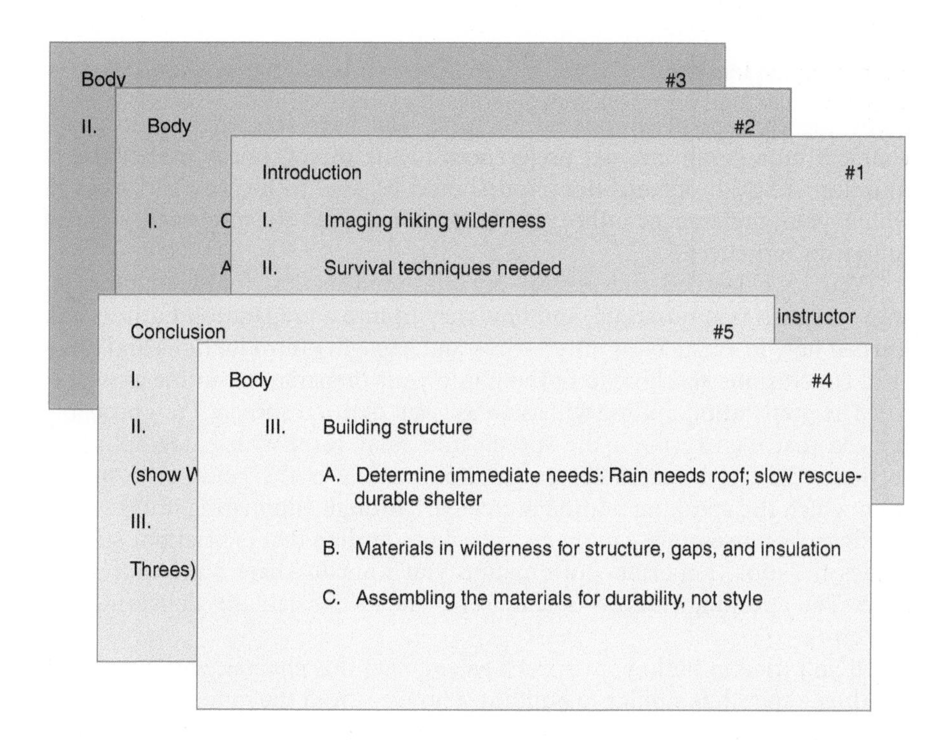

FIGURE **8.1** Sample Note Cards
Numbering your note cards will help you find your place should they become mixed up.

PRACTICE

The best way to practice an extemporaneous speech involves both the preparation outline and the speaking outline. After you have created both outlines, practice your speech no more than *three* times using your preparation outline. Practice out loud, standing up, and in front of a mirror starting from the *very first time.*

The first time you practice the speech, just try to say the entire speech as naturally as possible and while looking at yourself as much as possible in the mirror. During the next two practices, change the wording found on the page. Even if you change only a few words, get comfortable adjusting your words as you practice. Once you have practiced from the preparation outline three times, put it away—far away, so that you are not tempted to look at it while you continue practicing with the speaking outline.

Practice with your speaking outline as many times as you like. In fact, you should practice in a variety of settings, for friends and family, and while using your presentation aids. Practice several times by making yourself talk even if you can't remember what the original outline said. Simply focus on the message and use your keywords to remind yourself what is important. Chapter Twelve offers more practice and rehearsal techniques for refining your delivery. Remember that each time you practice your speech, say it a little differently. This will make presenting your speech much easier.

SUMMARY

Using the concept of contrastive rhetoric, you have learned how to adapt your culture's organizational preferences to the direct, linear preference of American English organization. You should be able to identify the areas in which your preferences either match or differ from the preferred style of American audiences.

You have learned the several organizational styles, for what types of speeches each is appropriate, and how they fit into a preparation outline. You learned how to create clear, interesting, and engaging introductions and powerful conclusions and how to fit them into your preparation outline as well.

The preparation outline will serve as your "written speech." You probably noticed that we never put the speech into essay form with paragraphs and sections. That is because the preparation outline is the completed speech from which the speaking outline is created. Through eliminating unnecessary words and phrases, you can make a speaking outline that is brief but still includes the most important information you want to share with your audience. The speaking outline is your set of notes for actually delivering the speech.

If you tried to build your speech as you read this chapter, you found that building a speech is similar to building a house—from the foundation of your specific purpose and thesis statement to the structure of the body to the windows and doors of the introduction and conclusion. If you have included all these components and put them together in a logical, clearly connected manner, your speech should be well constructed, solid, and easy to follow.

Discussion Questions and Activities

1. In this chapter, we discussed contrastive rhetoric. Get into a group with three of your classmates, and discuss what you know about the rhetorical styles in your home countries. What is the preferred style for organizing papers, arguments, and speeches in your home countries?
2. Outlining is highly stressed in English composition and public speaking classes in the United States. Write a brief essay on your prior experiences with outlining (if you have any). Were you encouraged to start with an "attention getter"? What was considered a good attention getter? A good conclusion? How did you move from one point to the next? How is outlining in your native country different from the way it is taught in the United States?
3. Which organizational pattern would be best suited for each of the following specific purpose statements?
   - To inform my classmates about the development of mariachi music in Mexico.
   - To inform my classmates about three of Picasso's most famous paintings.
   - To inform my classmates about how to make festive holiday picture frames.

- To persuade my classmates that instituting a $100 parking permit lottery is the best solution to the parking problem on campus.

4. After you have completed a first draft of your preparation outline, get together with three or four of your classmates, and go over each other's outlines. Proofread the outlines according to the guidelines provided in this chapter for creating effective outlines and organizing main points, introductions, and conclusions.
5. Consider everything you have learned in this and the three previous chapters. In what ways are the ideas and concepts similar to how you have been taught in the past to research, develop ideas, organize, write, or create speeches? In what ways are they different? Do you feel that there are cultural differences that influence the ways in which people create texts? Why? Why not? What other factors influence the manner in which one develops ideas into texts (whether written or spoken)?
6. As a class, choose a topic that everyone knows something about (e.g., local restaurants, cars, campus issues). Go around the room and have each student supply one fact pertinent to the topic. Then, as a group, arrange the facts into related sets. When the sets are of relatively equal size, write a main point for each set. Combine the main ideas of the various sets and write a thesis statement that ties the main points together. Outline a speech using the thesis, main points, and individual facts (supporting material) generated by the class.

Chapter Quiz

Matching

Place the letter of the term on the line next to the proper example.

a. Goal of the introduction **b.** Goal of the conclusion **c.** Chronological pattern

d. Problem-solution pattern **e.** Topical pattern **f.** Causal pattern

1. ______ An organizational pattern that has two main points: one that identifies the cause of a problem and one that identifies the effect of a problem.
2. ______ An organizational pattern that divides a topic into logical and consistent subdivisions.
3. ______ A speaker must establish his/her credibility.
4. ______ An organizational pattern that follows time or sequence order.
5. ______ A speaker must provide something for the audience to think about.
6. ______ An organizational pattern that has two main points: one that identifies a problem and one that identifies a way to solve the problem.
7. True or false: Before creating a speaking outline, it is best to create an essay from the preparation outline.
8. True or false: The speaking outline can include complete quotations, statistics, and the thesis statement.

9. Introductions and conclusions are important to speeches because
- **a.** they contain the content of the speech.
- **b.** they explain the thesis.
- **c.** they satisfy many goals and reinforce the key ideas.
- **d.** they help the rest of the speech make sense.

10. What is the primacy and recency effect?
- **a.** The idea that what audiences hear first and last has more impact than what they hear in the middle of a speech.
- **b.** The idea that the logic of human beings is derived from primates.
- **c.** The impact of presidential elections on the population.
- **d.** None of the above.

Sample Preparation (Full-Sentence) Outlines: Analyze the following speech outlines according to the guidelines set forth in this chapter for effective introductions, bodies, and conclusions. What organizational patterns did the authors use? What other evidence and research might they have included to make their speeches more interesting and credible? Are the speeches well adapted for a college audience? Were the sources properly cited? Is the Works Cited page done correctly according to MLA format?

Sample #1: Farah Pahlavi by Channelle Khoubian

General Purpose: To inform

Specific Purpose: To inform my classmates about Farah Pahlavi, the empress of Iran.

Thesis: Throughout her life as a well-known Iranian icon, Farah Pahlavi has played a great role in Iranian culture and the emancipation of women.

Introduction

I. "My strength, the power I wielded was, in one way or another, passed on to all Iranian women. During our time my Iranian sisters, formerly regarded as second class citizens, without the right to be heard, became more vocal and aware of their rights" (Pahlavi 16).
  A. This quote was written by Farah Pahlavi, who was reflecting on her accomplishment of emancipating Iranian women.
  B. Before her existence, Iranian women were suffering oppression.

II. How many of you know any Persian women?
  A. If you do, they will tell you the significant impact that Pahlavi has played in their lives.
  B. She has played a significant role in my life as well as my mother's, grandmother's, and even my great-grandmother's.

III. I have recently become more interested in learning about Pahlavi, and I even attended a conference she was holding here in Los Angeles.

IV. Farah Pahlavi is a well-known Iranian icon who played a role in shaping the culture of Iran and in emancipating the women of Iran.

(Transition: Let's begin by taking a closer look at her life.)

Body

I. Pahlavi has led a very fulfilling, yet heartbreaking life.
   A. According to the website IranChamber.com, Pahlavi had a very strict, education-filled childhood.
      1. She was born in Tehran on October 14, 1938, to Sohrab and Farideh Diba.
      2. Her father, Sohrab Diba, an Iranian Army officer and a law graduate of the Sorbonne, died when she was only nine years old.
      3. Her mother, Farideh Diba, took a huge interest in her education and she attended Tehran's Jeanne d'Arc and Razi schools, and then the Ecole d'Architecture in Paris.
      4. She studied there up to the time of her marriage to the Shah, Mohammad Reza.
   B. She met the Shah during a visit with the Iranian ambassador in France.
      1. Upon meeting the Shah she complained that the restrictions and regulations on Iranian currency complicated life for students studying abroad.
         a. The second time she met the Shah, he proposed to her and she accepted.
         b. They were married in Tehran on December 21, 1959.
         c. The couple had four children: Reza II, Farahnaz, Alireza, and Leila between 1960 and 1970.
      2. After the revolution of 1979, Pahlavi escorted her husband in exile.
         a. She stood by his side until his death on July 27, 1980.
         b. Her youngest daughter, Leila, recently committed suicide.
   C. She currently lives in France and Connecticut in the United States.
      1. She recently wrote a book about her marriage to the Shah, An Enduring Love: My Life with the Shah—A Memoir.
      2. The public has received this book very well.
      3. It is what actually inspired me to write this speech.

(Transition: During her reign, Pahlavi did many great things, including being a leader in the promotion of culture.)

II. As empress, Pahlavi was committed to the promotion of culture and social welfare.
   A. She led or participated in more than twenty educational, health, cultural, and charity organizations.
      1. Her work was not only through these organizations, but also through hands-on interaction with the people of Iran by frequently visiting even the most remote parts of Iran.
         a. By doing this, she obtained firsthand knowledge.
         b. She learned about the life, the challenges, and the aspirations of the farmers and other ordinary people.

2. Not only did she accompany her husband, the Shah, to every official visit abroad, she visited many foreign countries around the world on her own.
   a. Keep in mind, this was at a time when women didn't have many rights and it was uncommon for Iranian women to travel without their husbands.
   b. It was also at a time when it was uncommon for women to be involved in politics or foreign affairs.
3. Many of Iran's cultural and art movements of the last century can be attributed to Pahlavi's deep interest and involvement in the arts.
   a. As she attended exhibits and performances, other Iranians followed.
   b. She actively and successfully supported up-and-coming Iranian artists, specialized museums, and the preservation of ancient art collections.

(Transition: Her proudest accomplishment was the emancipation of Iranian women.)

III. Empress Pahlavi also pursued her interest in the emancipation of women.
   A. Before her reign, Iranian women had few rights.
      1. They were expected to be dutiful wives and mothers, but little more.
      2. She says, "It was hard to forget that, as a woman, my position was a delicate one. We were in a country where tradition was strong, in which many men could not yet accept unreservedly the same freedoms for women which they considered perfectly natural for themselves" (farahpahlavi.com 2006).
      3. As she set an example of what women were capable of during her reign, women increasingly became included in all spheres of society including the government.
         a. Women filled important offices in all areas of the administrations.
         b. Women could now be Parliament deputies, senators, ministers, ambassadors, lawyers, even judges.
         c. In addition, the King granted increased social and political rights including suffrage (ibid.).
   B. The increased inclusion of women coupled with the economic, social, and suffrage reforms occurring in Iran deeply altered the Iranian society with regard to women.
      1. She proved that women could have successful careers, serve society generously, and be homemakers all at the same time.
      2. Her purpose was to give women confidence and courage to raise themselves out of the subservient position.
      3. Although there are still many more changes to be made, Pahlavi helped pave the road and opened the doors for the newly empowered generation after her.

4. Though she was the First Lady of Iran, she considered her "importance to be measured only by the practical effect of what I accomplished for the improvement of our people" (Pahlavi 2006).

Conclusion

I. I hope all of you were able to see what an amazing woman Farah Pahlavi truly is.
II. The great changes she made in Iran and the Iranian culture are appreciated today, after almost twenty-seven years and an entire revolution.
III. I know that I am especially appreciative of what she did for the emancipation of Iranian women.

Works Cited

Empress Farah Pahlavi (Diba): A Promoter of Art and Women's Emancipation. 5 Apr. 2006 <http://www.iranchamber.com/personalities/fdiba/farah_diba.php>.
Pahlavi, Farah. An Enduring Love: My Life with the Shah. New York: Random House, 2000.
Pahlavi, Farah. "A Few Facts About Women in Iran." Official Site of Empress Farah Pahlavi. 2006. 2 Apr. 2006. <www.FarahPahlavi.org>.

Sample #2: Survival of the Fittest . . . Structure, by Nate Brown

Topic: Building a shelter in the wilderness

General Purpose: To inform

Specific Purpose: To inform my classmates about how to build an effective and comfortable shelter.

Thesis: To build a comfortable and effective shelter in the wilderness, it is important to choose a proper location, to prepare the ground, and finally to erect a structure.

Introduction

I. Imaging you are hiking or traveling through some wilderness area.
   A. You are having a great vacation until something goes wrong and you can't get out.
   B. Imagine being stuck in the desert or in the mountains.
      1. It is cold and snowing, or hot and dry.
      2. You have no immediate hope for being rescued.
      3. How will you survive until a search party finds you?
II. It is important to know some basic survival techniques because you can't always count on having some protective shelter to keep you safe, so knowing some simple shelter building techniques can save your life.
III. I was trained in survival techniques in my Army basic training.
   A. I also was an outdoor recreation major in college and studied survival skills extensively.
   B. I eventually became a teacher's aid and assistant instructor in that program, and then in survival programs outside of the college environment.

IV. In order to build a comfortable and effective shelter in the wilderness, it is important to choose a proper location, to prepare the ground, and finally to erect a structure.

(Transition: Let's begin by finding the right spot!)

Body

I. The first step in building a shelter is to choose a good location.
  A. Imagine a great shelter that gets flooded because it is in a dry riverbed or is blown away because it is exposed to the wind; therefore choosing a wise location could make the difference between life and death.
    1. Because one of the greatest threats in a survival situation is exposure to the cold, you want to choose a location that will avoid unnecessary coldness.
    2. You can avoid unnecessary cold by choosing your location at least one hundred feet above the valley floor. (Show visual: Thermocline)
      a. Since cold air sinks and warm air rises, the lower into a canyon or valley you are, the more cold air you will feel.
      b. At about one hundred feet above the floor is the first thermocline transition, where it may be at least ten degrees warmer.
  B. Being too cold can also occur with wind exposure, so choose a location for your shelter that avoids high wind areas. (Show visual: Typical wind flows)
  C. If you have chosen a location away from the threats of the cold air, you can also increase your chances of survival with a couple of other tips.
    1. Large boulders collect warmth from the sun all day, and then radiate that warmth at night, so a shelter next to one will be warmer.
    2. In any environment, when water falls, it will take certain predictable paths to lower ground—obviously, keep your shelter away from those paths of water drainage.

II. Once you have chosen a great location for your shelter, you need to do some preparation on the ground.
  A. The bare ground is actually very cold and will suck the warmth out of your body, so you need to lay down some insulating material.
    1. Pine needles, especially long pine needles, are a great form of insulation.
    2. Collect them from under trees until you can lay down about two feet of them on your shelter floor.
    3. The needles will compact significantly, so two feet at the beginning is necessary.
  B. Although warmth is obviously the most important part of the shelter, there is no reason why it cannot also be somewhat comfortable.
    1. Comfort leads to a positive attitude, which leads to greater chance of survival.
    2. To create a more comfortable shelter, you can contour the ground for your body shape.

a. The neck and the lower back need support.
b. That support can easily be created in a shelter by building bumps in the ground where your neck and back will be (show visual of body bump locations).
3. The needed size of these comfort mounds can be gauged by using the handwidth rule. (Show visual of handwidth rule.)

(Transition: You have a great location and a properly prepared floor, so now the only thing missing is the structure.)

I. Before erecting your shelter, you need to determine your immediate needs and the materials you can use.
A. First, you need to determine your immediate needs.
1. If there is a possibility of rain, you need a decent roof to keep the water away from your body.
2. If you feel that you will not be rescued within two days, then you should consider a more durable shelter that will help you survive longer.
B. The materials needed for building the structure can be found all around you in the wilderness.
1. Branches can be used to create the frame, walls, and roof of the structure.
2. Grass, branches, and leaves can be used to seal gaps and add insulation.
C. Assembling the materials is the last step.
1. Keep in mind that wind can be a strong force.
a. You don't want to have all your hard work blown away in the middle of a cold and rainy night.
b. If wind is a threat, erect a more stable shelter by using larger branches and thicker materials that have more weight.
2. Finally, remember that you are not being judged on style.
a. Keep the shelter simple.
b. If it keeps you safe from the wind, rain, and cold ground, then it is doing its job.

Conclusion

I. So you can see that in a survival situation, a little knowledge about location, ground preparation, and structure building can make the difference between freezing to death and surviving until you are rescued.
II. These skills I have covered are very basic.
A. If you want to learn some more advanced survival skills, I recommend the materials sold at the Hoods Woods survival school at www.survival.com (show web page image).
B. Through their video series, you can learn everything from catching fish with your hands to starting fire with nothing but sticks.
III. There are many threats to one's survival.
A. Remember that shelter may not be your immediate need.

B. In any survival situation, it is important to remember the Rule of Threes (show visual: Rule of Threes): You can live three minutes without air, three hours without shelter, three days without water, three weeks without food, and depending on your dating experiences, you can live three months without love.

Sample Key Word Outline from "Survival of the Fittest . . . Structure"

Introduction

I. Imaging hiking wilderness
II. Survival techniques needed
III. Me: Army basic training, outdoor recreation, assistant instructor
IV. To build a comfortable and effective shelter in the wilderness, choose proper location, prepare the ground, and erect a structure.

Body

I. Choose good location.
  A. Life and death: greatest threat; thermocline (show visual aid of thermocline)
  B. Avoid high wind (show visual of typical wind flows)
  C. More tips: boulders and water drainage
II. Preparation of ground
  A. Bare ground sucks warmth: pine needles
  B. Comfort greater survival: contour ground to body (Visual: body bump locations) and handwidth rule (Visual: handwidth rule)
III. Building structure
  A. Determine immediate needs: Rain needs roof; slow rescue—durable shelter
  B. Materials in wilderness for structure, gaps, and insulation
  C. Assembling the materials for durability, not style

Conclusion

I. Little knowledge can save you
II. Skills here basic: advanced survival skills www.survival.com (show web page image).
III. Immediate needs and Rule of Threes (show visual of Rule of Threes)

Chapter 8 Quiz Answers

1. f, 2. e, 3. a, 4. c, 5. b, 6. d, 7. False, 8. True, 9. c, 10 a.

CHAPTER 9 Using American English: A Review

CHAPTER GOAL

By the end of this chapter you will be able to identify and correct several common ESL grammar and language errors.

As a non-native speaker you already know that subtle changes in words, pronunciation, and grammar can impact how others understand us. Clearly, you have studied English grammar and vocabulary extensively, or you wouldn't be in this class, but even if you have studied English for several years, you probably still make some common mistakes simply because no two languages use language the same way. For that reason, this chapter offers some suggestions for improving your overall American English usage in terms of pronunciation, articulation, grammar, and word choice.

PRONUNCIATION AND ARTICULATION

If you are like many language learners, you are probably concerned about your accent and whether or not you are understandable to native speakers. First, you should realize that you are probably clearer than you think because most listeners can adapt quickly to various speaking styles with little trouble. However, when hearing a speech, listeners have less time to adapt and fewer opportunities to ask for clarification, so it is wise for you to spend some time ensuring proper pronunciation and articulation when preparing and practicing your speeches.

WHAT OTHERS SAY

"Sometimes it is hard for me to make certain sounds because Japanese doesn't have sounds that English has. For example, it is really hard for me to make a difference between "L" and "R" sound, simply because Japanese has only "L" and doesn't have "R" sound, even though we write "R," it is pronounced as "L". . . Moreover, for a non-native speaker, if the sounds don't exist in their native language, the sounds become just a noise for them."

—Riichi, Japan

"Giving a speech is hard, but what makes it hardest is my accent. Even though I know that everyone has an accent, every state has its own accent in the United States, I have been trying to get rid of my accent. Instead of improving other areas of my English, like writing or grammar, I have been trying to improve in an area that will not disappear like I always wanted. Taking speech made me realize that I will always have an accent and I have to accept myself as I am and my life will be easier. My accent is me, and I have to feel proud of it."

—Heiser, El Salvador

Although often used interchangeably, *pronunciation* and *articulation* have slightly different meanings. Pronunciation refers to how accurately one says individual words. For example, the word *February* ("FE-bru-ar-y") is often inaccurately pronounced by both native and non-native speakers as "FEB-u-ar-y" (eliminating the middle *r* sound). Articulation, a subset of pronunciation, refers to how clearly one says words, phrases, or sentences. For example, American English speakers are often accused of mumbling sentences such as: *Watchadoin?* Meaning "What are you doing?" Or *H'arya?* Meaning "How are you?"

Accent is the way in which people from various regions or backgrounds pronounce *and* articulate a given language. Most differences in accents are considered acceptable and are generally understood by others. You do not need to apologize for your accent. As long as you are understandable to the audience and you are using language appropriately and accurately, you can feel confident that the audience will adapt to your accent. Indeed, many people actually enjoy hearing unique and interesting accents. However, if your accent is particularly strong, you may want to practice standard pronunciations of words and phrases to improve listener comprehension. As you already know, small changes in pronunciation can sometimes mean embarrassing changes in meaning. For example, pronouncing *sheet* with a short *i* vowel sound (as in "sit") has a very different meaning than the appropriate long *e* vowel sound (as in "eat").

Dialect refers to a form of a language that has significant vocabulary, grammatical, and pronunciation differences. Dialect differences can create more difficulty in comprehension than accent can. For example, if you were trained in British English, you already realize that there are significant and confusing differences between the American and British varieties of English. Spellings vary (e.g., *color* vs. *colour; analyze* vs. *analyse; encyclopedia* vs. *encyclopaedia*), and the use of some verb forms differs (e.g., *Did you go to the store yet?* vs. *Have you gone to the store yet?* and *has gotten* vs. *has got*). Also, many English word meanings change from their use on one side of the Atlantic to their use on the other. In car terminology alone, the words *boot, lorry,* and *bonnet* in British English refer to the *trunk,* a *truck,* and the *hood,* respectively, in American English. Even within the United States, dialect differences can create comprehension problems due to pronunciation and word usage (see Figure 9.1). By using more formal, standard U.S. American English style, you can avoid most of these problems.

To ensure that you use standard American English pronunciation and word meanings, first check the suggested pronunciation and definition of words in a dictionary. Second, practice saying the word out loud several times to yourself until you feel comfortable saying the word in a sentence. Then, ask a friend, classmate, or teacher to listen to your speech, paying special attention to your pronunciation. Have him/her note any words that he or she

TONGUE TWISTERS

Reciting tongue twisters slowly and carefully can improve both pronunciation and articulation. A wonderful and inexpensive book of tongue twisters is the Dr. Seuss children's classic, *Oh, Say Can You Say* (Random House, 1979). You can find this book online or in any bookstore for under ten dollars.

CONSIDERING LANGUAGE

Sounds of Language

If your native language is:	You may not recognize the English sounds (see International Phonetic Alphabet guide below):	Similar sounds in your language are (notice the different meanings created):
Arabic	[p] as in pill or dip [g] as in got or gone [v] as in vine or strive [ɑ] as in all and caught	[b] as in bill or dib [k] as in cot or con [f] as in fine or strife No similar sound used
Japanese	[r] as in rock or rap	[l] as in lock or lap
Armenian, French, German	θ in thank or thought ð bathe or then	[t] as in tank or taught [d] as in bade or den

Source: Raja T. Nasr. *Applied English Phonology.* (Lanham: University Press of America, Inc., 1997.), 58–59.

FIGURE 9.1 **Dialect Regions of the United States:** Although there is great diversity within each of the dialect regions, the United States can be loosely divided into four general dialect regions.
General Northern: Used in more than half of the United States, this dialect is sometimes referred to as "General American" as well. Born in New England, this dialect began with the first settlers to the United States. The New England version of this dialect is most noted for the way *R*'s are dropped from words such as *park, dark,* and *farm,* which are pronounced *pahk, dahk,* and *fahm,* respectively. As one moves south into New York and west into Chicago and the Midwest, the dialect varies to include several equally distinguishable subdialects. Vocabulary includes *pocketbook* and *supper.*
Midland: Divided into North and South midland, this dialect category was developed primarily by Pennsylvanians moving westward. Other influences include German, Scotch-Irish, and English Quakers. Of particular influence is the grammar of the Pennsylvania Germans known as Pennsylvania Dutch (a mispronunciation of *Deutsch,* meaning "German", marked by a reordering of verb, noun, and prepositional phrases from the standard English construction. For example, instead of saying, "Carry your mother's bags through the door for her," they might say, "Carry your mother through the door her bags." Instead of "Slice a piece of ham with the knife on the counter for Mary," they might say, "Slice Mary with the knife on the counter a piece of ham." Vocabulary in this dialect region includes *dunken, fatcakes, molasses, flapjack, ragamuffin,* and *loophole.*
Western: The most recently settled dialect region in the United States, the Western region dialect is the least distinct and most overlapping of all the regions. In addition to claiming roots in each of the other dialects, this dialect borrows vocabulary from Spanish, cowboy/ranch jargon, surf jargon, and Native American languages (e.g., *adobe, hammock, corral, hightail, lasso, barrio, fiesta, parka, pay dirt, pan out, hang ten, patio,* and *tortilla*).
General Southern: This region encompasses the region that represented the Confederacy during the Civil War. Because it has been historically an agricultural region with little movement even within the region, this dialect has a large variety of subdialects and accents within the larger dialect. Influences contributing to the vocabulary and pronunciation particulars to this region include French, African languages, and Scotch-Irish (e.g., *goober, on account of, fussbox, savannah, Sunday child, catty corner, bad mouth, peruse, jambalaya, armoire, bayou, flitters, praline, greenhorn, kinfolks,* and *funky*).

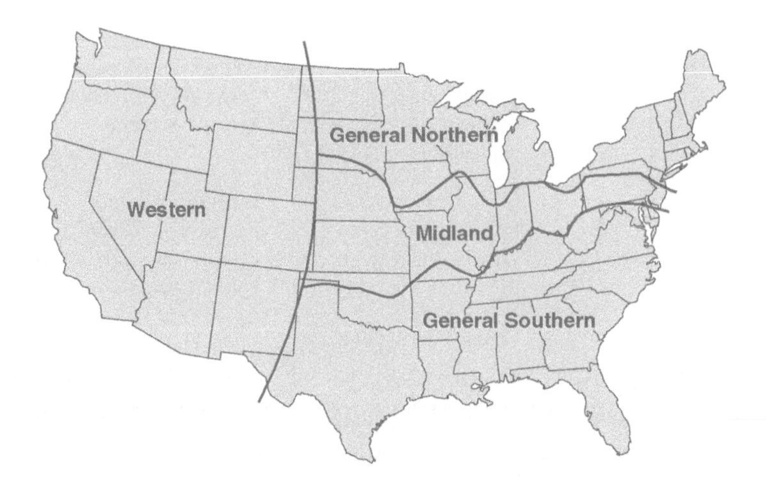

TABLE 9.1 **Pronunciation Guide**

Word	Conventional Phonetic Pronunciation Guide	Standard Dictionary Key	International Phonetic Alphabet
back, that	/a/	\a\	[æ]
father, palm	/ah/	\ä\	[ɑ]
far, mark	/a(r)/	\a\	[ɑr]
flaw, caught	/aw/	\o\	[ɔ]
bake, rain	/ay/	\a\	[eɪ]
less, men	/e/	\e\	[ɛ]
easy, ski	/ee/	\e\	[i]
trip, hit	/i:/	\i\	[ɪ]
life, sky	/i/	\i\	[aɪ]
flow, sew	/oh/	\o\	[o]
loot, through	/oo/	\ü\	[u]
out, how	/ow/	\au\	[aʊ]
boy, coin	/oy/	\oi\	[ɔɪ]
but, some	/uh/	\ə\	[ə]
put, foot	/u/	\u\	[ʊ]
yet, young	/y/	\y\	[j]
chew, chip	/ch/	\ch\	[tʃ]
sing, bring	/ing/	\N\	[ŋ]
shade, ash	/sh/	\sh\	[ʃ]
thick, bath	/th/	\th\	[θ]
this, bathe	/th/	\th\	[ð]

If you have trouble understanding the pronunciation key in your dictionary,

Click Here www.YourDictionary.com

In addition to providing pronunciation keys and definitions, this online dictionary provides audio samples of words pronounced by American English speakers.

TABLE 9.2 **Commonly Mispronounced Words**

Word	Common Mispronunciation*	Correct Pronunciation*
across	a-CRAWST	a-CRAWS
ask	aks	ask
asterisk	AS-tur-i:k	AS-tur-i:sk
athlete	ATH-uh-leet	ATH-leet
business	BI:D-nes	BI:Z-nes
candidate	KAN-i:-dayt	KAN-di:-dayt
comfortable	CUHMF-tur-bul	CUHM-fort-uh-bul
could have	CUD uhf	CUD hav
disastrous	di:-ZAS-tur-es	di-ZAS-truhs
duct tape	DUHK tape	DUHKT tape
electoral	ee-lek-TOR-al	ee-LEK-tor-uhl
escape	ex-SCAYP	es-CAYP
especially	ex-SPE-shuhl-lee; SPE-shuhl-lee	e-SPE-shuhl-lee
espresso	ex-SPRES-oh; ex-PRES-oh	e-SPRES-o
et cetera	ek-SET-ur-uh	et-SET-ur-uh
February	FEB-yoo-ayr-ee	FE-broo-ayr-ee
federal	FED-ruhl	FED-e-ruhl
film	FI:L-uhm	fi:lm
height	hith	hit
hill	hell	hi:l
interpret	i:n-TUR-pre-tayt	i:n-TUR-pret
library	LI-ber-ee	LI-brayr-ee
many	MAY-nee	MEN-ee
nuclear	NOO-kyu-lur	NOO-klee-ur
picture	PI:T-chur	PI:C-chur
prescription	pur-SKRI:P-shun	pri:h-SKRI:P-shun
probably	PRAWB-lee; PRAW-lee	PRAWB-uh-blee
realtor	REE-luh-tur	REEL-tur
pronunciation	pro-NOUN-see-ay-shun	pro-NUN-see-ay-shun
regardless	ir-re-GARD-less	re-GARD-less
says	sayz	sez
supposedly	su-POHS-ab-lee	su-POHS-ed-lee
thanks	taynks	thaynks
think	ti:nk	thi:nk
toward	tohrd	toh-WOHRD
vase	bays	vays
vehicle	BEE-hi:-kul	VEE-hi:-kul
Wednesday	WED-nes-day	WENS-day

*Using conventional phonetic pronunciation guide

did not immediately recognize or understand and point out any words that had unclear or confusing meanings.

Every language starts with a set of sounds called *phonemes*, but not all languages share or use all possible human sounds. Not being familiar with a particular phoneme or how to make its sound correctly can be both frustrating and embarrassing. Classic examples include the *th* (/ θ / and / ð /), /r/, and /l/. These sounds in English have unique pronunciations and do not exist in several other languages. If you encounter this problem, you may substitute the unfamiliar sound with a similar sound from your language (see "Considering Language").[1] Often, this works well for everyday conversation, but for more formal speaking situations you might want to practice difficult English sounds by referring to the pronunciation hints found in Chapter Two.

Below you will find pronunciation exercises to help you with some of the problem sounds. Table 9.1 provides pronunciation keys to help you decipher dictionary pronunciation guides as well as the International Phonetic Alphabet. Additionally, you will find lists of some of the most commonly mispronounced American English words with their proper pronunciation in Table 9.2.

GRAMMAR RULES

Native and non-native English speakers alike sometimes use grammar improperly. Improper use of grammar can confuse your audience and make understanding you more difficult. Some common grammar errors include using double negatives, shifting verb tense, and using pronouns inconsistently. As a non-native speaker of English, you might also have trouble remembering some of the rules of English grammar. Even more common for non-native English speakers is having difficulty remembering the exceptions to the grammar rules. As native speakers of any language, we learn the exceptions and the irregularities of our native language naturally and unconsciously. At a very young age, we know when we or someone else makes a mistake, but we may not be able to tell why it is wrong. Non-native speakers must not only learn a new language's rules but also memorize all the exceptions to those rules to speak the new language properly.

Some of the common problem areas for non-native English speakers include *subject-verb agreement, irregular verbs, articles,* and *prepositions*. In this section, we will not cover all the rules of English grammar but will touch briefly on some of the more common grammatical errors you might make.

HINT

Grammar Guide

If you don't already own one, buy yourself a good English grammar guide to refer to when you are writing or just for review.

Two texts that offer comprehensive reviews of and exercises in English grammar, punctuation and mechanics for both native and non-native English speakers are:

English Grammar in Context, by Kitty Dean (Allyn & Bacon, 2001)

A Writer's Reference, by Diana Hacker (Bedford/St. Martin, 2004).

Double Negatives

Using a double negative means using two words that indicate a negative (i.e., *no, not, never, nothing*). In English, when someone uses two negative words, the meaning of the phrase or sentence becomes positive. For example:

I don't have no talent means *I have talent.* The speaker meant *I don't have any talent.*

I wasn't doing nothing means *I was doing something.* The speaker meant *I wasn't doing anything.*

She doesn't want nothing means *She wants something.* The speaker meant *She doesn't want anything.*

When writing or speaking in English, if you intend to make a sentence negative, include only one negative word.

Verb Tense

Verb tense indicates when an action occurs—whether the action took place in the past, is taking place in the present, or will take place in the future. The most important thing to remember about verb tense is to be consistent. Changing tense can confuse the audience about when events occurred. For example:

CONSIDERING CULTURE

Hopi Language

Beyond helping us understand and be understood in a particular language, grammar is believed to actually shape and reflect a culture's thinking. Theorist Benjamin Whorf illustrated this relationship between culture, language, grammar, and thought by comparing European languages and the language of the Hopi (a Native American tribe) and the worldviews revealed through each.

According to Whorf, "Hopi language and culture conceals a metaphysics, such as our so-called naive view of space and time does . . . yet it is different."* European culture sees a clear distinction between space and time that is evident in the bipolar (either/or) nature of European language. Hopi culture sees the world and all that is in it as more or less relative. This is reflected in Hopi language by the rich vocabulary that reveals subtle differences in things and states of being. He tells us:

> One does not say "It is a hot summer" or "Summer is hot"; summer is not hot, summer is only when conditions are hot, when heat occurs. One does not say "this summer" but "summer now" or "summer recently." . . . Nothing is suggested about time except the perpetual "getting later" of it. And so there is no basis here for a formless item answering to our "time."*

*Benjamin Whorf, "An American Indian Model of the Universe," *Language, Thought, and Reality.* Cambridge: MIT Press 1956, 58.

TRY THIS

Using Negatives

When writing a negative sentence, you should use only *one* of the following negative words:

no	*nothing*	*nobody*	*scarcely*
not	*nowhere*	*no one*	*barely*
none	*neither*	*hardly*	*never*

Using the double negative rule, correct the following sentences where necessary:

You haven't seen nothing yet!

You barely have no time left to finish the exam.

I wish I hadn't left the car door unlocked.

This:

Last year, I did not understand how I could go to school and work at the same time. Just as I was about to give up and quit school, a friend offers me a free room to stay in while I finish the semester, so I take it and moved in right away.

Should be:

Last year, I did not understand how I could go to school and work at the same time. Just as I was about to give up and quit school, a friend offered me a free room to stay in while I finished the semester, so I took it and moved in right away.

© Rick Kirkman & Jerry Scott/King Features Syndicate.

FIGURE 9.2

And:

In the story, the boy is walking to the store to buy some candy for his friend, when suddenly, he saw a dog dash into the street. At the same time, a car swerved around the corner and, before the boy can do anything, the car hits the dog.

Should be:

In the story, the boy is walking to the store to buy some candy for his friend, when suddenly, he sees a dog dash into the street. At the same time, a car swerves around the corner and, before the boy can do anything, the car hits the dog.

Irregular Verbs

Irregular verbs frequently cause English-language learners difficulty because these verbs do not follow the regular English conjugation rules; hence they are *ir*regular. In all languages, native speakers learn the exceptions to the language's rules mostly unconsciously. They can hear what is *right* or *wrong*, but they can rarely explain why they know this. As a non-native speaker, you must simply learn and memorize the exceptions. Following is a quick review of the standard verb forms and some of the more common irregular verb forms. Note that the irregularity of these verbs occurs in the past tense and the past participle only. With the exception of the verb *to be,* these verbs behave regularly in the other tenses.

The standard verb forms are:

Infinitive	To jump
Present Tense	I/you/we/they jump; he/she/it jumps.
Past Tense	I/you/we/they jumped; he/she/it jumped.
Present Participle	I am jumping; you/they/we are jumping; he/she/it is jumping.
Past Participle	I/you/we/they have jumped; he/she/it has jumped.

The irregular verb *to be:*

Infinitive	To be
Present Tense	I am; you/we/they are; he/she/it is.
Past Tense	I was; you/we/they were; he/she/it was.
Present Participle	The present tense of *to be* is used in combination with other verbs to create the present participle (see the standard verb forms above).
Past Participle	I/you/we/they have (talked); he/she/it has (talked).

Other irregular verbs:

TABLE 9.3 Irregular Verb Forms

Infinitive	Past Tense	Past Participle
become	became	become
break	broke	broken
bring	brought	brought
build	build	built
buy	bought	bought
catch	caught	caught
come	came	come
cost	cost	cost
do	did	done
draw	drew	drawn
dream	dreamt	dreamt
drink	drank	drunk
drive	drove	driven
eat	ate	eaten
fall	fell	fallen
feel	felt	felt
find	found	found
fly	flew	flown
forget	forgot	forgotten
get	got	got
go	went	gone
have	had	had
hit	hit	hit
know	knew	known
learn	learnt	learnt
leave	left	left
lend	lent	lent
let	let	let
lose	lost	lost
make	made	made
mean	meant	meant
meet	met	met
pay	paid	paid
put	put	put
read	read	read
ride	rode	rode

(continued)

TABLE 9.3 (*continued*)

ring	rang	rung
run	ran	run
say	said	said
sell	sold	sold
send	sent	sent
shut	shut	shut
sing	sang	sung
sit	sat	sat
sleep	slept	slept
speak	spoke	spoken
spell	spelt	spelt
spend	spent	spent
swim	swam	swum
take	took	taken
teach	taught	taught
think	thought	thought
throw	threw	thrown
understand	understood	understood
wake	woke	woken
wear	wore	worn
win	won	won
write	wrote	written

Infinitive	To become	To draw	To hide	To see
Past Tense	became	drew	hid	saw
Past Participle (have/has)	become	drawn	hidden	seen

If you are unsure about a verb form, consult the irregular verb form chart in Table 9.3 or look up the word in the dictionary. The dictionary lists any irregular forms of verbs; if no forms are listed, you can assume that the verb is regular.

Subject-Verb Agreement

Sometimes when a sentence contains more than one noun, the speaker may match the verb to the wrong noun. The verb must match in both number and person to the subject of the sentence (i.e., who or what the sentence is talking about), not the other nouns in the sentence. For example, *The cups left in the living room needs to be carried into the kitchen* is incorrect. *Cups* does not match *needs*. The sentence should read, *The cups left in the living room need to be carried into the kitchen.*

As in our example, subject-verb confusion happens most frequently in the present tense with the "-s form" of the verb (e.g., *runs* vs. *run*). With only a few exceptions, the -s form of a verb is used when the subject of the sentence is singular, or contains only one person, place, or thing (e.g., *he runs*). Remember, plurals (more than one person, place, or thing) are created by adding an -s or an -*es* to the end of a noun (e.g., *one bird/two birds*), but this is not true with verbs (e.g., *She sings like a bird*). An easy way to remember this is to remember that between the subject and the verb, a sentence should have only one -s at the end of a word. For example:

Singular Subject/Verb	Plural Subject/Verb
She runs.	They run.
The car stops.	The cars stop.
The cat cries.	The cats cry.
Cynthia jogs every morning.	Cynthia and Andre jog every morning.

Exceptions to the -*s rule* include *to be* (see above for the proper present tense forms) and verbs that follow helping verbs such as *may, can, should, would, might,* and *must* (e.g., *may win, can help*), in which case you would use the non-s form of the verb: *She buys* versus *She should buy.* As always, when in doubt check the dictionary or ask a friend, classmate, or your instructor for help.

Pronouns

As you know, pronouns are words that take the place of nouns. Pronouns simplify texts and conversations by limiting how often we repeat recurring nouns. The noun that a pronoun refers to is called the *antecedent* (*ante-* means "before") because the noun usually appears before the pronoun that replaces it. Pronouns can become problematic when the same pronoun seems to refer to two different nouns:

> *Ruby and Madeline went to the movies last night, but she was disappointed that the movie she had wanted to see was sold out.*

In this example, it is unclear to whom *she* is referring—*Ruby* or *Madeline?* In this case, the first *she* should indicate whether the speaker is referring to *Ruby* or *Madeline.*

> *Ruby and Madeline went to the movies last night, but Ruby was disappointed that the movie she had wanted to see was sold out.*

Another common problem with pronouns occurs when the pronoun and antecedent do not agree. If the antecedent is singular, the pronoun must be singular also. This has become an especially common problem in the last twenty years in the United States, as we have moved away from the *universal he* as the generic singular pronoun. In the past, when we wanted to refer to people in general or to a typical member of some group, we would use the group name (e.g., *student*) or *one* to refer to all people as the antecedent, with the singular third-person masculine *he/him/his* as the pronoun. For example:

> *When one decides to pursue a higher education, he must ask himself whether or not he is prepared to accept the challenges and responsibilities a college education demands.*

Today, this is viewed as excluding women, so some speakers choose to use both the masculine and the feminine third-person singular pronouns:

> *When one decides to pursue a higher education, s/he must ask him- or herself whether or not s/he is prepared to accept the challenges and responsibilities a college education demands.*

Because this can sound awkward, some people make the mistake of substituting the singular third person with the *plural* third person, *they*.

> *When one decides to pursue a higher education, they must ask themselves whether or not they are prepared to accept the challenges and responsibilities a college education demands.*

The problem, of course, is that *one* clearly indicates a singular subject.

To avoid this problem, you have three choices. First, you can use both the masculine and feminine third-person singular pronouns together (e.g., *When one applies to a university, s/he must not forget to include the application fee*). It may feel awkward at first, but it is effective and accurate. Another related option is to use either *he* or *she* consistently throughout, but you should notify the audience about what you are doing first (e.g., "To save confusion, I will be using *she* as a generic pronoun").

Another alternative is to move away from the singular altogether and use the first-person plural (i.e., *we/us/our*) or the third-person plural (i.e., *they/them/their*). The first- and third-person plural forms avoid the masculine-feminine problem altogether.

Use:

> *When we decide to pursue a higher education, we must ask ourselves whether or not we are prepared to accept the challenges and responsibilities a college education demands.*

Or:

> *When students decide to pursue a higher education, they must ask themselves whether or not they are prepared to accept the challenges and responsibilities a college education demands.*

Just be sure to use the form you choose consistently. In other words, do not use them interchangeably. Again, the two most important rules to remember about pronouns are that you must indicate to whom the pronoun refers and you must be consistent when using generic pronouns.

Articles—A, An, The

A very common problem that non-native English speakers face is deciding when and how to use articles. This is partly because many languages, such as Korean, Chinese, Japanese, and many Slavic and African languages, simply do not use articles.[2] Hence, many of these speakers eliminate their use of articles altogether when they begin learning English. This can be quite problematic, considering that the use or absence of an article can seriously impact meaning. The difference between *a good book* and *the Good Book* is the difference between any enjoyable book and the Bible, for instance.

Articles are a special kind of adjective that tell us that a noun will follow soon. Choosing when and which article to use can be very confusing if English is not your first language because the rules are confusing and inconsistent. Native speakers learn it *by hearing them used appropriately* as they learn the language, but English-language learners must consciously learn the rules and the exceptions. Luckily, there are only three articles: *a, an,* and *the.* You need to decide only whether a noun needs *a, an, the,* or nothing at all. In any case, native speakers will understand your intent even if you use the articles incorrectly.

To decide when to use *a* or *an* versus *the,* first decide whether the noun is a *count noun* or a *noncount noun.* A count noun is any noun that can be counted, that is, an item that is one of many in a category (e.g., *a car* refers to any car out of all possible cars). A noncount noun refers to something that cannot be counted or that is conceptual or abstract (see Table 9.4). For example, *joy* is a feeling and cannot be counted or divided up. You feel joy, not *a joy.* Use *a* or *an* with singular count nouns and use nothing with noncount nouns. Avoid deciding whether a noun is a count or a noncount noun based

TABLE 9.4 **Count and Noncount Nouns**

Singular Count Nouns (use a or an)	Noncount Nouns (do not require an article)
application	anger
car	communication
eagle	education
garage	garbage
interview	information
king	knowledge
mountain	money
ovation	orange juice
student	snow
washing machine	warmth

*Hint: In English, most count nouns have only a singular form.

on your native language; what is considered a count noun in one language may not be in another.

If you are dealing with a count noun, you must then decide whether you should use *a* or *an*. You use *a* with count nouns that begin with a consonant and *an* with count nouns that begin with a vowel. Look back at Table 9.4. Which count nouns use *a*, and which use *an*? *Hint:* Four of the words use *an*, and the rest use *a!*

To indicate a certain amount with a noncount noun, you can pair it with a count noun:

Noncount Noun	Paired with a Count Noun and an Article
garbage	a bag of garbage
water	a glass of water
bread	a slice of bread
batter	an ounce of batter
joy	a moment of joy

You can use *the* with both singular count and singular noncount nouns when you are referring to a specific item in a category, not the entire category or any item in the category:

The garbage in the bin or *The bag of garbage by the back door*
The water on the steps or *The glass of water on the table*
The bread in the cupboard or *The slice of bread in the toaster*
The batter for the cake or *The ounce of batter in the measuring cup*
The joy of being a parent or *The moment of joy when I became a parent*

Do not use *the* when you mean "in general."

Instead of:

The candles add an ambient glow to any room.

Use:

Candles add an ambient glow to any room.

Like most English grammar and usage rules, there are many exceptions to the rules for using articles, but the specifics would be too comprehensive to discuss here. For now, try to pay attention to how and when native speakers use articles and listen for the exceptions.

Prepositions

Many students have told me that one of the most frustrating and confusing things about speaking English is using prepositions. Prepositions are used with nouns to define and describe the relationship of a noun or pronoun to another part of the sentence. They are abundant and inconsistent in English, and most prepositions have many meanings based on context, so if you were to look one up in the dictionary, you might find a dozen or more definitions for it.

Fortunately, there are only so many prepositions in the English language (fewer than 150, in fact), and of those, only nine prepositions are used most frequently. They are *at, by, for, from, in, of, on, to,* and *with.* Learning how to properly use these nine takes time and, in many cases, requires simple memorization because they often do not follow consistent rules.

Of the nine most common prepositions, *at, by, in,* and *on* tend to be the most problematic. Each can indicate time *or* place. When indicating time, we use *at* to designate a specific time of day: *We can meet at lunch.* We use *by* to indicate a deadline: *You need to finish the report by six o'clock.* We use *in* to indicate that something happens, happened, or will happen during or after a period of time: *I will be there in one week.* The word *on* refers to a specific date or day: *I returned the library books on Tuesday.*

When indicating location, we use *at* to designate a specific place or target: *I will meet you at my house at the corner of Elm and Pine; Trey threw the shirt at Trevor.* We use the word *by* to indicate proximity: *The school is by the big shopping mall downtown. In* specifies a geographic location or an enclosed space: *I will be in Australia over the winter break; put the cup back in the cupboard.* We use *on* to refer to placement on top of a flat surface: *Mary was on*

TABLE 9.5 Seventy-Two of the Most Commonly Used Prepositions in the English Language

about	between	minus	since
above	beyond	near	than
across	but	next	through
after	by	next to	throughout
against	considering	of	to
along	despite	off	toward
amid	down	on	under
among	during	onto	underneath
around	except	opposite	unlike
as	excluding	out	until
as well as	following	outside	up
at	for	over	up to
before	from	past	upon
behind	in	per	versus
below	inside	plus	via
beneath	instead	regarding	with
beside	into	round	within
besides	like	save	without

my street when the accident occurred; place the dish on the counter. Interestingly, we also use *on* to refer to entertainment and electronic media: *The show was on channel twelve; I heard it on the radio; I can get that information on the Internet.* In English we ride *in* cars, taxis, and trucks, but *on* planes, trains, and ships. Unfortunately, you will just have to memorize these!

CHOOSING THE RIGHT WORD

Word choice has a powerful influence on how an audience interprets a message. In Chapter Ten, we will discuss choosing words to increase a speech's impact, to avoid stereotypes, and to make a speech more interesting. Some words sound the same but carry different meanings (homonyms). Some words are very similar in sound and spelling, but carry different meanings (e.g., *blue* and *blew*). Some words have similar meanings and are used improperly. In this section, we will discuss how to avoid these common word choice mistakes.

Words that are often confused are called *word pairs*. Some of these words have related but subtly different meanings (e.g., *infer/imply, lie/lay*). Sometimes they represent different parts of speech (e.g., *affect/effect, council/counsel*). Sometimes they sound similar but actually have opposite or very different meanings (e.g., *explicit/implicit, prescribe/proscribe, elicit/illicit, eminent/imminent, accept/except*). Many word pairs sound the same but are spelled differently (e.g., *you're/your, to/too/two, their/they're/there*). When speaking, the audience will not know the difference. However, be sure to check the proper spelling of these word pairs so that your outline doesn't have any embarrassing word choice or spelling mistakes.

To improve the accuracy of your choice of words, become familiar with the Commonly Confused Word Pairs in Table 9.6. When using any of these words, look up each word and find its meaning and part of speech before using it in your speeches. Over time, you will learn when and how to use each word properly.

SUMMARY

The challenges of writing and delivering a speech may feel magnified by a lack of confidence in speaking American English. Insecurity about your accent or pronunciation can lead to problems of articulation and speaking loudly enough for the audience to hear you. Following the tips about pronunciation and articulation in this chapter will give you the reinforcement you need to clearly deliver your speech to your classmates. Remember, the key to ensuring that you are pronouncing each word correctly is to consult your dictionary and to practice your speech in front of a native speaker. As you practice correct pronunciation, your confidence will increase, and so will your intelligibility.

The grammar rules and all their exceptions can also make it difficult to learn and effectively use the English language. Reviewing the rules of English

TABLE 9.6 **Commonly Confused Word Pairs**

abject/object	bazaar/bizarre	desert/dessert	fatal/fateful
accede/exceed	bias/biased	device/devise	faze/phase
accept/except	biweekly/semiweekly	dilemma/difficulty	fearful/fearsome
actual fact/actually	borrow/loan	dialogue/discuss	fiscal/physical
adapt/adopt	both/each	disburse/disperse	flammable/inflammable
administer/minister	breath/breathe	discreet/discrete	flaunt/flout
advance/advanced	bring/take	discussed/disgust	flesh out/flush out
adverse/averse	by/'bye/buy	disinterested/uninterested	floppy disk/hard disk
advice/advise	cache/cachet	dominate/dominant	flounder/founder
adviser/advisor	callous/callused	done/did	foot/feet
affect/effect	cannot/can not	doubtlessly/doubtless	footnotes/endnotes
alliterate/illiterate	canon/cannon	dove/dived	for/fore/four
allude/elude	capital/capitol	downfall/drawback	for sale/on sale
allude/refer	caramel/carmel	drank/drunk	forceful/forcible/forced
allusion/illusion	carat/caret/carrot/karat	drastic/dramatic	forego/forgo
already/all ready	celibate/chaste	dribble/drivel	formally/formerly
altar/alter	cement/concrete	drier/dryer	fortuitous/fortunate
alternate/alternative	chuck/chunk	drug/dragged	foul/fowl
altogether/ all together	cite/site/sight	dual/duel	gone/went
alumnus/alumni	cleanup/clean up	dyeing/dying	good/well
ambiguous/ambivalent	click/clique	ecology/environment	got/gotten
amoral/immoral	close/clothes	elicit/illicit	grisly/grizzly
amount/number	coarse/course	emergent/emergency	hanged/hung
anecdote/antidote	collaborate/corroborate	emigrate/immigrate	hardy/hearty
angel/angle	compare to/compare with	eminent/imminent/immanent	heading/bound
anxious/eager	complement/compliment	empathy/sympathy	hear/here
apart/a part	continual/continuous	enormity/enormousness	heroin/heroine
appraise/apprise	contrasts/contrasts with	enquire/inquire	historic/historical
apropos/appropriate	council/counsel/consul	ensure/insure	hysterical/hilarious
aspect/respect	credible/credulous	envelop/envelope	idea/ideal
assure/ensure/insure	crescendo/climax	envious/jealous	impertinent/irrelevant
aural/oral	criteria/criterion	epigram/epigraph/epitaph	imply/infer
avocation/vocation	critique/criticize	exalt/exult	install/instill
awhile/a while	defuse/diffuse	exceptional/exceptionable	instances/instants
backslash/slash	degrade/denigrate	expresses that/says that	intense/intensive
barb wire/bob wire	democrat/democratic	fair/fare	interment/internment
bare/bear	depreciate/deprecate	farther/further	Internet/intranet

(continued)

TABLE **9.6** (*continued*)

into/in to	passed/past	reactionary/reactive	social/societal
itch/scratch	pawn off/palm off	real/really	sojourn/journey
it's/its	peace/piece	rebelling/revolting	sometime/some
late/former	peak/peek/pique	rebut/refute	spaded/spayed
later/latter	persecute/prosecute	recent/resent	stationary/stationery
lay/lie	personal/personnel	regard/regards	suit/suite
lead/led	perspective/prospective	regretfully/regrettably	summary/summery
leave/let	phenomena/phenomenon	reign/rein	taught/taut/thought
legend/myth	pole/poll	reluctant/reticent	taunt/taut/tout
less/fewer	populace/populous	repel/repulse	tenant/tenet
lighted/lit	pore/pour	resister/resistor	than/then
like/as if	pray/prey	reticent/hesitant	that/which
loose/lose	precede/proceed	revue/review	they're/their/there
lustful/lusty	precedence/precedents	risky/risqué	though/thought/through
mantle/mantel	precipitate/precipitous	rob/steal	threw/through
marital/martial	predominant/predominate	role/roll	throne/thrown
marital/martial	prejudice/prejudiced	root/rout/route	to/too/two
masseuse/masseur	premier/premiere	sail/sale/sell	toward/towards
may/might	premise/premises	sarcastic/ironic	troop/troupe
maybe/may be	prescribe/proscribe	say/tell	vary/very
medal/metal/meddle/mettle	principal/principle	seam/seem	verses/versus
medium/median	prophecy/prophesy	seen/saw	viola/voila
moral/morale	prostate/prostrate	select/selected	warrantee/warranty
nauseated/nauseous	proved/proven	sense/since	wary/weary/leery
onto/on to	purposely/purposefully	sensual/sensuous	weather/whether
oppress/repress	quiet/quite	service/serve	went/gone
ordinance/ordnance	ran/run	set/sit	were/where
oversee/overlook	rationale/rationalization	setup/set up	who/whom
parameters/perimeters	ravaging/ravishing	so/very	who's/whose

grammar is one way to continually hone your mastery of grammar. However, listening to and speaking English will improve your ear for the language even faster. In addition to your classes, grammar guides, and teachers, television and radio programs and commercials are a good way to identify American English language patterns and conventions. Many students report that watching children's shows such as *Sesame Street* helps them master the rhythm, pronunciation, and grammar exceptions of American English.

Remember, when writing or speaking in formal contexts such as classroom speeches, consult a writing guide and, as always, ask a native speaker to review your work for those common ESL mistakes. Each time you learn or relearn a rule, you are that much closer to eliminating making that mistake in the future.

Discussion Questions and Activities

1. Working in pairs, take turns pronouncing the words in Table 9.2 until you are confident that you are pronouncing each word correctly.
2. Practice saying the following tongue twisters out loud slowly until you can clearly pronounce each sound accurately (have your teacher help you with difficult sounds).
   - I think the then thirsty thing thought that Theo thought that they would thoroughly thank them.
   - Lindsey languished leisurely on the lovely lounge.
   - Robert read really rapidly to the roaring crowd.
3. In a small group, discuss with your classmates some of the problems you and they have experienced regarding pronunciation and articulation. Share suggestions of how each of you has worked to improve.

Chapter Quiz

For each sentence, choose the correct word from the provided choices.

Verb Tense

1. Maria **went/goes** to the store yesterday.
2. Yolanda **has speaking/has spoken** English for three years.
3. Stefano **bought/buyed** a new car for his mother.
4. I **am want/wanted** you to come with me to the carnival.
5. Earlier while we were walking home, I **see/saw** a dog **chase/chasing** a car.

Irregular Verbs

1. Takafumi **drived/drove** his car to school only once last week.
2. Yuliya **said/sayed/says** that she loved taking a speech class.
3. Noa **striked/struck** a bargain with the vendor on the new scarf she wanted.
4. Raul **throwed/threw** a party for all his friends when he graduated.
5. Ozge **has taken/has took** math twice before.

Subject-Verb Agreement

1. I **loves/love** to listen to opera in the morning.
2. Heiser **don't/doesn't** like rock 'n' roll.

3. Shelly **am/are/is** delighted that you **am/are/is** coming to the event.
4. Fai Hon and America **jog/jogs** every morning together.
5. Cassandre or Napoleon **takes/take** the trash out and **turns/turn** out the lights when leaving.

For each sentence below, put the correct word in the blank or leave the blank empty if no word is needed:

Articles: *A, An, The,* or Nothing

1. This is ______ easy question.
2. Please speak ______ little louder.
3. May I have your ______ phone number?
4. I have never seen ______ UFO.
5. May I ask you ______ question?
6. Is there ______ public telephone near here?
7. David is ______ best student in our class.
8. What is ______ name of the next station?
9. He has ______ my car today.
10. I went to ______ sea during my summer vacation.

Prepositions: *While, During, For*

1. He's been working ______ three weeks.
2. I fell asleep ______ the film.
3. Did you see Tom ______ your vacation?
4. We talked ______ an hour.
5. She watched TV ______ I cooked.
6. ______ our stay in London, we visited a lot of museums.
7. What did you do ______ you were in London?
8. I think I need to study French ______ a few months before I go there.
9. I came up with a great idea ______ I was thinking about my class.
10. He was out of work ______ six months before he found a new job.

Prepositions: *At, On, In*

1. The label is ______ the bottle.
2. Jack is waiting ______ the bottom of the stairs.
3. Our seats are ______ the third row.
4. Turn left ______ the light.
5. He's sitting ______ the sofa next to the piano.

6. I met Jack ______ the street.
7. He has a lot of beautiful pictures ______ the wall.
8. I live ______ the fifth floor of my apartment building.
9. We waited for over an hour ______ the bus stop.
10. Who is that woman ______ the photograph?

Correct the following sentences if needed:

Double Negatives

1. I don't want no help with this paper.
2. She never doesn't like to go shopping for clothes.
3. I don't want to not go to the party.
4. She has not eaten anything all day.
5. Mark can't hardly wait to visit his parents.

Chapter 9 Quiz Answers

Verb Tense 1. went, 2. has spoken, 3. bought, 4. wanted, 5. saw, chasing
Irregular Verbs 1. drove, 2. said, 3. struck, 4. threw, 5. has taken
Subject-Verb Agreement 1. love, 2. doesn't, 3. is, are, 4. jog, 5. takes, turns
Articles: A, An, The, or Nothing 1. an, 2. a, 3. blank, 4. a, 5. a, 6. a, 7. the, 8. the, 9. blank, 10. the
Prepositions: While, During, For 1. for, 2. during, 3. during, 4. for, 5. while, 6. During, 7. while, 8. for, 9. while, 10. for
Prepositions: At, On, In 1. on, 2. at, 3. in, 4. at, 5. on, 6. on, 7. on, 8. on, 9. at, 10. in
Double Negatives 1. ~~no~~, 2. ~~never~~, 3. ~~not~~, 4. none, 5. ~~'t~~

CHAPTER 10 Language

CHAPTER GOAL

By the end of this chapter you will be able to identify and employ several language tools appropriately, accurately, and interestingly.

Language is the most powerful tool we humans have at our disposal. Any language both affects and reveals the speaker's position in the world. Language choices can indicate background, attitudes, culture, and occupation. We make language choices every time we open our mouths to speak. Which specific language and words we use and how we put those words together will be influenced by the occasion, the reason we are speaking, the audience to whom we are speaking, and the style of our speaking. In other words, effective speakers tailor their message to the situation. In addition to appropriately adapting our speech to reflect the rhetorical situation, we also need to be certain that our choices accurately express the message we are intending and that we keep the attention and interest of our audience.

The difference between great speeches and average speeches is often how we use language. Using language inaccurately or inappropriately can confuse, offend, alienate, or simply bore the audience. On the other hand, using language well can enhance understanding and message retention. Vague language can be dull and boring, while interesting language can create rhythm, clarity, and vividness. Finding just the right words to convey your message may seem like a job for poets, writers, and professional speakers, but anyone can learn how to use language appropriately, accurately, and colorfully while still staying true to one's own style.

Let's begin with a discussion about the differences between oral and written styles of communication. In this chapter we will focus on how to use language to increase understanding and to avoid confusing or offending your audience. We will also explore some common linguistic devices that can make your speech more interesting and memorable. In addition, we will examine various figures of speech that can both illuminate a topic and alienate an audience, depending on the situation. Throughout the chapter, we discuss some of the particular language challenges that non-native speakers of English face when preparing and delivering a speech in English.

USING LANGUAGE APPROPRIATELY

How do you talk to your professors, your friends, your parents, and your boss? Do you write the same way that you speak? Do you use the same style of communication when you write an essay that you use when you write an e-mail? With whom do you use a formal style? With whom do you use a casual style? Would you use slang or "bad words" during a job interview? Do you use them with friends? Like all other aspects of speech preparation, you need to consider each aspect of the rhetorical situation to be sure that your language choices are appropriate to the context, the audience, the purpose, and you, the speaker. Of course, like all wise public speakers, you will avoid using language that is generally considered inappropriate in any situation.

Oral versus Written Language

Communication in all forms is goal oriented. Whether trying to inform, persuade, or entertain or whether we are in a conversation with friends, writing a formal essay, or making a speech, we create messages for a particular audience in a particular situation with a particular goal in mind. When writing a paper or preparing a speech, we research thoroughly, organize logically, and provide evidence abundantly to support our claims. Although writing, public speaking, and everyday conversation have many similarities, it is important to understand how they differ.

A reading audience has the advantages of being able to reread sections, look up unfamiliar words, and absorb the material at their own pace. For this reason, you may have found that reading a textbook is often easier than listening to a lecture. In oral or spoken communication, the listeners have only one chance to hear the message, especially in public speaking where the audience cannot ask for clarification or seek out definitions. On the other hand, written communication lacks the face-to-face, personal connection of oral communication and the benefit of nonverbal cues that clarify, reinforce, or emphasize the message. Therefore, we strive to make oral communication less complicated, more repetitious, less formal, and more personal than written communication.

Oral communication is less complicated than written communication because audiences have only one chance to understand a message (see Table 10.1). Speakers use simpler, easy-to-understand language and shorter, less complicated sentence structures. Long, complicated sentences and overly academic or technical language make quickly understanding oral language more difficult. Consider the following introductions to the same story on National Public Radio. The first is the oral introduction given over the radio. The second is the written introduction to the same audio story link on the NPR website:

> The Chinese government announced today that former president Jiang Zemin has resigned from his final post as head of the central military commission. The position now belongs to his successor, Hu Jintao. This peaceful transfer of leadership power to a younger generation completes an historic succession.[1]

Compare to:

> China completes its first peaceful leadership change in five decades, as former President Jiang Zemin relinquishes command of the Chinese military. The move completes the transfer of power to current President Hu Jintao, who also leads the Communist party.[2]

WHAT OTHERS SAY

The similarities that I noticed about language use in the United States and Romania is that in both countries public speaking is more conversational than a written paper, but it is more formal than everyday conversation. In a public speech one uses personal pronouns (as opposed to impersonal expressions), questions, active verbs and figures of speech.

The difference between my country and the U.S. is that in Romania you have to be very careful about speaking on the appropriate level of formality because people are VERY sensitive to things like that. There are specific personal pronouns that do not exist in the English language and that one has to use in addressing an audience.

—Gabriela,
Romania

TABLE 10.1 **Spoken versus Written Language**

- Spoken language is less formal than written language.
- Spoken language uses shorter sentences than written language.
- Spoken language uses more repetition than written language.
- Spoken language is more personal than written language.

Notice the simpler phrasing and word choices in the oral introduction: "has resigned," instead of "relinquishes command" and "The position now belongs to . . . " instead of "The move completes the transfer of power to. . . . "

To help the audience retain the message, oral English tends to be more repetitious than written English. If a reader misses an important idea, s/he can go back and reread the text to clarify and remember what the author said. When listening to a speech, however, an audience can neither go back nor ask for clarification in the middle of the presentation. That is why speakers often repeat key ideas several times and in several different ways. As we learned in Chapter Eight, previewing the main points, stating them clearly, providing transitions between the main points, and summarizing them at the end reinforce the main ideas of the speech through repetition.

Oral communication is less formal and more personal than written communication as well. Oral communication offers more direct communication with the intended audience. The speaker can make eye contact with individuals in the audience and can adapt to audience responses. When we speak, we tend to use more contractions such as *don't, it's, there's, isn't,* or *couldn't.* We use interactive wording such as greetings (e.g., *Good afternoon*), polling questions (e.g., *How many of you have ever taken a trip to Hawaii?*), tag questions (e.g., *don't you think?*), direct references to the audience (e.g., *I'm sure you, as students of this grand institution, can agree*), and personal references (i.e., *I, me, our, we, you*). This less formal and more personal approach, which is inappropriate for many types of written communication, allows the speaker to connect with the audience. Speeches that lack this personal connection or strive for too much formality often leave the audience feeling uninvolved, disconnected, or bored. This excerpt from former Hewlett-Packard CEO Carly Fiorina's speech at Tsinghua University is an excellent example of using the less formal and more personal style as well as using repetition and simple, direct language:

> Like any university students, I know for you the road ahead has much uncertainty. But if there is one thing I have learned from the past 20 years in this industry, it is that the principle you have learned inside the walls of Tsinghua is more true outside the university than inside. The principle I am speaking of is this: that great leaders, like great organizations, great companies, and great nations—great leaders are defined not simply by their capabilities, but by their character. Not just by the company they are, but by the company they keep. Not by success alone, but as Tsinghua teaches, with self-discipline and social concern in equal balance.[3]

Do not, however, make the mistake of being too informal and casual when giving a speech or presentation. Although speaking uses a less formal style, public speaking is still a more formal speaking situation than everyday conversation. When giving a speech, you still need to use more proper and formal language than you would use in everyday conversations. You also need to avoid slang, filler words, and incorrect or lazy grammar. You will not gain credibility or respect from your audience by introducing your speech like this:

> You know, I was thinking 'bout the whole global warming thing. You know, the way the earth is getting hotter every year by, like, one-tenth of a degree or somethin'. That might seem like a tiny smidge to you, but it totally adds up! We gotta do something about this or we are gonna be in big trouble. That is why I'm gonna tell you about all the mess that's created by global warming and how you can help stop it.

A more appropriate introduction might sound like this:

> As you have probably heard, the earth is getting hotter. According to the World Meteorological Organization, the earth is warming at a rate of one-tenth of a degree every year. That may not sound like much at first, but that small increase, according to a December 2003 *Newsweek* article, can be enough to wipe out one-third of all species by the year 2050. That is in our lifetime! That is why it is crucial for us to understand the causes and impact of global warming and what we can do to help.

One way to think about how formal your language should be during a speech is to consider how you would speak at a job interview or to a well-respected elder—comfortable, but carefully and respectfully.

Appropriate Language for the Rhetorical Situation

Speeches vary in their level of formality, familiarity, and directness, based on the rhetorical situation.

Formality versus Familiarity

Different venues demand different levels of formality. A house of worship would demand different language choices and speaking styles than a school auditorium. At a church or temple you would probably adopt a more formal, proper, serious style that stresses proper pronunciation and eliminates colloquial language. At the school auditorium, you might lean toward a more casual and relaxed language style. In the former context you might say, "Today, we have come together to celebrate the accomplishments of one of our own." In the latter, you might say, "It's great that so many of us could come out to celebrate the work of one of our own."

The occasion of the speaking event and your personal goals for the presentation also have an impact on formality and familiarity. Imagine giving a speech at a birthday party, a graduation, a sales presentation, a political rally, or a funeral. How would you adapt your language style to fit each of these different occasions? What would you be trying to accomplish? Would you want to create excitement, set a particular mood, honor the past, motivate for the future? Clearly, the level of formality, tone, and familiarity you would use would vary significantly from one occasion and purpose to another.

The size of the audience, the audience's expectations for the event, and the audience's level of familiarity and comfort with you, the speaker, also affect the types of language choices you will make in writing your speech. In general, the larger the audience, the more formal the language style you should use. As the audience grows in size, you will be expected to be less personal and familiar with the audience and to use a more proper style.

Finally, choose language that is appropriate for you. Do not try to use a level of formality with which you are unfamiliar and uncomfortable. When called upon to use a more formal style, use *your* more formal style. Aim to speak well, but use words that are familiar to you and that have meanings you are sure of. A mistake some speakers make is trying to sound "smart" or "sophisticated" by using a language style that they are not comfortable using. The result is that they look less smart and less sophisticated. Again, consider how you naturally adjust your communication style based on the different everyday contexts in which you speak—meeting friends at a fast food restaurant, meeting with your professor about a grade, or applying for a job.

Inappropriate Language

There are some language choices that are usually, if not always, inappropriate, such as sexist or racist terms, profanity, and slang. Most native speakers are familiar with these words and the inappropriateness of using them under any circumstances, especially in public speaking contexts. As a non-native speaker, you may not realize that some of these terms are, at best, inappropriate or offensive and, at worst, can be viewed as cruel or dangerous.

Sexist/Racist/Heterosexist

What is the least offensive way to refer to people who have very dark skin and black, curly hair? People with brown skin and brown eyes? People who speak Spanish? People who are romantically attracted to others of the same sex? People who are unable to see or hear or are in a wheelchair? Many people feel awkward and uncomfortable when they must choose a term that identifies a particular group of people by their physical attributes or a social category. This is often because racial and social categories are inaccurate and potentially demeaning and can lead to stereotyping, discrimination, and oppression. Any term that puts down, harms, or belittles others is called an *epithet*. Common epithets directed at individuals include *jerk*, *loser*, or *idiot*.

Effective and well-respected communicators avoid using these terms in any context. In place of these hurtful terms, choose terms that show respect for others. There are culturally sensitive and inclusive terms we can use when speaking about people from specific ethnic, social, or cultural groupings that are more likely than others to be received well; but it seems that what is considered the "right" term keeps changing, so how do you know which terms to use and when?

First of all, before choosing a term, ask yourself if identifying someone by a racial, gender, or social category is even appropriate. Many times we identify someone or a group of people unnecessarily. This can be offensive in and of itself. For example, it used to be common practice on the evening news to hear statements such as:

> A convenience store was robbed at gunpoint last night by three African-American men, believed to be in their late teens, whom authorities have arrested.

In this case, by identifying the race of the suspects, the speaker highlights and perpetuates the stereotype that blacks/African-Americans are criminals. If the authorities had still been seeking the suspects and were asking for the public's help, a description of the suspects that included their race would have been appropriate. However, this story did not necessitate a reference to race because the suspects were already in custody. Additionally, in the past it was common practice *not* to mention the race of suspects, in custody or not, if they happened to be white/European-American.

Similarly, it is usually unnecessary to say *woman doctor, male nurse,* or *policeman/policewoman.* In each case, the sex of the person is most likely irrelevant. We often use a signifying category to highlight or point out that some-

TABLE 10.2 **Inclusive and Sensitive Language**

Least	**More**	**Most**
husband/wife	spouse	partner
non-white	minorities	people of color
negro	black*	African-American*
Hispanic	Latino/a	specific country of origin
Oriental	Asian	specific country of origin
queer	homosexual	gay and/or lesbian
bag lady/bum	transient	homeless people
Indian	American Indian	Native American
Muslim**	Arab	Middle Eastern or specific country of origin
handicapped	disabled	people with disabilities
American	from the United States	U.S. American

*This is currently shifting again back toward a preference for black. Some have begun to deal with this uncertainty by saying *black or African-American* when they cannot ask which is preferred.

**Unless being used to describe someone who practices the Muslim religion.

how, this person is to be viewed as unusual, strange, or different. Instead, simply say *doctor, nurse,* or *police officer.*

Today, our sex no longer limits the occupations we can pursue. Women and men occupy a wide variety of positions that previously were considered the occupations of only one sex—police officers, firefighters, doctors, and lawyers. Sometimes, however, it is necessary to identify groups or individuals by these categories. If you were trying to distinguish between two doctors and you did not have either doctor's name, you might say the *male doctor* or the *female doctor* to distinguish between them.

It may be impossible to always use the *right* term for a group because groups often do not agree on what the best term is. The goal is to be as inclusive and accurate in your terminology as possible. When you choose culturally sensitive and inclusive language because you are concerned with the feelings and needs of the person or group in question, you can focus on what is most appropriate and sensitive in a particular situation. With that in mind, there are terms that are more likely to be well received than others. Table 10.2 provides a chart of some of the most common cultural identifiers.

Profanity

Profanity refers to the "bad words" in a language. I will not list or mention them here because, as in speech, they are inappropriate to use in writing. All languages have some form of profanity. In fact, many language learners often learn these words first. These are the words we use when we are angry, annoyed, shocked, or disgusted and the words we say with force and emotion. These are also the words that can upset and offend others.

As a rule, do not use profanity of any kind when giving a speech. The rare exception is when no other word can make the point you are trying to make. However, it has been my experience that when a student claims that the f-word is the only word that can make the point, we are often able to find a suitable, less offensive alternative. If you think you must use a profane word in your speech, talk to your instructor first. Many instructors have very strict rules about the use of profanity in the classroom. In other speaking contexts, err on the side of caution and avoid using profanity. Although it may shock the audience members or get their attention, it can also undermine your credibility, make you appear less intelligent, and cause your audience to stop listening to you. As my son, Adam, reminded me, "People use bad words because they are not smart enough to think of another way to say something."

Slang

Slang refers to the words and expressions people use in place of more standard, formal, or proper language. Slang terms and ways of speaking are constantly evolving and changing, so they lead to a sense of isolation or exclusion for the people who do not understand the terms. You may have that experience as you listen to friends and classmates talk. They may use terms and expressions with which you are unfamiliar or that defy the dictionary definitions. *Cool, bling, hood, yo, crib,* and *wussup* are all examples of slang expressions in use today with which you might be familiar.

"Is everything all right, Jeffrey? You never call me 'dude' anymore."

FIGURE **10.1**

> **TIP**
> **Eliminating Slang**
> To help you eliminate slang and filler words from your speech, audio record as you practice your speech. Then listen to your speech, paying particular attention to your use of slang and filler words. Keep practicing, recording, and listening until you can deliver the speech without any slang or filler words sneaking in.

Although slang is used frequently in everyday conversation and creates a sense of familiarity with others, it is not appropriate for use in public speaking. Audiences expect speakers to speak clearly and professionally, neither of which can be accomplished when using slang. As you prepare your presentation, proofread your work to make sure that you eliminate any slang terms or usages from your outline. Then, as you practice, be sure that you practice without adding slang back into your style.

A subcategory of slang is *filler words*. Filler words are words and phrases that a speaker throws between words or sentences to fill otherwise empty space or space where a pause might be found. Filler words and phrases include *OK, basically, you know, and, totally, like,* and *so*.

> So, ok, like basically, I'm going to do this whole, you know, presentation on marine mammals. And, basically, I found out that so many marine animals are, like, totally endangered because, you know, people have totally polluted the water, basically.

Consider this passage without fillers:

> I'm going to do this presentation on marine mammals. I have discovered that many marine animals are endangered because people have polluted the water.

CONSIDERING CULTURE

Considering Language: Contemporary American Slang

Here is a list of some of the more common terms you are likely to encounter. Be sure to avoid using any of these words when making a speech unless the term is necessary to make a point. Generally, slang is okay to use when talking to friends but not in formal conversation or public speaking. Before going on, do you know what these people are trying to say?

Yo, dawg, wassup? You're such an airhead! You missed a dope bash last night, dude.

ace (v): To do something very well. *I aced the test.*
airhead (n): An absent-minded or not very intelligent person. *That airhead just sat on my new hat.*
bash(n): A big party. *I had the greatest bash for my twenty-first birthday.*
bling (n): Expensive or flashy items, especially jewelry. *You can tell who the most successful rappers are by the amount of bling they wear.*
blue (adj): Sad, down, depressed. *Ever since I left home, I am missing my parents and feeling blue.*
brain (n): A smart person. *Ask the class brain; she got an A on the test.*
broke (adj): Lacking any money. *Paying for books and tuition has left me flat broke.*
chicken out (v): To back out of doing something because of fear. *He chickened out of the race at the last minute because he knew he would lose anyway.*
chocoholic (n): Someone who eats a lot of chocolate. *Hershey's was made for the chocoholic.*
cool (adj): A term to describe something as positive, good, terrific, or great. *You are a really cool person.*
dawg/dog (n): A friend. *Hey, dawg, how are you?*
dope (adj): A term to describe something as positive, good, terrific, or great. *With that new paint job, his car is dope.*
down/down with (adj): Agreement with, willing to, approving of. *Are you down with going to the store after the movie?*
dude (n): A person, usually a male. *How is the surf, dude?*
fishy (adj): Suspicious or untrustworthy. *There is something fishy about the way he keeps going to the closet to get things out of his coat.*
gab (v): To talk freely. *We gabbed on the phone for three hours.*
grub (n): Food. *I'm starving. Do you have any grub?*
loaded (adj): Drunk or high from drugs. *She showed up at the party already loaded.*
munchies (n): Snack food. *I will bring munchies to eat while we watch the football game.*
nuts (adj): Crazy. *Harry is nuts; he belongs in an institution.*
phat (adj): A term to describe something as positive, good, terrific, or great. *Alva's new car is phat.*
pissed/pissed off (adj): Very angry. *I was pissed when the teacher kept us in the class for an extra ten minutes.*
ride (n): Means of transportation. *Alva's new ride is fabulous.*
rules (v): Dominates as the best. *Public speaking class rules!*
snooze (v): To take a short nap. *I took a quick snooze after class.*
ticked off (adj): Angry. *Pei Ju was ticked off when she heard that Riichi could not drive her home.*
tight (adj): A term to describe something as positive, good, terrific, or great. *I love the new haircut; it's tight!*
trip (v): To overreact, lose control, be upset, or get angry. *Don't trip, dude. You're going to be okay.*
wacked (adj): Odd, weird, strange, or undesirable. *That teacher is wacked if she thinks I'm doing all that homework.*
wassup (greeting): Short for *What is up?* meaning *Hello, how are you/what are you doing?*
workaholic (n): One who works too much. *This new job has turned me into a workaholic.*
yo (greeting): A greeting or attention getter (substitute for *hello* or *hey*). *Yo, I'm over here!*

As you can see from the above examples, filler words make a speaker sound less confident and less prepared. Again, carefully practicing your speech will help you eliminate these inappropriate words.

USING LANGUAGE ACCURATELY

Consider the following:

The stately and mature Darbee Adriano strolled elegantly into the parlor like a swan gliding across a glittering lake. She smiled demurely at her many admirers, who were straining to catch a glimpse of their glorious benefactor.

Or:

The fragile old woman, Mrs. Adriano, meandered into the living room awkwardly. She managed an embarrassed grin as the guests turned to face her.

Each of these statements says roughly the same thing: *An older woman came into a room and noticed the people waiting to see her.* However, the mental image created by each description is very different. The language you choose to relay a message has a powerful impact on how your audience will understand and remember your message. Meanings can change significantly when you choose words that have slightly different meanings.

As a non-native English speaker, you may have found that choosing a word from the dictionary that seems to convey your ideas accurately can instead confuse your listeners or garner a giggle. This happens because even similar words sometimes have subtly different or even significantly different meanings. Words vary in their emotional impact, understandability, and precision.

Additionally, languages often have quirky ways of putting words and phrases together to mean something that might not translate correctly into other languages. These words can be especially troublesome for non-native speakers to learn and use effectively. In this section, we will look at the ways to improve your American English, focusing on language you might inadvertently use inaccurately.

Connotation and Denotation

Every word has at least two meanings. The *denotative meaning* is the most literal meaning of the word, the one that you would find if you looked it up in the dictionary. For example, *Merriam-Webster's Collegiate Dictionary* defines the word *dog* as "a highly variable domestic mammal closely related to the common wolf." This definition is simple, straightforward, and relatively clear. However, when you hear the word "dog," what do you see in your mind's eye? Do you picture a pit bull, a poodle, a puppy, a mutt, an unattractive person, a dishonest person, or a delicious meal? Does the word evoke positive, warm, and fuzzy feelings? A sense of fear and trepidation? Disgust? The word

TABLE 10.3 **How Word Choice Affects Meaning and Impact**

Words vary in:
Emotional impact: *dog* versus *pit bull*
Understandability: *confuse* versus *obfuscate*
Precision: *A lot of people were there* versus *110 people were there*

recalls your attitudes, memories, and feelings about dogs in general, even when someone says something as simple as, "Did you see that dog walking across the street?"[4] This second emotional and personal meaning is called the *connotative meaning* of the word (see Table 10.3).

Some words carry stronger connotative meanings than others (see Considering Language). The most powerfully connotative meanings are often associated with "bad" words, but many words can evoke powerfully negative

Considering Language

The Emotional Impact of Words

Some words carry more emotional impact, either positive or negative, than others with similar meanings. Following is a list of several groups of words with similar meanings that range from little emotional impact to either more positively charged or more negatively charged.

Neutral	Positive	Negative
dog	best friend	mutt
police officer	peace officer	cop
walk slowly	stroll	meander
elderly	mature	old
young	innocent	immature
mad	upset	furious
excited	animated	agitated
indigent	homeless	vagrant
house	home	dump
smell	scent	odor
situation	challenge	problem
tease	kid; rib	antagonize
average	normal	mediocre
still	at rest	stagnant
practice	custom	habit

HINT

Using a Thesaurus

Use a thesaurus only in conjunction with an English-to-English dictionary.

Using a thesaurus is a good way to find synonyms for commonly used words and to find words that offer different shades of meanings As a non-native speaker of English, you can use a thesaurus to expand your vocabulary and to find alternative words to avoid reusing the same word over and over again. This can be very effective, but it can also lead you to words that do not quite fit the meaning you are trying to convey.

By using a thesaurus in conjunction with an English-to-English dictionary, you can verify the differences in meanings among the word choices and be sure that you are using the word in the proper context.

It is also important to note that using a regular English dictionary is not the most effective way to find the proper English words for your speech. Many of these words and translations are outdated, archaic or inaccurate for the context. English-to-English dictionaries are more effective for helping you find just the right word for college-level work.

or powerfully positive reactions from people. Consider the difference between how it feels to hear someone say, "Hush" and how it feels to hear someone say, "Shut up." The different choices indicate a difference in meaning. *Hush* may conjure images of a mother gently and lovingly soothing a baby or gently reminding a child to settle down, whereas *shut up* is more likely associated with anger, frustration, or even threat.

When choosing the right words for your speech, carefully consider the connotations of your words to make sure that they convey the mood and feelings you want to create. Depending on the type of speech you are giving, you may want to minimize or maximize the emotional impact of your language choices. In informative speeches, you generally do not want to reveal your personal biases during the speech. For example, in an informative speech designed to introduce the audience to two sides of a political issue, you want to avoid using words that reveal your opinions about the issue. In ceremonial or special occasion speeches, speakers try to tap into audience members' emotions to make them excited or sentimental. If you are giving a ceremonial or special occasion speech, you will want to use words that are inspiring and sentimental. Persuasive speeches, too, often rely on evoking audience emotion in order to inspire the listeners to action. Additionally, it is expected that a speaker will reveal biases in a persuasive speech.

Indiscriminate Language

To improve the accuracy of your communication, avoid using indiscriminate language. Indiscriminate language does not make distinctions among people, actions, or members of a category. It does not allow for subtlety, exception, or individuality. Instead, indiscriminate language uses sweeping generalizations, static evaluations, and absolutes.

Sweeping generalizations are statements that claim to be a general truth about a large group or category but are based on limited, inaccurate, or incomplete evidence. Stereotypes are sweeping generalizations: *Women are better communicators than men, so women obviously would make better negotiators than men.*

Static evaluations describe a person or thing in terms that indicate how the person or thing always is—in other words, a description that is unchanging. For example, *Adrian is domineering* indicates that Adrian, in general, is domineering. Conversely, *Adrian dominated the discussion* means that in one particular conversation, Adrian might have been domineering, but in general this is not the case. Static evaluations say that an action or behavior is part of another's personality instead of being a one-time or momentary thing. Statements involving static evaluations often use the term *is*.

Absolutes, words that leave no room for exceptions, are often used to make sweeping generalizations and static evaluations. Words such as *always, never, all, none, every, nobody,* and *everyone* suggest extremes that don't allow for exceptions. Rarely is something true of *all* people, and rarely does something *never* happen. When we use absolutes we usually mean that something often happens or hardly ever happens, not actually that something *always* or *never* happens.

The biggest problem with sweeping generalizations, static evaluations, and absolutes is that because they are inaccurate, they make the speaker look less skillful. If the audience can think of even one exception to the statement, the speaker has lost credibility. Even a seemingly positive statement such as *All parents love and want to protect their children, so it is unthinkable that this mother would have purposely harmed her children* may not be accepted because most people can think of examples of parents who do not seem to love their children and who fail to protect and even harm their children. Although the speaker's sentiments are hopeful, they are unrealistic.

To avoid making sweeping generalizations, describe only what you have witnessed or can prove with evidence and research. As we have discussed throughout the book, using stereotypes and manipulating supporting material are unethical and lead to a loss of credibility. To avoid making static evaluations, avoid using the word *is* to describe a person or thing unless you are *certain* that it is a description that is relatively unchanging, like height, career, or coloring: *He is six feet tall; she is an accountant; the box is red.* Ask yourself if there is a time or circumstance in which the description would not be accurate. If you can think of one, then describe the characteristic as something that is situational or temporary: *He was uncharacteristically speaking loudly; she arrived late for the fourth time; the box doesn't usually sit on the table.*

Finally, to avoid using absolutes, replace them with relative language. *Relative language* is more accurate and believable than absolutes are. Words such as *many, often, frequently, rarely, occasionally, most,* and *few* more accurately reflect most circumstances.

Instead of: *Teachers are never in their offices when they say they will be.*

Try: *My teachers are often not in their offices when they say they will be.*

Additionally, you should be sure to use the most accurate relative language for your purposes by adapting the wording to fit the reliability of the information. If the information is highly reliable and you have research to back up the claim of reliability, you can use words such as *certainly* and *surely.* When the information is less reliable, use terms such as *probably* or *perhaps* or even *highly probable.* When the information is not very reliable and you want to stress that it is not reliable, use *supposedly* or *apparently.*[5]

You can also improve your accuracy and believability when you are expressing an opinion by using provisional language. Remember, just because something is true for you, that does not mean it is true for all people. *Provisional language* indicates that the information you are providing is opinion or is what you personally believe based on your experience or faith. Provisional language allows for exceptions or alternative opinions, whereas absolutes and certainty do not: *I have found that, I believe that,* or *In my opinion,* are examples of provisional language. Use provisional language when the information is not clearly opinion. If the information is obviously an opinion,

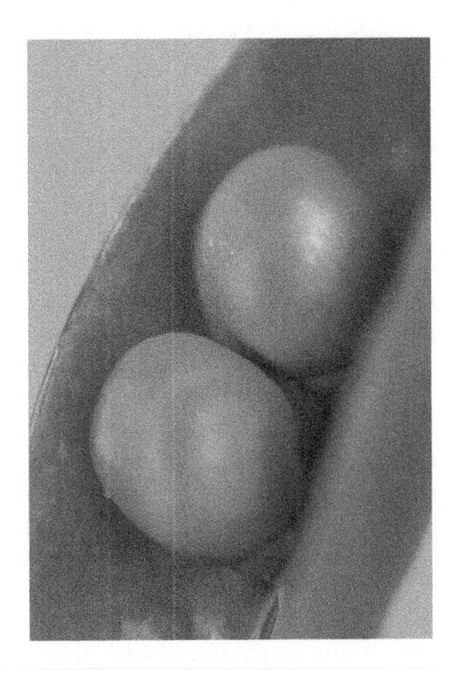

Every language has sayings and figures of speech that don't make literal sense. For example: Just like two peas in a pod.

you do not need to use provisional language; in fact, using it in that case will weaken your overall argument.

Remember that you are responsible for the information you pass on to your audience. You want to support the information you provide only to the extent that you believe it yourself and can prove it to be true.

Idioms, Figures of Speech, and Sayings

Few things can be more frustrating to learn and use in another language than the expressions common to the language and/or culture. *Expressions* are unique groupings of words that communicate an idea, thought, or feeling. You may have asked someone what something meant, and he or she responded, "Oh, it's just an expression." Some common expressions heard on U.S. college campuses today are, "You want to hang out?" or "I'll catch up with you later." Expressions, which include idioms, figures of speech, and sayings, can be problematic for non-native speakers to master. Using expressions inaccurately can be one of the more embarrassing language mistakes language learners make.

Idioms are a type of expression that do not follow a set of rules (indeed, they often contradict the rules) and have to be memorized when learning a new language. For example, *catch up* in the example above is an idiom that means, for example, "I will meet you later, but first I have something else I need to do."

Idioms can be very confusing for language learners because idioms rarely translate word for word and generally just have to be memorized over time. As you learn to understand many idioms from the context of speech and try to use them yourself, you may make frequent mistakes by mixing up similar-sounding idioms or incorrectly separating the words of an idiom. For example, *catch, catch on, catch some, catch up*, and *catch up with* each have different meanings:

I didn't catch what you were saying = I didn't hear what was said or I missed a portion of what you were saying.

I didn't catch on to what you were saying = I didn't understand your hint or joke.

I need to catch some sleep = I am tired and need to go to sleep.

I will catch up to you after the show = I will meet you after the show.

I got a chance to catch up with my sister during her visit = I learned during my sister's visit what she has been doing lately.

Learning which construction to use can be frustrating. Paying close attention to the idioms you hear and how they are used can help you use them properly. Additionally, you will find a glossary of some of the most common idioms and other expressions in the Glossary of English Expressions at the end of the book in Appendix A.

A *figure of speech* is an expression that takes an abstract thought, idea, or concept and makes it easily understandable through a creative and nonliteral use of words. A figure of speech is a succinct way to convey a lot of meaning in only a few words; it can also be a gentler way of conveying something negative. To *pull an all-nighter* means to stay up all night studying. To *pull someone's leg* means to deceive someone by telling him/her a fantastic or unbelievable story for the purpose of teasing that person. *A quick study* is a person who learns very quickly.

I had gotten so far behind in my reading for the class that I had to pull an

CONSIDERING CULTURE

Proverbs, Sayings, and Idioms

Proverbs, sayings, and idioms of a language often reveal the beliefs, values, and attitudes held by the cultures using that language. Some sayings convey meanings that hold true in a variety of cultures. For example the Wén-yán literary tradition of classical Chinese has two sayings that have similar meanings to two English counterparts:

Tigers do not breed dogs = Like father like son

Calamities do not occur singly = When it rains it pours

Adapted from: David Crystal, *The Cambridge Encyclopedia of Language*, (Cambridge: Cambridge University Press, 1987) p. 312–313.

Proverbs from Around the World

Proverbs are short sayings with a long history that express a simple truth or offer advice. Following is a list of several proverbs from around the world. Read each and try to determine what message each is trying to convey and what values are being expressed. Then do research by asking classmates or friends or by looking online to find the true meanings.*

God gave teeth; He will give bread.
—Lithuanian
Better a mouse in the pot than no meat at all.
—Romanian
Better to light a candle than to curse the darkness.
—Chinese
The country rooster does not crow in the town.
—Swahili
Do not push the river, it will flow by itself.
—Polish
Walk till the blood appears on the cheek, but not the sweat on the brow.
—Spanish
Every beetle is a gazelle in the eyes of its mother.
—Moorish
You can't wake a person who is pretending to be asleep.
—Navajo
From a thorn comes a rose, and from a rose comes a thorn.
—Greek
The go-between wears out a thousand sandals.
—Japanese
Good fences make good neighbors.
—American
He who wants a rose must respect the thorn.
—Persian
If work were good for you, the rich would leave none for the poor.
—Haitian
You may laugh at a friend's roof; don't laugh at his sleeping accommodation.
—Kenyan
Don't empty the water jar until the rain falls.
—Philippine
Turn your face to the sun and the shadows fall behind you.
—Maori
If you scatter thorns, don't go barefoot.
—Italian
Experience is the comb that nature gives us when we are bald.
—Belgian

The Quotations & Sayings Database, http://www.quotesandsayings.com/proverbial.htm (retrieved February 7, 2005).

all-nighter just to pass the exam.

So you were only pulling my leg when you told me that class is canceled?

Maria is such a quick study that she learned to program the Tivo in less than five minutes.

Anyone can create a figure of speech using metaphors, similes, and hyperbole. We will discuss these literary tools more thoroughly in the next section on creating vividness in a speech. For now, just remember that when you use a figure of speech, be sure that you are creating the image you intend. Often, figures of speech, like other expressions, do not translate well from one language to another. They can even paint an inaccurate picture of what you are trying to communicate. Instead, create figures of speech using the logic and meanings of the English language, or briefly explain figures of speech that you translate from your native language to English.

Sayings are the phrases and terms people use to offer a quick piece of advice. Every language and culture has sayings, called *proverbs,* that are passed down from one generation to the next and summarize many of the key values and beliefs of the culture. Sayings offer a concise way to pass along a complicated or esoteric idea simply and memorably. One of my favorite sayings is, "You can't step into the same river twice." Literally, this refers to the idea that a river is constantly moving water, so if you take your foot out and put it right back into the river, it is a different river because the water that was there only moments before has already moved on. What this saying conveys is that the world is constantly changing, so even if you do the same things or go to the same places over and over again, the experience will not be exactly the same each time.

Another favorite saying of mine is, "Don't count your chickens before they are hatched." Literally, this means that if you had a bunch of fertilized chicken eggs, you shouldn't count them as the chickens you will have because you never know how many will actually hatch and grow into healthy chickens. This saying emphasizes that you cannot count on what you don't already actually have in your possession, no matter how certain at the moment the future may seem. You need to wait and see what actually transpires.

Using expressions in speeches can be an effective way to quickly transmit information to an audience in a colorful manner. However, there are two reasons you need to be careful not to overuse sayings and proverbs. First, they can become tiresome or clichéd (a phrase that has lost its effectiveness due to overuse). Still, an occasional, well-placed saying or proverb can summarize your ideas eloquently. Frequently, speakers use well-known sayings or proverbs as part of an attention getter or as the closing remarks in a speech. A second reason to avoid overusing sayings is that sayings can be confusing. That is, unless you are certain that your audience is familiar with the saying and its meaning, you might confuse them or lose their interest.

This is also true of figures of speech. Unless they are immediately recognizable or understandable or you are planning to explain them, you should avoid using them. Remember, unlike written communication, oral communication does not allow a listener to go back or look up what the speaker has said.

A good storyteller can paint vivid pictures with her words.

Finally, as with all language use, make sure you are using expressions accurately. Changing even a single word can change the meaning significantly and can leave your audience confused or giggling inappropriately. Check with your instructor or a native speaker about the pronunciation and word order you are planning to use to ensure that you use them properly. This will help you avoid making any embarrassing mistakes.

 MAKING LANGUAGE INTERESTING

In addition to using language appropriately and accurately, you must also make the language interesting. Audiences can be lulled to sleep by a dense and dry speech that drones on, sentence after sentence, like a grocery list of things they need but don't necessarily want to buy. Audiences enjoy and retain speeches that create vivid imagery and a sense of rhythm. They like to feel involved in the speech and part of the action. You can enhance audience interest and understanding by using simple language tools, called *linguistic devices,* that are designed to add vividness and create rhythm.

Creating Vividness

Have you ever read a book that was so descriptive that you could *see* in your mind what the author was describing? Or a story so real that you felt like you were actually there? Using vivid language paints a picture in the audience's mind and helps them enjoy and remember the speech because they can clearly imagine what the speaker is saying. Speakers create vivid imagery through the use of *description, metaphor, simile, hyperbole, alliteration,* and *irony.*

Description

Description puts into words what the speaker has seen, heard, smelled, felt, tasted, or otherwise experienced through the senses. Good description is specific rather than general and uses brief, clear sentences. In short, good description uses colorful but simple wording. What do you picture in your mind when I tell you that I arrived to my office this morning using my regular transportation? You might have a vague understanding of what my school looks like—probably like any other nondescript school—and you might try to guess what this form of transportation might have been; but you are largely left to your own imagination as to how I got to school or what my school looks like. However, if I told you:

> At ten minutes to class time, I trotted out the front door and down the three steps of my little 1950s beach bungalow onto the tree-lined street. The sun was shining brightly as I briskly walked the short block to school. As I entered the back gate and passed the new swimming complex, I could hear the coach's whistle calling the swim team out of the pool. I passed the newly planted football field and the new red rubber track as I made my way through to the gym. As I emerged on the other side of my shortcut, I waved at fellow colleagues, smiled hello to current and former students, and found myself at the faded-blue single-story temporary building that houses my office.

From this description, you have a much more accurate picture of my journey to school on a typical morning. This second description is specific and descriptive. The use of adjectives and adverbs (e.g., *red, old, tree-lined, briskly, newly,* etc.) and concrete wording (e.g., *swimming complex, track, football field, single-story,* etc.) helps the reader see what I see when I walk to school. Descriptive words such as adjectives and adverbs can give color and life to your descriptions. Saying, "I walked briskly to school on my tree-lined street" paints a much clearer picture than simply saying, "I walked to school."

More specific wording is called *concrete language.* Concrete language has a clearer one-to-one relationship with people, places, and things than does more general, or *abstract,* wording and gives an audience a more precise picture of what the speaker is talking about. Words run on a continuum from more general and abstract to more specific and concrete. For example, *animal* is much more abstract than *dog* is, but *dog* is more abstract than *poodle.* A *black male standard poodle* is even more concrete than just *poodle.* Think of it this way:

Martin Luther King, Jr. used linguistic devices effectively to move millions to action.

More General ______________________________ More Specific

Abstract *Animal* *Dog* *Poodle* *Black standard poodle* Concrete

When using description, choose easy-to-understand words. Remember, in oral communication, you want to be easily understandable. Overly complicated word choices can sound contrived or lead to confusion, so you might want to choose *red* over *crimson, insensitive* over *stolid, noisy* over *raucous,* and *complicate* over *obfuscate.*

Metaphor, Simile, Hyperbole, Alliteration, and Irony

Several ways to create interest are through the use of linguistic devices such as metaphor, simile, hyperbole, alliteration, and irony. Both metaphor and simile are used to make comparisons between two seemingly dissimilar things. When using metaphor, you compare the two things as if one *is* the other: *My love is a tidal wave rolling over in crashing waves.* The comparison is implied. Similes make comparisons more explicitly than metaphors by using the terms *like* or *as: He was as cold as ice.*

Both metaphors and similes concisely convey a depth of meaning and emotion poetically. Metaphors can be especially useful in helping the audience recall the topic long after you are done speaking because metaphors simplify complicated or esoteric ideas into simple comparisons.[6] They can also help us make the unfamiliar familiar through comparisons with experiences we are likely to know and understand. Shakespeare and other artists gave the world many famous and often-repeated metaphors and similes:

> All the world's a stage and all the men and women merely players.–Shakespeare, *As You Like It*
>
> Death lies upon her like an untimely frost.–Shakespeare, *Romeo and Juliet*
>
> The perfect sky is torn.–Natalie Imbruglia, "Torn"
>
> Everyday is a winding road.–Sheryl Crow, "Everyday Is a Winding Road"
>
> You are the wind beneath my wings.–Bette Midler, "Wind Beneath My Wings"

Metaphors are often laced throughout a speech to make a larger point. Martin Luther King, Jr., does this beautifully in his speech "I Have a Dream." The title itself previews the metaphor of his dream, which is not a literal dream that he had while he slept, but instead his hope for the future of race relations in the United States. He incorporates many other metaphors into this speech as well. In one metaphor, he brings home the point that African-Americans in the United States have been treated badly and not recognized or included as full citizens of the country and that they have been marginalized by the rest of society.

> But one hundred years later, the Negro still is not free. One hundred years later, the life of the Negro is still sadly crippled by the manacles of segregation and the chains of discrimination. One hundred years later, the Negro lives on a lonely island of poverty in the midst of a vast ocean of material prosperity. One hundred years later, the Negro is still languished in the corners of American society and finds himself an exile in his own land.[7]

When using similes and metaphors, be sure to use them logically and not to *mix metaphors*. When making comparisons, be sure they accurately reflect the point you are trying to make. Also, avoid inappropriately putting two unrelated metaphors together, such as:

> He is not the brightest bulb in the drawer.

These two often-repeated metaphors are actually:

> He is not the brightest bulb in the shed.
>
> He is not the sharpest knife in the drawer.

Hyperbole is exaggeration used to make a point or create an effect. When you use hyperbole, you are not trying to convince the audience that what you are saying is actually true or meant literally. You are simply trying to create an effect: *The spiders in Australia are as big as mice!* Hyperbole can be effective when used sparingly and well. Sometimes, however, hyperbole is misunderstood as the improper use of absolutes (e.g., *Nobody was there! Everybody is trying it!*) or as exaggeration to stretch the truth (e.g., *There must have been fifty people there!*—when there were actually about thirty). Overuse and misuse of hyperbole can lead to a loss of credibility and cause the audience to distrust what the speaker is saying.

Alliteration is the repetition of the same sound at the beginning of a series of words: *She was calm, cool, and collected despite the constant complaining of her counterparts*. Alliteration creates an easy way for the audience to remember a list or the main points of a speech: *Don't forget the three "R's": reduce, reuse, and recycle.* Politicians know this well, as we can see from Bill Clinton's acceptance address in the 1992 Democratic National Convention where he sums up his domestic policy using alliteration:

> Somewhere at this very moment a child is being born in America. Let it be our cause to give that child a happy home, a healthy family, and a hopeful future.[8]

Irony is a language device that involves a contradiction between what is said and what is intended to be understood. For example, a teacher might say to her students, "I know you must be disappointed that I need to postpone the exam for two weeks," knowing the class was not prepared for the test. Irony can be useful to engage the audience's thinking, to avoid saying the obvious while still pointing it out, or to create humor in a presentation. Irony can be especially useful in persuasive speeches in which the audience is either in agreement with the argument or is skeptical about the argument but not entirely hostile to it. Irony should be avoided with hostile audiences, however, because it can actually cause them to hold more strongly to their beliefs.[9]

Although description, metaphor, simile, hyperbole, alliteration, and irony are not the only linguistic devices available for creating vividness in a speech, these are some of the easiest ways to start playing with the English language to create impact and style. As a non-native speaker, you may want to add only one or two of these devices at first until you become more comfortable using them. Or you may want to import some of the figures of speech from your native language. Just be sure, however you decide to stylize your speech, that your message remains clear and memorable to the audience.

Creating Rhythm

In addition to making the language more interesting through the use of various figures of speech, you will also want to create rhythm in your speech. *Rhythm* is the somewhat predictable pattern created in a speech. A speech with good rhythm creates a mood and a pace for the speech that are predictable and satisfying. Rhythm helps the audience anticipate where the speaker is going and when. You can create rhythm through stylistic devices such as repetition and antithesis.

Repetition is the repeating of a word, phrase, or grammatical structure in a speech. Repetition creates rhythm and predictability because the audience comes to expect the repetition. It also reiterates a theme or idea. Many famous speeches are famous in part because of their use of repetition. Returning to Martin Luther King, Jr.'s "I Have a Dream" speech, one thing that makes this speech so memorable is the repetition of "I have a dream." Ironically, Robert F. Kennedy's speech announcing the death of Martin Luther King, Jr., offers another excellent example of repetition:

> What we need in the United States is not division. What we need in the United States is not hatred. What we need in the United States is not violence and lawlessness; but is love and wisdom and compassion toward one another, and a feeling of justice toward those who still suffer within our country whether they be white or whether they be black.[10]

This quote also offers an example of antithesis. *Antithesis* is the juxtaposing of two contrasting ideas to create a balance—in other words, taking two opposing ideas and placing them in adjacent phrases, sentences, or paragraphs to create balance. In the example above, Kennedy uses antithesis by proposing first what the United States does *not* need—division, hatred, and violence—and then proposing what we *do* need—love, wisdom, compassion, and justice. Another example of antithesis comes from Richard M. Nixon's "Inaugural Address," where he uses a series of four antitheses:

> We find ourselves rich in goods but ragged in spirit, reaching with magnificent precision for the moon but falling in a raucous discord on earth. We are caught in war wanting peace. We're torn by division wanting unity.[11]

Creating a Personal Style

Finally, your language choices can also help you create a personal style that will help you connect with your audience. Audiences respond more favorably to speakers they perceive as more personal with and connected to the audience. Using personal pronouns—*I, we,* and *you* instead of *one* or *people*—is a good start to personalizing your speech.

Involve the audience in your speech by referring to specific people in the audience, asking questions, or having audience members do some small activity. If you know the names of some of the audience members, and especially if the other audience members are likely to know the names, too, you can refer to them specifically or offer acknowledgment: *I can't thank Drs. Robar and Ogata enough for giving me the chance to speak to you today.*

Questions can also involve the audience in your speech. You can ask polling questions (see Chapter Four) and have audience members raise their hands. You can occasionally include tag questions to encourage the audience to nod in agreement (e.g., *We all want what is best for our children, right?*). You can even ask the audience members to participate and have them look at the people sitting next to them or do some small activity such as standing up, closing their eyes, or repeating after you. Including the audience in your presentation is a great way to keep them energized and engaged.

SUMMARY

Attending to the language you use in your speech is the last step before practicing the speech and refining it for the big day, but you don't have to wait until the speech is completed to begin thinking about the language choices you will make. As you write your speech, think about the best ways to construct your message in terms of choosing your words, adapting your language to the oral communication context, and ensuring that you are using language accurately, appropriately, and interestingly.

As you consider your language choices, ask yourself if you are using the most appropriate language and level of formality for the time, place, audience, and purpose of the speech. Is your speech free of sexist and racist language, profanity, and slang? If not, adjust accordingly.

Ask yourself if you are using language accurately for the speaking situation. Are the connotations of the words matched to the connotations you feel? Do they reveal feelings that you would rather not reveal? Is your speech free of indiscriminate language choices, absolutes, and sweeping generalizations? Are you using idioms and sayings correctly?

Ask yourself if the language you are using is interesting. Have you created vividness through the use of various linguistic devices? Are your descriptions specific and colorful? Have you included any metaphors, similes, or other linguistic devices? Have you created a sense of rhythm by using repetition or antithesis? Are you using a personal style that engages and involves the audience?

You will probably not answer "yes" to all of the above questions. It would not be appropriate to use every linguistic or stylistic device in every speech. In the same way that every speech needs to be adapted to the speaking situation, the language choices also need to be tailored to the needs of the particular audience, occasion, and topic. Simply asking yourself the above questions can go a long way toward helping you adapt the language choices in your speech appropriately, accurately, and interestingly.

Discussion Questions and Activities

1. To practice using abstract and concrete language, put the following words in order from the most abstract to the most concrete:

   Yellow 2004 Ford Mustang, Automobile, Transportation, Sports Car, Yellow Sports Car

   Flowers, Pink Tulips in a Clear Vase, Plant, Tulips, Spring Flowers

   Person, Male Comedian, David Letterman, Entertainer, Talk Show Host

2. In this chapter we discussed ways to make the language of your speech more colorful and interesting. Discuss with your classmates how language is used in your first language to create vividness and rhythm. Can you think of examples of how the various language tools discussed in this chapter (antithesis, metaphor, alliteration, etc.) are used in your first language? What is difficult about trying to use these tools in English? What is easy about it?
3. Obtain a copy of Martin Luther King, Jr.'s "I Have a Dream" speech from http://www.americanrhetoric.com/speeches/Ihaveadream.htm or from www.stanford.edu/group/king/index.htm and identify at least two examples of each of the following language tools:

description	simile	repetition
metaphor	alliteration	antithesis

4. Rewrite your most recent speech using as many of the language tools discussed in this chapter as possible. Once you have rewritten the speech, turn it into a keyword outline. Practice giving the speech using the language tools as naturally as you can. What difficulties did you experience? Why? How can you both incorporate more interesting language and be able to use a keyword outline without memorizing the speech? Talk to your classmates about possible solutions.
5. Discuss the implications of using the various types of inappropriate language (racist, sexist, or foul language; name-calling; and slang) in a speech. What effect does this language have on the audience? On the speaker? On others who are not present? What can a speaker do to ensure that the language in the speech is appropriate and effective?

Chapter Quiz

1. Spoken language differs from written language in each of the following ways EXCEPT:
   - **a.** Spoken language is less formal than written language.
   - **b.** Spoken language uses longer sentences than written language.
   - **c.** Spoken language uses more repetition than written language.
   - **d.** Spoken language is more personal than written language.
2. Speeches that lack this personal connection or strive for too much ______ often leave the audience feeling uninvolved, disconnected, or bored.
   - **a.** balance
   - **b.** informality
   - **c.** formality
   - **d.** inappropriateness

3. Which of the following terms would be inappropriate to use in a classroom speech about immigration?
   a. Naturalized citizens
   b. Undocumented workers
   c. Immigrants
   d. Illegal aliens
4. True or false: When Ramon bristles just from the sound of the word "pit bull," he is responding to the denotative meaning of the word.
5. *Here today, gone tomorrow* is an example of:
   a. an idiom.
   b. a figure of speech.
   c. a saying.
   d. indiscriminate language.
6. What are the four types of language you should NOT use in a speech because they could offend the audience and harm others?
7. Which of the following language tool(s) add(s) rhythm to a speech?
   a. antithesis
   b. alliteration
   c. parallel structure
   d. concrete language

Speech for Analysis

Great speakers are considered great largely because of their ability to use language artfully. Research a great speaker from anywhere in the world, and analyze one of his or her speeches in terms of the use of language. Is the language effective, appropriate, accurate, and interesting? What language tools does the speaker use? Provide specific examples.

Chapter 10 Quiz Answers

1. b, 2. c, 3. d, 4. False, 5. c, 6. sexist, racist, heterosexist, profanity, 7. c.

CHAPTER 11 Presentation Aids

CHAPTER GOAL

By the end of this chapter you will be able to select, create, and utilize presentation aids appropriately and effectively.

John spent three weeks constructing an exact model of Dealey Plaza, the scene of President John F. Kennedy's assassination. The detail and care with which he constructed the scene of the crime were breathtaking. From the car carrying the President and Mrs. Kennedy, to the book depository, to the grassy knoll, he wanted his model to give the audience a three-dimensional understanding of what happened on that fateful day in 1963.

On the day of John's presentation, he called upon the audience to gather around the four-by-six-foot model resting on a table. He made sure that everyone could see his beautiful handiwork. His audience gasped in admiration at the incredible detail of every plant, tree, and rock. Then John began his speech.

Almost immediately, John realized he had a serious problem. Although he had researched his presentation carefully, he had rushed through the writing of his actual speech the night before the presentation. He had spent so much time working on the visual aid that he had not given himself enough time to write and practice his speech.

His words fell from his lips awkwardly. He forgot important points; he became disorganized, and he panicked. In an attempt to salvage a modicum of respect, John turned to his audience and said, "Did I tell you that this model took me three weeks to make?"

John learned a valuable lesson that day: A presentation aid cannot take the place of a well-planned and rehearsed speech. For his next speech, John took his instructor's advice and wrote his speech before he made an equally fabulous presentation aid. He then practiced his speech several times and ended up giving a terrific presentation to an enthusiastic audience.

In Chapter Seven, we discussed supporting materials and found that well-chosen supporting materials bring a speech to life, make an argument compelling, and make an audience laugh, cry, or cheer. You will remember that there are six categories of supporting materials. The first five represent the information you use in the text of your presentation, including facts, examples, statistics, quotes, and comparisons. The sixth category consists of the "extras" you include to help your audience understand what you say and to make the presentation more interesting—visual aids, audio material, videotape, aromas, and samples for your audience to taste, touch, or take home. We call this category *presentation aids*.

Because presentation aids are not actually part of the written speech but are planned, created, and developed after you write the speech, presentation aids represent a special category of supporting material. Although you should keep your eyes and ears open for possible presentation aids as you research and begin writing your speech, you will not choose the aids until after the writing is complete. In this chapter, we will discuss the purpose and advantages of including presentation aids in your speech, the kinds of information you can include in your aids, the best ways to present the information, and the ways to prepare and use your presentation aids.

PURPOSE OF PRESENTATION AIDS

The old saying in English "A picture is worth a thousand words" means that sometimes presenting a simple picture or image can be more effective in communicating an idea than using a lot of words to explain it. Providing the audience with sensory information in addition to the words of the speech increases clarity, interest, retention, credibility, and self-confidence.

Research has found that the majority of audiences feel that helpful visual elements are an important component of any presentation and that they learn valuable information from good visual elements in others' presentations.[1] No matter what language a speaker is using, presentation aids increase clarity. This can be especially helpful to non-native speakers who are concerned about their accent and pronunciation. By providing a physical representation of your point, the audience has more than one way to understand your message. A poster can clarify key terms for the audience, thus helping them to more quickly adapt to your speaking style.

Presentation aids also make a speech more interesting. They give your audience something else that reinforces and clarifies your message. The more you keep the audience's attention, the more likely they are to understand and remember your message. Studies have shown that when people use more than one sensory channel to take in information, they learn and retain that information better.[2]

Presentation aids increase speaker credibility as well. Audiences respect speakers who have clearly invested time and energy into preparing professional, clear, and relevant presentation aids and who handle the aids with confidence and poise. In other words, if you look like you have put the effort into researching, preparing, and practicing with your presentation aids, the audience will be more likely to believe that you know what you are talking about.

Additionally, by taking the time to do a good job preparing and practicing with your aids, you will feel more confident and self-assured as you give your speech. Students frequently report feeling more comfortable as a result of having presentation aids to work with. They claim that presentation aids refocus their attention to the message and away from negative self-talk and help them remember their speeches. Again, the more confident you look and act (even if you aren't feeling confident), the more credibility the audience gives you and the more confident you will actually begin to feel.

As a non-native speaker of English, you will gain some extra advantages using presentation aids. As noted above, you can rely on visuals to clarify your main points if you are concerned about your accent or pronunciation interfering with audience comprehension. Visuals reduce the focus on you and your accent and give the audience another place to focus their attention.

Because you might have had to rely on nonverbal messages as you were learning a new language, you are also likely to have a good understanding of the types of sounds, smells, and pictures that transcend language and culture and communicate *universal messages*. Human suffering, joy, love, and sorrow can often be shared through a picture or a song.

FIGURE **11.1**

Pie Charts are graphs in the shape of a circle that is cut into pieces to show the relative frequencies or percentage portion of each part to the whole. This particular graph does not tell us how much money was earned in each of the categories, but it does tell us proportionally where the money came from.

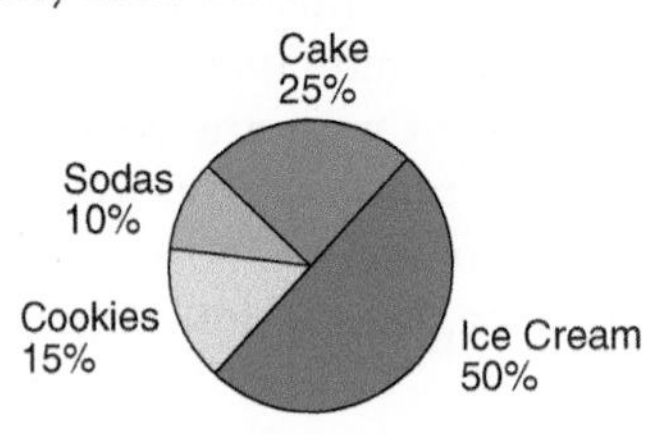

Annual Distribution of Sales, 2005

Line Graphs show a relationship between one dependent variable and one independent variable. They are good for showing trends or changes over time. This particular graph shows us that ice cream sales increase over the summer months.

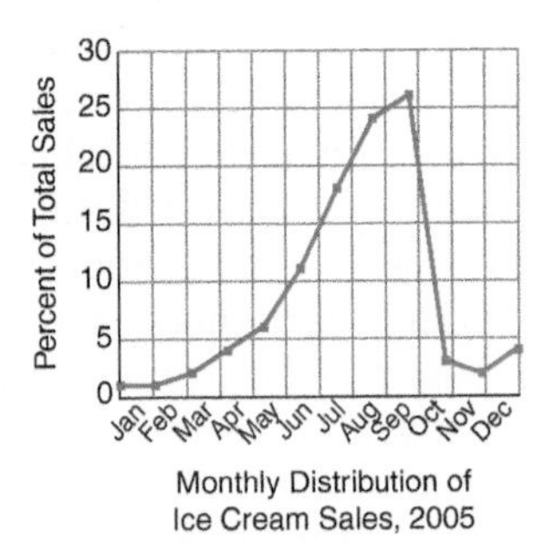

Monthly Distribution of Ice Cream Sales, 2005

Bar Graphs show a comparison between two or more things. This chart shows us the difference in dollar amounts earned by each product.

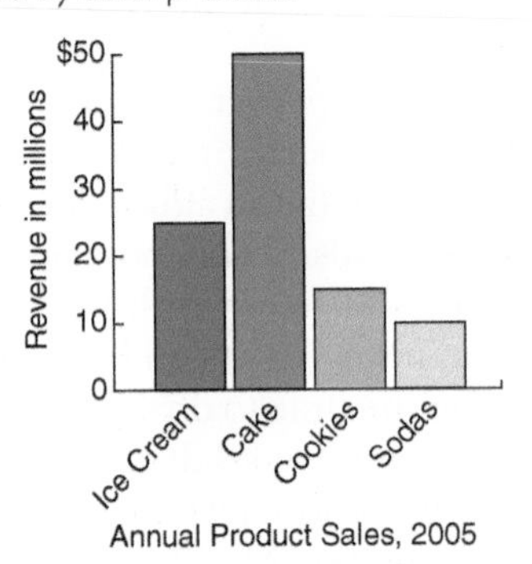

Annual Product Sales, 2005

You can also use your presentation aids to draw upon your culture and your creativity to show the audience a little about who you are. Using graphic styles and colors that are associated with your cultural background—including your own artwork, photographs, or belongings—can help bridge the gap between your culture and those of the audience. Connecting with the audience makes the speaking experience easier and more enjoyable for you and more interesting for them.

However, you don't want to include presentation aids just to have them; you want to include them because they support your verbal message. A good rule to follow when deciding whether to use a presentation aid is to use one only when you need to make a point, to summarize large amounts of information, or to show a visual relationship (see Figures 11.1, 11.2, and 11.3 for some examples of visual aids you might want to create).

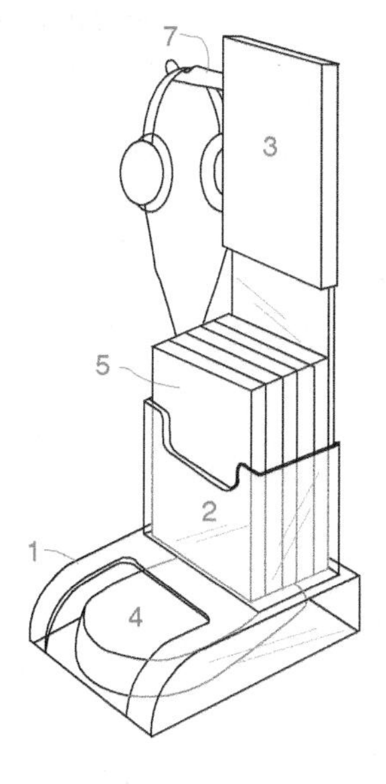

FIGURE 11.2 **Diagrams** demonstrate or explain how something works through a sketch, a drawing, or an outline.

WHAT TO USE

Sarah used a map to indicate the migration route of the monarch butterfly. Declan used a timeline to show the development of rock 'n' roll in relation to national and international events. Sabrina showed photographs of starving children to persuade the class to donate to a children's fund. Yerin brought in a hand-painted Persian vase to illustrate the ancient art of vase painting. Morgan used a pie chart to show how student tuitions are budgeted at her university. Donovan wore his car racing uniform while discussing the safety improvements implemented by NASCAR, including those on the uniform.

What you choose as a presentation aid is limited only by your purpose and your creativity. In choosing what visual to use, be aware of the benefits and drawbacks of each type. See Table 11.1 for a list of the types of presentation aids and the benefits and drawbacks of each.

Choosing the Right Media

As you may have noticed, some types of presentation aids can be shown only one way. For example, you would show food, objects, and models as they are. You would not need to mount them on a poster or videotape them. You would simply share them directly with your audience. Other aids require choices about how to show them. Graphs can be mounted on posters, copied onto transparencies, or incorporated into a computer-generated presentation

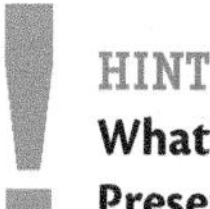

HINT

What Not to Use as Presentation Aids

Some items just don't make good presentational aids, especially for classroom speeches:

- Alcohol
- Drugs
- Weapons
- Offensive graphics (judged by audience)
- Potentially dangerous animals (unless you are a trained expert in the handling of the animal and you have proper permits and permission for having such an animal on the premises)
- Potentially dangerous chemicals

If you are unsure, check with your instructor.

Learning Style	Learn Through...	These Learners...
Visual Learners	seeing	need to see body language and facial expression learn best from visual displays including: diagrams, overhead transparencies, videos, flip charts and handouts prefer to take detailed notes to absorb the information
Auditory Learners	listening	learn best through lectures, discussions, talking, and listening interpret meanings through tone of voice, pitch, and speed often benefit from reading text aloud and using a tape recorder
Tactile/Kinesthetic Learners	moving, doing, and touching	learn best through a hands-on approach enjoy actively exploring the physical world enjoy color highlighters and take notes by drawing and doodling

Source: Adapted from http://www.nwlink.com/~donclark/hrd/learning/styles.htm and http://www.ldpride.net/learningstyles.MI.htm

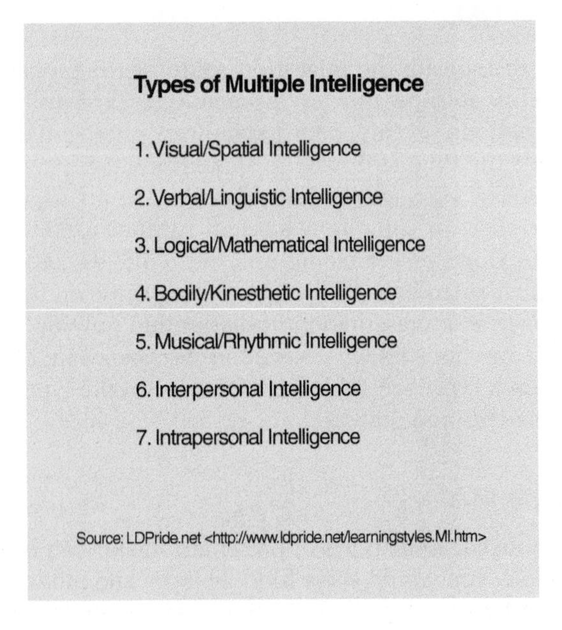

FIGURE 11.3 **Charts and posters** are a good way to summarize large amounts of information.

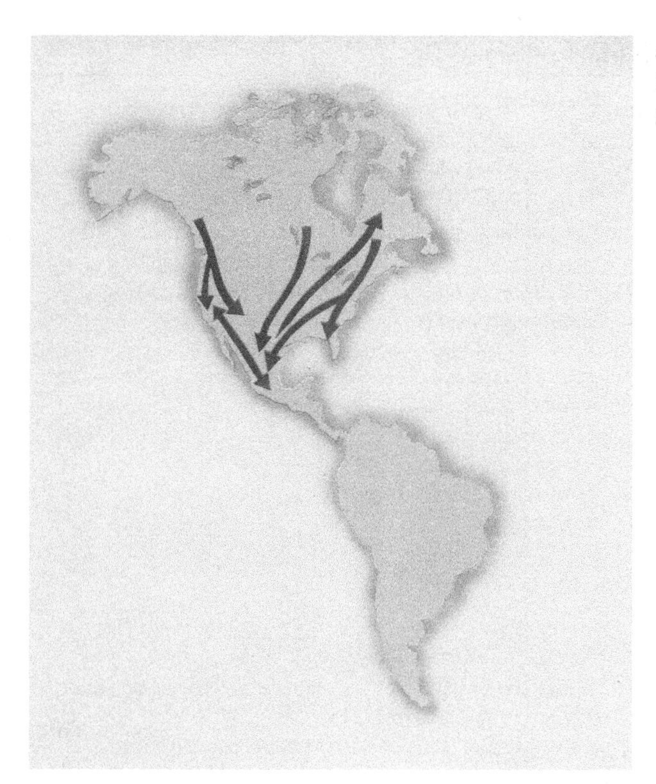

A map showing the traveling route of the migrating monarch butterfly helped students understand the great distance traveled by these little wonders.

program such as PowerPoint. Your choices range from simple and low-tech to complex and high-tech.

Using Your Own Body

For her speech on the Hanbok, the traditional Korean dress, Yoon wanted to display an actual Hanbok. Her choices included hanging the dress in the front of the room, having a volunteer wear the dress, or wearing the dress herself. She decided that hanging the dress up for the audience to see would not display how beautiful the dress looks when it is worn. Having a volunteer wear the dress was too complicated because she had to find someone who could fit into the dress and was willing to model. She also feared that having another person on stage with her might be distracting to the audience. If Yoon wore the dress herself, she would have to put it on before her speech, and the audience might see it before she was ready to show it to them, which would ruin the surprise. In the end, Yoon decided to wear the dress herself. She dressed before class and wore a long coat over the dress until it was her turn to speak. Her speech was a success.

TABLE 11.1 **Presentation Aids: Types, Benefits, Drawbacks, and Tips**

Types	Benefits	Drawbacks	Tips
Objects: Actual item being discussed (a costume, a person, an animal, etc.) to explain, demonstrate, or clarify.	•The audience doesn't have to imagine because it is in front of them. •Can add interest and variety to the presentation.	•Live objects can be unpredictable and unreliable. •May be too small, large, or complex for audience to see clearly. •Can be distracting to audience if "too interesting."	•If the object is large, use a table or desk to display the object high enough for the audience to see. •For smaller objects, hold the item up in your hand and be sure to show it to all areas of the room.
Models: Life-sized, large-scale, or small-scale versions of real objects (a human torso, a cutaway model of a cargo ship, a model of a sugar molecule) when the real objects are too small, too large, impractical, unavailable, or inappropriate to use.	•Provide the appropriate size and detail for effectively discussing the object. •Can add interest and variety to the presentation.	•Can be costly and time consuming to make. •May not accurately represent the actual object. •May still be difficult to see from the back of the room.	•Same as Objects.
Photographs and Illustrations: Pictures, drawings, and images that show things like types of flowers, styles of architecture, artwork, places, and people.	•Provide vivid visual support. •Can show places, people, and things that otherwise could not be seen.	•Often too small to see. •Tempts speakers to hand them around. •Often not explained well or necessary.	•Enlarge and mount on poster board. •Transfer to slides and project them onto a screen. •Copy onto transparency film and show on an overhead projector. •DO NOT pass around or show them from books.
Diagrams: A type of drawing that is used to show the shape, parts, layout, or workings of something, such as a floor plan, the parts of a guitar, or the respiratory system (see Figure 11.2).	•Inexpensive and easy to draw. •Show only the information you want the audience to see. •Can be used at various points in the speech.	•Can look sloppy or unprofessional if not created carefully.	•Diagrams that are computer generated and printed onto transparency film can be shown on an overhead projector. •Draw on paper and mount on poster board.
Graphs: A type of diagram that shows relationships between variables. There are several types of graphs; line, bar, and pie are among the most common (see Figure 11.1).	•Provide visual representation of statistical data and their significance. •Can show changes over time, divisions of wholes, and comparisons between variables.	•Can be too small to see, confusing, or too complicated. •May try to cover too much information. •May not adequately explain the meaning or significance.	•Same as Diagrams. •Be sure to make the number values large enough to be visible from all areas of the room. •Be sure to include a legend and labels where necessary.

Types	Benefits	Drawbacks	Tips
Charts: A set of words, symbols, and images that lists or summarizes key information or shows relationships among components. For example, the steps to make a budget, the components of a good resume, a play chart in hockey (see Figure 11.3).	•Can clarify steps or processes quickly. •Provide information your audience can write down quickly.	•May cover too much information and overwhelm the audience. •May be messy and unprofessional.	•Same as Diagrams and Graphs.
Maps: A drawing of all or part of a geographic area or place. Maps can be used to show transportation routes in towns or cities, borders between countries, immigration patterns, topography, and voting trends.	•Can be tailored to the speech to illustrate the speaker's point clearly. •Can show vast areas in a small space. •Can highlight significant landmarks easily. •Add interest and variety to the speech.	•If you rely on available maps, they might be too detailed and too small for the audience to see relevant information. •Difficult to draw accurately if not artistic.	•Transfer to slides. •Draw on poster board. •Download from Internet and make transparencies.
Audio Clips: Sound samples of other people talking, songs, sound effects, etc.	•Can bring to life lyrics, music, sounds, and quotes in a way that simply explaining or quoting cannot do.	•If too long, will lose audience interest. •Can be awkward to handle during the presentation. •Need to explain significance. •Equipment may be unreliable or unusable.	•Edit each clip down to 45 seconds or less and put only the clip(s) you are using onto a tape or CD. •Cue the tape or CD to the proper sound clip before beginning your speech.
Video Clips: Clips from movies, television shows, home movies, events, etc.	•Can exemplify a point or show an example in a way that description cannot.	•Same as Audio Clips.	•Edit each clip down to 45 seconds or less and put only the clip(s) you are using onto a videotape or DVD. •Cue the videotape or DVD to the proper clip before beginning your speech.
Food and Drinks: Useful for providing samples of dishes discussed, recipes taught, or ceremonies explained.	•People are often very happy to eat, so using food or drinks creates interest and enthusiasm. •Add powerful reinforcement to description and explanation.	•Audience may dislike the taste or refuse to try. •Can be difficult to distribute quickly. •Can be disruptive.	•Prepare servings in advance. •Distribute either at the beginning or at the end. •If distributing the samples during the speech, enlist volunteers to make distribution quick. •Clean up afterward.

Aaron was asked to teach a group of beginning gymnasts how to do a proper handstand. He decided that the best way to accomplish this was to demonstrate how to do each step himself.

Lindsey showed a third-grade class how to say, "I love you" in sign language by modeling the correct movements with her hands.

Using your own body is a convenient way to include presentation aids in your speech. You can use your own body by wearing a costume as Yoon did, demonstrating a skill as Aaron did, or modeling a movement as Lindsey did. Using your own body is also a reliable presentation aid because you can't forget your body at home, your body will work if the electricity goes out, and water will not make your body wrinkle, fade, or disintegrate. However, before choosing to use your own body as the medium for your aid, ask yourself the following questions:

- *Can I perform the action or demonstration properly even when I am nervous?* Nerves can make a voice quiver, hands shake, or knees wobble.
- *Is there enough room for me to effectively demonstrate or perform the action?* You may have limited space for large movements, or you might be situated close to steps or furniture.
- *Will everyone in the audience be able to see the action clearly?* In large audiences or flat rooms, people behind the first two or three rows may not be able to see the action clearly enough to understand, especially if the action takes place close to the ground.
- *Can I effectively coordinate my actions with what I am saying to the audience so that I don't waste time and my words are understandable?* Activity may cause you to become out of breath, to have awkward pauses or hesitations, or to turn away from the audience and not be heard.

If you answered "no" to any of these questions, you might want to reconsider using your own body as your presentation aid.

Using the Audience

One of the most effective ways to gain an audience's attention is by engaging them actively in your presentation. Having the audience clap, shout, look at each other, shake hands, stand up, or close their eyes enlists audience cooperation and attention. Be careful not to ask them to do anything that is embarrassing, dangerous, or inappropriate, and be certain that whatever participation you seek is relevant to a particular point you are trying to make. Also, be aware that the audience may not cooperate. Speakers have asked audiences to stand up, close their eyes, or change positions, only to be faced with blank stares, or worse: hostile glares. You don't want to be in the position of begging for cooperation or alienating your audience. Ask politely and cheerfully and reassure them that you won't be asking them to do anything embarrassing.

Chalkboards/Whiteboards

Most classrooms, meeting rooms, and lecture halls come equipped with chalkboards or whiteboards. You have witnessed your instructors using them during a lecture to clarify a point, sketch quick drawings, list key terms, or outline an idea. However, in presentations of less than ten minutes or so, you should avoid using chalk- or whiteboards. Writing on boards is time consuming, requires turning away from the audience, and is often sloppy. Avoid using the board unless a specific question comes up during your speech that you can explain only by using the board. Otherwise, prepare visuals in advance to show while you are speaking.

Handouts

When you have a lot of information or complicated concepts to explain, or you want to provide your audience with something to take home after the presentation, consider using handouts. Handouts allow you to give your audience a visual aid on which they can write notes and take home. It allows you to explain the significant aspects of your presentation while leaving more detailed information for the audience to review later.

Handouts can be challenging to incorporate into your speech if you are not prepared. The audience may be confused as to which page you are referring or become distracted by reading ahead while you are talking. So when preparing handouts, be sure that each page is clearly numbered so that you can direct your audience easily to the sections you are discussing. Also, distribute the handouts facedown before your presentation and ask the audience not to turn them over until you instruct them to do so. This way, the audience stays focused on you. When you are ready to discuss a page, direct the audience to the page and section you want them to see: "Turn to the bottom of page three in your handout." When you are finished discussing the handout, be sure to have audience members turn it facedown again. If you are not going to refer to the handouts during the presentation, you can distribute them at the end of your speech and let the audience know what kind of information they will find so that they will be more likely to read it.

Posters

If you are the creative type, you might want to spend some time developing a poster featuring one or two simple charts, graphs, lists, or photos. The advantages of using posters include the opportunities to prepare and practice with the visual in advance of your presentation and the opportunity to express some of your creativity.

When making a poster, there are several guidelines you should follow to make your poster look more professional, interesting, and easier to read. Use foam board instead of cardboard. Foam boards are more expensive than card-

Posters can be colorful, clear, and informative. Just remember to make them neat, professional, and uncluttered to be most effective.

board, but they are sturdier, easier to work with, and more professional looking than cardboard. They don't fall over when placed on an easel, the corners won't wear down as quickly, and they don't wrinkle. On all posters, make sure you premeasure and lay out your lettering and graphics before committing to the designs with ink and glue. Once you write on the poster, you cannot take it off. For more tips on preparing effective presentation aids see Table 11.3.

Transparencies and Slides

Many speakers prefer using overhead or slide projectors to show a series of visual aids. Virtually anything that can be photocopied or printed on a computer can be made into a transparency because transparency film can work in place of paper in most printers and photocopy machines. Place the transparency in the paper tray and print as you normally would.

Transparencies can be in color or black and white and offer the added benefit of allowing you to write directly on the transparency while you are discussing it. When preparing transparencies, make sure that both text and im-

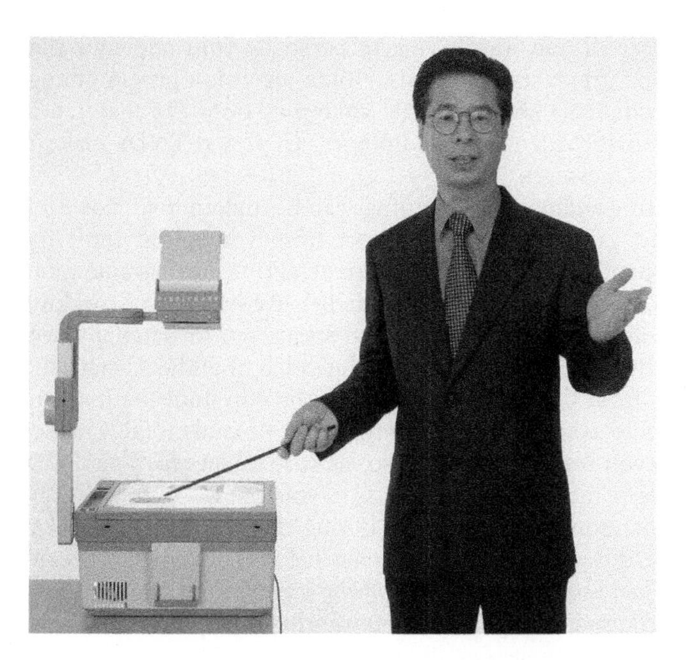

Using an overhead projector allows you to face the audience and to show graphics, maps, lists, and pictures that would be hard to include on a poster.

ages are large enough for everyone in the audience to be able to read. Visuals aren't effective when you must say, "I know you can't see this, but. . . . "

Speakers once used slides frequently during a speech, but today we are seeing fewer slide presentations and more overhead projectors and computer-generated presentations. Nonetheless, slides offer an excellent way to show photographs because you can adjust the size to fit the size of the room. However, slides can be expensive to produce, and projectors are sometimes difficult to obtain. If you plan to use slides, be sure to find out if a projector is available and arrive early to test and practice with the equipment before your presentation.

As with any electrical or mechanical equipment, always have a contingency plan in the event of power or equipment failure—expect the unexpected! Bring an extra light bulb for the projector, and have handouts of your transparencies just in case you can't use the projector (it's a good idea to provide handouts of transparencies anyway).

Audiovisual Recordings

An audio recording of whale sounds, a funny scene from a movie, a popular television ad, or a series of outtakes from a popular movie can offer vivid, interesting, dynamic, and persuasive support to presentations. For example, you could play a portion of a song by Julio Iglesias to show an example of his

TIP
How to Use Transparencies and Overhead Projector Effectively

- Discretely number your transparencies in case they become mixed up.
- Use a 36-point font when creating transparencies to ensure readability.
- Position a piece of paper between each transparency for easier handling.
- Position the transparency before you turn on the projector, and check the first image on the screen before you begin your presentation.
- Place transparencies on the machine faceup so that you can read the words, not facedown so the words are backward.
- Point with a pencil or pen, not your finger. This looks unprofessional and imprecise. Remember, your hand movements will be projected onto the screen as well as the image.
- Unless you are showing only a few transparencies in fast succession, turn off the projector between each one.
- When uncovering one line or section of a transparency at a time , lay a piece of paper under the transparency so that the transparency does not slide. This will also allow you to see the text of the transparency while the audience cannot.

passionate singing style. If you were trying to persuade your audience that people of color are underrepresented in prime-time television programming, you could compile videotape showing brief examples from the major networks' prime-time shows. Video- and audiotapes, CDs, and DVDs make it easy to create powerful messages.

The benefits of using audiovisual recordings can be undermined, however, by ineffective use. To gain the greatest impact from your clips, limit the amount of time you spend on a single clip. The general rule is to have no more than forty-five seconds of audiovisual recordings per five minutes of speaking time. Remember, the audience came to hear you speak, not to watch a video. This time should include the time it takes for the video or audio to start and stop. In other words, from the moment you begin the clip until the moment you stop the clip should take no more than forty-five seconds total. Practice and editing will help you reach this goal. Also, be sure to cue the tape, DVD, or CD before you begin the speech, and be sure you know how to use the equipment. Nothing is more distracting and boring than to watch a speaker fumble with equipment that he or she has never before encountered. I can't stress this enough: *When using electronic equipment with which you are unfamiliar, practice your speech using the equipment in advance of your presentation.*

Computer-Generated Presentations

PowerPoint, PowerPoint, PowerPoint. Some speakers love to use PowerPoint slide shows when giving speeches. In recent years, business professionals, students, and instructors alike have embraced the idea of eye-popping graphics, animated transitions, and heaps of bullet points to outline a speech from opening line to closing remarks. Many of us have been subjected to them as well. The ease with which a speaker can make beautiful, full-color, professional slides has led to overuse, misuse, and even abuse of this new technology. PowerPoint has become so overused and misused that many instructors, businesses, and professional speakers have banned its use entirely. However, I believe that banning its use, as an old saying goes, "throws the baby out with the bathwater," meaning that in ridding ourselves of what we do not want, we also rid ourselves of what we want and need. As Andrew Wahl claimes in *Canadian Business Magazine*, "PowerPoint doesn't kill presentations: people kill presentations."[3]

PowerPoint presentations should not be used for presentations that are shorter than thirty minutes (many even say sixty minutes). If your presentation is thirty, forty-five, sixty, or more minutes long, then feel free to use PowerPoint; but use it carefully. As Doug Carter warns, "You, the presenter, need to be the center of attention. . . . The more your audience interacts and relates with you, the more likely they'll also embrace your ideas."[4] Again, the audience is there to hear you speak, not to watch a slide show. See Table 11.2 for some tips on using PowerPoint slides.

TABLE 11.2 **How to Use PowerPoint Slide Shows Effectively***

- Get comfortable with the technology; you will look awkward if you don't know what you are doing.
- Don't use a slide unless you absolutely have to: The focus should be on you, not on your slide show. One slide for every three to five minutes is plenty.
- Know what you are talking about: Do not read or repeat the PowerPoint slide.
- Less is more in slide design:
  - Set off important numbers with color.
  - Use no more than five points per slide and five or six words per line.
  - Present detailed tables, charts, or columns of numbers as handouts, not on slides.
  - Use little animation and few transitions: Too much animation detracts from a speech—it is boring and time consuming.
- Avoid clip art that is commercially available. Create your own using a digital camera or scan pictures from magazines and books.
- Don't show the slide prematurely: Wait until it comes up, pause, and then discuss it.
- Use the "B" key to black out the screen when you are not talking about a slide.
- Rehearse: Practice and experiment in private, and rehearse with the technology thoroughly.
- Don't turn off all the lights: Leave some lights on so that the audience can take notes.

* PowerPoint guidelines adapted from: Andrew Wahl, "PowerPoint of No Return," *Canadian Business Magazine* 76, no. 22 (November 23, 2003): 131–133; Fraser P. Seitel, "Every Picture Tells a Story," *United States Bander* 102, no. 7 (July 1992): 55; and Marilyn M. Helms, "The Key to a Strong Presentation Is in the Details," *Presentations* 17, no. 5 (May 2003): 58.

HOW TO USE PRESENTATION AIDS

When using presentation aids, you need to consider preparing the aids as well as actually using them in your speech. The most important considerations before preparing your presentation aids are the audience, you, your time, and cost. As always, consider your audience at each step, asking yourself whether this is the best way for you to make your point to this audience. However, you can't lose sight of how the presentation aid impacts you.

Weigh your decisions about presentation aids against how much money and time you are willing to invest in making them. In my experience, students don't usually have too much money or time. Students have received high scores using economical presentation aids while others have received low scores using much more expensive and time-consuming ones. Remember John? Tables 11.3 and 11.4 offer specific guidelines for preparing and using presentation aids.

Presentation aids are termed "aids" and not "replacements" for a reason. No audiovisual clip, object, or action can take the place of a well-planned, researched, and rehearsed speech, but aids do add interest and help to clarify

TABLE 11.3 **Guidelines for Preparing Presentation Aids**

Content

- Summarize, not duplicate, your speech on a visual aid.
- Include only one idea per visual aid.

Lettering and Fonts

- Make fonts large enough for your audience to be able to read them (use fewer words if necessary).
- Make letters at least two inches high for readability on posters.

Color

- Use colors and shades consistently.
- Make sure text color contrasts with background color, with the greatest contrast between the title and the background. Black or dark blue on white is effective.
- Limit colors to no more than three so not as to confuse and clutter the message. Use tints of fewer colors instead.

Graphs and Charts

- Use chart legends sparingly; instead, put labels and figures on the bars themselves.
- Highlight the most important part of a pie chart or graph by giving it a brighter color; use shades of that color on the rest.
- Divide a pie chart into no more than eight slices; if more are needed, use another chart.

Graphics and Pictures

- Avoid diagonal and checkered patterns in color graphics; they are hard to see and can make the audience dizzy.
- Use only one arrow to draw attention to a single point. Using too many arrows has no impact.
- If you must enlarge or shrink an image, maintain the natural aspect ratio (the ratio between height and length).

Other Guidelines

- Proofread spelling, spacing, and grammar carefully!
- Cite the source of your information on the bottom of the visual aid.
- Practice, practice, practice using your presentation aids until you can use them

your points. You never know what might happen the day of your presentation: The equipment may malfunction, you might forget your handouts at home, or the electricity might go out, leaving you on your own. If you are confident enough in your speech, you can still give an excellent presentation without the help of presentation aids.

SUMMARY

Presentation aids, the sixth category of supporting materials, help both the speaker and the audience. They increase clarity and audience interest in the presentation, making your speech more meaningful and memorable. For the

TABLE 11.4 **How to Use Presentation Aids Effectively and Professionally**

- Cover or conceal your aids until you are ready to use them. Place the presentation aids out of the way, but easily accessible.
- Place visual aids where they are visible to all audience members, and do not stand in front of the visual.
- Introduce and explain the aid before you reveal it: "This graph demonstrates how. . . ."
- Reveal the presentation aid and explain its significance or how it relates to your point clearly: "As you can see here, violent crime has exploded since. . . ."
- Maintain eye contact while discussing your aid: Don't stare at the presentation aid or turn your back to the audience.
- Put the aid away when you are finished with it.

speaker, presentation aids build credibility and confidence. As a non-native speaker, you may also find that a presentation aid helps you relax, knowing that your aid will help the audience get used to your speaking style more quickly without their missing important information.

In Chapter Seven, we said that speakers should use only the supporting material that is directly related to the point they are trying to make. Otherwise, it can distract from the speech instead of enhance it. The same advice is true for your speech aids: Choose only the best, most relevant, interesting, and meaningful presentation aids. Prepare them carefully, making sure that they are big enough to be seen clearly from all areas of the room and are neat and legible, and that you explain their significance to the audience.

Finally, remember not only to choose and prepare your presentation aids carefully, but also to practice with them thoroughly so that you become comfortable with them and can manage any challenges you might face. Presentation aids are there to enhance your speech, making it more understandable, meaningful, and memorable. If they distract, are irrelevant to, or take over the presentation, you should not use them. Your presentation should never rely on the presentation aids because you never know when something might go wrong. Remember, expect the unexpected, and you will be prepared!

Discussion Questions and Activities

1. Think about the last time an article, speech, or story moved you. What kind of presentation aids did the author use? What did you find the most interesting, memorable, and/or compelling? Why? What other presentation aids might the author have included that would have made the story or argument even more powerful? What kinds of visual support do you generally find to be the most persuasive or convincing? Is this a personal preference or a cultural preference? Why?
2. After creating and practicing alone with your presentation aids, meet with three or four classmates to practice your speeches using your presentation

aids. Provide each other with clear, honest, and useful suggestions for improving both the speeches and the uses of presentation aids.

3. Based on a recent lecture in one of your classes, create a PowerPoint presentation that makes the lecture more interesting and easier to follow. Use the fewest number of slides possible, following the guidelines for PowerPoint presentations in this chapter. Present the lecture to a classmate as if you were the teacher. Did the PowerPoint presentation help you present the information? How? Was it difficult to talk and manage the slide show at the same time? Talk to your classmate about what s/he thought of your presentation and discuss ways it could have been improved.
4. Read the speech at the end of this chapter, and develop a visual aid that clarifies and creates interest in the speech.
5. Watch your local evening news and analyze the use of presentation aids. Do the aids help you understand the story? Do the presentation aids support the story or dominate the story? Are they effective? Do the aids convey the same story as the words, or do the aids simply add visual interest (something to look at while the anchor talks)?
6. Analyze the presentation aids used in your classmates' speeches. Choose one speech and answer the following: Which of his/her visuals did you find the most effective? Why? What could the speaker have done to improve the effectiveness of the visuals? If this speaker were to redo this speech, what advice would you give this speaker for developing new visual aids? Why?

Chapter Quiz

Matching

Place the letter of the presentation aid that would best suit the claims and types of information below.

a. Photographs **b.** Chart **c.** Model
d. Line graph **e.** Timeline **f.** Pie chart

1. _____ "The teenage smoking rate is increasing at an alarming rate."

2. _____ The frescoes in the Sistine Chapel

3. _____ Vincent Van Gogh's love life: date of first heartbreak, date of second heartbreak, start and end of relationship with Sien, love affair with older woman

4. _____ "This university relies most heavily on its tuition for funding."

5. _____ "There are three things you can do to reduce your stage fright."

6. _____ The location of the O-ring malfunction in the space shuttle *Challenger*

7. True or False: It is always preferable to use PowerPoint presentations over transparencies.

8. True or False: When choosing supporting materials, you should first choose the supporting materials that will be in the text of your speech and then decide on your presentation aids.
9. True or False: When making a poster, you should try to use no more than three colors.
10. Which of the following is true about creating presentation aids?
    a. Aim to duplicate the content of your speech.
    b. Include no more than three ideas per visual aid.
    c. Letters should be no more than two inches high.
    d. Limit the variety of colors to no more than three.

Speech for Analysis

Read the following speech and decide where the speaker should include visual aids. Suggest the types of visual aids and what information should be included on each. Discuss your choices.

Giraffe Women
by Wai Kwong

What do you think of this woman? This is quite strange to us. Is she crazy? My first impression is that she is crazy, but now I know better. Most people call them long-necked or giraffe women, but, in fact, they belong to the tribe called Padaung.

Although the history of the Padaung is sad and the method of wearing the brass rings around the neck is painful, the Padaung still continue their custom because of many reasons. Let's talk about their history first.

Padaung has a sad and unfortunate history. They are originally from Burma, the yellow region of the map. A theory program called beauty guilty mentioned that there were 7,000 people in Padaung in Burma 30 years ago. However, some of them escaped from the political turmoil and migrated to Thailand, which is next to Burma. The number of Padaung in Thailand is very low. There are only 300 people in Thailand of the Padaung people and only 51 of them maintain this custom of wearing the brass rings around their necks.

So how and when do they wear the brass rings around the necks? The method of wearing the brass rings around the necks looks simple, but it takes a long time to complete and it is very painful. According to the website of the People of the World Foundation, they start to wear the brass ring from 5 years old. After 10 years old, they add one more ring around their necks for each passing year. Their necks grow longer until they are totally matured. That is around 25 years old.

The maximum number of bands to wear is about 37 and the total mass is around 5 to 10 kg. These two math books are about 5 kg. I think nobody of us likes to carry this heavy book to school every day. However, the Padaung need to wear this weight of rings every day, even when they sleep or work. So you can imagine how they can be painful. In fact, they have to decide whether or not to wear the rings at 10 years old. After 25 years old, they can't take off the rings until they die, otherwise it is dangerous to their lives. Because at this time their necks will be very weak. In fact, the rings do not make their necks longer; they just make their necks look longer. This is just a visual illusion.

Let's take a look at this picture. These are people who are not wearing the rings. The angle between the neck and the shoulder is about 110°. However, after wearing the rings, the heavy mass of the rings pushes down the collarbone and the range of the shoulders. So the angles between the neck and the shoulders of the Padaung are larger than people who do not wear the rings. This is about 150°. As a result, the collarbone and the shoulder become part of the neck.

Why do they want to have this suffering? There are many reasons for them wearing the rings. One is they want to prevent a tiger attacking them in the forest. The other one is that they believe they are the descendants of the phoenix, so they want to make their neck longer to imitate the phoenix. The other reason they want to make their neck longer is to make them more unattractive to avoid being captured by other enemy tribes. However, another reason is opposite to this. The Padaung think that a long neck is a sign of beauty and they can attract a better husband. Nowadays, a reason for them to do this is tourism. They are very popular for tourists to visit now in Thailand and this has become their main income.

In conclusion, even though the custom of the Padaung may seem crazy at the first impression, the custom is not easy and comfortable to maintain. Actually the Padaung have many cultural and historical reasons for wearing these brass rings around the neck. So this is proof that all countries have their own beliefs and customs and we should not judge others but respect others' customs because we do not know the history of them. Thank you.

Chapter 11 Quiz Answers

1. d, 2. a, 3. e, 4. f, 5. b, 6. c, 7. False, 8. True, 9. True, 10. d

CHAPTER 12 Delivery

CHAPTER GOAL

By the end of this chapter you will be able to identify and practice proper vocal and non-vocal delivery techniques.

The human face reveals our deepest emotions.

Alessandra spent weeks researching, organizing, and writing her speech. Ever since her marine biology class, she had been interested in the destruction of the world's coral reefs, so for her informative speech she chose the effects of pollution on coral reefs. After many hours of preparation and with the help of a fabulous visual aid, Alessandra was certain she would do a great job.

Unfortunately, Alessandra's visual aid took longer to put together than she had expected, so it wasn't finished until the night before the presentation. Out of time and tired, she decided to run through the speech once the night before and once on her way to class in the morning. She figured that since she had researched the topic so thoroughly and had spent so much time putting it together, she would have no problem getting through the speech smoothly. She was wrong!

The speech began strongly enough, at least through the attention getter. However, Alessandra mumbled and stuttered through the rest of the speech, staring at her limited notes and hoping for some cue to remind her what to say next. She completely forgot to show her visual aid. She found herself clutching the podium and nervously shifting from foot to foot. As she finally found some words to end the speech, she snatched up her papers and scurried back to her seat, embarrassed and disappointed.

As a language learner, you already know that communicating effectively in a new language means more than simply learning its vocabulary and syntax. Communicating successfully in any language requires effective and accurate use of both the verbal and the nonverbal components of communication and the culture. Verbal communication refers to that part of communication that uses language. Written language, spoken language, singing, and sign language are all forms of verbal communication, whereas gestures, facial expressions, and body posture, for example, are components of nonverbal communication.

Nonverbal communication includes all the communication cues surrounding verbal communication that are not actual language. Gestures, facial expressions, vocal cues, use of space, and eye movements are a few examples of nonverbal behaviors. Both verbal and nonverbal communication can be either vocal (using the voice) or non-vocal (not using the voice). (See Table 12.1.) Thus far, we have mostly discussed the verbal aspects of public speaking. In this chapter, we will focus on the nonverbal aspects of public speaking—the "delivery" of the speech.

One of the common mistakes speakers make is spending a lot of time writing their speech and little to no time practicing their delivery. Preparing for the delivery of the speech is as important as any other part of speech preparation. A good delivery can make a mediocre speech better, and a poor delivery can make an excellent speech hard to listen to and even boring.

In this chapter you will learn the following:

- The four types of speech delivery
- Ways to refine and improve speech delivery through practice
- The importance of proper pronunciation and articulation
- Ways to improve sentence and word stress
- Vocal aspects of speech delivery (e.g., rate, volume, pitch, variety, and pauses)

TABLE 12.1 **Vocal/Non-Vocal; Verbal/Nonverbal**

	Verbal	**Nonverbal**
Vocal	Spoken language Singing	Vocalics (vocal cues) Screaming Laughing Humming
Non-Vocal	Written language Sign language	Gestures Eye movements Use of space Touch

- Non-vocal aspects of good speech delivery, including eye contact, facial expressions, body movements, and gestures
- More on the best ways to practice

Let's begin by examining some of the particular concerns you may have as a non-native speaker.

SPECIAL DELIVERY CONCERNS OF NON-NATIVE SPEAKERS

As a non-native speaker, some of your greatest public speaking concerns probably have to do with delivery. You may be concerned with clarity, stuttering, finding the right words at the right time, meeting the expectations for proper body movements and gestures, and your accent, among other things. In this chapter, you will find specific suggestions on the preferred delivery style used in the United States and in most of the English-speaking world, but first let's look at one of the most common cross-cultural nonverbal mistakes people sometimes make: the use of specific gestures.

As you know, cultures differ in more than language; a small, meaningless gesture in one culture can have a powerful meaning in another, even when the two cultures share a common language. For example, the "peace sign" or "V for Victory" sign created by making a "V" with the index and middle fingers and the palm facing away from the person making the sign is perfectly acceptable in the United States, Great Britain, and Australia. However, if one were to turn the hand around and face the back of the hand toward others, this would be quite offensive in Great Britain and Australia, but would be relatively meaningless in the United States. Knowing which gestures are offensive within a given culture is very important for avoiding uncomfortable misunderstandings. The "Considering Culture" chart below provides a summary of the most inappropriate gestures used in English-speaking countries as well as a few other gestures that audiences around the world might find unacceptable.

If you are concerned about your accent, you may make the mistake of rushing through your presentation, speaking too softly, or simply finding a way not to have to speak. Unfortunately, none of these tactics will help you improve either your public speaking or your clarity. Instead, concentrate on the content and organization of your message, and practice proper pronunciation and articulation in front of a native speaker if at all possible.[1] If you can't find a native speaker to guide your clarity, then use the dictionary and web sources to perfect your pronunciation of difficult words. Slow down your delivery and speak loud enough for everyone in the room to hear you.

DELIVERY STYLES

There are four basic styles of speech delivery commonly used in the United States: memorized, manuscript, impromptu, and extemporaneous. Logically, the memorized style refers to when a speaker memorizes his/her speech word

CONSIDERING CULTURE

Gestures Around the World

Like words, the meanings of gestures change from culture to culture. The following list will help you become familiar with some common gestures used in the United States and around the world and their meanings.

Gesture	Meaning in U.S.	Meaning Elsewhere
Raised fist	Can either mean "power" or indicate anger	None
Lifting the middle finger with the back of the hand pointing out	Vulgar, aggressive, and offensive	Much of the Western world now recognizes this as an obscene gesture. Other parts of the world see it as meaningless.
Pointing	Indicates where something is or what someone is talking about; can be seen as rude when pointing at another person	Can be viewed as rude in many places in the world.
Head nodding: moving the head up and down	Indicates "yes," agreement, or encouragement to the speaker	In Bulgaria, the opposite is true: Nodding indicates "no" or disagreement.
Head shaking: moving the head back and forth (from the right to the left)	Indicates "no," disagreement, or confusion	In India, one long side shake indicates agreement or encouragement to the speaker to continue.
"OK": Creating a circle with the thumb and index finger with remaining fingers sticking up toward the sky	Indicates "OK" or that "everything is good"	In Brazil, Russia, and Germany it is a vulgar insult. In Japan it refers to money or coins, and in France it refers to zero.
"Thumbs up": Clenching hand in a fist with the thumb sticking out and pointing up toward the sky	Another way to say "OK" or to indicate pride or agreement	In Germany and Japan it is used for counting (1 and 5, respectively). In Nigeria, Australia, and Iraq it is a very vulgar insult.
"Hook' em horns": Extending the index and pinky fingers with thumb holding the two middle fingers down	Texas pride or the devil's horns	In Italy it is a reference to one's spouse being unfaithful. In Africa it is a curse. In Brazil and Venezuala it is a good luck sign.
Extending index finger and making circular motion at temple	Crazy (also in Germany)	In Argentina it signifies a phone call.
Waving open hand back and forth	Hello/good-bye	In Europe this means "no."
Showing the sole of your shoe	When done inadvertently (putting one's feet up on a desk), this is meaningless in the United States	In Saudi Arabia, Egypt, Singapore, and Thailand, this is an insult.

Politicians and newscasters frequently use teleprompters when speaking.

for word and delivers the speech entirely from memory. This is the style used by politicians, actors, and others when a speech is very short or when it must be precise. The benefit of using a memorized speech is that all the words are carefully chosen and crafted ahead of time, leaving the speaker with nothing to decide at the moment of delivery. The risks of using a memorized delivery include forgetting the lines, sounding monotone or scripted, and creating a sense of distance between the speaker and the audience.

Manuscript delivery refers to reading a speech word for word from a paper or from a teleprompter (i.e., the electronic device used in television that displays the words to a speaker such as a politician or newscaster). The benefit of using the manuscript style is that the speaker has every word in front of him/her, so s/he is not likely to go blank or forget what to say. Similar to memorized speaking, manuscript speaking can lead to a monotone voice and a distance between the audience and the speaker. Furthermore, speakers sometimes lose their place when using a manuscript, pages become mixed up, and speakers sometimes misread or mispronounce the words.

Impromptu style is often thought of as speaking "off-the-cuff," with little or no preparation. Actually, impromptu speaking is a limited-preparation activity that is "not something that just happens; rather, it is something that can be planned for and taught."[2] It is a very natural style that uses the speaker's personality and enthusiasm to connect directly with the audience. The key to delivering successful impromptu presentations is to choose two or three main points that directly support a clear thesis.

Extemporaneous speaking uses the best of the other three delivery styles. An extemporaneous speech is well planned, crafted, researched, and practiced like manuscript and memorized speeches, but the speaker chooses the actual words as he or she is speaking, as in everyday conversation and in impromptu speaking. However, the extemporaneous speech differs from conversation and impromptu speaking in that a great deal of preparation precedes the delivery of an extemporaneous speech. Additionally, an extemporaneous speech is not written word by word, as is a manuscript or an essay, but rather as an outline of only the major points (see Chapter Eight). The use of the keyword outline helps the speaker stay focused and accurately provide facts, statistics, and quotes without having to read everything word for word. In this way, extemporaneous speakers are free to be conversational and natural, as well as organized and knowledgeable.

Many new speakers fear using an extemporaneous style because they think that if they don't have all the words for the speech in front of them, they will forget what they have to say. This is far from the case; the use of too many notes or relying on your memory under times of increased excitement and anxiety is more likely to confuse you than to help you. If you plan, prepare, and practice your speech using an extemporaneous style, you will have all the notes you need to get through your speech. The key to successful extemporaneous speaking is practice, so be sure to allow yourself enough time before each speech to practice thoroughly.

VOCAL ASPECTS

The vocal aspects, also called *vocalics*, of good delivery include such things as pronunciation, articulation, word and sentence stress, volume, rate, pause, pitch, and conversational tone. Together, these aspects create a rhythm or a cadence to your speech that keeps it lively, interesting, and easy to follow. The vocal aspects of a speaker can also influence how the audience feels, not only about the message but also about the speaker, such as how much they like or trust the speaker.[3] In Chapter Nine we discussed ways to improve pronunciation and articulation, so in this chapter we will focus on the other aspects of good vocal delivery.

Word Stress

English is a stressed language, in which some words and syllables within words are spoken with more force than others. This means that speakers spend more time on some words and syllables than on others. Conversely, syllabic languages, such as Japanese, French, and Italian, do not use word stress. These languages say each syllable with the same amount of stress or force, giving equal importance and time to each, yet they do have variation in which words in a sentence are stressed.

Many stressed languages have very clear and consistent rules regarding where to put the stress on a word, which makes it easy to discern one word from another after a little practice. Spanish, for example, has only two rules

TABLE 12.2 **Syllable Stress Rules in English** (stressed syllables are indicated by all caps)

Word stress rules apply only to words containing more than one syllable.	*Car, dog,* and *thin* have only one syllable, so no stress rules apply.
Place the stress on the first syllable in most two-syllable nouns and adjectives.	AU-to, POO-dle, SKIN-ny
Place the stress on the last syllable in most two-syllable verbs (with the exception of two-syllable verbs ending in *–ing*).	cre-ATE, con-CLUDE, for-GIVE (exceptions: DRIV-ing, WASH-ing)
Place the stress on the second-from-the-last syllable when the words end in *–sion, -tion,* or *–ic.*	di-VER-sion, po-LU-tion, met-a-BOL-ic, su-per-SON-ic
Place the stress on the third to the last syllable when the words end in *–al, -cy, -gy, -phy, -sy* and *–ty.*	sen-SA-tion-al, in-DE-cen-cy, a-NAL-o-gy, phi-LO-so-phy, hy-POC-ri-sy, QUAN-ti-ty
Place the stress on the first part in compound nouns (nouns made by combining two or more nouns).	BOOK-case, DUST-pan, GREEN-house, UN-der-gar-ment
Place the stress on the second word in compound adjectives and verbs (adjectives and verbs made by combining two words).	ab-sent-MIND-ed, up-COM-ing, o-ver-HEAT, un-der-ES-ti-mate

for deciding where to place the accent in a word: (1) Words that end in a vowel, in *-n*, or in *-s* are stressed on the next-to-the-last syllable (e.g., *nada* is "ná-da"; *hablan* is "há-blan"; and *hombre* is "hóm-bre"). (2) All other words ending in consonants are stressed on the last syllable (e.g., *beber* is "be-bér," and *recogedor* is "re-co-ge-dór"). Exceptions to the two rules use a written accent to indicate where to place the stress (e.g., *está, teléfono*). Unfortunately, the rules for English stress are not as consistent, concise, or predictable.

Generally, there are several major rules governing word stress in English (see Table 12.2). However, it is important to remember that, like most English rules, there are many exceptions to each of these rules. The best way to learn the rhythms of English stress is to learn the stress of each word as you learn the word. The dictionary indicates which syllable to stress within the pronunciation guide with an accent mark (∏) after the proper syllable ("créd-it"), by capitalizing the stressed syllable ("CRED-it"), or by bolding the stressed syllable ("**cred**-it").

Sentence Stress

Whereas word stress indicates which one syllable in a word will be stressed, sentence stress indicates which words within a sentence will be stressed. We identify two types of words in sentences when we talk about stress: *content* and *function* words. Content words are the "important" words in the sentence that carry the significant meaning of the sentence. The function words are the words that give the sentence structure, but add little meaning to the sentence. Consider the following sentence:

> **Last night**, **I walked** to the **store** to buy some **ice cream** because I was **craving** something **chocolate**.

In this sentence, the words in bold are the content words. The other words are the function words. The content words are the words that a speaker stresses, the words that are more carefully pronounced and articulated. The function words are the words that a speaker is more likely to mumble, garble, or speed through.

The good news is that when listening to an English speaker, you can discern most of the intended meaning by listening to the content words that are stressed and usually pronounced more slowly and carefully than the rest of the words. Practice listening to native English speakers on television or on the radio. Think of it as listening to the melody of the language. Language is rhythmic and flowing, so in time, the natural flow of the language will become second nature to you. When practicing your speech, work on stressing the appropriate syllables and the important words to help your audience follow along and understand you.

Volume

The volume of speaking refers to how loudly or quietly one speaks. When giving a speech, you need to be sure that you are speaking loudly enough for everyone in the room, including those in the back row, to hear every word, but not so loudly that you are yelling. More people have a tendency to be too quiet rather than too loud. To ensure that you are speaking with a loud enough volume, begin your speech by actually speaking to the back row of the audience. Think of it this way: If you were trying to talk to a friend who is across the street, you would naturally speak louder to throw your voice far enough for your friend to hear you. Similarly, when you focus on speaking to the back row, your voice will naturally be louder.

Remember, you can observe audience members' nonverbal feedback to judge if they can hear you or not. If audience members are turning their ears toward you, leaning forward, or looking like they are straining to hear you, this is a good indication that you are speaking too softly.

Luckily, there is a fairly broad range of acceptable volumes that allows your audience to hear you clearly but is not perceived as being too loud. Aim to match your volume to the mood you are trying to create while making sure that you are always loud enough to be heard. A louder volume creates passion, excitement, and anticipation; a softer volume creates solemnity and seriousness.

Rate

The rate of speaking refers to how quickly or slowly you speak. Some speakers speak very quickly, so quickly, in fact, that the audience (native and nonnative speakers alike) may have trouble keeping up with the message. Other speakers speak so slowly that the audience becomes restless and bored waiting to hear the rest of the message. U.S. Americans typically use a fairly quick rate of speech (about 125 words per minute), but we also like well-placed pauses to give us time to think. When practicing your speech, be sure that your speaking rate is fast enough to keep the audience's interest and slow enough for the audience to take in and understand your message.

Research has shown that planned speaking such as a speech results in a person using a speech rate twice as fast as for unplanned or natural speech, such as a conversation with a friend.[4] If you are a *fast-talker*, one who speaks very quickly (more than about 135 words per minute), you will need to pay special attention to slowing down when you practice. Fast-talking is often the result of feeling anxious and wanting to get through the speech as quickly as possible. To avoid rushing, remember to *pause* (briefly stopping before moving on) before you begin speaking and to breathe deeply and slowly. When practicing your speech, you can tape-record yourself to get an idea of how you sound to others. Practice until you feel that you can present your speech at a reasonably slower rate. Then practice in front of a friend, roommate, or family member and ask that person to notice the rate at which you speak. Finally, write, "SLOW" in the margins of your speaking outline to remind yourself to take your time.

If you are a *slow-talker* (fewer than 110 words per minute), you will need to learn to pick up the pace to keep your audience's interest. Slow-talking is often the result of feeling insecure and self-conscious or worrying that you won't be able to remember the words. To bring your speech up to speed, practice the speech several times, forcing yourself to keep talking even when you feel at a loss for words. When you practice, overcompensate for your insecurity by pretending that you feel *very* confident. Act confident and soon you will feel confident. Remember, the way you practice the speech will be very similar to how you will perform the speech, so practice as if you are the most confident and comfortable speaker in the world. That confidence will carry over to your speech.

In addition to making the speech interesting and intelligible, the speaking rate sets the pace, rhythm, and tone of the speech. In general, the slower one speaks, the more serious, ceremonial, or somber a mood one will create. Eulogies, commencement addresses, and memorial speeches are often marked by a slower rate of speech and the use of more pauses. This allows the audience more time to savor the words and to consider what the speaker is saying.

A fast rate of speech, on the other hand, creates excitement, passion, joy, or anticipation. Motivational speeches, speeches of celebration, and acceptance speeches use an accelerated tempo, short words and sentences, and high energy, which encourage the audience to feel the speaker's excitement and to join the celebration. The key to using rate effectively to create mood is to change your rate throughout the speech to match the ideas and points you are making at the time.

Pauses

As mentioned above, the use of pauses can help slow down the rate of speech, but they can also be used to create tension, anticipation, and impact in a speech when strategically placed throughout a speech. A pause, you might remember, is a brief break in speaking, a short moment of silence between words or sentences that slows down the speaker and provides the audience a moment to think. Read the following out loud:

> Imagine yourself sleeping soundly in your bed. All the world is quiet. When suddenly you hear a loud CRASH! And you realize the crash was the sound of your kitchen window breaking. Someone is breaking into your house. What do you do?

Now, say it again, but pause where indicated:

> Imagine yourself sleeping soundly in your bed. (PAUSE) All the world is quiet. (PAUSE) When suddenly you hear a loud CRASH! And you realize the crash was the sound of your kitchen window breaking. (PAUSE) Someone is breaking into your house. (LONG PAUSE) What do you do?

Did you notice the difference in the tension created by the second example? As you write your speech, you should also plan pauses by placing the word "PAUSE" (in all caps) after key points, before or after transitions, and anywhere you want the audience to stop and think for just a second.

Although pauses can add impact, they can also be overused or misused. Your speech rate can become awkward and halting if you infuse the speech with too many pauses, add vocalized pauses, or use filler words. To avoid an awkward speech rate, use pauses for impact only occasionally, and learn to avoid using vocalized pauses and filler words.

Vocalized pauses are the nonword sounds we make between words and sentences to fill empty space as we try to think of the next word or formulate the next sentence:

> I was, uh, thinking that, ah, I, uh, might want to, um, try to, uh, convince you to, ah, donate blood.

Filler words, like vocalized pauses, fill up space with extra words that don't actually mean anything in the sentence:

Basically, I was, you know, thinking that, like, I, basically, might want to, you know, try to convince you to donate blood, basically.

Although most people use filler and vocalized pauses from time to time and although these pauses are a natural part of everyday conversation, when used too much they can make a speaker seem unsure, less intelligent, and unprepared. To reduce their use, practice your speech very slowly the first few times, being careful not to use any filler or vocalized pauses whatsoever. You may find that you have to speak–only–one–word–at–a–time–to–eliminate–the–extra–words–and–sounds, but by going slowly, you retain control over what you say. Once you have mastered your speaking, increase your delivery speed with each subsequent practice until you can say your entire speech at a normal rate without using unnecessary pauses or filler words.

Considering Language

Emotions in another language

Matching the expression of emotion with the mood and tone of a the speech is vital to a speaker's credibility. However, it is important to know that not all cultures have the same understanding of emotions. In fact, not all languages even have a word that is equivalent to the English word "emotion." For example, Tahitians and the Ifaluks of Micronesia do not have such a word. Furthermore, not all cultures view individual emotions equally. The Japanese view "considerate" and "lucky" to be emotions, but in English we do not. Additionally, the Japanese emotion of *amae* (presuming upon another's love), the Bengali *obhiman* (sadness caused by a loved one's insensitivity), and the Spanish *verguenza ajena* (feeling shame for the actions of others) are unique emotions to those languages.*

*James Russell "Culture, and the Categorization of Emotions," *Psychological Bulletin* 110, no. 3 (1991): 426–450.

Pitch

Pitch refers to the relative highness or lowness of one's voice. Like musical instruments, voices move up and down the scale. Some people have naturally higher-pitched voices, while others have naturally lower-pitched voices, and everyone uses a variety of pitches to convey mood, attitude, and tone. Like slowing a speech down and lowering volume, lower pitch is associated with a more serious mood, while higher pitch is associated with excitement and anticipation.

The opposite of adjusting one's pitch is called *monotone*. Monotone speakers sound like they are reading or as if they memorized their speech. A monotone voice is boring to the audience, so pay special attention to adjusting your pitch to create a more natural flow of speech.

Conversational Tone

The aim of extemporaneous speaking is to use our best conversational tone when speaking. That is not to say that we should speak as informally as we do in everyday conversation, but that we should speak naturally. From the audience's perspective, a conversational tone feels like the speaker is simply talking to them spontaneously. A conversational quality is relaxed, clear, yet still organized with just the right amount of formality and professionalism. This is achieved by combining all the elements of good vocal delivery into *vocal variety*.

Vocal variety refers to altering volume, rate, pause, and pitch throughout a speech to match the mood and tone of the presentation. The best way to achieve this is to carefully plan the speech and to practice it thoroughly. You can do this by practicing from a keyword outline and saying it differently each time you practice. Choosing different ways to convey the same ideas each time keeps the delivery fresh, gives you practice creating sentences to express the same idea in a variety of ways, and builds your speaking confidence without relying too heavily on notes. When we create new ways to say the same things, we are more likely to sound conversational because we are, in fact, using speech spontaneously.

NON-VOCAL ASPECTS OF GOOD DELIVERY

In addition to the vocal aspects of good delivery, an effective speaker also pays attention to the non-vocal aspects of good delivery. In the United States, audiences like lively, enthusiastic speakers who move around and show expression. You can meet audience expectations by paying attention to your appearance, gestures, bodily movements, facial expressions, and eye contact.

Appearance

Before you even begin speaking, your audience has made assumptions about you and what they can expect from your speech. These assumptions are made largely from what they already know about you and how you look. If the audience knows you well, your appearance will be less important, but if they don't know you well, your appearance can have a powerful effect.

If you were going on a job interview, to a meeting with a religious leader, or to a special celebration, you would be expected to dress appropriately for the occasion. This is also true for all kinds of speeches, including classroom presentations. In other words, whether the instructor tells you or not, how you dress and handle yourself will likely have an impact on your grade. Your appearance refers to how you dress, stand, and carry yourself.

In general, the rule for how formally a speaker should dress for a presentation is *one up*. That is, you should dress one degree more formally than your audience dresses. If your audience is likely to be wearing jeans and T-shirts, you should wear khakis and a polo or button-down shirt. If you audience will be wearing khakis and button-down shirts, you should wear dress pants and a tie or a skirt and professional blouse. If your audience will be wearing casual business attire, you should wear professional business attire. As the speaker, you are in a special position relative to the audience—one of power. You should honor that position and your audience by dressing to reflect the special nature of the event and your position in the event.

Most public speaking instructors do not expect their students to arrive on speech days wearing a suit and tie or a dress, nylons, and heels; however, jeans, T-shirts, shorts, athletic shoes, flip-flops, baseball caps, and sunglasses are definitely not appropriate. Ask your instructor what s/he expects so that you are absolutely sure, but if you can't, err on the side of caution and aim for at least the khakis and a button-down shirt or blouse.

WHAT OTHERS SAY

"Another thing that I like about speech class is that it teaches us not only about speaking, but appearance. Because appearance is the first thing that someone notices and uses to judge another person, it is good to know what to wear in speeches. Even though I am not a person who prejudges people by their attire, it is a fact that people will see first how someone looks. Listening to someone who wears typical California college clothes—flip-flops, which make terrible sounds by the way, surfer shorts, ultra-mini skirts, ultra low rise jeans—wouldn't be a good experience."

—Ozge, Turkey

For tips on how to speak in front of a camera, including clothing suggestions,

Click Here http://public-speaking.org/public-speaking-tvvideo-article.htm

The Advanced Public Speaking Institute offers advise, tips, and funny anecdotes about all aspects of public speaking, including personal appearance.

Other clothing to be avoided during a presentation includes hats, large or loud jewelry, coats, sweatshirts, nylon jackets, overly revealing clothing, and items placed on the head, behind the ear, or in the hair. Wearing hats (with the exception of religious headwear) indoors in the United States is generally considered inappropriate, although in recent years the wearing of baseball caps both indoors and out has become increasingly more acceptable in informal settings. Additionally, hats tend to cover the face or draw attention away from the speaker's face, so on speech days, leave your hats at home.

Jewelry that is large, loud (several metal bracelets knocking into each other), or overly bright can also become a distraction. Also, be careful to avoid playing with your jewelry while you speak. Common jewelry mistakes

Remember, when choosing your clothes, jewelry, and accessories for your speech, you don't want the audience to pay more attention to what you are wearing than to what you are saying.

include spinning rings, stroking necklaces, or sliding bracelets up and down the arm. On speech days, either leave your jewelry at home or choose pieces that add to the professionalism of your appearance without calling attention to themselves and away from you and the presentation.

On colder days, it is not uncommon for students to wear coats, sweatshirts, or nylon jackets to class. This is fine, until they try wearing them during a speech. Outerwear is made for outdoors, not indoors, so coats, jackets, sweaters, and the like can give the impression that the speaker has just barely arrived or is in a hurry to leave as soon as the speech is over. Additionally, outerwear typically constrains movement, causing the speaker to look stiff and uncomfortable. Finally, some outerwear, especially nylon jackets and windbreakers, makes considerable noise when one moves. This noise can be very distracting and even drown out what the speaker is saying. Before it is your turn to speak, take off any outerwear so that you have more freedom of movement and the audience doesn't get the impression that you would rather be outside in the cold than giving a speech.

At the other extreme of self-presentation is overly revealing clothing. For every one person who wears too many clothes at the lectern is a speaker who looks like s/he forgot to get dressed. Choose clothing that covers at least the tops of your arms and chest (this is true for both men and women) and does not reveal too much leg. Clothing that is either too small or designed as beach- or evening wear can draw audience attention away from your speech and onto the revealed body parts. In short, choose clothing that is complimentary and tasteful, without calling attention to itself or to your body.

Lastly, avoid putting anything on your head, behind your ears, or in your hair that doesn't belong there. Favorite "headpieces" include sunglasses, cigarettes, pencils, and pens. Leave these items at your seat. If you must bring a pen or pencil to the lectern, avoid holding it while you speak. Most people will spin, twirl, or click pens or pencils they are holding. Set down any necessary writing utensils and all other objects while you are speaking except when you are actively using them as part of your presentation.

You should also know that dressing appropriately for your presentation can boost your confidence and your sense of professionalism, making the transition from classmate/student to confident speaker easier and more believable. Think about the last time you "dressed up" for an event. You probably carried yourself differently—a little more upright and confidently than when you wear your everyday clothes, right?

Gestures

One of the questions new speakers ask frequently is, "What do I do with my hands?" It seems strange that we can use our hands all day every day without thinking about them and how to use them appropriately—until we are giving a speech, that is. Suddenly, our hands feel like two large, awkward appendages that are in the way or hanging oddly at our sides. As in using other

Hold your hands relaxed in front of you at about waist height to keep them ready for action, but also keep them out of your way as you begin to speak.

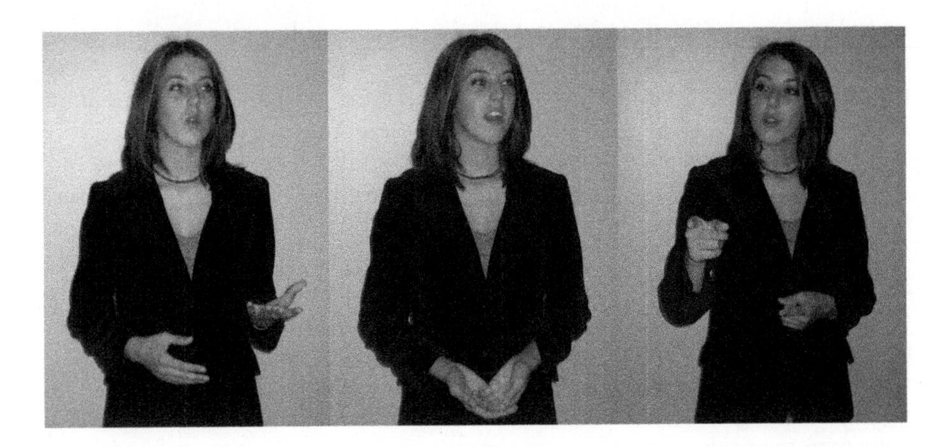

nonverbal aspects of good delivery, the answer is not to let your hand gestures distract the audience, but to use them to enhance your presentation.

First, learn how to keep your hands from becoming a distraction. Flipping and stroking your hair, touching your face, scratching your head, or tugging on your clothes are common distractions. How can you keep your hands from wandering off during your presentation? I advise keeping your hands off the lectern. Resting your hands on, grasping the sides of, leaning on, or wrapping your body around the lectern has never been necessary to keep a lectern from getting up and walking out of the room. Indeed, most lecterns prefer to stay in the room and listen to your speech, so leave the lectern alone. After you walk up to the front of the room, place your notes on the lectern so that you can easily see them, and then take a half step back to place the lectern just beyond a comfortable reach. This will allow you the freedom to move more easily as your speech progresses and will reduce your tendency to hold onto the lectern.

In general, you should keep your hands under your control. One way to control your hands is to bend your arms at the elbows and hold your hands loosely, one on top of the other, in front of your waist (see the photo). This keeps your hands comfortably out of the way when you are not using them and keeps them ready to be used if and when you need them.

As you become more comfortable as a speaker, you will begin to use gestures naturally. Do not resist using your hands when this happens. In fact, including well-placed gestures in a speech can actually improve audience understanding.[5] As a non-native speaker of a language, gestures can be especially helpful to both the speaker and the audience in conveying and understanding the message, respectively.[6] Allow your hands to move naturally as long as they are not fidgeting needlessly. Also allow your hands to punctuate a sentence, count out a list (indicating numbers with your fingers), or emphasize an idea. When your gestures follow your words and the intent of your speech, they add vibrancy and clarity to your ideas.

Body Movements

Just like your hands, the rest of your body can undermine your poise and distract the audience when it makes unnecessary and unwanted movements—fidgeting, swaying, wiggling, and pacing. To control unwanted body movements, start by walking up to the lectern with as much confidence as possible. Remember, even if you don't feel confident, pretend that you do! Your audience won't know the difference. Stand up straight without hesitation and walk assertively to the front of the room. Confidently place your notes on the lectern, step back slightly, and take a brief moment to make sure that you are standing in the proper speaking stance (see "Try This").

As you begin your presentation, make sure to maintain a comfortable stance throughout the speech, paying special attention to any wayward movements. Avoid tapping, swinging, or moving your feet unless you are actively taking steps. Avoid twisting your torso back and forth or leaning on one hip. Keep your head straight without tilting it to one side or the other. In short, make every movement count. If you catch yourself moving needlessly, simply stop and reassume the proper speaking stance. Eventually, this position will become natural.

When you become more comfortable, try moving around a bit more. For example, try taking a few steps toward one side of the room. Stop, make a point, and then take a few steps toward the other side of the room. Stop, make a point, and then move back toward the podium to briefly check your notes for the next point. Moving away from the podium focuses the audi-

The Proper Speaking Stance

1. Stand up as if you are talking to friends. Where are your feet? Your hands? Your head? Do you feel balanced? Can you move easily from this position to other positions? Does this position foster confidence?
2. Now, stand up like you are giving a speech. Balance your weight evenly on both feet. Straighten your legs but do NOT lock your knees (locking your knees reduces blood flow and increases the chances of fainting). Straighten your back up through your neck and hold your head high. Roll your shoulders back and down. Place your hands in the starting position. You should feel balanced and comfortable in this position.
3. Now try taking a step to the left. Then take two steps to the right. Each time you move return to the upright balanced position.

This is the proper stance for public speaking. It is confident, relaxed, and formal. Practice standing and moving in this position as you practice your speech. You will find that your confidence will increase, as will your credibility with your audience.

ence's attention on you, shows the audience that you are confident and comfortable, and allows you to connect more directly with your audience. Additionally, the extra movement helps make you feel more confident and comfortable because it uses up some of the extra energy in your system.

Facial Expressions

Of all the non-vocal aspects of delivery, a speaker's facial expressions, especially eye contact, are among the most important. Research has shown that audiences focus more on a speaker's face than on his or her gestures or body movements.[7] A speaker whose facial expressions contradict or do not reflect what he or she is saying may be viewed as unreliable, untrustworthy, and insincere. Remember, too, that there are cultural differences that govern the use of facial expressions (see "Considering Culture").

CONSIDERING CULTURE

Facial Expressions

In the 1960s and '70s, researcher Paul Ekman and other researchers* found that there are seven principal facial expressions that are created and understood by people of all cultures: happiness, anger, disgust, sadness, surprise, fear and Interest.

Although this research has shown that much of human emotion and the display of that emotion is universal across cultures, cultural differences still do exist. Subsequent research has shown that facial expressions of emotions seem to contain subtle nonverbal "accents" that are culture-specific. In other words, "emotions may be expressed in a manner largely consistent with universal prototypes, but there can still exist subtle cultural differences in the appearance of these universal emotions."**

Additionally, some cultures are more outwardly expressive than others. Some cultures enjoy very pronounced and free expressions of internal states, while other cultures are more reserved and tend to minimize the expression of emotion. In the United States, we appreciate a moderate amount of emotive expression. Big smiles are appreciated and seen as a sign of openness and a positive attitude when used in conjunction with content that is upbeat and friendly. On the other hand, a big smile that seems too big for the occasion or overly friendly can be seen as insincere.

*Paul Ekman, W. V. Friesen, M. O'Sullivan, A. Chan, I. Diacoyanni-Tarlatzis, K. Heider, R. Krause, W. A. LeCompte, T. Pitcairn, P. E. Ricci-Bitti, K. Scherer, M. Tomita, and A. Tzavaras, "Universals and Cultural Differences in the Judgments of Facial Expressions of Emotion," *Journal of Personality and Social Psychology* 53 (1987): 712–717; and Paul Ekman, E. R. Sorensen, and Wallace V. Friesen, "Pancultural Elements in Facial Displays of Emotions," *Science* 164 (1969): 86–88.

**Abigail A. Marsh, Hillary Anger Elfenbein, and Nalini Ambady, "Nonverbal 'Accents': Cultural Differences in Facial Expressions of Emotion," *Psychological Science* 14, no. 4 (2003): 373–376.

As you practice your speech, watch yourself in a mirror to make sure that your facial expressions match the tone and mood of your message. If you have a tendency to smile too much, practice using a more appropriate expression. Make notes in the columns of your speaking outline to remind yourself about the expression you want to present. If you tend to underexpress (i.e., you tend not to express emotions very obviously or have an unexpressive style), work on increasing your expressiveness. Looking in the mirror, practice making happy, sad, surprised, confused, and angry faces. Exaggerate the expressions until each expression is unique and easily discernable from the others.

Eye Contact

In the United States as well as in much of the Western world, direct eye contact is viewed as a sign of trustworthiness and confidence. Avoiding making eye contact is interpreted as a sign of insincerity or insecurity. In other parts of the world, however, making direct eye contact is seen as rude and inappropriate. If you come from a culture that discourages eye contact, making eye contact may be one of the more difficult aspects of public speaking for you to master. When speaking publicly in the United States, you will need to look directly into the eyes of your audience throughout your speech.

There are two aspects of eye contact that you need to attend to: room coverage and length of hold. Room coverage refers to looking at people in all areas of the room. Sometimes speakers find one or two people to look at and proceed to give the entire speech to them. This makes the rest of the audience feel left out. When giving a speech, find people in all areas of the room to become your eye contact anchors. Your anchors can also be those folks with "smiling faces." There are usually several people who will look at you and smile as if to say, "I am interested and listening to every word you say." Use these people as anchors.

Once you find your smiling faces or anchors, look from person to person every few seconds. Look at the back left person, then at the middle person, then at the front right person, then at the front left, back right, middle, back left, etc. Keep moving around the room to your various anchors so that no part of the room feels left out.

You also need to be sure to hold eye contact long enough to actually see and make contact with the person. Beware of darting your eyes from one person to the next without actually seeing them. This hardly counts as making eye contact. Hold eye contact for at least one full second with each person as you move your eyes around the room. One second is long enough for you to see the person and for that person to feel you looking at him or her. You will find that the longer you can hold your gaze and connect with each person, the more support you will actually feel from the entire audience. Audiences like to feel included in the speech, and eye contact is the best way to bring them in.

TABLE 12.3 **Tips for Good Delivery**

1. Use a conversational tone that varies your volume, rate, and pitch.
2. Avoid making distracting sounds with your mouth, hands, feet, and voice.
3. Avoid wearing distracting clothes.
4. Avoid distracting mannerisms.
5. Hold your hands loosely and comfortably in front of you at about waist high.
6. Stand up straight with both legs straight and knees UNLOCKED.
7. Take three seconds to gather your thoughts and get settled before beginning.
8. Speak in a loud, clear voice.
9. Make eye contact with a variety of people in all areas of the room.
10. Enjoy the attention!

The most important thing to remember about delivery is to avoid doing anything that distracts your audience's attention away from what you are saying. You want the audience to listen to and think about what you are saying, not about what you are wearing, how you are speaking, or the way you are moving. Planning and practice can ensure a lively and clear speech delivery. See Table 12.3.

Practice

You may have noticed that one theme has emerged throughout this book: practice, practice, practice. All the research and writing in the world will not prepare you for the actual delivery of your speech as much as effective practice will. Practice reduces anxiety, smooths out language difficulties, and helps you control your body. In Chapter Eight, we briefly discussed how to practice using both the preparation and the keyword outlines. In this section we will review the practice tips from Chapter Eight as well as include the practice tips from throughout this chapter and the rest of the book to help you make the most of your practice sessions.

Remember that you should practice your speech from your preparation outline three times, out loud, and standing in front of a mirror. Each time, change the wording a little to avoid memorizing your speech. During each practice, try to make eye contact with yourself in the mirror as much as possible. After you have practiced three times, put the preparation outline away and continue practicing with the keyword outline only. Remember to practice in front of family and friends using your visual aids as if you were giving the speech to your real audience.

As a non-native speaker, you should follow the above advice and what follows. While practicing from your preparation outline, try tape-recording your speech as you practice in front of the mirror so that you can hear what you sound like. Listen for your pronunciation, articulation, pitch, volume, and rate. When you begin practicing from your keyword outline, tape your

Practicing in front of a mirror is a good way to monitor your facial expressions and to practice making eye contact.

speech again. Remember that when you are speaking from a keyword outline, you should continue speaking even if you can't remember what to say—just stay focused on the message and keep talking. Listen for the flow of your speech. Practice until you are able to give the speech without stopping, hesitating, or adding filler or vocalized pauses. Again, you should use different wording each time to keep your tone of voice conversational and natural.

After you feel that your speech has an even flow that sounds conversational, videotape your practice session. Watch your speech to see if you are managing your body movements, using natural gestures, engaging in eye contact, and avoiding distracting sounds and mannerisms. Practice with the videotape until you feel that you are in control.

Once you feel comfortable speaking to only yourself, practice your speech in front of other people at least one or two times. This works best if at least one of your audience members is a native English speaker. You will find that your speech sounds and feels very different when you do it in front of an audience than when you do it for yourself. It should. When you speak in front of an audience, you can imagine what it sounds like to them in a way that you cannot imagine when you are by yourself. Ask your audience to give

Practicing in front of a friend who is a native English speaker can help you identify any pronunciation or articulation problems.

HINT

Videotape a Practice Performance

Videotape a practice performance of your speech. Watch the tape twenty-four hours after taping it and do an informal evaluation of your speech. Write down three things you liked about your speech and three things you would like to improve. Then practice your speech again with the video camera to see if you can improve your problem areas.

you an honest critique especially in terms of your areas of most concern. You can even give them a checklist (see Table 12.4) to fill out as you speak. Afterward, discuss with your practice audience how you can improve your delivery. Repeat this process.

This practicing process will also help you avoid "going blank" during your actual presentation because you will have already worked through finding the right words in front of an audience. However, if you still happen to go blank or forget what you want to say during your presentation, don't panic. There are things you can do. First, turn to your visuals or your notes; both should contain "at a glance" notes to help you remember what you want to say. You can repeat the last thing you said to give your mind a chance to remember. You can also pause for a moment and ask, "Are there any questions at this point?"[8] Remember, the best way to avoid this possibility is to prepare thoroughly without memorizing your presentation.

SUMMARY

A friend of mine recently had to give her first classroom presentation. If she'd had the choice, she would have avoided giving a presentation at all because she is very afraid of public speaking. Before the presentation, she spent hours

TABLE 12.4 **Speech Delivery Checklist**

Give this checklist to your practice audience members to fill out.
Was my message clear?
What was the main point of my speech?
Did I have any distracting mannerisms? Explain.
Did I engage in enough eye contact? Explain.
Did I rely too heavily on my notes? Explain.
Did I stand up straight and look confident? Explain.
Did I mispronounce any words? Explain.
Was my language clear and my accent unobtrusive? Explain.
Were my sentences grammatically correct? Explain.
Did I handle my visual aid professionally?
Could you see the visual aid clearly?
Did the visual aid add to your understanding of my speech?

writing and fine-tuning her presentation, and she practiced it over and over again. Every time she started to feel nervous, she practiced. After the presentation, I asked her how her presentation had gone. She proudly exclaimed that she got an A on the presentation and was surprisingly calm while giving it. She said she believed that the practice she had done had made her speech a success. Her teacher had commented that she looked comfortable and natural in front of the class. My friend even said she "kind of enjoyed it!"

Some people are born public speakers: comfortable, natural, and interesting on the stage. Most of us have to learn how to look good at the lectern. Preparation and practice are the keys to successful extemporaneous speaking. As you practice your delivery and gain more experience in public speaking, you will find that managing your vocal nonverbal delivery skills, volume, rate, pitch, and conversational tone will become easier, as will your ability to manage your non-vocal delivery skills. Eye contact will serve to make you feel more connected to the audience and more open to receiving their support. Your hands and body will settle into natural movements that won't take away from what you are saying but instead add energy and emphasis. With thorough preparation and practice, you will look intelligent, confident, natural, and comfortable. You may even find that you enjoy the experience.

Ultimately, "you cannot get any better if you do not speak regularly."[9] Join a speaking organization such as Toastmasters International, or join the speech and debate team at your college. Accept any opportunity to say a few words. This more than anything else will help you become a more confident, comfortable, and natural public speaker.

Discussion Questions and Activities

1. Partner with a classmate, and take turns practicing your speeches for each other. The observer should take notes on the speaker's delivery strengths and weaknesses as discussed in this chapter. After each practice, offer each other only two suggestions to work on for the next run-through. Keep practicing until each of you can give the speech confidently with few delivery errors.
2. In groups of four or five, discuss the differences among various cultures in terms of good speech delivery. What is considered good eye contact, body movement, vocalics, etc., in each of your home countries? How does that affect your ability to be good audience members in the United States? How can learning about the different delivery standards help you better adapt your style to diverse audiences?
3. Eye contact is very important when speaking publicly in the United States. Discuss with your classmates how eye behavior and practices vary from culture to culture. Include a discussion on the specific eye behavior practices of your home culture.
4. Tape-record yourself practicing your speech using a keyword outline. Run through the speech three times in a row, being sure not to stop in the middle of each run-through. Then compare the three versions. Which did you like best? Why? What did you do well each time? What would you like to improve in your vocal delivery based on hearing these recordings? How can you use what you have heard to improve your overall vocal delivery?
5. Practice your speech one time as you would normally. Then practice your speech in front of a mirror using only a keyword outline. Try to maintain eye contact with yourself throughout. How did it make you feel to practice while seeing yourself? Did you notice anything different about how you stood, moved, or sounded? What accounts for the differences when using only the keyword outline and the mirror?
6. Watch a speech on videotape or TV (you can also find several speeches today online). Analyze the speaker's delivery skills in terms of both the vocal and the non-vocal aspects. Did the speaker articulate clearly? Did s/he express enthusiasm and commitment to the topic through his/her vocalics? Did the speaker control his/her body movements well? Was s/he dressed appropriately? Did s/he minimize distractions from her/his delivery style?

Chapter Quiz

1. Nonverbal communication includes:
   - **a.** vocal, but not non-vocal, aspects.
   - **b.** non-vocal, but not vocal, aspects.
   - **c.** neither vocal nor non-vocal aspects.
   - **d.** both vocal and non-vocal aspects.

2. True or false: The four basic types of speech delivery commonly used in the United States are: memorized, manuscript, impromptu, and extemporaneous.
3. Which of the following is the accurate pronunciation in the United States of the word *encyclopedia*?
   - **a.** en-CY-clo-pe-di-a
   - **b.** en-cy-CLO-pe-di-a
   - **c.** en-cy-clo-PE-di-a
   - **d.** EN-cy-clo-pe-di-a
4. All of the following are tips for good delivery EXCEPT:
   - **a.** Avoid making distracting sounds with your mouth, hands, feet, and voice.
   - **b.** Avoid wearing distracting clothes.
   - **c.** Avoid distracting mannerisms.
   - **d.** Hold your hands rigidly behind you at about waist high.
5. True or false: As long as you have fully prepared your speech and can deliver it well, it doesn't matter how you dress.
6. True or false: Vocal cues, use of space, gestures, facial expressions, and eye movements are all forms of verbal communication.
7. Gestures, facial expressions, and body posture are components of ______.
8. To deliver your speech the best possible way, you should remember to:
   - **a.** speak in a loud, clear voice.
   - **b.** avoid wearing distracting clothes.
   - **c.** avoid making distracting sounds with your mouth, hands, feet, and voice.
   - **d.** All of the above.

Chapter 12 Quiz Answers

1. d, 2. True, 3. c, 4. d, 5. False, 6. False, 7. nonverbal communication, 8. d

CHAPTER 13 Informative and Special Occasion Speeches

CHAPTER GOAL

By the end of this chapter you will be able to distinguish among the purpose, format, and delivery of a variety of informative and special occasion speeches.

Consider the following speech titles:

"On the Move: Why People Immigrate"
"Locking Down the Borders: Stopping Illegal Immigration at Its Source"
"Can You Tell Me How to Get to Chicago? The Meanderings of a Wayward Immigrant"

Each of these speeches makes use of the same general topic, immigration, but each has a different general purpose (to inform, to persuade, or to entertain). The first speech is an informative speech about the various reasons people immigrate from one country to another, the second is a persuasive speech advocating tightening border security, and the third is an entertaining speech about the trials and tribulations of being an immigrant in the United States.

In Chapter One, we listed the three categories of speeches: informative, persuasive, and special occasion; and in Chapter Five we discussed how to write a general and a specific purpose for each. You might find it odd that we are fully discussing the various types of speeches at the *end* of a book on public speaking, but the information in the previous twelve chapters applies to each of the three categories of speeches. This chapter and the next will discuss the differences among these speeches and some of the special considerations you will have when preparing and delivering each kind of speech.

To review: Every time we speak, we do it for one of three reasons—to inform or request information; to persuade or to ask to be persuaded; or to entertain or to ask to be entertained. The same is true for public speaking. When we give a speech, we are informing, entertaining (giving *special occasion speeches*), or persuading. In this chapter we will discuss the first two of these three categories of speeches and the U.S. American preferences for organizing, supporting, and preparing informative and special occasion speeches. Then in Chapter Fourteen we will fully examine persuasive speaking.

INFORMATIVE SPEECHES

Informative speeches teach audiences about a particular topic. They explain, demonstrate, report, define, clarify, and describe the topic so that the audience can better know and understand it. For example, you may have heard of *nanotechnology*, but you might not understand what it is, how it is used, or why it is important. A speaker may introduce the material to you by defining what it is, explaining how it is important, or clarifying why you need to know about it. A speaker could also demonstrate how nanotechnology works, report on the most recent research in nanotechnology, or describe new applications that use nanotechnology.

Types of Informative Speeches

There are six major topic areas of informative speeches: objects, people, places, processes, concepts, and events. Each type lends itself to a variety of organizational patterns (see Chapter Eight). In the following pages, we will

CONSIDERING CULTURE

What Is Accepted as Evidence

Cultures vary in terms of what they find to be acceptable or believable evidence. Whether you are making an informative or a persuasive speech, it is important to use evidence that your audience will find logical and compelling.

Following is a list of preferred evidence by country. Remember, all individuals in a country or from a particular culture may not be moved by the same forms of evidence. Similarly, using additional forms of evidence may reinforce and lend more credence to a culture's preferred evidence.

Country	Preferred Evidence
Australia, Canada, England, Finland, Switzerland, United States	Objective facts
Belarus	Personal feelings, speaker credibility
Bolivia, Chile, China, Israel, Malaysia, Mexico, Russia, Singapore, South Korea, Taiwan, Thailand	Personal feelings, religious and ideological faith, objective facts
Columbia, El Salvador, Uruguay	Personal feelings
Costa Rica, Ecuador, Egypt, Greece, Honduras, India, Indonesia, Italy, Kuwait, Nicaragua, Pakistan, Panama, Paraguay, Peru, the Philippines, Portugal, Saudi Arabia, Spain, Sri Lanka, Turkey, Venezuela	Personal feelings, religious or ideological faith
Czech Republic, Denmark, Romania, Ukraine	Personal feelings, objective facts
France, Japan	Objective facts, speaker credibility, feelings
Germany, the Netherlands, New Zealand, Norway, Poland, Sweden	Objective facts, ideological faith
Guatemala	Personal feelings, religious faith, tradition

discuss the various topic areas of informative speeches and the possible organizational patterns you might use for each.

Objects

Speeches about objects discuss animals, plants, or things, both living and nonliving. Almost anything you can touch, taste, hear, see, or smell is an object. Speeches about objects need to be clearly focused, because rarely can we fully discuss all aspects of an object in the limited time allowed for a speech. Consider an object as simple as a chicken's egg. You could talk about the parts of the egg, various egg recipes, how chickens hatch eggs, or the nutritional information of eggs. You could not possibly talk about all these ideas in one speech, so you must narrow your specific purpose like we discussed in Chapter Five.

Using the examples above, we could organize some of our egg topics spatially:

Specific Purpose: To inform my audience about the parts of an egg.
Thesis: An egg is made up of an outer shell, inner membranes, the albumen, and a yolk.

I. The outside of the egg is called the shell.
II. Beneath the shell are the outer and inner shell membranes.
III. Inside the inner shell membrane is the albumen or white of the egg.
IV. The innermost section of the egg is called the yolk.

Or topically:

Specific Purpose: To inform my audience about the nutritional value of eggs.
Thesis: Eggs are a good source of protein, vitamins, and minerals.

I. Eggs are high in protein.
II. Eggs contain many important vitamins.
III. Eggs are a good source of minerals.

Or topically like this:

Specific Purpose: To inform my audience about artificial incubation of eggs.
Thesis: Temperature, humidity, ventilation, and turning are four critical factors in incubating eggs artificially.

I. You must maintain a constant temperature when artificially incubating eggs.
II. You must maintain the right percentage of humidity when artificially incubating eggs.
III. You must provide adequate ventilation when artificially incubating eggs.
IV. You must turn the eggs at regular intervals until the final few days of incubation when artificially incubating eggs.

People

The villains, heroes, and martyrs of history; the literary and artistic giants throughout time; the celebrities and politicians of today; and even the up- and-coming sports figures of tomorrow provide fascinating and insightful topics that thrill and intrigue us. People love to learn about other people. We love to be inspired by those who have overcome great difficulty, and we wonder at those who have caused harm. Speeches about people can offer a wealth of possible topics.

Having trouble finding a good speech topic?

Click Here http://www.hawaii.edu/mauispeech/html/infotopichelp.html

The University of Hawaii's Topic Selection Helper site offers lists of ideas in general subjects, popular themes, and procedures.

Speeches about people can focus on individuals or groups of people: John Lennon or the Beatles; Sammy Davis, Jr., or the Rat Pack; Marshall Applewhite or the Heaven's Gate Cult; Pope John Paul II or popes of the twentieth century. You can also compare two or more people: George W. Bush and William J. Clinton; Mother Teresa and Florence Nightingale; Jim Carrey, Robin Williams, and Mike Myers. As a non-native speaker you have the advantage of being able to discuss a variety of people from your home country or culture with whom your audience in the United States might not already be familiar.

WHAT OTHERS SAY

"*I had nightmares about my first speech when the day was coming closer. Sometimes I had dreams about organizing the speech. These days, I do not have nightmares, but I actually brainstormed some things during my sleep for my informative speech. . . . The next speech is really challenging, but I am looking forward to do my best.*"

Hiroko, Japan

Like in speeches about objects, when giving speeches about people, you need to clearly focus on one aspect of their lives: their education, childhood, contributions, or achievements, for example. Also, it is not appropriate to simply state the information one would find in an encyclopedia. As we discussed in Chapter Seven, encyclopedias are not considered appropriate for college-level research. Your speech may include common facts about the individual or group in question, but those facts should not be the only information you present. To make a speech about a person interesting, it is a good idea to mix factual information with stories and anecdotes from the person's life to illustrate your points.

Speeches about people are most often organized in topical or chronological order. If you were to do a speech about the Beatles, you might organize it chronologically:

Specific Purpose: To inform my audience about the Beatles' progression to superstardom from the 1950s to the 1970s.

Thesis: From the late 1950s in England to the 1970s, the Beatles were one of the world's most famous bands.

I. The Beatles began their journey to fame in the late 1950s in Liverpool, England.

II. The Beatles skyrocketed to fame upon arriving in the United States in the early 1960s.

III. The Beatles reached their height of fame in the early 1970s shortly before breaking up.

Or topically:

Specific Purpose: To inform my audience about the ways the Beatles revolutionized music.

Thesis: The Beatles revolutionized the recording techniques of rock 'n' roll, the rock 'n' roll music tour, and rock 'n' roll music itself over the course of their rise to stardom.

I. The Beatles revolutionized recording techniques.
II. The Beatles revolutionized the rock 'n' roll music tour.
III. The Beatles revolutionized the music of rock 'n' roll.

Occasionally, you might choose to do a speech about people spatially:

Specific Purpose: To inform my audience about where the Beatles' fame developed.

Thesis: The Beatles' fame started in England, increased in Germany, and peaked in the United States.

I. The Beatles got their start in Liverpool, England.
II. The Beatles defined their style while performing in Germany.
III. The Beatles found their greatest success in the United States.

Places

Speeches about towns, cities, countries, historical landmarks, natural wonders, and specific locations on the Earth or in space can all be considered speeches about places. You might consider places to be objects because when you are standing in a place, you are actually touching that place with your feet, but we are looking at speeches about places separately because places are unique from other objects. Places can exist currently (Tehran, Iran) or historically (Babylon, Babylonia), or can be real (the Great Wall of China), imagined (Wonderland), or hypothetical (the lost city of Atlantis).

Speeches about places are usually best organized spatially, chronologically, or topically. Imagine that you were giving a speech about Manhattan's nightlife. You could organize it spatially as follows:

Specific Purpose: To inform my audience about the world-class nightlife that can be found all over the city of Manhattan.

Thesis: From uptown jazz to midtown theaters to downtown nightclubs, Manhattan offers world-class nightlife.

I. Uptown Manhattan boasts jazz and dinner clubs.
II. Midtown Manhattan is famed for its theaters.
III. Downtown Manhattan offers a full range of nightclubs and eclectic restaurants.

Using the same topic with a different focus, you can organize your speech chronologically:

Specific Purpose: To inform my audience about the development of

Manhattan's famed nightlife.
Thesis: Manhattan's famed nightlife began in the 1800s with the first theaters, grew in the early 1900s with the advent of cabarets, and exploded with the introduction of jazz clubs in the 1940s.

I. In the early 1800s, Manhattan's famed theater district, Broadway, was born.
II. In the early 1900s, Manhattan cabarets became the first true "nightclubs."
III. In the 1940s, jazz became central to Manhattan's nightlife.

You can organize the speech topically like this:

Specific Purpose: To inform my audience about how to plan a great night out in Manhattan.
Thesis: Beginning with a Broadway show, catching a jazzy dinner, and then going out dancing is one way to have a fabulous night in Manhattan.

I. A night out in Manhattan begins with a trip to Broadway for a show.
II. Manhattan's jazz dinner clubs are a great place for a late dinner and music.
III. All-night dancing can be found in one of the many famed Manhattan nightclubs.

Notice how the general topic is the same, but the organizational patterns lead the specific speech content in different directions. In the first speech, the audience can expect to learn the various areas of the city and for what they are known in terms of nightlife. The second speech gives the historical development of nightlife in Manhattan. The third speech is more like a travel guide giving the audience an idea of what they can do while they are in Manhattan.

Which speech would be most interesting to you? Unless you have plans to visit New York City in the very near future, you would probably find the first two topics more useful and interesting. In general, travel guide–type speeches are better left to travel professionals. For academic speeches, travel suggestions tend to be shallow and irrelevant. Instead, aim to provide insight into a place so that your audience members can feel that they have actually learned something.

HINT
Talking about Home
When doing a speech about your home country, avoid presenting it like a travel guide would or covering features that everyone is sure to already know about. Talk about something unique in your country or little-known aspects about some of its more famous landmarks. This way, you can build on the knowledge your audience already has.

Processes

Process speeches teach an audience how to *do* something or explain how a complicated process is done. I refer to these two kinds of process speeches as the *how-to speech* (also called a *demonstration speech*) and the *how-it-is-done speech* (also called a *speech of explanation*). In the how-to speech, the speaker teaches the audience members a skill or technique so that they can actually perform the skill themselves. Examples include:

Specific Purpose: To inform my audience how to make an origami crane.
Specific Purpose: To inform my audience how to make festive holiday frames.

Specific Purpose: To inform my audience how to change the oil in a car.
Specific Purpose: To inform my audience how to make double-chocolate fudge brownies.
Specific Purpose: To inform my audience how to remove stubborn stains.

How-it-is-done speeches take a complicated process that the audience probably does not understand and explain it so that they are better informed. The aim is not for the audience to be able to do the process but for them to be able to understand it. Have you ever watched children's television shows like *Sesame Street* or *Mister Rogers' Neighborhood*? These shows often include segments on how things are made, like orange crayons or packaged candy bars. On Saturday mornings, you can still see a segment called *School House Rocks* wherein an animated bill explains how a legislative bill becomes a law in the United States.[1] These are examples of how-it-is-done presentations. In the classroom, I have heard speeches on how the electoral college system works, how overnight shipping is accomplished, and how the immigration system decides who gets a green card.

The how-it-is-done process speech explicitly connects the explanation of the process and the outcome of the process in terms of what the audience will find the most interesting. For example, a process speech on how aircraft safety systems work can show the audience how safe they are when they fly even if something goes wrong. The specific purpose for this speech might be: *To inform my audience about how aircraft safety systems protect passengers.*

Both how-to and how-it-is-done speeches are usually arranged chronologically, walking the audience through each step from start to finish. For example:

Specific Purpose: To inform my classmates how to apply to graduate school.
Thesis: There are three key steps to successfully applying to graduate school.

I. The first step in applying to graduate school is to find the school that is right for you.
II. The second step in applying to graduate school is to research the admissions process at the schools you want to attend.
III. The third step in applying to graduate school is to submit your application with the proper documentation.

Sometimes, however, process speeches should be arranged topically:

Specific Purpose: To inform my audience how aircraft safety systems protect passengers.
Thesis: Aircraft safety systems protect passengers in three ways.

I. Aircraft safety systems address aircraft icing concerns.
II. Aircraft safety systems address electromagnetic threat concerns.
III. Aircraft safety systems address digital system concerns.[2]

The key to a successful process speech is to make the material meaningful and significant to the audience. Adult audiences may not appreciate a speech on how to make brownies as much as a speech on how to become a more effective listener. Also, process speeches, particularly the how-to speech, rely heavily on presentation aids to help the audience learn the process. Be sure that your aids are clear, relevant, professional, and easily visible to all audience members.

Concepts

Concept speeches explore ideas, theories, hypotheses, issues, and beliefs without putting forth an opinion. Concept speeches focus on abstract ideas rather than concrete things or events. Examples of concept speeches are those that discuss or explain religions or belief systems (e.g., Buddhism, Islam, Christianity, etc.); scientific or psychological theories (e.g., evolution, dream interpretation, quantum physics, etc.); political systems (e.g., democracy, communism, monarchies, etc.); and controversial issues (e.g., abortion, stem cell research, same-sex marriages, etc.).

Although the speaker may discuss others' opinions about the concepts, he or she does not advocate a position or reveal an opinion about the topic. This can be difficult, especially when discussing a controversial issue. Instead, the speaker should simply, clearly, and objectively explain the various positions held and their key arguments.

Concepts and theories tend to be vague and quite complicated; therefore, you should aim to focus your speech on just the ideas you want to clarify, define, or explain and do so in a straightforward, easy-to-understand way that is appropriate to your time limit. Concept speeches are usually arranged topically:

> Specific Purpose: To inform my classmates about the four Myers-Briggs preferences.
> Thesis: There are four Myers-Briggs preferences that reveal different personality profiles.
> I. The first Myers-Briggs preference is extroversion/introversion.
> II. The second Myers-Briggs preference is sensation/intuition.
> III. The third Myers-Briggs preference is thinking/feeling.
> IV. The fourth Myers-Briggs preference is judgment/perception.

When discussing an issue, you might want to arrange it topically, according to each side's position:

> Specific Purpose: To inform my classmates about the controversy over stem cell research.
> Thesis: The controversy over stem cell research is based on the differing opinions of what constitutes "human."
> I. Those who oppose stem cell research believe that it is unacceptable to use embryos fertilized in the lab because they are human.
> II. Those who support stem cell research believe that it is acceptable to use embryos fertilized in the lab because they are not yet human.

Informative speeches can be a wonderful way to learn about cultural differences surrounding common traditions. Here a Chinese-Malay Babas couple is wearing the traditional Chinese wedding costume.

Events

Speeches about events can discuss anything that has happened, is happening, or will happen. Events include a cultural ritual or custom (e.g., a quinceñera, Chinese wedding ceremonies, a bris, or the May Day celebration); a historic event (e.g., the Armenian Genocide, the fall of Rome, or the sinking of the *Titanic*); or commonplace events (e.g., tea parties, the first day of school, or commuter traffic). Because diseases *happen* to us, they are also considered events.

Event speeches can be arranged chronologically, topically, causally, or in problem-solution order. Event speeches about cultural rituals or customs and historic events are often chronologically arranged:

Specific Purpose: To inform my audience about the Six Etiquette for arranged Chinese marriages.

Thesis: There are six steps in the Six Etiquette for arranged Chinese marriages.

I. The first two steps in the Six Etiquette for arranged Chinese marriages are the request for marrying the bride and the request for the bride's and groom's birthdates.

II. The third and fourth steps in the Six Etiquette for arranged Chinese marriages are the initial gifts and the formal gifts for the bride's family.

III. The fifth step in the Six Etiquette for arranged Chinese marriages is the selection of the wedding date.

IV. The sixth step in the Six Etiquette for arranged Chinese marriages is the wedding day itself.[3]

Or:

Specific Purpose: To inform my audience about the stages of the Apartheid era in South Africa.
Thesis: The Apartheid era in South Africa began in 1910, sparked opposition and reaction from the 1940s through the 1980s, and was finally abolished in the 1990s.

I. The Apartheid era in South Africa began in 1910 with the passing of laws that curtailed the rights of the black majority.
II. In the 1940s and '50s, nonviolent opposition to Apartheid became more organized and vocal.
III. From the 1960s through the 1980s, the government banned the ANC, sparking more subversive and covert opposition tactics and more government violence against protestors.
IV. In the 1990s, the new president of South Africa announced the end of Apartheid, and the ANC returned to South Africa to work with the government in transitioning to general elections based on universal suffrage.

Some event speeches are topically ordered:

Specific Purpose: To inform my audience about the reasons for the increased traffic in our city.
Thesis: The increase in traffic in our city can be attributed to three things.

I. One reason for the increased traffic in our city is the decrease in public transportation options.
II. A second reason for the increased traffic in our city is the increased average commuting distance traveled.
III. A third reason for the increased traffic in our city is the ongoing public works projects, which are closing down lanes and diverting traffic.

> **TIP**
> **Process Speech Visual Aids**
> When giving a process speech, make a series of visual aids that show the stages or steps of the process vividly and clearly. Be sure the aids are large enough and positioned well enough for everyone in the audience to be able to see. Practice giving the speech to someone who doesn't know or understand the process, using your visuals to find out whether they aid in learning the process.

Diseases are often presented in causal order:

Specific Purpose: To inform my audience about the causes and effects of breast cancer.
Thesis: Breast cancer is caused by both environmental and biological causes, and has significant physical, psychological, and emotional effects.

I. Breast cancer has both environmental and biological causes.
II. The effects of breast cancer are physical, psychological, and emotional.

Diseases are also often presented in problem-solution order:

Specific Purpose: To inform my audience about the efforts to reduce new cases of heart disease in the United States.
Thesis: Since heart disease is on the rise in the United States, the American Heart Association has launched a campaign to reduce new cases through education.

I. Heart disease is on the rise in the United States due to poor eating and exercise.

Developing Topics

Choose a general topic from one of the topics listed below, and develop a specific purpose statement and a thesis statement for each type of informative speech discussed in this section. Which of your potential speeches seems the most interesting to you? To your audience?

Teenage pregnancy	Skateboarding	International travel
Test taking	Classical music	Energy conservation
Photography	Soccer	Skin cancer

Although many general topics can be worked into any of the speech types, most topics fall more easily into one type of informative speech than the others.

II. In an effort to reduce new cases of heart disease in the United States, the American Heart Association has started a campaign to educate the public on good eating and exercise habits.

Don't feel as though you *must* use any of these organizational patterns if you find another pattern that works better for your speech. The key for every informative speech is that it is logical and clear so that the audience leaves your speech feeling as though they understood your topic and learned something of value.

SPECIAL OCCASION SPEECHES

Think about the most important moments you have had in your life so far. No matter what culture you are from, chances are good that the most significant moments in your life have been celebrated or commemorated with speeches. We call these speeches *special occasion speeches* because they can make special occasions more special and more memorable.

Of the three categories of speeches—informative, persuasive, and special occasion—special occasion speeches are the ones that you will *want* to be asked to give in your life. Why? Because being asked to give these speeches indicates that you are someone special. Commencement speeches are given by the academically successful. Wedding toasts are given by best friends and loving parents. Eulogies are given by those loved and respected by the deceased. Award speeches are both given by those at the top of a field and given to those showing excellence. Retirement speeches come at the end of long and successful careers. Memorial speeches are given by heroes and community leaders. As much as you may fear giving a speech, you should relish the request to give one on a special occasion.

Although special occasion speeches often inform or persuade, they are not intended to do either. Rather, they are intended primarily to entertain and give meaning to an event. Because special occasion speeches are as numerous and varied as the events they mark, we will not discuss all the different types here; but we will go over some of the more common ones you are likely to encounter in your life and offer some general tips for preparing special occasion speeches.

Speeches of Introduction

Someday you may be asked to introduce another speaker to an audience. In this case, you are giving a speech of introduction. Speeches of introduction are brief and designed to generate excitement for the speaker.

Brevity

Speeches of introduction are brief, seldom longer than two or three minutes, although in a few cases they may be much longer. The idea is that you are preparing the audience for the speaker, not speaking for the speaker. Speaking too long takes attention away from the speaker (the opposite of the purpose of the introduction speech), takes time away from the speaker, and irritates the audience. One public speaking consultant advises that the speech should be no more than 250 words in length and two minutes long.[4]

The exception to the brevity rule is when the speaker will be giving a long or keynote address, as in the case of a lecturer-of-the-year speech. If the speaker is expected to speak for an hour or more, the introduction may be as long as ten or fifteen minutes in order to adequately establish why the speaker has been asked to give the address, including the speaker's accomplishments.

Generating Excitement for the Speaker

Speeches of introduction fulfill the same four goals as an introduction at the beginning of one of your own speeches. They get the audience's attention, relate the significance of the speaker to the audience, reveal the topic of the speaker's presentation, and establish the speaker's credibility. Remember, you will probably want to focus the attention of the audience on the front of the room and familiarize them to the occasion. People may just be getting settled in their seats or finishing their meals. In any case, the audience's attention may not be focused on you or on the upcoming speaker when you stand at the lectern. You will need to gently get their attention before you begin with the formal introduction. Phrases such as, "Welcome," "Good afternoon," or "Hello" work well to summon the audience's attention.

Next, tell the audience why they should be excited to hear the speaker. Explain how lucky they are to be there, how excited you are, or what an honor it is to be able to listen to this particular speaker. You may want to combine this step with revealing the topic to the audience so that they know what to expect.

Next, you will need to explain the speaker's credibility relative to the topic he or she will discuss and give the reason the speaker was asked to speak on the particular occasion. Finally, you will need to reveal the speaker's name. Saving the speaker's name for last is a fun way to create drama and excitement. Also, saving the name for last cues the audience to applaud appropriately. Following is an example of a speech of presentation:

> Good evening, and welcome to our President's Circle Distinguished Lecturer series. Tonight we are so lucky to have with us one of the top marine biologists in the United States, who will be discussing coral bleaching and how it impacts global climate.
>
> Receiving his PhD in marine biology from UCLA, our speaker's specialty is coral reefs and the impact of environmental factors on coral health. He was a pre-med student at UCLA before switching his major in his senior year. When asked why he switched to marine biology when he was so close to finishing his pre-med requirements, he told me that he had to change his major after his first scuba dive. He said, "As soon as I went underwater and looked around, I knew this was it. I immediately changed my major to marine biology and I've never regretted it."
>
> His studies have taken him around the world, from Europe to the Caribbean to the Hawaiian Islands to the South Seas. Currently, he is involved in a project that takes groups of undergraduate students to Australia to research the Great Barrier Reef at one of the world's foremost marine biology research stations on Herron Island. However, today we are lucky enough to have him here in the States. It is my honor to introduce Dr. Garen Baghdasarian.

The most important point to remember when giving a speech of introduction is to provide all of the information accurately. Verify with the speaker the pronunciation of his or her name if at all possible and make sure that the details of his/her accomplishments are accurate. Nothing is more embarrassing or uncomfortable for the upcoming speaker, the audience, and the introducer than when the introducer mispronounces the speaker's name or attributes the wrong accomplishments and degrees to the speaker.

Speeches of Presentation and Acceptance

Speeches of presentation and acceptance tend to go together. Speeches of presentation are given to present awards or gifts to deserving recipients, and speeches of acceptance are given by the recipients of awards or gifts. Like speeches of introduction, speeches of presentation and acceptance are brief, rarely longer than five minutes. Exceptions to the brevity rule are acceptances to lifetime achievement awards or other significant awards like the Nobel Prize.

Speeches of Presentation

Speeches of presentation often have to meet three goals: explaining the award or gift, explaining why the recipient is getting the award, and thanking other competitors, if any. If the audience is unfamiliar with the award, you need to explain the origin and/or purpose of the award and the criteria for winning the award if the award is given after a competition. Then you will need to review the recipient's accomplishments as they relate to the award and the award's criteria. If others competed for the same award, you must remember to thank the other competitors. Here is an example of a speech of presentation for a high school's most prestigious scholarship:

> We have come to the final scholarship award of the evening. Every year, the Brower family offers a $5,000 scholarship in honor of Michael G. Brower to the senior who best fulfills Michael's legacy of excellence. As the first student body president at Standmont High School, Michael exemplified excellence in every aspect of his life. He showed excellence in his education by maintaining a 3.8 GPA throughout his high school career and being a member of the National Honor Society and the California Scholarship Federation. His excellence here at Standmont High extended beyond the classroom into his participation in campus leadership, sports, and clubs. Not only was Michael the first student body president; he was also an outstanding athlete. As captain of both the baseball and wrestling teams, Michael led his teams to winning seasons his senior year. He was also an active member of many clubs on campus, including the chess club and the glee club. Outside of school, Michael displayed excellence in the extensive volunteer work he did for the local homeless shelter. Michael carried with him the hopes and dreams of our school as he graduated with the designation "Most likely to succeed."
>
> After graduating in 1990, Michael carried his excellence overseas to fight for his country as a Marine. Sadly, two months after his deployment to the 1991 Gulf War, Michael was killed. The Brower family established this award to memorialize Michael and to foster excellence in his name. Honorees must exhibit excellence academically as well as through service to the school and the community. This year's recipient definitely fulfills those requirements.
>
> Although our school is lucky to have many students who would do honor to Michael's name—and, believe me, the selection committee was impressed by all of this year's nominees—we could choose only one for the award. This year's recipient has a 4.0 GPA, not including adjustments for her many AP classes! She earned this while working part time for her parents all four years. Like Michael, she is a member of the National Honor Society and California Scholarship Federation, even holding an of-

Awards ceremonies offer us the opportunity to learn what works and what doesn't when giving an acceptance speech. In the United States, we like to see people be excited, grateful, and humble when they accept their awards.

fice in each. She is an active member in student leadership as a class senator and student body treasurer. When not working after school and on the weekends, our recipient is busy volunteering at the local Red Cross, the Food Pantry, or the children's program at the Department of Parks and Recreation.

Truly, this year's recipient has done great honor to the memory of Michael G. Brower and to this school. Ladies and gentlemen, the 2007 Michael G. Brower Memorial Scholarship of Excellence goes to Natalie Solis.

Speeches of Acceptance

Have you ever watched an award show on television? They are very popular in the United States, especially during the early months of the year. The Academy Awards, the Grammy Awards, the MTV Music Awards, and the

Tony Awards are a few examples. People watch award shows to find out if their favorite performers and television programs won and to watch the acceptance speeches, which can be funny, inspiring, and touching. But they are also brief.

As the counterpart to speeches of presentation, speeches of acceptance offer gratitude for an award or gift. These speeches are brief, but they must accomplish at least two goals. First, the speaker must thank those who bestowed the gift. Second, the speaker must thank those who helped him or her earn the accomplishment. Who is the first to be thanked at the Academy Awards? The Academy, of course! When thanking those who have helped you win the award, you need to stay focused on those who actually helped you. Leave out your third-grade teacher, your dog, and your dry cleaner, unless your dry cleaner ran down to the movie set in the middle of the night to pick up a stained costume and returned the dress just in time to shoot the scene the next day *and* that very dress is the reason you are winning the Best Costume Design award!

Most acceptance speeches will be only two to three minutes long, and should typically be shorter than the presentation speech that precedes it. However, acceptance speeches can be longer and can include some insight into the recipient when the award is a significant one, such as a lifetime achievement award or a humanitarian award. Following is an example of an acceptance speech given by the reciptient of the scholarship presented on page 314.

> Thank you. Thank you so much. I would first like to thank the Michael G. Brower family for making this award possible and keeping the memory of Michale and his legacy alive. I would also like to thank the selection commitee for noticing me and my hard work. Knowing all the other amazing students at this school, I feel humbled by this honor.
>
> High school can be difficult. The pressures to conform, the temptations to stray from the path, and the worries about what to wear offer a constant challenge to keeping focused on what is truly important. But I made a commitment when I started high school that I would give everything I had to doing this well. I promised myself I would give up parties and dances and hanging out with friends in order to get the grades and earn the money to pursue my dream of going to Columbia University. The funny thing is, although it was difficult, it was much more fun, even fulfilling, than I would have imagined. Plus, I have received an endless supply of help and support along the way. For that, I would like to thank my friends who also gave up the weekend parties and dances to volunteer with me at the food pantry and at the park. Not only did we do some great work, we had a blast doing it! You guys are the best.
>
> I want to thank all my teachers who challenged me, encouraged me, and gave up their lunch hours to tutor me through the rough spots. I especially want to thank Mrs. Ackerman for helping me get through calculus when I thought it was hopeless. You knew I could do it even when I didn't.

I want to thank Jason Young at the food pantry who on my first day showed me how to set aside my discomfort and fear so that I could greet the people with compassion and respect. I will carry the lessons I have learned from you throughout my life.

Toasts

Toasts are given throughout the world by raising a glass, saying a few words, and drinking a sip. Toasts are generally informal, very brief speeches in honor of someone, an event, or an idea. You are probably already familiar with and have participated in toasts both here and in your home culture. Although they are similar around the world, there are a few guidelines for giving and receiving toasts in the United States that you should be aware of so that your toasts are meaningful and memorable.

In the United States, toasting is generally considered an informal speech. With the exception of weddings, in which the best man offers the first toast,

Toasting is a great way to become more comfortable with public speaking. The next time you are at an event or dinner with friends, try standing up and saying a few words in honor of the occasion.

Considering Language

What to Say When Toasting

The rules of toasting vary from country to country and from culture to culture. So if you ever find yourself at a Greek wedding, a Mexican baptism, a Chinese dinner party, or the like, you will want to know what it is you are expected to say or do when the time comes. Some cultures simply have a word or two to say with few other rules for guests or the honorees. Other cultures have guidelines for all the participants. Here are just a few examples from around the world:

Country	When Giving the Toast	When Honored by Toast	When Participating in Toast
China	Toast guests with highest ranking first. Say, *Kan pei* or *Gan bei*, which mean "Bottoms up!" or "Drain the glass."	Say, *Xie xie* and drink as much as the person honoring you.	In China it is not customary to clink glasses before drinking.
France	Say, *A votre santé*, which means "To your health," but offer one to the host only after being honored by the host first.	Say, *A la votre*, which means "And to yours."	Offer a toast only if one has first been given in your honor by the host.
Hungary	Say, *Egészségére*, which means "Cheers."	Thank the person offering the toast and thank the host(s) for the event.	
Mexico	Say, *Salud*, which means "Health."	Say, *Thank you* and repeat *Salud*.	
Norway	Say a few words thanking the hosts or giving honor to the event, ending with *Skål*.	Return the toast with a few words of your own and end with *Skål*.	During smaller events, it is common for a variety of people to give toasts.
Poland	Say, *Za przyjazn*, which means "For friendship."	Say, *Dziekujje bardzo*, which means "Thank you very much." Then lift your glass and say, *Na zdrowie*, which means "Cheers."	Follow the lead of the honoree. Lift your glass and repeat, *Na zdrowie*.
South Korea	Toast the hosts of the event using formal titles and names. *Kun bae* means "Cheers."	Say, *Thank you*, (name the person giving the toast), and thank the hosts for the event.	Say, *Kun bae*.
Sweden	Toast only your host or anyone who is your senior, unless they toast you first. Do not drink until the host has started the festivities by saying, *Skoal*.	Say, *Tack* and a few additional words.	In smaller settings, it is appropriate to complete the toast in pairs. If you are a woman, look to your left; if you are a man, look to your right. Raise your glass to the person you see

first toasts are usually initiated by the host of an event. After the host has given a toast, others are then free to offer their own. Everyone in the room is expected to lift her or his glass in response to the toast. Although "clinking" glasses is customary in the United States, it is necessary only to touch glasses with all guests in smaller parties and to touch glasses with the people on either side of you at a larger event.

Toasts should be from the heart, but do not be afraid to use humor. Toasts should show the audience and the honoree that you care about and appreciate the person, but they should not include inside jokes or references that few in the room will understand. Instead, use a story that paints the honoree in a positive light. You will definitely want to avoid embarrassing the honoree or others in the room.

If you have the opportunity to plan the toast in advance, take the time to write it with as much care as you would any other speech. Before you begin writing, decide on your specific purpose and the thesis or theme of the toast. Research by reminiscing and talking to others to find stories about the honoree, or find a meaningful quote to use. If this is a wedding toast or for another cultural ritual, be sure to investigate the particular guidelines for toasting at the occasion in that culture. In the United States, wedding toasts made by the best man or maid of honor tend to be humorous and touching. Toasts from the parents tend to be sentimental and sweet.

When it is time for you to give the toast, begin by getting your audience's attention. You can simply say in a voice loud enough to be heard by interested parties, "I would like to propose a toast!" If the room is large and people are talking, you can begin by *gently* tapping on the side of your glass with your knife and then announcing that you would like to propose a toast.

Once you have everyone's attention, be sure to speak clearly, sincerely, and respectfully. Match your facial expressions to the mood you want to create. As you begin to speak, hold the glass about shoulder height and look directly at the honoree. As you progress, you can glance around the room, but be sure that the majority of your eye contact is with the honoree. As you approach the end of your toast, raise your glass to about head level and end with a prepositional phrase that captures your theme. For example: "To Rachel and Jeffrey as they begin their lives together." "To your health." "To a long and successful career." At that point, the audience will know to raise their glasses, after which you may take a sip.

If you are the recipient of the toast and you are sitting when the toast is proposed, you should stay sitting even though others should stand. At the end of the toast, you should not drink. The toast is in your honor; drinking would be like applauding your own speech. Think of it this way: If the bride and groom were to drink after every toast given in their honor, they would not remember the reception! After the toast, you can say thank you or offer your own toast in return. You may drink when you return the toast or for subsequent toasts for other people.

Commencement speeches are a time to reflect and to look forward. Often, colleges and universities ask celebrities, politicians, and other dignitaries to speak at graduation.

Commemorative Speeches

Commencement addresses, memorial speeches, eulogies, and dedications honor and remember special days, heroes, important events, and lost loved ones. Commemorative speeches celebrate, memorialize, honor, and observe events, people, ideas, and institutions and also mark special occasions by inspiring audiences, rekindling pride and sentiment for the event or person, and providing a focal point for an event. As such, they tend to be longer than other special occasion speeches, often ten, fifteen, twenty minutes or longer!

Commemorative speeches should be very well researched, planned, and written out in advance of the event to allow yourself plenty of practice. You should give special attention to the creative, even poetic, use of language. Because of the emotional significance of these speeches and the need for vivid and emotional language, commemorative speeches are often delivered manuscript style. They are written out and then delivered word for word. This is why plenty of practice is a must. You don't want to *sound* or *look* like you are reading.

Commemorative speeches also aim to entertain, so you should use a variety of supporting materials that create color and imagery. However, as with all speeches, before you begin writing, decide on your specific purpose and thesis or theme. Choose three or four main ideas to advance your theme, and then choose supporting materials that will bring your theme to life. Supporting material for these speeches may include references to great heroes and historical events, quotes from famous authors, and memories of past events.

SUMMARY

In this chapter, we explored informative and special occasion speeches. We learned that informative speeches aim to teach the audience about a subject through clear focus and careful organization of the main points. We learned about the variety of informative speeches one can make, how to best organize them using the various organizational patterns we learned about in Chapter Eight, and how to apply the patterns to each of the six types of informative speeches: objects, people, places, processes, concepts, and events

We discovered how important special occasion speeches are, not only to make our events special, but also to make our lives richer and more meaningful. We learned that it is an honor to be asked to give one of these special speeches. Then we explored some of the various types of special occasion speeches that we are most likely to encounter in our lives, no matter where in the world we live. We learned how to bring together the components of organization, language use, and delivery to create powerful and meaningful presentations for the joyful, important, and sacred moments of life.

Knowing what kind of speech you are planning to write can be very helpful in organizing, researching, and preparing your speech to fit the rhetorical situation. Often, the speech type—whether informative, special occasion, or persuasive—and the specific type within each provide us with clues about which organizational patterns will be the most useful, which types of supporting materials we might want to find, and which language choices might work best. Understanding the differences between and within each type of speech can help guide our speechmaking now and in the future.

Discussion Questions and Activities

1. In groups of four or five, generate a list of ten informative speech topics that would be interesting to and appropriate for each of the following audiences:
   - An audience of one hundred fourteen- to seventeen-year old boys.
   - An audience of twenty recent college graduates.
   - An audience of sixty-five parents of toddlers.
   - An audience of 1,500 first-year college students.
   - An audience of fifteen pre-adolescent girls (nine to eleven years old).

   Explain why these topics would be interesting and appropriate for each audience.
2. Quickly think of a skill, trick, or procedure that you know how to do and that can be easily taught to someone else. Develop a three- to five-minute process speech to teach your classmates how to do the skill.
3. Write a brief informative speech about someone in your life whom you consider successful. Then write the speech as a speech of dedication. How are the

speeches different? What kind of supporting material did you use in the first speech that was different from what you used in the second? How were your specific purposes different in the two speeches? How did the language change from one speech to the other?

4. If you could win any award in the world (Nobel Peace Prize, Lifetime Achievement Award, Humanitarian-of-the-Year Award), what would you want it to be? Imagine that you have won that award. Write a speech of presentation honoring you for that award. Then write a speech to accept the award.
5. With a partner and the speeches you wrote in question four, have your partner present you with the award using the speech you wrote. Then accept the award, giving your acceptance speech. Then present the award to your partner, who should accept it with his/her acceptance speech.
6. Using the guidelines for commemorative speaking, write a five-minute graduation/commencement speech for your own college graduation. Pay particular attention to word choice and language techniques (see Chapter Ten for ideas).
7. At your next dinner with friends or family, propose a toast to the host or chef of the meal, using the guidelines for giving toasts in this chapter.

Chapter Quiz

Matching

Identify which kind of speech each of the following thesis statements represents.

a. Commemorative speech **b.** Concept speech **c.** Event speech
d. Object speech **e.** Speech of introduction **f.** Process speech

1. ______ Growing nasturtiums is as easy as 1-2-3.

2. ______ Sparked by the death of Hu Yaobang, China's largest nonviolent political protest began with protesters occupying Beijing's Tiananmen Square to voice their discontent and ended with a violent government crackdown in 1989.

3. ______ Sigmund Freud's Structural Model of Personality divides the personality into the id, the ego, and the superego.

4. ______ Charles M. Schulz taught us wisdom through wit, insight through innocence, and compassion through his comics.

5. ______ As you enter the gates to downtown Disneyland and make your way through the various lands within, you will discover that Disneyland is a world unto itself.

6. ______ Ladies and gentlemen, the President of the United States.

T/F, Multiple Choice, Fill-in

1. List the six types of informative speeches.

   ____________________ ____________________ ____________________

   ____________________ ____________________ ____________________

2. True or false: Process speeches can be categorized into two types—how-it-is-done and how-long.
3. The type of informative speech that explores ideas, theories, hypotheses, issues, and beliefs without offering an opinion is called
   - **a.** process.
   - **b.** concept.
   - **c.** event.
   - **d.** object.
4. True or false: Informative speeches help explain the topic in order to persuade and entertain the audience.
5. Speeches of ______ are given to present awards or gifts to deserving recipients, and speeches of ______ are given by the recipients of awards or gifts.
6. All of the following are types of speeches EXCEPT:
   - **a.** informative
   - **b.** persuasive
   - **c.** special occasion
   - **d.** compulsive
   - **e.** none of the above
7. The purpose(s) of speeches of introduction include:
   - **a.** To prepare the audience for the speaker
   - **b.** To give the speaker more time when s/he is not ready
   - **c.** To generate excitement for the speaker
   - **d.** Both a and c
   - **e.** None of the above

Speeches for Evaluation

Informative Speech for Evaluation: Evaluate the following informative speech. What are the specific purpose and thesis statements? Does the speaker establish her credibility and relate the topic well to a college audience? What types of supporting material does the author use? Are there other kinds of supporting materials she could have included? Is there anything she could have left out? Did the speech hold your interest? Why? What language techniques does she employ to make the speech more interesting? What other techniques could she have used?

A Midsummer Day
by Linda Augustine

(Alarm rings, turn on lights.) I guess it's time for everyone to wake up. Good morning, everyone. Today, everyone in this classroom is about to experience their first Midsummer Day ever. For me, on the other hand, this is going to be the twenty-first time I'm going to celebrate midsummer because I have been celebrating this since the year I was born. You better get ready because in the upcoming seven minutes, we are going to celebrate this day through a lot of dancing, singing, and eating typical Swedish dishes because that is what we Swedes do during Midsummer Day in the middle of June, surrounded by a lot of different flowers.

One of the main points during this important day is the dancing. We do the dancing around a Midsummer pole and we sing around the pole in costumes. The main costume we wear was created by a Swedish designer named Martha Jurgensen in the 1950s. The national outfit contains three different colors: white, blue, and yellow. Jurgensen was a feminist who created this costume as a counterweight to the fashion tyranny that was going on during these years, which included uncomfortable clothes, and impractical female dresses. So these costumes fit us perfectly when we do the dance around the Midsummer pole.

The Midsummer pole looks like this. The pole actually symbolizes a male sex organ. I guess all of you are wondering what this has to do with a Midsummer Day. Well, actually, this day is about rebirth and regrowth, and it's about Mother Nature's fertility. I guess you will have to use your imagination. To raise the pole, we gather friends, family, and neighbors in one place every year the same and we raise it during the morning, so we can stand there and watch it every day.

During the Midsummer Day we have two main songs that are always being sung. These two songs are _____ and _____. If I'm going to translate this it will be something like, "The fox is hurrying off the ice," and "The small little frogs." When we sing the songs some of the adults make something we call schnapps. After this song, I will tell you why. (Two women sing and dance.)

Now you might understand why we need something called schnapps. Schnapps is sort of like a shot. It will have different kinds of flavors. We also need this for all the games we will play. We play games such as tug-of-war and something we call balance a potato on a spoon. Two teams in two lines put the spoon in the mouth and the potato on the spoon and then run as fast as possible and as long as possible. The one who drops the potato first loses. It is as simple as that.

There are a lot of other activities going on during this day, that is why it is important to eat. We eat several times during this day. Our main dishes are herring, potato, meatballs, strawberries, and salmon. You have a food sample in front of you, and I want you all to taste it. What you are eating is raw fish that is pickled in dill on whole wheat bread and that is what we eat on Midsummer Day, probably about five of these favors. The two most wanted products are the fresh potatoes and the strawberries because these are seasonal products and very wanted during the rest of the year and they are very hard to get. Most of the meals are eaten in picnic form because it is important to stay outside.

That brings me to the third point about Midsummer Day, the flowers and the nature. It is important to be part of the nature during this day and we always stay outside no matter what the weather is. It is said that June can cure illness, that there is power in the love, and that the love is shown in the flowers. And the water can take away all the bad. That is why the Swedes wear a garland of flowers during a Midsummer Day. There is also a myth that if a virgin girl jumps over three crosses and three fences in silence by herself and picks seven different flowers and then sleeps with these flowers under her pillow the night before a Midsummer Day, she will dream about her future husband. I did this and dreamt about Brad Pitt.

I guess after all this garland binding, all this dancing around, singing, and eating these typical Swedish dishes, you are about to get a bit tired, so I guess it is time for me to thank you for participating in my Swedish holiday. Good night (turn off light).

Special Occasion Speech for Analysis: Analyze the following special occasion speech.

For Aaron
by Gary Squier

Aaron, when I considered what message to give to you on your Bar Mitzvah, I decided to first consider the messages I've given you these last thirteen years. I put myself into your shoes—or ears. "What does Dad have to say to me?" *Have you done your homework? When are you going to practice clarinet? Don't multitask. Stay focused. Get out of Hannah's room. Clean your room. Don't play with doors. Don't play with your retainer. Put the CDs back into their sleeves. Don't leave your stuff in my office. Stop goofing around.*

Well, those are not very satisfactory messages. What I should have said instead, or at least in addition, is what was in my heart. What you should have heard more of was: *I love it when you figure out how to make waffles from scratch. I'm proud of your accomplishments in Scouts—long hikes, fifty-mile bike rides, canoeing in treacherous weather without complaint. I'm proud of you taking on leadership as co-editor of the school yearbook. It's OK that you'd rather fix my computer than play tennis with me. I'm proud of your willingness to figure out the bus system to get to UCLA computer camp. I'm impressed at your mastery of everything mechanical and electronic in the house. I'm impressed by your gentle nature and kindness.*

What can I say today that might be useful to you in years thirteen to one hundred? Follow two of the core aspects of who you are: your goodness and your intense curiosity. Whatever drives you to read the owner's manual for our Honda Odyssey, to sleep, laptop on your stomach, Ethernet cord trailing off your bed logged onto HowThingsWork.com. Whatever steers you to the stack of ads in the Sunday *Times* and results in you knowing every camera model, tent style, and where to buy them at the best price.

Let that curiosity be your light. Let that goodness be your compass. And you'll do fine on the path before you—but you'd better finish your homework! And try to look behind the stream of demands you hear from me and mom to see the love, admiration, respect, and wonder for you that lives in our hearts.

Chapter 13 Quiz Answers

Matching: 1. f, 2. c, 3. b, 4. a, 5. d, 6. e

T/F, Multiple Choice, Fill-in 1. Objects, places, people, processes, concepts, and events, 2. False, 3. b, 4. False, 5. presentation, acceptance, 6. compulsive, 7. d.

CHAPTER 14 Persuasion

CHAPTER GOAL

By the end of this chapter you will be able to construct a logical, well-organized persuasive speech that employs a variety of proofs and that is free from logical fallacies.

What is the difference between the two thesis statements below?

- The history of capital punishment in the U.S. justice system tells a story of racism.
- Capital punishment needs to be abolished from the U.S. justice system due to its history of racism.

The first statement is more appropriate for an informative speech on the racist aspects of capital punishment. The second statement is appropriate for a persuasive speech calling for a change in policy—the end of capital punishment in the United States.

Persuasion is an important part of our everyday lives, and to use it more effectively, particularly in formal speaking situations, we need to understand how it differs from informative speaking and learn the various types, styles, and tools of the persuasive speech.

First, let's define *persuasion. Merriam-Webster's Collegiate Dictionary* defines persuasion as "the act or process of moving another to a belief, position, or course of action." In other words, we use persuasion to convince others to believe, think, or do something that they might not otherwise believe, think, or do. For example, if I wanted you to join your college's debate team, and you wanted to join the track team instead, I would have to provide all the reasons I think it would be better for you to join the debate team. If you finally decide to join the debate team, I would have been successful in persuading you.

Persuasion doesn't always seek to move us to action, as in the example above. Sometimes we simply want people to agree with our opinions or to see the world the way we see it. Arguing that one movie is better than another or that the government should pass a certain law are also examples of persuasion that we encounter every day.

SIGNIFICANCE OF PERSUASION

Persuasion is an important part of our everyday lives. We use persuasion and are the targets of persuasion not only every day, but hundreds of times every day! Think about where you have been, whom you have seen, and what you have done today. Did you drive or walk along streets in a commercial area of town? Did you listen to the radio? Watch television? Pass people on the streets or in your classrooms or at work who were wearing clothing with logos on them? Did you use any products that had the company's logo or trademark on them? Did you eat at a restaurant or get fast food? Go to any stores? If you answered "yes" to any of these questions, you were the target of potentially thousands of persuasive attempts in the form of advertising, in addition to any direct appeals from family, friends, co-workers, and strangers. Persuasion surrounds our lives.

Realizing this should not create paranoia or fear in you. Contrary to popular belief, persuasion is not a "bad" thing. Persuasion is part of being human and adds to the collective knowledge and greater good of humanity. In fact, the research you study in school is a form of persuasion. Scientists and theorists use their best evidence from experiments and research to persuade others in their field that their explanations most reasonably explain certain phenomena. It is this form of persuasion that has led to the growth of human knowledge and understanding.

On a less grandiose level, we need persuasion in our everyday lives to help us reach our goals and meet our needs. You use persuasion when you apply for jobs, to graduate schools, and for scholarships; when you need to question a grade or ask for an extension on an assignment; and when you need to borrow money.

Although the same principles and rules of good public speaking apply, persuasive speaking differs from other public speaking in the extent of responsibility the speaker has to the audience. Because a persuasive speaker is asking the audience to change or act in some way, the persuasive speaker is held to the highest ethical standards. When the speaker stands to gain something from the audience's compliance, the speaker must take great care not to manipulate or deceive the audience in any way.

Additionally, because the speaker is asking the audience to make a choice that follows the speaker's wishes, the speaker is acting as a leader. This gives the speaker relatively more power than the audience, which means the speaker has a responsibility to protect the best interests of the audience. Finally, persuasive speaking often relies on rousing the audience's emotions to move them to action. However, speakers must take great care not to frivolously play with the audience's emotions.

TYPES OF PERSUASION

We have already stated that every time you speak, you are informing, persuading, or entertaining. Similarly, when you persuade you are using one of three types of persuasive claims or propositions: fact, value, or policy. In this section we will look at each persuasive proposition and at some of the more effective ways to organize these propositions in speeches.

Propositions of Fact

Propositions of Fact
Assertions made about the truth or falsity of a statement.

Did the defendant kill his wife? Is there a God? Will the Los Angeles Dodgers win the next World Series? For each of these questions, there is one, and only one, answer, and these answers would come in the form of propositions of fact: *The defendant did not kill his wife. There is a God. The Dodgers will win the next World Series.* Factual propositions, then, propose or claim that something is true, was true, or will be true or that it is false. I could claim, for instance, that there are aliens from Pluto attending this school, but it seems clear that this "truth claim" would be found to be false. The problem is that sometimes we *don't know* (i.e., only the defendant knows if he killed his wife or not), *can't know* (i.e., we won't know for sure that God exists until we have died and perhaps not even then), or *don't know yet* (i.e., we will find out in several months whether the Dodgers win or lose the Series or don't even make it to the postseason).

When we know the truth about something, we state facts that are verifiable. We often use facts to support arguments or when informing our audience. When we are persuading someone of the truth or falsity of something that may be difficult or impossible to prove definitively, we propose the truth of the situation using a proposition of fact. In this way, *propositions of fact* are aimed at convincing people that one answer to a question is more likely to be true than other answers. They are statements that answer questions that have definite true or false, yes or no answers that we are unable to know at this moment in time or that are very difficult to prove. If there were no possibility of dispute on a proposition of fact, we would no longer need courtrooms, and gambling would be an easy way to get rich.

Because we may never know the one true answer to a question of fact, the best we can do is provide our best evidence and reasoning to support our case. Although similar to informative speeches that provide a variety of supporting materials to explain and clarify the facts about a subject without taking a position, persuasive speeches on questions of fact advocate for one possible version of what is true by taking a firm stand. Whereas an informative thesis statement might say, *One religious view of creation is that the universe was created in seven days by God,* the proposition of fact thesis would say, *God created the universe in seven days as it was taught in the Bible.*

Because of this similarity to informative speeches, you can organize a proposition of fact speech using the same organizational patterns—that is, topically, spatially, or causally.

Most arguments containing propositions of fact do not always stop there. Often, speeches start with a proposition of fact to support a proposition of value or policy.

Propositions of Value

Propositions of Value
Assertions that make a value judgment about the worth or righteousness of a policy, action, or object.

State-sanctioned gambling is morally wrong. Capital punishment is just. Shrek *is the best children's movie of the past ten years.* Each of these statements represents a *proposition of value.* Propositions of value go beyond a factual claim (a description of reality) and include an opinion or conclusion about some aspect of reality. For example, it is a fact that Yosemite Park is located in California, but a proposition of value might claim that Yosemite Park is the most beautiful of our national parks. Note that the park must exist in order to be beautiful; therefore, we say that each proposition of value *includes* propositions of fact.

Propositions of value are claims that aim to modify the way people think or feel about a subject. They express an opinion about what is right or wrong, good or bad, fair or unfair, easy or difficult, smart or stupid, beautiful or ugly. That is, they contain ideas *about* something or someone. Because they involve personal opinion, they cannot be proved right or wrong. However, we may still be successful in convincing others to agree with our opinion of something. These propositions can be argued alone or as a basis for speeches urging audience action.

Although we talked about several organizational patterns in Chapter Eight, there are some patterns that are specific to persuasion. One of these is criteria-satisfaction.

The criteria-satisfaction organizational pattern is used in persuasive speeches aimed at making value judgments. The speaker establishes a set of criteria for the evaluation and then defends the reasons that a particular object, person, philosophy, event, or situation meets or exceeds the criteria. The criteria-satisfaction organizational pattern is found in movie and book reviews and in some legal arguments.

Your first main point establishes the criteria for evaluation. The second main point evaluates the person, object, or event based on those criteria. Say, for example, that you want to argue that *Shrek* is the best children's movie released in the past ten years:

Specific Purpose: To persuade my audience that *Shrek* is the best children's movie released in the past ten years.

Thesis: Because of its excellent production, performance, and moral value, *Shrek* is the best children's movie released in the past ten years.

I. An excellent children's movie must have outstanding production, performance, and moral value.

II. *Shrek* has outstanding production, performance, and moral value.

Propositions of Policy

Child molesters and child killers should be given life sentences without the possibility of parole. Our university should end the dorm curfew. The state legislature of New Mexico should pass a law prohibiting cockfighting. Each of these statements represents a proposition of policy. Propositions of policy are claims that aim to modify a rule, regulation, or specific course of action. They include facts and values but go beyond them and suggest whether or not something should be done. For example, one might argue that Yosemite should limit the number of visitors to the park in order to preserve its pristine beauty. Note that the statement assumes that Yosemite exists (fact) and that it is worth preserving (value), and goes on to advocate what should or should not be done.

Propositions of Policy
Assertions that advocate for a particular solution to a problem or for a specific course of action to be taken.

Propositions of policy seek either passive agreement or immediate action. Sometimes your audience is not the group you want to actually take the action, but just a group of people you want to agree with you so that they can spread the word or put pressure on those who would take the action. We call this *passive agreement.*

If you are asking the audience in front of you to take the action, you are presenting a policy speech that asks for *immediate action.* This does not mean that you are asking the audience to take action immediately. They may not

Politicians use policy speeches to convince each other, the public, and other governments to adopt or defeat specific policies. Here former U.S. Vice President Al Gore urges attendees at a Global Environmental Action Conference to support his agenda to reduce greenhouse gas emissions.

take the action until a later date. For example, you may give a policy speech asking the audience to have only two children. You are not asking them to go out and have two children right away, but you are asking them to follow your preference to limit their children to two whenever the time comes for them to make that choice.

If you are from a traditionally high-context culture that prefers to avoid direct statements and, in particular, direct requests, you may find the U.S American persuasive style to be too direct, even rude. However, you can adapt your style to the U.S. American preference for directness by saving your direct request for action until the end of your speech. Use your evidence and reasoning to lead the audience to your conclusion, and then ask them to comply at the end. With a little experience, you will find that American audiences appreciate a direct style because it *informs* them of exactly what you are expecting of them.

Both types of policy speeches must address the *needs, plan,* and *practicality* of the action you are advocating. Unless you are speaking about a problem on which complete agreement exists, you must show your audience that a problem truly exists and will continue to exist and grow if something is not done

Considering Language

Lost in Translation

Advertising is one of the most pervasive forms of persuasion. Companies spend billions of dollars on advertising every year to persuade us to buy their products. As many of these companies gain success in their home countries, they venture abroad to the international markets, taking their advertising campaigns overseas. Unfortunately, they don't always recognize that translation is a tricky thing. A few well-known blunders include:

- Swedish vacuum cleaner Electrolux translated their slogan "Nothing Sucks Like an Electrolux" into English, not realizing that "sucks" is a term meaning "poorly made" or "inferior."
- A T-shirt maker improperly translated "I saw the Pope" (el Papa) as "I saw the potato" (la papa).
- An Italian campaign for Schweppes tonic water inadvertently translated the product's name into Schweppes toilet water.

Translation problems such as these are common for anyone trying to persuade people using a language that he or she is not completely comfortable with. Many times in persuasion we use euphemisms, axioms, sayings, and idioms that do not translate between languages.

To help us translate, sometimes we can turn to online translation sites such as http://www.appliedlanguage.com/free_translation.shtml. However, this can lead to embarrassing mistakes as well. For example, I entered, "Don't throw the baby out with the bathwater" to be translated into Arabic. Then I entered the Arabic translation to be translated back into English. I was surprised to receive, "The child does not throw outside with the [bthwtr]" as the translation!

to remedy it. You can't expect people to donate blood, support a tuition increase, or sign up for a beach cleanup unless you have first proved that a serious problem exists that affects them. In the case where others are advocating a change of policy and you are advocating for the status quo, you will instead need to argue that a problem does *not* exist.

You will also need to carefully explain your solution or *plan* and how it addresses the problem. If other solutions are being advocated, you will further need to convince the audience that your plan is the best available solution to the problem. Also, be sure to address any concerns about how the plan would be implemented and how it would be paid for, and other specific details that might raise audience concerns.

Finally, you will need to discuss the practicality of your plan, explaining to the audience how your plan is the easiest and most beneficial solution to the problem and addressing any concerns regarding unintended consequences. One technique is to show how the same or a similar plan has been successfully used to address the same type of problem somewhere else. In this way, you can show how the plan has worked well and identify other side benefits resulting from implementing the plan.

When presenting a policy speech, you can organize the speech using problem-solution, problem-cause-solution (see Chapter Eight), or comparative advantage order. Following are examples of each.

Problem-Solution

Specific Purpose: To persuade my audience to implement a first-year-student alcohol awareness program to address the problem of underage drinking on our campus.

Thesis: Because underage drinking has become such a major problem on our campus, the school administration needs to implement an alcohol awareness program for incoming freshmen.

Main Points:

I. Underage drinking has become a major problem on our campus.

II. The school administration needs to implement an alcohol awareness program for incoming freshmen.

Problem-Cause-Solution

Specific Purpose: To persuade my audience to boycott music videos that portray women negatively.

Thesis: To combat the rise in violence toward women, we need to boycott music videos that negatively portray women.

Main Points:

I. Negative attitudes and violence toward women is on the rise among seventeen- to twenty-five-year-olds.

II. Music videos that celebrate the objectification of women as instruments of pleasure for men have played a major role in this increase.

III. We need to boycott artists who negatively portray women in their videos.

Comparative Advantage

Another persuasion-specific organizational pattern, comparative advantage organization, is used in persuasive speeches given to an audience who agrees that a problem exists but disagrees on the proper solution. The comparative advantage pattern compares two or more possible solutions to the problem, showing how one solution is the best alternative compared to the others.

TABLE 14.1 Monroe's Motivated Sequence

I. Attention step: Gains the attention of the audience, tells them who you are and why they should listen to you, and gives them an indication of what you are about to discuss.
II. Need step: Shows the audience that a need or a problem exists and how it affects them.
III. Satisfaction step: Offers a solution to the problem. Shows a step-by-step plan and how it will solve the problem.
IV. Visualization step: Shows the audience how practical and beneficial the plan is and how individual audience members will benefit from taking the proposed action.
V. Call to action step: Calls for the audience to take the proposed action and reminds them how to do so.

Specific Purpose: To persuade my audience that hybrid electric cars are a better alternative to gas-powered cars than strictly battery/electric cars.

Thesis: Hybrid electric cars are a better alternative to gas-powered cars because they can travel farther (without refueling or recharging) and are less expensive than battery/electric cars.

Main Points:

I. Hybrid electric cars can travel farther than strictly battery/electric cars because they do not need to be recharged.
II. Hybrid electric cars are less expensive than battery/electric cars both in the short and the long term.

Monroe's Motivated Sequence

Monroe's Motivated Sequence, another persuasion-specific organizational pattern, is a five-point pattern that speakers use when they are calling for the audience to take a specific action.[1] If you listen to commercial radio or watch commercials on TV, you are already familiar with Monroe's Motivated Sequence because it is used extensively in advertising. Monroe's sequence anticipates the audience's questions: Who are you and what do you want? Is there a problem here? What can I do about it? What is in it for me? What do you want me to do?

When asking for immediate action, Monroe's Motivated Sequence walks audience members through each step of gaining their attention and trust, establishing that a problem exists, showing them a workable plan to address or solve the problem, explaining the practicality of the plan and what additional benefits they can enjoy if the plan is adopted, and finally asking for action from them.

The speech is organized into five main points that answer these questions. Unlike the other organizational methods, Monroe's sequence does not include a separate introduction and conclusion in the outline because they are contained in Steps I and V, respectively (you will find a sample Monroe outline at the end of this chapter). For now, let's look at the basic parts of Monroe's Motivated Sequence (see Table 14.1). Following is an example of a speech organized using Monroe's sequence:

Specific Purpose: To persuade my audience to become regular blood donors.

Thesis: Becoming a blood donor is easy and saves lives.

Main Points:

I. Like many of you, I have had the unfortunate experience of losing a loved one unnecessarily.

II. Blood supplies in our state and across the nation are critically low.

III. Donating blood regularly at the local Red Cross can save lives.

IV. Donating blood is easy to do and offers many benefits.

V. Please make an appointment this week to start donating blood at the local Red Cross.

MAKING A PERSUASIVE ARGUMENT: LOGOS, ETHOS, PATHOS, AND MYTHOS

Building a persuasive argument that truly moves the audience to change their beliefs or actions takes more than just organizing the main points logically. A speaker also needs to employ a variety of persuasive tools that support the argument. We call these persuasive tools *proofs*. Proofs are the various types of evidence that a speaker uses to establish the truth of an argument. The four types of proofs a speaker can use are logos, ethos, pathos, and mythos.

Persuasive arguments are constructed by arranging claims, premises, and evidence in believable and compelling ways. A claim, as we discussed above, is what the speaker is arguing for. It is the central or major proposition of the argument and is expressed in the form of the thesis statement or central idea.

Even though it was Aristotle, the father of Western public speaking, who named the first three types of proofs, all cultures use these same proofs, albeit in different ways, to create persuasive arguments. The key to learning how to create persuasive arguments in American English is to learn the audience's preferences for each type of proof.

Logos

Logos is the logic that persuaders use in constructing their arguments. The logic of a speech consists of the ways in which evidence and reasoning are used—or as Aristotle said, the "logical arrangement of the argument."[2] Evidence is anything used to verify the truthfulness or accuracy of a premise or claim. Reasoning is the way in which the evidence, premises, and claims

CONSIDERING CULTURE

Deductive and Inductive Reasoning

Although there are many forms of reasoning and logical arguments used in the United States and around the world, the two most frequently discussed and taught in the United States are deductive and inductive reasoning.

Deductive reasoning has been considered the most "airtight" argument because when and if the premises are true, the audience must accept the conclusion. In other words, if the audience agrees with each of the premises, then they must agree with the conclusion. Often, deduction starts from a general principle and then moves to a more specific factual example that leads to the claim. We refer to this form of reasoning as reasoning from principle. One classic example of this is a categorical syllogism:

Premise 1:
All men are mortal.
Premise 2:
Socrates is a man.
Claim:
Socrates is mortal.

Inductive reasoning is less absolute than deductive reasoning because it employs one or more premises that are inferential instead of factual. Because of this, inductive arguments lead to probable truths of a claim. Frequently, these arguments start from or include a more specific example and then move to a general claim, but not always. This form of inductive reasoning is referred to as reasoning from specific instances. An example of this is:

Premise 1:
Mariko is from Japan.
Premise 2:
Rice is a staple food in Japan.
Claim:
Mariko eats rice.

Notice that the claim is only probable; it is not necessarily true. Mariko might be an exception. The more likely or believable the premises are, the more likely the audience will be to accept the claim.

The difference between an inductive and a deductive argument is probability. That is, the conclusion of an inductive argument is said to be more or less probable depending on the quality and quantity of the evidence.

are put together in the argument. Together, the evidence and reasoning of an argument constitute the logic. What counts as logic varies by culture: Different cultures find different kinds of evidence and reasoning more or less persuasive.

In Chapter Six, we discussed various forms of evidence that we can use to support the main points of a speech. In persuasion, the main points are often in the form of premises, which are a type of evidence that act as the building blocks of an argument; they are the minor propositions of an argument from which the conclusions are drawn. In some arguments (known as *deductive arguments*, see "Considering Culture"), the speaker offers premises that the audience agrees to first and that lead the audience to accept the speaker's conclusion. For example:

Premise 1: *Children should respect their parents.*

Premise 2: *Contradicting one's parents in public is disrespectful.*

Conclusion: *Children should not contradict their parents in public.*

Notice how the argument leads easily, clearly, and directly from Premises 1 and 2 to the conclusion.

When the premises are not easily agreed upon, the speaker needs to prove the premises with further evidence. That is when the premises look more like main points that need to be supported by further evidence:

Main Point I: *Children should respect their parents.*

Subpoint A: *Parents know more than their children about the world.*

Subpoint B: *Without respect, children will not learn from their parents.*

Main Point II: *Contradicting one's parents in public is disrespectful.*

Subpoint A: *Contradicting someone can lead to embarrassment.*

Subpoint B: *Embarrassing a parent shows disrespect.*

Conclusion: *Children should not contradict their parents in public.*

The quality of the individual premises and evidence and how they are linked together determine the quality of the argument. Persuasive arguments need to be both true and valid to be considered *good arguments.* An argument is true if each of the premises is shown or is believed to be true. We already know that all the evidence you use in a speech needs to be true for ethical and credibility reasons.

To be valid, the premises and other evidence must also link together in a reasonable way. An argument is considered valid if the premises guarantee the acceptance of the conclusion. The example above is a good illustration of a valid argument that goes from the general to the specific. It begins with a general premise: *Children should respect their parents;* links to a second premise that is more specific: *Contradicting one's parents in public is disrespectful;* and ends with a conclusion that the audience must accept if they have already accepted the two premises: *Children should not contradict their parents in public.*

Interestingly, an argument does not have to be valid for it to be true. For example:

Premise 1: *Children should respect their parents.*

Premise 2: *Parents should not be mean to their children.*

Claim: *Children should not be mean to their parents.*

Each of these premises and the conclusion seems self-evidently true. However, they do not link together in a reasonable or logical way. On the other hand, an argument can be valid but not true. For example:

Premise 1: *Children should not respect their parents.*

Premise 2: *Contradicting one's parents in public is disrespectful.*

Claim: *Children should contradict their parents in public.*

This argument is valid, but it is not a good argument. It follows logically from the premises to the conclusion, but few if any people would argue that the premises or conclusion is true under normal circumstances. The important thing to remember here is that your arguments need to be both true and valid.

Ethos

Ethos is a speaker's credibility—how believable and trustworthy a speaker is in terms of his/her competence and character. Is the speaker qualified to speak on this subject? Does the speaker have the necessary credentials or experience to qualify as an expert? Has the speaker done extensive research? Does the speaker have a reputation for being believable? Can he/she back up claims with believable evidence from a trustworthy source? Does the speaker seem confident and prepared? These questions emphasize the need for credibility in public speaking.

Throughout this book we have talked about the importance of credibility when giving a speech. We have talked about having credible sources for supporting material, establishing credibility in the introduction, and reinforcing credibility through confident delivery. Credibility is important for gaining and maintaining audience interest and to ensure that an audience believes the information being presented. However, credibility is especially important when trying to persuade. An audience is unlikely to believe or emulate a speaker they do not see as credible.

There is some evidence that certain people are granted more credibility from audiences than others, based on such things as attractiveness, charisma, openness, sex, and attire,[3] and speakers can improve their overall credibility by paying special attention

WHAT OTHERS SAY

Growing up in Hong Kong, once a colony of the British Empire, logic, reasoning, and evidence take a great role in persuasion. In China, people tend to be moved easily by emotional appeals. For example, there is a Chinese saying that there are no bad parents in the world. To us, it is absolutely clear that most, but not all, parents do good to their children. Children have to go along with their parents even if the parents make some serious mistakes, or the children will be blamed for not obeying their parents. In a speech, if the speaker can catch the emotional things like love to parents, children, or country, generally people will agree with the speaker even though the evidence is not strong.

—Kenny,
Hong Kong

to establishing their competence and character. As a non-native English speaker, you may be particularly concerned about the role of accent in speaker credibility. Studies do show that initially, audiences grant more credibility to speakers who have the same accent. However, by attending to the content of your message and managing your pronunciation, you can overcome this initial challenge. In fact, there is evidence that when a speaker who has an accent is clear and well organized, the accent actually boosts the speaker's credibility.[4]

Competence is a speaker's knowledge and expertise on a subject. A speaker needs to establish that he or she knows what s/he is talking about. A speaker can convey his or her competence several times and in several ways before, during, and after the speech.

First, a speaker needs to *act* like s/he knows what s/he is doing. As we discussed in Chapter Twelve, you can increase your perceived competence through a strong delivery that begins the moment you arrive on speech day. Before the speech begins, you should look calm, self-assured, and relaxed. A shaking leg, darting eyes, and a pained expression tell the audience that you lack self-confidence, are ill-prepared, or are unprofessional. To demonstrate competence before your speech, move fluidly, smile, and pay attention to what others are saying and doing until it is your time to speak. Avoid making unnecessary, fidgeting movements or wiggling in your seat. When it is your turn to speak, stand up with determination and confidence. Do not rush or meander to the podium. Get settled, acknowledge the audience calmly, and begin with a strong, clear voice.

During the speech, be sure to speak with a loud and clear voice that is devoid of hesitations and awkward pauses. Use your hands to gesture freely and avoid clinging to the podium. At the end of your speech, pause briefly, gather your materials, and make your way back to your seat confidently.

Second, you increase your perceived competence by what you say. If you are from a culture that discourages talking or bragging about oneself, having to talk about yourself may create some discomfort for you. However, you should know that in the United States and in many other English-speaking and Western cultures, self-promotion is viewed positively in certain contexts, public speaking being one of them. Remember, many English-speaking countries are high on individualism (see Chapter One), meaning that they have a preference for individual achievement and personal success; and many are low context, meaning that messages tend to be explicit and direct. Therefore, to successfully increase your credibility while giving a speech in American English, you will probably need to mention, at least briefly during your introduction, why you are knowledgeable about your topic. Many researchers believe that establishing your credibility in the first two minutes of a persuasive presentation is crucial to gain and keep audience attention.[5] Explicitly state your interest, special training, or experience you have with the subject, or any special research you have conducted. For example:

> My interest in diabetes began when I was fourteen years old and my mother was diagnosed with the disease. The news changed our whole

> lifestyle from the way we ate to the way we spent our free time. Gone were Friday-night burgers, colas, and movie rentals; in their place were grilled fish, mineral water, and an invigorating after-dinner walk. This lifestyle change and the fear of losing my mother prematurely led me to research this deadly disease, and I have found that early intervention is the best cure. That is why I am here to convince you to dramatically reduce the amounts of sugar and fat in your diets and the apathy in your lifestyles to avoid becoming the next generation of diabetes victims.

During your speech, you can emphasize your knowledge of the subject by referring to the research that supports your claims.

Third, you can increase your perceived competence by finding common ground with your audience. Identify the ways in which you and your audience are the same and are affected in similar ways by the topic. People like to talk and listen to people they perceive to be like themselves:

> I know what you are thinking: "I don't have enough money as it is. I have rent, a car payment, school fees, and I have to eat. Besides, I have plenty of time to save later." I used to think that, too. I was broke all the time. My expenses always seemed to be growing. Where would I find the extra money to put away? Then one day in my junior year of high school, a friend convinced me to take ten dollars out of every paycheck and deposit it. She said that I wouldn't even miss it if I never had it in my hands. She was right. I slowly increased the amount I was saving. Currently, I am putting away about two hundred dollars a month. The key has been depositing the money before I ever see it. I don't know about you, but once I see the money, I find a way to spend it!

Speakers trying to persuade also need to be perceived as honest. A speaker's perceived trustworthiness is called *character.* First and foremost, speakers increase their perceived trustworthiness by building a reputation of being honest and reliable. Additionally, make sure that your claims, especially the claims that seem less believable, can be verified, and do not manipulate or stretch the truth in any way. Finally, addressing counterarguments and reasonable concerns honestly and openly tells the audience that you have nothing to hide and are therefore believable. Speakers who hide facts, manipulate details, or give vague explanations undermine their trustworthiness.

Pathos

Pathos is the emotional appeals that persuaders use to motivate people. Although statistics, facts, and testimony can be compelling, and although a good delivery from a believable speaker can increase credibility, some arguments just won't convince an audience until the audience is moved emotionally.

Emotional appeals are intended to make an audience *feel.* When a speaker can make an audience cry, laugh, become angry, or feel guilty, the audience is more likely to take an action or change their attitudes than when they hear just a series of facts and statistics.

Advertisements often resort to emotional appeals because they are quick and powerful. This advertisement from the American Cancer Society ran in the 1970s to try to convice the heavily smoking American people to quit smoking by trying to create guilt in the readers.

Negative emotions such as fear, anger, sadness, and guilt are the feelings most often evoked in speeches. These emotions are useful for moving an audience because once the speaker has established the emotion, the audience knows that they can feel better (i.e., less afraid, angry, sad, or guilty) by

Emotions can be a powerful persuasive tool. Advertisers have been aware of this for years.

Click Here http://www.bellsystemmemorial.com/bellsystem_ads-1.html to see examples of a successful advertising campaign from the 1970s. In 1979, AT&T launched one of the most successful ad campaigns of the last century. In an attempt to improve the company's image after a series of takeovers and acquisitions, the company began an ad campaign that showed sad and lonely grandparents moping around until their grandchildren called. "Reach out, reach out and touch someone" urged the audience to pick up the phone by making the audience feel guilty. Long-distance calls increased dramatically, and AT&T's image improved after this ad campaign hit televisions and magazines across the United States.

adopting the position or policy advocated by the speaker. For example, after a persuader presents a fear-invoking message, such as the risks of breast cancer, she offers a solution for avoiding the risks, such as self-examination or a healthier diet. Minimally to moderately frightening messages are most effective for bringing about behavior change in the audience. However, highly fear-inducing messages sometimes have the opposite effect.[6]

Positive emotions such as joy, compassion, hope, and pride can also be powerful persuaders. In this case, the good feelings a person has can be maintained by following the speaker's prescriptive. For example, pride in one's country can be used to encourage young men to join the military.

When using emotional appeals, you must abide by the highest of ethical standards because it is dangerous to play with the emotions of others. To ensure that your emotional appeals are ethically sound, use emotional appeals in conjunction with solid evidence and reasoning, and use only the emotional appeals that are directly related to your topic and purpose.

Mythos, or the Narrative Approach

A fourth persuasive proof, *mythos,* is narrative proof or storytelling. The narrative approach refers to both a logical form of evidence and an organizational style. Storytelling is almost as old as humanity.[7] Early civilizations used storytelling to pass on wisdom from one generation to the next. Today, we still love to hear a good story.

As a communication tool, narration is effective because it is interesting, repeatable, clear, easy to follow, and easy to remember. Stories and their important lessons can be easily passed from one audience to the next or from one generation to the next. Listening to a story feels less like being taught and more like being entertained.

Using narration in a speech can help you stay focused and keep the audience's attention. A well-told story can draw an audience in, bring a subject alive, and convey a great deal of information succinctly and interestingly. Additionally, the love of stories crosses all cultural lines and brings audience and speaker closer.

Storytelling can help a speaker connect with the audience and encourage new ways of looking at information. As such, Vincent Kituku advises each speaker

> to remember that the story can be even more powerful if you find ways to encourage audience members to pick apart a parable and explore the parts of the story that are relevant for them. You will be surprised to find that the same tale can mean different things to different people.[8]

Whether you choose to present your whole speech as a story or use one or two brief stories to make your points clear, narratives, according to Roderick P. Hart:

1. Disarm listeners by enchanting them. . . .

2. Awaken within listeners dormant experiences and feelings. . . .
3. Expose, subtly, some sort of propositional argument.[9]

Narrative has these effects because the features of narrative cause people to listen and reason differently than they do when hearing other forms of speech. First, narrative follows a natural timeline that compels us to hear the ending after we have heard the beginning of a story. Just think about how difficult it is to walk away from a TV show that is not finished or to put down a good book in the middle of a chapter. We need to know how the story ends.

Second, narratives are stories about other people. We love to hear about people who are like ourselves, who have overcome great obstacles, or who have contributed great things to the lives of others. We can identify with their everyday concerns, their challenges and battles, and their successes. Because we see ourselves in the stories we hear, they touch us personally.

Third, through description, narratives transport us from the here and now to a place more wonderful or terrible than the present moment. We enter the realm of our imaginations and become the characters of the story.

Fourth, narrative transcends cultural barriers because it is primitive and speaks to the child in us. We first learned about the world, life, and our culture from the stories our parents told us and the books we read.

Finally, the lessons we learn from stories are not obvious or dictatorial. We the listeners feel as though we take part in creating the meaning. Well-told stories offer a comfortable form of learning and persuasion that does not force understanding or agreement, but instead charms us into understanding or agreeing.

Narrations can also be told from the heart. As noted above, stories have a natural, even predictable, organization that walks both speaker and audience chronologically from the beginning, through the middle, and to the end. This predictability makes remembering the important details of the story easier for the speaker, so speakers do not have to rely heavily on notes. Think of some of the stories you like to tell and retell. No matter how many times you share the story, the details are roughly the same and you have little trouble remembering how the story goes. It's like giving a speech from a keyword outline: You just talk. Having said that, there are a few things you need to know about using a narrative approach in your speeches.

For a narrative to be effective, it must contain both *probability* and *fidelity.*[10] Narrative probability is the coherency of the story—that is, whether or not a story "holds together." Is the story believable as it is told? Does the story make sense as a logical whole, or does it have inconsistencies? Make sure your story makes sense. When the details of a story do not correspond, the credibility of the speaker suffers, as does the ability of the audience to continue listening. For example, the other day I was watching a news story about a girl who was to be reunited with her father for the first time since she was one year old. The story was very moving, but the narrator repeatedly said, "This thirteen-year-old girl will see her father for the first time in thirteen years . . . the last time she saw her father, she was only one year old." I kept telling myself, "That is impossible; if she hasn't seen him in thirteen years, and she was one when she last saw him, she would have to be fourteen!" This small mathematical discrepancy kept me from fully focusing on the story. Therefore, remember that even small inconsistencies can distract your audience.

Narrative fidelity is the truthfulness or reasonableness of the story. Unlike the need for internal consistency of likelihood, fidelity looks at the reasonableness of the entire story. Is the story plausible? Could it happen? Are the values and lessons put forth consistent with the audience's values and beliefs? Is the story logical and well reasoned? A story that contradicts common sense or the audience's beliefs and values will not be believable and will undermine the speaker's credibility.

DIFFERENCES IN PERSUASIVE STYLE

As mentioned above, cultures have different preferences for evidence and how arguments are put together. These preference differences are called "persuasive styles."[11] The three persuasive strategies that make up a culture's persuasive style—based on a culture's values, communication norms, and cultural patterns—are quasi-logical, analogical, and presentational.

Quasi-Logical

Although in the United States we refer to our preferred persuasive style as *logical*, this highly structured, direct, and linear style is actually an example of the *quasi-logical* persuasive style. We call it *quasi*-logical because it is not the only way to be logical, not because it is only partially logical. Each of the persuasive styles is, in fact, logical in its own way. The quasi-logical persuasive style is the preferred, but not the exclusive, style used in many Western cultures. This style is derived from the formal logic introduced by Aristotle and conforms to the Western rhetorical tradition discussed in Chapter One and in this chapter. It relies on objective evidence such as witnesses, expert testimony, and statistics and is often arranged deductively. The key word here is *objective*. Users of the quasi-logical style believe that truth can be discovered through evidence that is beyond the speaker's or listeners' influence, opinion, or feelings. The quasi-logical style relies most heavily on the proof of logos.

Presentational

The *presentational style*, conversely, relies more heavily on personal experience, feelings, and emotions. Cultures that prefer this style trust human experience and the emotional appeals of the persuader more than objective evidence. Latino, Middle Eastern, and African-American cultures often prefer this style of persuasion.

The manner in which the information is presented is more important than the evidence in the presentational style. Emotional, creative uses of lan-

HINT

How to Incorporate Narrative into Your Speech

- Weave case studies, brief analogies, or examples into your speech to make a point.
- Keep stories simple. Avoid complicated and irrelevant details.
- Be careful in choosing which elements of the story to include. Shocking your audience may get their attention, but gruesome or upsetting stories can make them stop listening.
- Use clear transitions when moving from your speech to the story and back to your speech so that the audience can follow along.
- Practice, practice, practice. Know the story well enough that you can remember it without the help of notes. Then tell it in your own words, from the heart. A story told sincerely has more impact than a story recited precisely.

Source: Executive Communications Group, http://ecglink.com/, on CFO.com, http://www.cfo.com/article.cfm/3002412/2/c_3046495?f=insidecfo.

guage and a dynamic delivery style encourage the audience not only to hear the argument but also to experience it. If the speaker can successfully compel the listeners to feel, taste, and see what he or she is saying, then the audience members will believe the speaker because they have experienced it for themselves. Specific details such as exact numbers and precise facts are not as important to either speaker or listeners as the emotions the speech evokes. The presentational style, then, relies more on the proof of ethos than on either pathos or logos.

Analogical

George Kennedy, in his book *Comparative Rhetoric,* claims:

> Argument from example is probably the most common form of reasoning widely used all over the world. Examples are drawn from mythology, from analogies with nature, and from events of the past known to an audience.[12]

This reliance on stories, analogies, and parables to make an argument is known as the *analogical* style. The analogical style, as you have probably guessed, relies on the narrative approach.

The values of tradition and collectivism underlie the analogical style. Audiences who prefer this style of persuasion find tradition and the experiences of others or heroes from the past to be more persuasive than facts and statistics or an eloquent speaker. The stories are designed to tap into the emotional logic of the audience. Along with relying on mythos, this persuasive style makes use of pathos as well.

It is important to note that not everyone from a culture will prefer the same persuasive style and that people from all cultures can and do use elements of all three persuasive styles, often in combination. Therefore, you must remember that different cultures will tend to privilege one form of persuasive style over another, and adapt your speeches accordingly. In the United States you will often find that the most persuasive arguments are first developed using the quasi-logical approach, but as we have seen throughout this book, arguments in America still depend on strong delivery and language skills and use many emotional components. In fact, many arguments are won using emotional stories that contradict the facts. The key is to use a variety of methods and styles to adapt to the audience at hand.

> **HINT**
> **Checking for Faulty Reasoning**
> One good way to check for faulty reasoning is to play the devil's advocate (a person who argues the other side of an argument to test the soundness of the logic and reasoning). Read through your speech as if you were a strong opponent to the ideas or policies being advocated. Identify the claims and arguments that are most likely to be challenged by the opposing side, and then make the necessary corrections or adjustments.

AVOIDING COMMON ERRORS IN REASONING: LOGICAL FALLACIES

When an argument's reasoning does not follow the premises, even when the premises are true, we call this a *logical fallacy.* The premises, even the conclusion, may be true, but the argument is considered invalid if the conclusion does not follow logically from the premises. Unfortunately, we are bombarded with logical fallacies every day that on first glance seem to make sense. Advertisers, politicians, and even our friends, family, and ourselves can fall into these logical traps, so we need to learn how to spot this faulty kind of reasoning.

Following is a brief list of some of the more common logical fallacies (and a few of my favorites) that people use when trying to persuade. (*Note:* There are dozens more not listed here; see "Click Here" for a link to additional logical fallacies.) Learning to recognize these errors in reasoning will help you become a more critical consumer of persuasion and will help you avoid making the same kinds of mistakes.

- **Ad hominem**—Latin for "to the man." A logical fallacy that attacks the people making an argument instead of the argument itself. Example: *Why would you believe a bunch of low-life drug-abusing hippies? Clearly all they want to do is make marijuana legal so they can party.*
- **Appeal to tradition**—A logical fallacy that asserts that something should be done because that is the way it has been done in the past. Example: *I don't see a need for a new high-tech computerized filing system. The old filing system has served us well for over fifty years.*
- **Bandwagon**—A logical fallacy that urges people to adopt a policy or engage in an activity because other people are already doing it. This is the argument teens often use on their parents or friends to gain compliance. Example: *You have to go to the concert on Saturday; everyone will be there.*
- **Begging the question**—A logical fallacy that attempts to prove the truth of a claim by using one or more premises that assume the very thing needing to be proved. It is a way of restating the claim in different words through the premises rather than using them to support the claim. In other words, you already assume to be true what you are trying to prove. Example: *You should vote for Fai Hon as student body president because he is the best candidate.*
- **Composition**—A logical fallacy that assumes that what is true of the parts is automatically true of the whole. Example: *Juan is a great guy. Jane is a wonderful person. They would make a great couple!*
- **Division**—A logical fallacy that assumes that what is true of the whole is automatically true of the parts. This is the opposite of the fallacy of composition. Example: *Humans have color. Humans are made up of atoms; therefore, atoms must have color.*
- **False dilemma (also called the *either/or dilemma*)**—A logical fallacy that claims that only two possibilities exist when in fact there are more possibilities. Example: *Either you are with us or you are with the terrorists.*
- **Hasty generalization**—A logical fallacy in which an inference is made about an entire population from only a sample of that population. Example: *After surveying ten of my classmates around campus, I have found that students on this campus are in favor of banning soda sales at our school.*
- **Non sequitur**—Latin for "does not follow." A logical fallacy in which the claim or conclusion does not follow the premises of the argument.

Non sequitur arguments simply do not make logical sense. Jokes are sometimes based on non sequiturs, such as, *Is it farther from here to New York or by bus?* You could say that all logical fallacies are in some way non sequiturs because on further examination, the conclusions do not follow from the premises. Example: *Our campus is very large and spacious; therefore, we must be able to double the size of the student body to increase revenue.*

- **Post hoc ergo propter hoc**—Latin for "after this therefore because of this." A logical fallacy that assumes that because one event occurred before another, the first event is necessarily the cause of the second. This is a fallacy of causal reasoning or attributing cause and effect when in reality the first event may not have any connection to the second. Example: *After she logged onto the computer, the electricity went out. Her computer must have caused the blackout.*
- **Cum hoc ergo propter hoc**—Latin for "with this therefore because of this." A logical fallacy closely related to the post hoc fallacy, except this one assumes that because one event occurs simultaneously with another event, one must be the cause of the other. Example: *Every time I go to a baseball game, our team loses. I had better not go to tonight's game or they will lose.*
- **Red herring (also called *changing the subject* or *misdirection*)**—A logical fallacy that diverts attention from the issue at hand by bringing up a seemingly related issue or a new subject that does not actually support the argument in question. Example: *I don't understand why the court is chasing after me for a few delinquent parking tickets when the chief of police is costing the city millions due to the ongoing corruption scandal.*
- **Slippery slope**—A logical fallacy that claims that one step in a particular direction will inevitably lead to an unstoppable series of steps and end in the worst-case scenario. Example: *We cannot legalize same-sex marriage because it would lead us down the road toward bestial marriage, polygamy, and legalized incest and pedophilia.*

Using the logical fallacies above as a guide, read the editorial section of your local newspaper and see if you can find and identify examples of each of the fallacies described.

To learn more and find more types of logical fallacies on Wikipedia,

Click Here http://en.wikipedia.org/wiki/Logical_fallacy

SUMMARY

In this chapter, we explored the various types of persuasive speeches. Although different from informative speeches in that instead of simply teaching, they advocate for a position, belief, or action, persuasive speeches are an important part of our everyday lives. We learned the three kinds of persuasive speeches: fact, value, and policy. We also learned about the various proofs we have at our disposal to support our persuasive arguments: logos, ethos, pathos, and mythos. And we learned how different cultures place different values on the various types of evidence and reasoning we can use.

By learning the forms of and the processes involved in persuasive speaking, we can be better prepared to persuade others and to evaluate others' attempts to persuade us. As a final note on persuasion, even if you never give a persuasive speech, learning to recognize persuasion and how it serves to influence us can provide you with a valuable tool and a first defense against falling victim to less ethical persuaders.

CONCLUSION

In concluding this chapter, we end our exploration of the important elements of public speaking in the United States and other English-speaking countries. The most important thing to remember when speaking to any audience is that what you have to say is important for the audience to hear. Treat the preparation, practice, and delivery of the message with the respect that it deserves. Try to hear the message as the audience is likely to hear it, and make every effort to tailor the message to their ears. Support your message with evidence that you can be proud to present and with presentation aids that tell your audience that you really believe in what you are saying.

If you respect your message and your audience, they will respect you. Whatever trouble you fear because English is not your first language will fade away as you focus your efforts on tailoring your message to your specific audience. Good luck and speak well. Peace.

Discussion Questions and Activities

1. Find an opinion piece in your local newspaper and analyze the arguments the writer uses. How is the article organized? What types of proof (logos, ethos, pathos, mythos) does the author use? Can you find any logical fallacies? Is the article convincing? Did the author change your mind about the issue? Why or why not?
2. Every culture has a preferred way of trying to persuade others. In the United States we favor logic, reasoning, and evidence along with emotional appeals. What are the favored ways of persuading and making an argument in your home culture? What similarities and differences in logic and reasoning do you notice between the U.S. American style of persuasion and your culture's?

3. In this chapter we discussed the U.S. American preference for the quasi-logical persuasive style; however, some would cite advertising campaigns and claim that this style is no longer preferred. Watch several commercials and analyze the arguments put forward. What type of arguments are employed? What is the predominant persuasive style, if any? What accounts for the differences in this type of persuasion?
4. Using the narrative approach, write a brief persuasive speech to convince an audience to donate blood.
5. Identify a TV or radio commercial that uses Monroe's Motivated Sequence. Outline the argument using proper outlining technique.

Chapter Quiz

Matching:

Identify which kind of speech each of the following thesis statements represents.

a. Proposition of fact	**b.** Proof by logos	**c.** Proposition of policy
d. Proof by pathos	**e.** Proposition of value	**f.** Proof by ethos

1. _____ As a Fortune 500 executive, I can honestly say that getting my degrees was the best decision I ever made.
2. _____ Given the difficulty of finding the right house in the right neighborhood for the right price, you should use a realtor when buying a home.
3. _____ Imagine the pride in your father's eyes when he sees you march across that stage, diploma in hand!
4. _____ With breathtaking scenery and a wide variety of adventures and attractions, Vancouver Island is the best place to vacation in Canada.
5. _____ Given the new pitching staff and the organization's renewed commitment to building teamwork, the Dodgers will definitely make it to the playoffs this year.
6. _____ You should stay in college because a recent study proved that people who go to college are happier and more successful than those who don't.

T/F, Multiple Choice, Fill-in

1. Which of the persuasive styles is distinguished by personal experience, feelings, and emotions? _______________
2. The claim "If we give in on the number of volunteer hours we are willing to accept, the next thing you know, they will be asking to decrease our supplies budget, then reducing our overall funding" is an example of which type of logical fallacy?
   a. Bandwagon
   b. Post hoc ergo propter hoc
   c. Ad hominum
   d. Slippery slope

3. True or false: Mythos is the proof discovered by Aristotle that relies on historical precedence to prove an argument.
4. True or false: A non sequitur is a logical fallacy in which the conclusion does not follow the premises of the argument.
5. The persuasive style relied upon most in the United States is the
   a. quasi-logical.
   b. ontological.
   c. analogical.
   d. presentational.
6. Monroe's Motivated Sequence is best used for which of the following types of persuasive speeches?
   a. Propositions of fact about something that will happen in the future
   b. Propositions of policy asking for passive agreement
   c. Propositions of value on an issue of taste
   d. Propositions of policy asking for immediate action
7. When dealing with a proposition of policy, what three things must you address?

   ____________ ____________ ____________

Speech for Evaluation

Read the following persuasive speech outline and answer these questions:

- What type of persuasive arguments is the speaker trying to make (proposition of fact, value, or policy)?
- Is the specific purpose clear?
- Identify the thesis in the speech. How do you know that is the thesis? Is it an appropriate thesis for the argument being made? Is the argument appropriate given the thesis?
- Give examples of the various kinds of proofs used in the speech (logos, ethos, pathos, mythos).
- Identify and give examples of the dominant persuasive style used in the speech. Do you think these are the most appropriate choices given the topic? For what audiences would this persuasive style work best?

Sample Outline for Monroe Motivated Sequence Speech

Too Much Exposure: Limiting Access to Online Pornography
By Nate Brown

I. Attention
  A. I took a computer class once and one day the professor was talking about new technologies of search engines.
    1. At that time the newest and best search engine wasn't Google, but was something called HotBot, so the teacher instructed us to use the computers in front of us to go to Hotbot.com.
    2. By mistake, I typed Hotbod.com, which turned out to be a site filled with graphic pornography.
    3. I was an adult, as we all were, and it was an honest typing mistake, so it was really not that big of a deal, but imagine if I had been a ten-year old boy trying to get to that search engine and making that same mistake.
    4. It is that scenario that leads me to believe that pornography on the Internet is a problem that must be dealt with.
  B. Pornography has been around for all of recorded history, because if history can be recorded in the form of writing or painting, so too can erotic words and images.
    1. In a September 2000 article in *American Heritage* by Frederick Allen, pornography and media technology have always gone hand in hand.
      a. The invention of the printing press was soon followed by the printing of erotic literature.
      b. The invention of photography was soon followed by the taking of dirty photographs.
      c. The invention of movies was soon followed by the filming of X-rated movies.
    2. The invention of the Internet, and its saturation into so many homes, now makes the dissemination and consumption of pornography more available and more convenient.
    3. It is this convenience that makes online pornography such a problem because it is too easily accessible to children.

(Transition: The protection of children is obviously of great importance, and they are at risk because of online pornography.)

II. Need
  A. Online pornography is too easily accessible to those children that look for it, and let's not kid ourselves; many of them are looking for it.
    1. Minors that seek to view pornography by buying magazines or movie tickets are likely to face some form of age-verification check.

2. With online pornography, there is no such reliable obstacle.
   a. Although some online pornographic websites require an age check, there is an apparently unlimited amount of online pornography that does not.
   b. Kids can find everything from soft-core nudity to graphic sexual violence, says Janet Kornblum in the January 2006 *USA Today.*

B. What is even more disturbing is that many children are unintentionally exposed to online pornography.
   1. Just like the Hotbod.com example from my own experience, many children had a similar experience when they tried to study the Whitehouse by going to Whitehouse.com, which until recently was a pornographic website.
      a. It is true that public pressure on the owners of that website finally induced them to remove the pornographic content, but that kind of accidental exposure should never be possible in the first place.
      b. Unwanted exposure to pornography is not always as innocent as stumbling across the wrong websites.
   2. Sometimes, kids are the victims of aggressive adult solicitation from others on the Net.
      a. According to the Crimes Against Children Research Center at the University of New Hampshire, as reported in the July 2000 *eWeek,* "About 20 percent of youths ages 10 to 17 received a sexual solicitation online in the last year, and 25 percent had unwanted exposure to sexually explicit photos online."
      b. Carrie Kirby in a June 2000 article for the *San Francisco Chronicle* reports, "1 in 5 youths online face invitations to engage in cybersex or receive other risqué solicitations."

(Transition: Now that we know that kids are exposed to adult material online, the question is, "So what?" If they are not harmed by it, then why should we care?)

C. The fact is that they are harmed by this exposure at such an early age because exposure to pornography teaches some undesirable lessons to kids.
   1. It teaches that unprotected sex is normal and desirable because according to Gary Webb in the May 2001. *Yahoo! Internet Life,* most graphic sexual pornography shows sex without the use of condoms.
   2. More shocking, however, is that kids exposed to graphic pornography at an early age exhibit undesirable aggressive and sexual tendencies when they become adults.
   3. Cynthia Stark reports in the Summer 1997 *Social Theory & Practice* journal, "Recent studies have indicated that exposure to violent pornography fosters positive attitudes toward rape and other forms

of sexual violence and that such attitudes can lead to desensitization to sexual violence."

(Transition: If this is not what we want for our kids, then something needs to be done to curb the exposure of kids to online pornography.)

III. Satisfaction
- A. It is time for some more regulation of online pornographic material.
  1. We already have the Communications Decency Act of 1996, which makes it illegal to knowingly disseminate pornography to minors.
  2. Either this Act is ineffective or is unenforceable because I see no reduction of the amount of adult material that is easily accessible online.
  3. Neither do I see any real obstacles to the solicitation of minors by Internet predators.
- B. I propose several safety measures be put in place and enforced to protect our children from Internet pornography.
  1. First, a special domain extension should be created just for adult oriented material.
     - a. Just like we have the .com, org, .net extensions, adult websites could be relegated to the .xxx domains.
     - b. That would make it easier to avoid accidental exposure to the material and to block it from a computer or network entirely.
  2. Second, the age verification checks should be mandatory on all adult websites.
  3. Third, Internet predators should face more aggressive regulation and prosecution.
     - a. The U.S. should enforce these regulations through heavy fines and incarceration.
     - b. Internet predators should be tracked down using the logs and files generated at the Internet providers and phone companies.
  4. Finally, recognizing that the Internet is very difficult to regulate, and that there will continue to be owners of pornographic websites that refuse to comply with these regulations, pressure can be put on the companies that supply the connectivity to these websites.

IV. Visualization
- A. This can be accomplished if we, the concerned citizens of this country, just take a few minutes to tell our representatives it is time to stop protecting the offenders and start protecting our children.
  1. By taking just a few minutes to write a letter, make a phone call, or send an email to your representative you can help stem the tide of children's exposure to pornography.
  2. You can find your representatives with just a few mouse clicks by going to: http://www.house.gov/writerep/ and putting in your state and zip code.

a. This site provides you with email access, addresses and phone numbers.
b. When I tried it, it took less than one minute to get all the information I needed.
3. Doing this takes little time and no money, but if we all do it and encourage our friends and families to do the same, it can have a powerful influence.

B. You may not get anything personally for your efforts.
1. There are no medals handed out for doing the right thing.
2. But you can feel good knowing that you have taken a stand to protect children everywhere.

V. Action

A. Because online pornography is so readily accessible to minors, because exposure can lead to undesirable effects, and because Internet predators pose a real threat, it is reasonable to support regulations that restrict that content.
1. Keep in mind that these regulations are not an unreasonable infringement on our freedom of speech.
a. Pornography will continue to be available, but less so for children.
b. Just like the adult movie theaters or magazine stands that check for ID are not violating our freedom of speech, neither will these online regulations.
2. We can live in a world with adult material that does not threaten our children.
a. If we wanted to legalize prostitution for example, we would not want prostitutes hanging out at the lunch counters of our junior high schools, would we?
b. If we wanted to legalize drugs, we would not want free cocaine samples being mailed to our homes, would we?
c. And if we want legal and accessible pornographic material for adults, we should not make it easily available to children through our home computers.

B. Write to your political representatives and let them know that you want them to help protect your children.
1. Let them know that free pornography without age verification should not be available on children's computer screens.
2. Let them know that we can balance adult freedom of speech with the desire to keep our children safe.
3. Let them know that it is time they did what is right and that they should support these regulations of online pornography.
4. Our children deserve it.

Works Cited (MLA Style)

Allen, Frederick. “When sex drives technological innovation.” American Heritage Sep 2000: 19–20.

eWeek. Editorial. July 10 2000. Vol. 17 Issue 28, p48.

Kirby, Carrie. “‘Startling’ number of kids solicited for sex on Internet.” SFGate.com. 9 Jun 2000. http://www.sfgate.com/cgi-bin/article.cgi?file=/chronicle/archive/2000/06/09/MN36265.DTL

Kornblum, Janet. “Porn ‘tidal wave’ puts parents to test.” USA Today 30 Jan 2006: 10d.

Stark, Cynthia. “Is pornography an action? The causal vs. the conceptual view of pornography’s harm.” Social Theory & Practice. 23:2 (1997): 277–306.

Webb, Gary. “Sex and the internet.” Yahoo! Internet Life May 2001: 88.

Chapter 14 Quiz Answers

Matching: 1. f, 2. c, 3. d, 4. e, 5. a, 6. b

T/F, Multiple Choice, Fill-in: 1. Presentational style, 2. d, 3. False, 4. True, 5. a, 6. d,
7. Need, plan, practicality.

Appendix A

Glossary of English Expressions

antsy: nervous; unable to sit still
at the eleventh hour: almost too late
back down: retreat from a position in an argument
back out: desert; fail to keep a promise
back out of: desert; fail to keep a promise
back up: move backwards
bad-mouth (verb): to talk negatively about someone
be up and running: functioning
bear down on: lean on; browbeat
bear on: have to do with
bear up: endure
bear up under: endure
beat (adj.): tired
beat around the bush: to avoid being direct; avoiding the truth
beats me: I do not know
before long: soon
bent out of shape: angry; upset
bite off more than one can chew: to have more to do than one can handle
blabbermouth: someone who can't keep a secret
blow in: drop in to visit unexpectedly
blow one's top: to lose one's temper
blow over: pass without doing harm
blow up: explode; lose one's temper
break a leg!: Good luck (it is considered bad luck to say good luck to actors about to perform)
break down: analyze; list the parts of separately
break in on: interrupt
break into: go into a house or room forcibly; suddenly; begin; bring about: cause to happen; interrupt
bring off: accomplish
bring on: cause
bring out: publish; emphasize
bring over: bring
bring to: revive
bring up: raise; care for from childhood
broke: to not have any money
brush out: brush the inside of
buck(s): money
bug (verb): to irritate or annoy
bull-headed: stubborn
burn down: destroy by burning
burn the midnight oil
burn up: consume by fire
bushed: very tired
buy out: by the other person's share of a business
buy up: buy the whole supply of
call for: come to get; require
call off: cancel; order away
call up: telephone; summon for military service
calm down: become calm
came about: happen
can't make heads or tails of: to not understand something
care for: like; guard; supervise; maintain
carry on: continue as before; misbehave
carry on with: continue
carry out: fulfill; complete; accomplish; perform
carry over: carry; continue at another time or place
catch on: understand
catch one's eye: notice something or someone (usually because it is attractive)
catch some Zs: sleep
catch up: cover the distance between oneself and a moving goal
check out: leave; pay one's bill
check up: investigate
check up on: examine; verify
cheer up: cause to become cheerful
chew up: chew thoroughly
chicken: a scared person
chop up: chop into small pieces
chow: food; to eat
chow down: to eat quickly
clean off: clean the surface of
clean out: clean the inside of
clean up: clarify; tidy
clear out: clear the surface of; leave
clear up: become clear
close down: close permanently
close up: close temporarily
come across: find accidentally
come along: accompany; make progress
come along with: accompany; make progress
come back: return
come by: find accidentally; visit someone in his home
come down with: become ill with
come out: appear; make a social debut; reveal one's homosexuality
come out with: utter; produce
come over: come to someone's house, to where someone is
come through: succeed
come to: regain consciousness
come up with: utter; produce
cool (adj.): good; interesting; worth paying attention to
cost (someone) an arm and a leg: very expensive
couch potato: someone who is lazy
count in: include
count on: rely on
count out: exclude
count up: calculate; count; add to a total
cram: to study at the last minute for an exam
cross out: eliminate
cut down: reduce in quantity
cut in: interrupt a dancing couple to dance with one of the partners
cut in on: interrupt
cut it out!: stop
cut off: interrupt; sever; amputate

cut out: eliminate; delete
dicey: unsure; volatile
die away: fade; diminish
die down: fade; diminish
die off/out: disappear; become extinct
disagree with: cause illness or discomfort to
ditch class: to not attend class without an excuse
do away with: abolish
do without: deprive oneself of
down in the dumps: feeling depressed or sad
drag one's feet: to move slowly
draw up: write; compose (a document)
dress up: don fancy or unusual clothes
drive back: return by car
drop in: visit someone casually without planning
drop in at/on: visit casually without planning
drop out: abandon some organized activity; leave; quit
drop out of: leave; quit
drop over: visit someone casually
dust out: dust the inside of
easy does it!: be careful
eat up: eat completely
elbow grease: extra effort
face up to: acknowledge
fall back on: use for emergency purpose
fall behind: not progress at required pace
fall behind in: lag; not progress at required pace
fall off: decrease; lose weight
fall out with: quarrel with
fall through: fail; not be accomplished
far-fetched: unlikely; outlandish
feel blue: feeling sad
feel puny: feeling sick
fender-bender: a minor car accident
figure out: interpret; understand
figure up: compute
fill in: complete (a printed form); substitute
fill in for: substitute for
fill out: complete (a printed form)
fill up: fill completely (a container)
find out: discover; learn
fix up: repair; arrange in a suitable manner
fly back: return by air
fly over: fly to where someone is
for ages: for an extended period of time
get a kick out of something
get across: cause to be understood
get ahead: make progress
get ahead of: surpass; beat
get along: have a friendly relationship
get around: circulate; move about; evade; avoid
get away: escape
get away with: do something wrong without being caught or punished
get by: manage; either just barely or with a minimum of effort
get by with: manage with a minimum of effort
get down to: become serious about; consider
get going: leave
get in: enter
get it: understand
get off: descend from; leave
get on: mount
get on one's nerves: annoy; irritate
get on with: proceed with
get on/along: progress; be compatible
get one's wires crossed: miscommunication
get out of hand: lose control of
get through: finish
get through with: terminate, finish
get up: rise
get up and go: energy
give back: return
give out: become exhausted
give out: distribute; announce
give up: surrender; fail to finish
go back: return
go back on: desert; fail to keep (a promise)
go for: like a great deal
go in for: be interested in; participate in
go off: explode
go on: happen; continue
go on with: continue
go out: stop burning; leave one's residence
go over: go; succeed; review
go with: harmonize with; look pleasing together
go without: abstain from
grab a bite: get something to eat
grow up: mature
had better: should
hand down: deliver; pronounce formally; leave as an inheritance
hand over: yield control of
hang around: remain idly in the vicinity of
hang up: replace a telephone receive on its hook; suspend; make late
hard feelings: feeling angry or sad due to an exchange with another person
have on: be dressed in
have over: entertain someone informally at one's home
head honcho: person in charge; the person with decision-making authority
hear from: receive a communication from
hear of: learn about (sometimes accidentally)
hit on: discover accidentally; to flirt
hit the books: study
hit the hay: go to bed
hit the sack: go to bed
hold off: delay; restrain
hold on: grasp tightly; persevere; wait while telephoning
hold on to: grasp tightly
hold out: continue to resist; persevere; persist
hold out against: resist
hold up: delay; rob; threaten with a weapon
how come?: Why?
if I had my druthers: If I have a choice, I would rather
in the black: having more money than one owes
in the red: owing more money than one has coming in
jump all over someone: to verbally attack someone
jump the gun: to make a hasty decision; to act hastily
junk mail: unwanted advertisements through the mail
keep an eye on: to watch someone or something
keep at it: persevere at
keep on: continue
keep one's chin up: to stay positive in spite of difficulties

keep one's fingers crossed: to hope for
keep one's nose to the grindstone: to work very hard
keep to: persist in; continue
keep up: continue; keep the same pace
keep up with: maintain the pace of
kid: a child; to tease
kind of: somewhat
know something backwards and forward: to know something very well
know something inside out: to know something very well
leave out: omit
lend someone a hand: to help someone
let down: disappoint
let out: release from confinement; make larger (in sewing)
let sleeping dogs lie: don't mention something that will upset people if there is no reason
let up: diminish in intensity
let-down: disappoint
lie down: recline
light up: light; illuminate thoroughly
live down: live in such a way as to cause something to be forgotten
live from hand to mouth: barely making enough money to survive
live on: support or sustain oneself by means of
live up to: maintain the standard demanded of
look after: take care of
look back on: remember nostalgically
look down on: feel superior to
look forward to: anticipate
look in on: to check someone who may need help
look on: be a spectator
look up to: respect; admire
lose track of: unable to follow along
make a mountain out of a mole hill: exaggerating a negative situation
make out: progress; succeed
make over: remake
make up: become reconciled
make up for: compensate for
make up one's mind
move over: move to the side
nosh: food
not on your life: no possible chance
nuke: nuclear weapon
nuts: crazy
on the cutting edge: at the forefront of technology
on the dot: to arrive exactly on time
once in a while: occasionally
pan out: turn out well; be successful
pass on: die; transmit
pass out: become unconscious; distribute
pass up: not take advantage of (as an opportunity)
pay back: repay
pay off: discharge a debt completely; give someone his final pay
pick on: tease; bully
pick up: come to meet an escort; lift with hands or fingers; learn casually;
play down: minimize
play up: emphasize
play up to: flatter for personal advantage
point out: indicate
pooped (adj.): tired
pretty (adv.): having a substantial size, value, or extent (e.g. it was a pretty long drive)
pull an all-nighter: stay up all night
pull in: arrive
pull someone's leg: to innocently tease or trick someone by telling a lie
pull through: survive (barely)
push across: cause to be understood or accepted
put off: postpone
put on: dress in; deceive or fool
put up: preserve (food); receive as an overnight guest
put up with: tolerate
quiet down: be quiet
r and R: Rest and relaxation
raining cats and dogs: A very strong rainstorm
read up on: search out information on
ride over: ride to where someone is
rinse off: rinse the surface of
rinse out: rinse the inside of
rub the wrong way: to annoy or irritate
rule out: eliminate
run against: compete against in an election
run away: escape; leave; leave quickly without permission
run away with: leave; escape from
run down: slowly lose power so as to stop functioning; disparage; hit with a vehicle
run for: campaign for
run off: cause to depart; reproduce mechanically; depart quickly, drain
save up: accumulate
savvy: to be well informed about practical matters
see about: consider; arrange
see off: accompany someone to the beginning of a trip
see through: complete; in spite of difficulties
see to: arrange; supervise
sell out: sell the ownership or responsibility
send back: send to a place where formerly located
send over: send to where someone is
set up: arrange
settle on: decide on; choose
settle up: pay one's bills or debts
shoot the breeze: have a conversation just for enjoyment
show off: boast by words or actions
show up: arrive; appear unexpectedly
shut off: cause to cease functioning
shut up: stop talking
sleep on it: to think about something before making a decision
slow up: reduce speed
someone's made his/her bed; now let her/him lie in it.
sort of: similar to something else, but not quite the same
so-so: mediocre
spell out: enumerate; state in detail
stand by: wait; be prepared to assist
stand for: represent; permit
stand up: fail to keep an appointment or date; stand; rise from sitting; last; endure
stand up for: support; demand
stand up to: resist
stay over: remain at someone's house overnight or longer
step aside: move to one side
step on it!: hurry; go faster
stick to: persist
stick up for: support; defend
sweep out: sweep the inside of
take after: resemble
take back: return; retract a statement

take down: remove from a high position; write from dictation
take in: understood; fool; deceive; make smaller (in sewing)
take it easy: relax
take off: leave the ground
take over: assume command
talk back: answer impolitely
talk back to: answer impolitely
talk over: discuss
tear down: destroy
tear up: tear into small pieces
tell off: scold; reprimand
tell on: report misbehavior to authority
think over: consider
think through: consider from beginning to end
think up: create; invent
throw away: discard
throw over: reject
throw up: vomit
tie up: tie securely or tight
tire out: cause to be exhausted
touch on: mention briefly
touch up: repair
try on: put on a garment to verify the fit
try out: test
turn around: turn so that one is facing another direction
turn down: refuse; lower the volume
turn in: go to bed
turn into: become
turn out: produce; force into exile, extinguish (a light); come; appear, as at a public meeting
turn up: arrive; be found unexpectedly
two-faced: a person who maniputively tells two people different things to gain favor
under the weather: feeling ill or sick
until hell freezes over: forever
until you're blue in the face: saying something repeatedly
used to it: comfortable with; it's familiar
wait on: serve
wait up: slow down and wait for me
wait up for: not go to bed while waiting for
wake up: awaken
walk back: return on foot to where one was
walk over: walk to where someone is
was my face red!: embarrassed
wash off: wash the surface of
wash out: fade or disappear from washing; wash the inside of
watch out: be careful
watch out for: be careful for
wear off: fade; disappear through use or time
wear out: use until no longer usable; tire greatly
wear out one's welcome: to stay longer than one should
wet behind the ears: inexperienced; novice
what's up?: What is happening?
wind up: finish, tighten the spring of a watch or machine
wipe off: wipe the surface of
wipe out: wipe the inside of; decimate
wishy-washy: indecisive
with bells on: enthusiastically
work out: solve
would just as soon: would rather
write down: record
write out: write down every detail; spell out
write up: compose; prepare (a document)
yes-man: a person who will say yes to anything his/her superiors say
yucky: something that is disgusting
yummy: tastes good
zilch: nothing; zero
zip your lip: stop talking

Appendix B

Additional Speeches for Analysis

Who Then Will Speak for the Common Good?

1976 Democratic National Convention Keynote Address
By Barbara Jordan

Thank you ladies and gentlemen for a very warm reception.

It was one hundred and forty-four years ago that members of the Democratic Party first met in convention to select a Presidential candidate. Since that time, Democrats have continued to convene once every four years and draft a party platform and nominate a Presidential candidate. And our meeting this week is a continuation of that tradition. But there is something different about tonight. There is something special about tonight. What is different? What is special? I, Barbara Jordan, am a keynote speaker.

When—a lot of years passed since 1832, and during that time it would have been most unusual for any national political party to ask a Barbara Jordan to deliver a keynote address. But tonight, here I am. And I feel—I feel that notwithstanding the past that my presence here is one additional bit of evidence that the American Dream need not forever be deferred.

Now—now that I have this grand distinction what in the world am I supposed to say? I could easily spend this time praising the accomplishments of this party and attacking the Republicans—but I don't choose to do that. I could list the many problems which Americans have. I could list the problems which cause people to feel cynical, angry, frustrated: problems which include lack of integrity in government; the feeling that the individual no longer counts; the reality of material and spiritual poverty; the feeling that the grand American experiment is failing or has failed. I could recite these problems, and then I could sit down and offer no solutions. But I don't choose to do that either. The citizens of America expect more. They deserve and they want more than a recital of problems.

We are a people in a quandary about the present. We are a people in search of our future. We are a people in search of a national community. We are a people trying not only to solve the problems of the present, unemployment, inflation, but we are attempting on a larger scale to fulfill the promise of America. We are attempting to fulfill our national purpose, to create and sustain a society in which all of us are equal.

Throughout—throughout our history, when people have looked for new ways to solve their problems and to uphold the principles of this nation, many times they have turned to political parties. They have often turned to the Democratic Party. What is it? What is it about the Democratic Party that makes it the instrument the people use when they search for ways to shape their future? Well I believe the answer to that question lies in our concept of governing. Our concept of governing is derived from our view of people. It is a concept deeply rooted in a set of beliefs firmly etched in the national conscience of all of us.

Now what are these beliefs? First, we believe in equality for all and privileges for none. This is a belief—this is a belief that each American, regardless of background, has equal standing in the public forum—all of us. Because—because we believe this idea so firmly, we are an inclusive rather than an exclusive party. Let everybody come!

I think it no accident that most of those emigrating to America in the 19th century identified with the Democratic Party. We are a heterogeneous party made up of Americans of diverse backgrounds. We believe that the people are the source of all governmental power; that the authority of the people is to be extended, not restricted.

This—this can be accomplished only by providing each citizen with every opportunity to participate in the management of the government. They must have that, we believe. We believe that the government which represents the authority of all the people, not just one interest group, but all the people, has an obligation to actively—underscore actively—seek to remove those obstacles which would block individual achievement—obstacles emanating from race, sex, economic condition. The government must remove them, seek to remove them.

We—we are a party—we are a party of innovation. We do not reject our traditions, but we are willing to adapt to changing circumstances, when change we must. We are willing to suffer the discomfort of change in order to achieve a better future. We have a positive vision of the future founded on the belief that the gap between the promise and reality of America can one day be finally closed. We believe that.

This, my friends, is the bedrock of our concept of governing. This is a part of the reason why Americans have turned to the Democratic Party. These are the foundations upon which a national community can be built. Let's all understand that these guiding principles cannot be discarded for short-term political gains. They represent what this country is all about. They are indigenous to the American idea. And these are principles which are not negotiable.

In other times, I could stand here and give this kind of exposition on the beliefs of the Democratic Party and that would be enough. But today that is not enough. People want more. That is not sufficient reason for the majority of the people of this country to vote Democratic. We have made mistakes. We realize that. We admit our mistakes. In our haste to do all things for all people, we did not foresee the full consequences of our actions. And when the people raised their voices, we didn't hear. But our deafness was only a temporary condition, and not an irreversible condition.

Even as I stand here and admit that we have made mistakes, I still believe that as the people of America sit in judgment on each party, they will recognize that our mistakes were mistakes of the heart. They'll recognize that.

Now—now we must look to the future. Let us heed the voice of the people and recognize their common sense. If we do not, we not only blaspheme our political heritage, we ignore the common ties that bind all Americans. Many fear the future. Many are distrustful of their leaders, and believe that their voices are never heard. Many seek only to satisfy their private work—wants; to satisfy their private interests. But this is the great danger America faces—that we will cease to be one nation and become instead a collection of interest groups: city against suburb, region against region, individual against individual; each seeking to satisfy private wants. If that happens, who then will speak for America? Who then will speak for the common good?

This is the question which must be answered in 1976: Are we to be one people bound together by common spirit, sharing in a common endeavor; or will we become a divided nation? For all of its uncertainty, we cannot flee the future. We must not become the "New Puritans" and reject our society. We must address and master the future together. It can be done if we restore the belief that we share a sense of national community, that we share a common national endeavor. It can be done.

There is no executive order; there is no law that can require the American people to form a national community. This we must do as individuals, and if we do it as individuals, there is no President of the United States who can veto that decision.

As a first step—as a first step, we must restore our belief in ourselves. We are a generous people, so why can't we be generous with each other? We need to take to heart the words spoken by Thomas Jefferson: Let us restore the social intercourse—"Let us restore to social intercourse that harmony and that affection without which liberty and even life are but dreary things."

A nation is formed by the willingness of each of us to share in the responsibility for upholding the common good. A government is invigorated when each one of us is willing to participate in shaping the future of this nation. In this election year, we must define the "common good" and begin again to shape a common future. Let each person do his or her part. If one citizen is unwilling to participate, all of us are going to suffer. For the American idea, though it is shared by all of us, is realized in each one of us.

Now, what are those of us who are elected public officials supposed to do? We call ourselves "public servants" but I'll tell you this: We as public servants must set an example for the rest of the nation. It is hypocritical for the public official to admonish and exhort the people to uphold the common good if we are derelict in upholding the common good. More is required—more is required of public officials than slogans and handshakes and press releases. More is required. We must hold ourselves strictly accountable. We must provide the people with a vision of the future.

If we promise as public officials, we must deliver. If—if we as public officials propose, we must produce. If we say to the American people, "It is time for you to be sacrificial"—sacrifice. If the public official says that, we [public officials] must be the first to give. We must be. And again, if we make mistakes, we must be willing to admit them. We have to do that. What we have to do is strike a balance between the idea that government should do everything and the idea, the belief, that government ought to do nothing. Strike a balance.

Let there be no illusions about the difficulty of forming this kind of a national community. It's tough, difficult, not easy. But a spirit of harmony will survive in America only if each of us remembers that we share a common destiny. If each of us remembers, when self-interest and bitterness seem to prevail, that we share a common destiny. I have confidence that we can form this kind of national community. I have confidence that the Democratic Party can lead the way. I have that confidence.

We cannot improve on the system of government handed down to us by the founders of the Republic. There is no way to improve upon that. But what we can do is to find new ways to implement that system and realize our destiny.

Now I began this speech by commenting to you on the uniqueness of a Barbara Jordan making a keynote address. Well I am going to close my speech by quoting a Republican President and I ask you that as you listen to these words of Abraham Lincoln, relate them to the concept of a national community in which every last one of us participates:

"As I would not be a slave, so I would not be a master." This—this—"This expresses my idea of Democracy. Whatever differs from this, to the extent of the difference, is no Democracy."

Farewell to Song Leaders

By Sarah Hemmert

The curve of your hearts, are the same curves of your bodies. The bodies that move to the beats we create. The bodies that move in 10 different ways. Do you all remember the camp we connected at? Do you remember the bus seats we shared? Do you remember the first impressions we imprinted on each other soon realizing they were a little off mark? Do you remember the first time we thought of each other as one? As friends? Where we had each others' backs no matter what? Do you remember our first game, feeling stupid and displaced together and laughing afterwards about how humiliated we felt? But do you remember our last game we shared feeling confident, happy, proud and friends, laughing afterwards of how accomplished we were at that moment?

Do you know how beautiful you are? How all of your eyes, although concentrated on the next step, seem to understand the girl next to you or even across the room? We tend to look on each other as sisters, friends and teammates. 10 sisters, 10 friends, 10 teammates.

Amanda, keep making the faces that put us in the moment. Keep putting your good heart into the music. You taught me how to get excited, energized and confident.

Sarah, keep smiling, kissing the crowd, giving every motion a life. You taught me how to be a loyal friend and teammate and how to see the good in people.

Tilly, keep teaching us your grace in movement and your laugh that cheers us up and makes us laugh with you. You taught me how to laugh to anything and everything.

Alexa, keep making up dances and songs that keep us entertained and bonded. Keep your goofy, fun attitude. You taught me uniqueness and how to brighten someone's day.

Arianna, keep shaking your stuff. Keep chuckling to things others would be too serious to appreciate. You taught me I can be beautiful with imperfections, and things, no matter how bad, are always somehow okay.

Aisha, keep singing, flipping your hair and working so hard to be the best you can be. You taught me how to work hard, how to be myself and what it feels like to be truly loved by someone.

Vianney could not make it here tonight, but I want her to keep filling us all with amazement with her voice that gives us chills and fills our hearts with pride. She taught me sisterhood and true support.

Denise, keep working your butt off. Keep finding the beat inside your heart to produce amazement for everyone to see. You taught me to find power and strength within myself.

Tobin, keep creating, dancing, and keep making these teams of friends, no matter where you are. You taught me. You taught me how to dance, to live with others, and you taught me to try, do and create.

As for me, I'll keep dancing, I'll keep in touch. I hope I taught all of you something.

Thank you for being the people I need in my life. I love you girls and will never forget the 100 things you all shared with me and taught me through all of the truths and wonders we shared this year. You girls loved me and made me the person I am today. I would love to spend the next year with all of you dancing side by side at pep rallies and competitions, but I know that when I walk close to the stadium and hear the crowd going wild with the words "Fire it up big blue," under the screams, I'll know it's my girls. When I climb up the stairs into the bleachers instead of down to the field, I'll look at the track below and see the same nine, eight or seven passionate girls I spent my senior year with. I'll look at you with such appreciation, love and pride, eager to see the new dances and cheers.

For those of you who are graduating next year good luck, you will do great and go so far. You will feel the same way I do now, proud of your team, your accomplishments and friendships. When you make your way to the stadium you will go up the stairs and join me in the bleachers where we will look together at the girls left, We will smile and feel happy for them and proud that we were once part of that. Thank you.

Endnotes

Chapter 1

1. Andrew Zekeri, "College Curriculum Competencies and Skills Former Students Found Essential to Their Careers," *College Student Journal* 38, no. 3 (September 2004): 412–422.
2. "English project set to move beyond talk." *South China Morning Post* (May 12, 2001), http://infotrac-college.thomsonlearning.com.
3. J. Michael Sproule. *The Heritage of Rhetorical Theory* (Boston: McGraw Hill, 1997), 6.
4. Ibid.
5. Aristotle, *On Rhetoric*, trans. George A. Kennedy (New York: Oxford University Press, 1991).
6. Sherwyn P. Morreale and Philip M. Backlund, "Communication Curricula: History, Recommendations, Resources," *Communication Education* 51, no. 1 (January 2002): 4.
7. Ibid., 5.
8. Xing Lu and David A. Frank, "On the Study of Ancient Chinese Rhetoric/Bian," *Western Journal of Communication* 57 (Fall 1993): 447.
9. Ibid., 450.
10. Ibid.
11. Ibid., 453.
12. S. K. Lao, *His-pien Chung-kuo Che-hsueh Shih.* [New Complied Version of Chinese History of Philosophy]. (Taipei: San Min Books, 1984), 380, quoted in Lu and Frank, "On the Study of Ancient Chinese Rhetoric/Bian," 454.
13. Confusius in Zhu, Li. Personal Thoughts on Public Speaking. (2004).
14. Sproule, *The Heritage of Rhetorical Theory,* 8.
15. Larry A. Samovar and Richard E. Porter, *Communication Between Cultures*, 5th ed. (Belmont, CA: Thomson Wadsworth, 2004), 50.
16. Edward T. Hall, Beyond Culture (Garden City, NY: Anchor Books/Doubleday, 1976), 91
17. Geert Hofstede, *Culture's Consequences: International Differences in Work-Related Values*, 2nd ed., (Beverly Hills, CA: Sage, 2001), xix.
18. Geert Hofstede, "The Cultural Relativity of the Quality of Life Concept," in *Cultural Communication and Conflict: Readings in Intercultural Relations*, 2nd ed., G. R. Weaver, ed. (Boston: Pearson, 2000), 139.

Chapter 2

1. James C. McCroskey, "Classroom Consequences of Communication Apprehension," *Communication Education* 26 (1977): 27.
2. Bruskin Associates, "What Are Americans Afraid Of?" *The Bruskin Report,* no. 53 (1971).
3. Douglas H. Powell, "Treating Individuals with Debilitating Performance Anxiety: An Introduction," *Journal of Clinical Psychology* 60, no. 8 (2004): 801–808.
4. James C. McCroskey, *Introduction to Rhetorical Communication,* 5th ed. (Englewood Cliffs, NJ: Prentice-Hall, 1986), 24.

5. J. A. Daly, A. L. Vangelisti, and S. G. Lawrence, "Self-Focused Attention and Public Speaking Anxiety," *Personality and Individual Difference* 10 (1989): 903–913.
6. Camille D. Smith, Chris R. Sawyer, and Ralph R. Behnke, "Physical Symptoms of Discomfort Associated with Worry about Giving a Public Speech," *Communication Reports* 18, no. 1–2 (April/October 2005): 31–41.
7. Gail Fann Thomas, Walter G. Tymon, and Kenneth W. Thomas, "Communication Apprehension, Interpretive Styles, Preparation, and Performance in Oral Briefing," *The Journal of Business Communication* 31, no. 4 (1994): 314.
8. Susan Zarrow, "Picture Yourself Successful; Visualization Works," *Prevention* 42, no. 3 (March 1990): 16.
9. Lawrence R. Wheeless, "An Investigation of Receiver Apprehension and Social Context Dimensions of Communication Apprehension," *The Speech Teacher* 24, (1975): 263.
10. Charles D. Spielberger, *Manual for the State-Trait Anxiety Inventory (Form Y)* (Palo Alto, CA: Consulting Psychologists Press, 1983); and Elaine K. Horwitz, M. B. Horwitz, and J. A. Cope, "Foreign Language Classrooom Anxiety," *The Modern Language Journal* 70 (1986): 125–132.
11. Elaine K. Horwitz, "Language Anxiety and Achievement," *Annual Review of Applied Linguistics* 21 (2001): 112–126; and Peter D. MacIntryre, "How Does Anxiety Affect Second Language Learning? A Reply to Sparks and Ganschow," *The Modern Langauge Journal* 79 (1995): 90–99.
12. Peter D. MacIntyre, Kimberly A. Noels, and Richard Clement, "Biases in Self-Ratings of Second Language Proficiency: The Role of Language Anxiety," *Language Learning* 47, no. 2 (1997): 272–278.
13. Robert McCrum, William Cran, and Robert MacNeil, *The Story of English* (New York: Penguin, 1992), 1.
14. Ibid.
15. I recommend Diana Hacker's *A Writer's Reference,* 5th ed. (Bedford/St. Martin's, 2004), which offers extensive rules on all aspects of writing and includes a comprehensive section on ESL trouble spots that many students have found particularly helpful.

Chapter 3

1. Richard L. Johannesen, *Ethics in Human Communication,* 5th ed. (Prospect Heights, IL: Waveland Press, 1996), 2.
2. Virginia L. Downie, Personal interview, April 20, 2004.
3. Stephen E. Lucas, *The Art of Public Speaking,* 7th ed. (New York: McGraw Hill, 2001), 40.
4. George W. Bush, "President Delivers 'State of the Union Address,' " *The White House,* January 28, 2003, http://www.whitehouse.gov/news/releases/2-003/01/2003012819.html.
5. Sen. Ted Kennedy quoted in Dana Bash, "Democrats Want Uranium Claim Probed," CNN.com, July 9, 2003, http://www.cnn.com/2003/ALLPOLITICS/07/-08/sprj.irq.bush.sotu/.
6. "The Celebrated 'Roots' of a Lie," *New York Post* (January 16, 2002). NewYorkPost.com, http://www.nypost.com/cgi-bin/printfriendly.pl (retrieved March 28, 2004)
7. Carolyn Matalene, "Contrastive Rhetoric: An American Writing Teacher in China," *College English* 47 (1985): 803. 789–808.

8. Lenora C. Thompson and Portia G. Williams, "But I Changed Three Words! Plagiarism in the ESL Classroom," *The Clearing House* 69, no. 1 (September–October 1995): 27–29.
9. Lise Buranen, "But I *Wasn't* Cheating: Plagiarism and Cross-Cultural Mythology," in *Perspectives on Plagiarism and Intellectual Property in a Postmodern World,* Lise Buranen and Alice M. Roy, eds. (New York: State University of New York Press, 1999), 69.
10. Virginia L. Downie, *Together: A Relationship Survival Kit* (Upland, CA: Real Life Publications, 2002), 6.
11. Ibid.
12. "International Student Enrollment Growth Slows in 2002/2003, Large Gains from Leading Countries Offset Numerous Decreases," *Institute of International Education,* November 17, 2003, http://opendoors.iienetwork.org/?p=36523.
13. Dennis M. Kratz and Abby Robinson Kratz, in Michael Packard, "Listening for Sounds of Success: Tips for Effective Listening," *RV Business* 48, no. 7 (October 1997): 18.
14. Euen Hyuk (Sarah) Jung, "The Role of Discourse Signaling Cues in Second Language Listening Comprehension," *The Modern Language Journal* 87, no. iv (2003): 563.
15. John Field, "Promoting Perception: Lexical Segmentation in L2 Listening," *ELT Journal* 57, no. 4 (October 2003): 327.

Chapter 4

1. Gina Lucente-Cole, "Delivering an Effective Presentation," *Public Relations Quarterly* 49, no. 4 (Winter 2004): 42.
2. Stephen E. Lucas, *The Art of Public Speaking,* 7th ed., Instructor's Edition (New York: McGraw Hill, 2001), 104.
3. Myron W. Lustig and Jolene Koester, *Intercultural Competence: Interpersonal Communication Across Cultures,* 3rd ed. (New York: Addison Wesley Longman, Inc., 1999), 35.
4. Ibid.
5. Elizabeth Urech, *Speaking Globally* (Dover, NH: Kogan Page Limited, 1998), 189.
6. Ibid., 189.
7. Ibid., 160.
8. ACLU Washington. *About the ACLU,* http://www.aclu-wa.org/about.html (retrieved April 25, 2004).
9. Federal Bureau of Investigation Website. *FBI Priorities,* http://www.fbi.gov/priorities/priorities.htm (retrieved April 25, 2004).
10. Robert S. Mueller, III, "The New FBI: Protecting Americans Against Terrorism," *ACLU 2003 Inaugural Membership Conference,* June 13, 2003, http://www.aclu.org/Conference/Conference.cfm?ID=12909&c=256 (retrieved April 25, 2004).
11. Eric Lichtblau, "F.B.I. Leader Wins a Few at Meeting of A.C.L.U." *New York Times,* June 14, 2003, http://www.nytimes.com/2003/06/14/politics/14ACLU.html?ex=1083038400&en=8080cf1e640c8c10&ei=5070 (retrieved April 25, 2004).
12. Patti A. Wood, "What Are They Thinking? How to Read and Respond to Your Audience's Body Language," *Consulting to Management* 16, no. 4 (December 2005): 28–29.

Chapter 5

1. John A. Daly, Anita L. Vangelisti, Heather L. Neel, and Daniel P. Cavanaugh, "Pre-performance Concerns Associated with Public Speaking Anxiety," *Communication Quarterly* 37, no. 1 (Winter 1989): 39–53.
2. Andrew Rosenbaum, "Chart the Course of Your Negotiation," *Harvard Management Communication Letter* 6, no. 8 (July 2003): 3–4.
3. Asha Tickoo, "On Variable Temporal Passage in Storytelling: Identifying Constraints and Evidencing Constraint Violation in the Narratives of Second-Language Writers," *Text* 23, no. 1 (2003): 129–163.
4. Carolyn Boiarsky, "The Relationship Between Cultural and Rhetorical Conventions: Engaging in International Communication," *Technical Communication Quarterly* 4, no. 3 (Summer 1995): 245.

Chapter 6

1. From the *National Diet Library Newsletter, #133,* National Diet Library (October 2003), http://www.ndl.go.jp/en/publication/ndl_newsletter/133/334.html (retrieved July 14, 2004).
2. Danny Sullivan, ed., *Search Engine Watch* (September 2003), http://searchenginewatch.com/reports/article.php/2156481 (retrieved July 23, 2004).
3. "Additional Crime Facts at a Glance." *National Crime Victimization Survey, Bureau of Justice Statistics* (August 24, 2003), http://www.ojp.usdoj.gov/bjs/gvc.htm (retrieved July 23, 2004).
4. American Cancer Society, *Cancer Prevention and Early Detection Facts & Figures 2004,* 5.
5. Michael Coren, "NASA Turns to Deep Sea Training for Space," *Science and Space.* CNN.com, http://www.cnn.com/2004/TECH/space/07/23/aquarius.habitat/index.html (retrieved July 23, 2004).

Chapter 7

1. Sten Odenwald, "What Is the Speed of the Earth's Rotation?" *Ask the Space Scientist*, NASA Image/Poetry Education and Public Outreach Program, http://image.gsfc.nasa.gov/poetry/ask/a10840.html (retrieved July 25, 2004).
2. "What Is Nanotechnology?" *National Nanotechnology Initiative*, National Nanotechnology Coordination Office, http://www.nano.gov/html/facts/whatIsNano.html (retrieved July 25, 2004).
3. Interview w/Donna Bauman August, 2004. Executive at of Canada
4. Leslie Valdivia, "Misconceptions about Alcoholism." In-class speech, April 2002.
5. Jacques Duchesneau, "Notes for a Speech," *International Trade and Technology Summit*, Canadian Air Transport Security Authority (CATSA), (June 24, 2004), http://www.catsa-acsta.gc.ca/english/media/speech_discours/2004-06-24.htm (retrieved July 27, 2004).
6. U.S. Department of Transportation, National Highway Traffic Safety Administration, "State Alcohol Related Fatality Report 2002." DOT HS 809 673 (December 2003): 9, *National Center for Statistics and Analysis* (retrieved July 27, 2004).
7. National Coalition to Abolish the Death Penalty, "Deterrence . . . Fact or Fiction," http://www.ncadp.org/html/fact5.html (retrieved July 27, 2004).
8. Hunter G. Hoffman, "Virtual-Reality Therapy," *Scientific American* (August 2004): 60.

9. Martin Luther King, Jr., "I Have a Dream." Washington, D.C. August 28, 1963.
10. "Ryan Matthews Is 115th Death Row Inmate Freed," Death Penalty Information Center, http://www.deathpenaltyinfo.org/ (retrieved August 9, 2004).
11. "The Death Penalty in the United States," *The Clark County Prosecuting Attorney Death Penalty page*, Clark County Prosecuter, http://www.clarkprosecutor.org/html/death/dpusa.htm (retrieved August 9, 2004).
12. "Highlights from the Condition of Education 2004: Postsecondary Education," National Center for Education Statistics http://nces.ed.gov//programs/coe/highlights/h5.asp (retrieved August 10, 2004).

Chapter 8

1. Nathan Stormer, "Articulation: A Working Paper on Rhetoric and Taxis," *Quarterly Journal of Speech* 90, no. 3 (August 2004): 275.
2. Alexandra Rowe Henry, *Second Language Rhetorics in Process: A Comparison of Arabic, Chinese, and Spanish* (New York: Peter Lang, 1993), 101.
3. Robert B. Kaplan, "Cultural Thought Patterns in Intercultural Education," *Language Learning* 16 (1966): 15.
4. Clayann Gilliam Panetta, *Contrastive Rhetoric Revisited and Redefined* (Mahwah, NJ: Lawrence Erlbaum Associates, Publishers, 2001), 5.
5. Jan Corbett, "Contrastive Rhetoric and Resistance to Writing," in *Contrastive Rhetoric Revisited and Redefined,* Clayann Gilliam Panetta, ed. (Mahwah, NJ: Lawrence Erlbaum Associates, Publishers, 2001), 34.
6. A Mohammed Akram A. M. Sa'Adeddin, "Text Development and Arabic-English Negative Interference," *Applied Linguistics* 10 (1989): 36–51.
7. Ibid.
8. M. G. Clyne, "Cultural Differences in the Organization of Academic Texts: English and German," *Journal of Pragmatics* 11, no. 2 (1987): 239.
9. Ann Lowry, "Style Range in New English Literatures," in *The Other Tongue,* 2nd ed., Braj B. Kachru, ed. (Urbana, IL: University of Illinois Press, 1992), 296.
10. Tad Simons, "Great Beginnings," *Sales and Marketing Management* 157, no. 9 (September 2005): 40–45.
11. Clarence Darrow *The Story of my Life* 1932 New York: Charles Serebners over for 10c 1-3: References for Table 8.3 10d Claire Deal "Preparing & Delivering and Presentations: Organizing and Quttening your topic" (9/15/01) Retrieved on 2/17/07 from http://people.hsc.edu/facutty-staff/cdea/students/orgaout.htm
12. Nelson Mandela, "Nobel Peace Prize Address," *Social Justice Speeches Project* (December 10, 1993, http://www.edchange.org/multicultural/speeches/mandela_nobel.html (retrieved August 26, 2004).

Chapter 9

1. Mitchell R. Burkowsky, *Teaching American Pronunciation to Foreign Students* (St. Louis, MO: Warren H. Green, Inc., 1969), 7.
2. "Typical ESL Problems," *University Writing Center, Cal State L.A.* (November 26, 2004), http://web.calstatela.edu/centers/write_cn/esltyp.htm.

Chapter 10

1. Liane Hansen, "China's Former Premier Cedes Final Post," Oral Introduction (September 18, 2004), *Weekend Edition* on NPR.org. Audio. http://www.npr.org/rundowns/rundown.php?prgId=10&prgDate=current.

2. "China's Former Premier Cedes Final Post," Written Introduction (September 18, 2004), *Weekend Edition* on NPR.org. Audio. http://www.npr.org/rundowns/rundown.php?prgId=10&prgDate=current.
3. Carly Fiorina, Address to Tsinghua University, Beijing, China, March 11, 2004.
4. I thank Dr. Peter Marston for sharing this example with me. This has been a very useful and successful example for explaining the connotation/denotation distinction to my students for the past several years.
5. Yamuna Kachru, "Culture, Style, and Discourse: Expanding Noetics of English," in *The Other Tongue: English Across Cultures,* 2nd ed., Braj B. Kachru, ed. (Urbana, IL: University of Illinois Press, 1992), 340.
6. Vincent Muli Wa Kituku, "Tapping the True Power of a Metaphor Requires Creativity," *Presentations* 17, no. 7 (July 2003): 58.
7. Martin Luther King, Jr., "I Have a Dream," Washington, D.C. August 28, 1963.
8. William J. Clinton, "Our New Covenant: 1992 Democratic National Convention Acceptance Address." New York. July 16, 1992.
9. Kathryn M. Olson and Clark D. Olson, "Beyond Strategy: A Reader-Centered Analysis of Irony's Dual Persuasive Uses," *Quarterly Journal of Speech* 90, no. 1 (February 2004): 45.
10. Robert F. Kennedy, "Remarks on the Assassination of Martin Luther King, Jr." Indianapolis, IN. April 4, 1968.
11. Richard M. Nixon, "First Inaugural Address." Washington, D.C. January 20, 1969.

Chapter 11

1. Candie Jones, "Good Intentions, Bad Presentations," *Chronicle of Philanthropy* 18, no. 17 (June 15, 2006): 34–35.
2. Marguerite Foxon, "I Know You Can't See This But. . . . ," *Training* 29, no. 11 (November 1992): 47.
3. Andrew Wahl, "PowerPoint of No Return," *Canadian Business Magazine* 76, no. 22 (November 23, 2003): 131.
4. Doug Carter, "Avoiding PowerPoint Poison," *Proofs* (November 2005): 67.

Chapter 12

1. H. Dennis Beaver, "They Don't Like My Accent," *ABA Banking Journal* (May 2006): 49.
2. Susan M. Fredricks, "Teaching Impromptu Speaking: A Pictorial Approach," *Communication Teacher* 19, no. 3 (July 2005): 75–79.
3. Lois L. Hinkle, "Perceptions of Supervisor Nonverbal Immediacy, Vocalics, and Subordinate Liking," *Communication Research Reports* 18, no. 2 (Spring 2001): 128–136.
4. Angel A. Portalatín Martínez, "Fluency and the Planned and Unplanned Speech of Spanish-English Bilinguals," master's thesis, University of Puerto Rico, 2004.
5. Sandra C. Lozano and Barbara Tversky, "Communicative Gestures Facilitate Problem Solving for Both Communicators and Recipients," *Journal of Memory & Language* 55, no. 1 (July 2006): 47–63.
6. Marianne Gullberg, "Some Reasons for Studying Gesture and Second Language Acquisition," *International Review of Applied Linguistics in Language Teaching* 44, no. 2 (2006): 103–124.
7. Marianne Gullberg and Kenneth Homqvist, "What Speakers Do and What Addressees Look At," *Pragmatics & Cognition* 14, no. 1 (2006): 52–82.

8. C. Peter Giuliano and Frank J. Carillo, "Going Blank in the Board Room: What to Do When You Forget What to Say," *Public Relations Quarterly* (Winter 2003): 35–36.
9. Paul Evans, "20 Public-Speaking Tips for Clarity, Connection and Confidence," *Presentations* 19, no. 12 (December 2005): 38.

Chapter 13

1. Dave Frishberg, "I'm Just a Bill, Sitting on Capitol Hill," *School House Rocks,* 1972.
2. "Aircraft Flight Safety Research," *Galaxy Scientific: Innovative Technical Solutions,* April 14, 2005, http://www.galaxyscientific.com/areas/safetech/acs3.htm.
3. "Traditional Chinese Wedding Customs," *Chinese Poems,* April 14, 2005, http://www.chinese-poems.com/wedcus.html.

Chapter 14

1. Virginia M. McDermott, "Using Motivated Sequence in Persuasive Speaking: The Speech for Charity," *Communication Teacher* 18, no. 1 (January 2004): 13–14.
2. Aristotle, *On Rhetoric.* Trans. George A. Kennedy (New York: Oxford University Press, 1991).
3. Deanna D. Sellnow and Kristen P. Treinen, "The Role of Gender in Perceived Speaker Competence: An Analysis of Student Peer Critiques," *Communication Education* 53, no. 3 (July 2004): 286–296.
4. H. Dennis Beaver, "They Don't Like My Accent," *ABA Banking Journal* (May 2006): 49.
5. Tad Simons, "Great Beginnings," *Sales and Marketing Management* 157, no. 9 (September 2005): 40–45.
6. David R. Roskos-Ewoldsen, H. Jessy Yu, and Nancy Rhodes, "Fear Appeal Messages Affect Accessibility of Attitudes Toward the Threat and Adaptive Behaviors," *Communication Monographs* 71, no. 1 (March 2004): 49–69.
7. Joanna Slan, *Using Stories and Humor: Grab Your Audience* (Boston: Allyn & Bacon, 1998), 5–6.
8. Vincent Kituku, "When Using Stories, Capitalize on Perspectives," *Presentations* 19, no. 6 (June 2005): 50.
9. Roderick P. Hart, *Narrative and Reasoning, Modern Rhetorical Criticism* (Glenview, IL: Scott Foresman, 1990).
10. Walter R. Fisher, *Human Communication as Narration: Toward a Philosophy of Reason, Value and Action* (Columbia, SC: University of South Carolina Press, 1987), 68.
11. Barbara Johnstone, "Linguistic Strategies for Persuasive Discourse," in *Language, Communication, and Culture: Current Directions,* Stella Ting-Toomey and Felipe Korzenny, eds. (Newbury Park, CA: Sage, 1989), 139–156.
12. George Kennedy, *Comparative Rhetoric: An Historical and Cross-Cultural Introduction* (New York: Oxford University Press, 1998), 225.

Glossary

absolutes: Words that leave no room for exceptions, are often used to make sweeping generalizations.

abstract language: Words that have a general, non-specific relationship to the people, places, and things they refer to than do more concrete terms.

abstract: a brief overview of a book or article used to quickly identify the key subject areas and conclusions of the work.

abstractive thinking: A manner of processing new information using a variety of sources to imagine or visualize the new ideas or concepts; going beyond what one has experienced and relate a new idea to general principles.

accent: The way in which people from various regions or backgrounds pronounce and articulate a given language.

achievement-nurturance: The cultural taxonomy that distinguishes to what degree achievement traits versus nurturing traits are valued and rewarded among cultures.

adrenaline: One of the "fear" hormones that is released into the blood stream when a person feels fear or senses danger.

alliteration: The repetition of the same sound at the beginning of a series of words.

American Psychological Association (APA): often refers to the APA's standards for writing and reference.

analogical: A logical style that relies on stories, analogies or parables to make an argument.

analogy: A comparison between two different things that are in some ways similar.

- *Figurative*: An analogy that finds similarities between seemingly unrelated things.
- *Literal*: An analogy that makes comparisons to events, times, places, and people that are actually very similar.

annotation: A brief summary, note, comment, or explanation about a text.

antithesis: The juxtaposing of two contrasting ideas to create a balance.

articulation: How clearly one says words, phrases, or sentences; a subset of pronunciation.

associative thinking: A manner of processing new information by relating new ideas and concepts to personal past experiences.

audience analysis: Examining a potential audience to better understand their experiences and emotions in order to adapt a message to them.

bibliography: A list of resources at the end of a text that indicates where the author found his/her information and other possible sources for further information on the subject.

body: The main section of the speech that contains the main points and supporting material.

Boolean searching: A method of combining search terms in a database using *and, or* and *not*.

brainstorming: An idea generating technique used to develop creative solutions to a problem or for generating topic ideas for a speech.

call number: A number used to organize and locate materials, such as books, magazines, and journals, in a library.

canons of rhetoric: The set of five principle rules for preparing and delivering a speech developed in the early Western rhetorical tradition. They are: invention, arrangement, style, memory, and delivery.

captive audiences: 1. An audience that is in attendance because of a sense of obligation or requirement (e.g. attending traffic school). 2. An audience that is so interested in the presentation that they can't pull themselves or their attention away.

card catalog: Traditionally, the alphabetical listing of all materials in the library on small cards by author, subject, or title used to locate materials in the library.

causal organization: The organizational pattern that shows a cause and effect relationship. The causal pattern has two main points: one that identifies the cause of a problem and one that identifies the effect of a problem.

channel: The means by which a message travels from the sender to the receiver.

chronological organization: The organizational pattern that follows a time or sequence order.

circulation (circulation desk): The location in the library where one applies for a library card, checks out books, or returns books.

citation: A notation that identifies the source of information that includes the author, publisher, title, and date.

cite: To document or give credit to a source of information; to quote a person or mention an example as proof or support.

co-culture: Groups of people within a larger culture (dominant culture) that have notably different characteristics, values, beliefs, behaviors, and norms from the larger culture, while still sharing many of the characteristics, values, behaviors and norms of the larger culture.

colloquial: Informal language that is used in everyday conversation.

communication apprehension: The fear and/or anxiety associated with communicating with another person or persons.

communication competence: The ability to communicate appropriately and effectively.

comparative advantage: The organizational pattern that compares two or more possible solutions to the problem showing how one solution is the best alternative compared to the others.

comparative rhetoric: The study of rhetorical traditions across cultures in societies around the world and over time.

conclusion: The last section of the speech that summarizes the speech's main ideas.

concrete language: Words that have a close one-to-one relationship with the people, places, and things they refer to than do terms that are more general.

connectives: Words, phrases, or sentences that link the various sections and main points of a speech together.

connotation: The emotional, personal meaning of a word that varies from person-to-person.

context: All the influences that surround and affect a communication interaction, such as the time, place, and occasion, and the cultural, psychological and historical context of the interaction.

contextual audience analysis: A type of audience analysis that considers the contextual influences of the speaking situation, such as time of day and venue.

contrastive rhetoric: The study of writing styles across cultures to identify varying rhetorical structures.

cortisol: One of the "fear" hormones that is released into the blood stream when a person feels fear or senses danger.

count Noun: A noun that represents something that can be counted individually.

count: A number indicating how many there are of something.

credibility: The relative believability and trustworthiness of the speaker.

criteria-satisfaction organization: The organizational pattern used in persuasive speeches aimed at making value judgments wherein the speaker establishes a set of criteria for evaluation and then evaluates something based upon those criteria.

cultural patterns: The imbedded system of beliefs and values within the people of a culture that work in combination to provide a model for perceiving and behaving the world.

culture: A group of people that share the same beliefs, values, norms, and behaviors across time.

database: A computerized collection of related information organized for rapid search and retrieval.

decode: The process of translating a message that has been sent into an understandable idea based on the receiver's experience.

deductive reasoning: A type of argument that often begins with general and accepted principles then moves to specific conclusions wherein if the premises are true, the conclusion must be accepted.

demographic audience analysis: A type of audience analysis that considers categorical influences, such as ethnicity, sex, religion, or political affiliation, on one's audience.

demographics: A list of general characteristics of a particular group of people, audience or segment of the population.

denotation: The most literal meaning of a word; the definition of a word found in the dictionary.

dialect: A form of a language that has significant vocabulary, grammatical and pronunciation differences.

dispositional audience analysis: A type of audience analysis that considers the attitudes of the audience toward the speaker, the occasion, and the topic.

due date: The date by which borrowed library materials should be returned or renewed.

emphasizers: Phrases and words that highlight important ideas for the audience.

encode: The process of translating an idea into a message that can be sent.

epithet: A word or phrase that is abusive or disparaging.

ethics: A system of moral principles that govern proper behavior.

ethos: One of Aristotle's proofs that refers to the speaker's credibility; the character and competence of a speaker.

etymology: The origins, history, development, and evolution of words or parts of words.

examples: Specific references or stories that illustrate and clarify a point, idea, theory, skill or opinion.

- *Brief Examples*: relatively short examples designed to clarify a small point or single word or idea, often ranging from one word to a sentence long.
- *Extended Examples*: Longer examples that offer greater detail and support a larger point.
- *Factual Examples*: Examples taken from actual events, people, or things. Based in reality.
- *Hypothetical Examples*: Examples that are invented by the speaker, not based in reality.

expert: An individual with special education or experience with regard to a particular field or topic.

expressions: Unique groupings of words that communicate an idea, thought or feeling.

fact: Something that is undeniably true; a piece of information that can be proven to exist or to have happened.

faith, feeling and fact dimension: The types of evidence people feel is the most credible, relevant, and meaningful; what a culture is likely to value most as *truth*—belief in a religious, political or moral ideal, subjective feelings or objective facts.

feedback: Any verbal or nonverbal message that the receiver sends to the sender as a response to that message.

fidelity: A narrative term that refers to the reasonableness or truthfulness of a story.

fight versus flight response: The most fundamental human fear response to fear and danger that tells the person to either run/retreat or to stand and fight.

figure of speech: An expression that takes an abstract thought, idea, or concept and makes it easily understandable through a creative and non-literal use of words. A figure of speech is a creative and succinct way to convey a lot of meaning in only a few words, or it can be a gentler way of conveying something negative.

filler words: Words and phrases a speaker throws between words or sentences to fill otherwise empty space or space where a pause might otherwise be found.

fixed-alternative questions: Survey questions that ask respondents to choose between one or two choices, usually *yes, no,* and *maybe* (or *unsure*).

general purpose: The overriding goal of the speech expressed in the infinitive verb form that guides the development of the topic. A general purpose can be to inform, to persuade, or to entertain.

government publication: An official document issued by a government agency.

group communication: Communication among three or more people, usually in work or decision making groups.

hate speech: Language and speech that attacks or disparages a group of people based on membership in a particular ethnicity, religion, sexual orientation, or other social group.

heterogeneous audiences: Audiences representing a wide diversity of origins, backgrounds, experiences, and attitudes.

high context cultures: Those cultures that rely more heavily on the contextual cues of a communication interaction to discern much of the meaning.

hit: A web page or source retrieved that match specific search criteria when searching for information on a database or on the Internet.

homogenous audiences: Audiences made up of people with similar backgrounds, attitudes, and experiences

homonyms: Two or more words that have the same sound or are pronounced the same, but have different meanings.

homophobic language: Discriminatory language based on sexual preference.

hostile audience: An audience that is not favorable to the speaker and/or the topic or position of the speech.

hyperbole: An exaggeration used to make a point or for its effect.

hyperventilation: Breathing too rapidly causing light-headedness and possibly fainting.

idioms: A type of expression that does not follow a set of rules and often contradict language rules; an expression that cannot be understood from the individual words used, but must be learned as a whole.

immediate action: A type of proposition of policy that asks the audience to take a specific action.

inclusive language: Language that considers and includes often excluded or marginalized groups.

indiscriminate language: Language that does not make distinctions about people, actions, or members of a category.

individualism-collectivism: The cultural taxonomy that distinguishes between cultures that focus more on individuals versus those that focus more on groups.

inductive reasoning: A type of argument that makes general conclusions based on specific examples or observations.

inference: Believing something to be true based on available evidence and reasoning; an implied *truth*; drawing a conclusion based on evidence and reasoning.

integrity: The unwavering commitment to high moral or ethical principles and behavior.

interface: The computer document or webpage where a user inputs search terms to retrieve information; a graphic or text-based display by which a user navigates through a program or application digitally.

interference/noise: Anything that changes, distorts, or obstructs the message from being received as intended. There are three kinds: physical, physiological, and psychological.

interlibrary loan: A library program that allows users to borrow books and materials from other partner libraries.

internet: A worldwide system of networks that interconnects computers.

interpersonal communication: Communication between two people.

intrapersonal communication: Communication with oneself.

introduction: The beginning section of the speech that gains the audience's attention, relates the topic to the audience, establishes the speaker's credibility, and previews the main points.

irregular verbs: Verbs that do not follow the regular conjugation rules of a language.

keynote speaker: The main speaker at an event or the person who delivers the most important speech at an event (esp. at a conference, convention, or political event).

keywords (also key words or subject terms): The words you use to find the information in a database. Keywords are usually drawn from the terminology used in the field of study in question.

laypeople: Everyday people who have no particular expertise in terms of education or work experience with regard to a particular topic, but do have relevant personal experiences, reactions, and emotions.

library classification system: The manner in which a library collection is organized so that allows people to find materials quickly and easily.

- Dewey Decimal System: The most widely used library classification system in the world.
- Library of Congress Classification System: The library classification used by the United States' Library of Congress as well as most academic libraries.
- National Diet Library System (NDLC): The library classification system used in Japan.

loan period: The length of time library materials may be borrowed.

logical fallacy: A mistake in reasoning; when an argument's reasoning does not follow the premises even when the premises are true.

logos: One of Aristotle's proofs that refers to the logic and reasoning of an argument.

low context cultures: Those cultures that rely more heavily on the actual words spoken in a communication interaction to discern much of the meaning.

mass communication: Communication that is directed toward large numbers of people, usually the general public. It is often characterized as being one-way as it is difficult for feedback to be given.

message: An idea that has been encoded into a form that can be received by others.

nonverbal communication: Communication that does not use language.

organizational communication: Communication among larger groups of people (from 15 up to several hundred) within the context of an organization or network.

metaphor: A non-literal comparison between two seemingly very different things. A type of analogy between two things that are similar in some respects by claiming that the first thing *is* the second.

metasearch engines: A search tool that searches several search engines simultaneously and provide the results of all the searches on one page.

microform: A storage format that reduces the images of articles and books for compact storage and easy retrieval. Microform requires special machines supplied by the library for reading the material.

mind mapping: A brainstorming technique that starts with a general subject, that one builds upon by free association and connecting the ideas graphically.

mixed metaphors: The inappropriate combining of two unrelated metaphors together.

Modern Language Association (MLA): often refers to the MLA's standards for writing and reference.

Monroe's Motivated Sequence: The five point organizational pattern used in persuasive speeches that call for a specific action from the audience.

mythos: A proof that refers to storytelling or narrative as a form of evidence for an argument.

narrative: The storytelling approach to argumentation.

neutral audience: An audience that is neither favorable nor unfavorable toward the speaker and/or the topic or position of the speech.

noncount noun: A noun that represents something that cannot be counted individually or that represents a concept or abstract idea.

nonverbal communication: Communication that does not employ the use of language—written, signed, or spoken.

nonverbal feedback: Responses to messages from others that are given with out the use of language.

objective evidence: Information that is based on factual information without regard to personal experience, opinions, or feelings.

Online Public Access Catalog (OPAC): A card catalog system that users can access through the Internet to locate materials in the library's collection.

open-ended questions: Survey questions that allow for detailed and open responses from respondents.

operational definition: A context specific definition tailored specifically by the speaker to clarify a particular term is to be understood for that discussion.

opinion: A personal view, preference, or attitude about an issue; judgment based on personal feelings, experiences and preferences; personal judgment.

organizational pattern: The manner in which speech or essay main points are logically organized.

overdue: A term that indicates that the book you checked out passed the return date. You will usually incur fees if you turn in library materials after the due date.

paraphrase: The act of putting someone else's words into one's own words.

passive agreement: A type of proposition of policy that asks the audience to simply agree with the speaker's policy plan; Passive agreement does not ask the audience to take action.

pathos: One of Aristotle's proofs that refers to the use of emotional appeals as evidence in an argument.

peer review: A system of review used to evaluate academic and professional research and writing before being accepted for publication.

phonemes: The individual sounds of a language that when combined make the words of the language.

plagiarism: An act of plagiarizing.
plagiarize: To use someone else's ideas or words as if they were one's own.
power distance: The cultural taxonomy that distinguishes cultures based on the relative acceptance people within a society have for large power inequities.
preparation outline: An extended outline of a speech used to prepare and organize the speech into full sentences.
presentational aids: Visual, audio, tactile and experiential supporting materials that are used in addition to, to complement or to reinforce the evidence provided in the speech text.
presentational style: A logical style that relies on personal experience, feelings, and emotions to persuade.
preview: A brief statement that indicates the main idea of the information that will follow.
previews: Statements that give the audience information about what is about to be discussed.
primacy: The first message received in a communication.
primary sources: Information you gather that comes from the actual event or individual(s) you are studying.
probability: A narrative term that refers to the coherency or likelihood of a story being real or realistic.
problem-solution organization: The organizational pattern that has two main points: one that identifies a problem and one that identifies a way to solve the problem.
profanity: Language or gestures that show disrespect for religion or God.
profanity: The "bad words" in a language; language that is offensive or disrespectful.
pronunciation: How accurately one says individual words.
proposition of fact: An assertion that is made about the truth or falsity of a statement.
proposition of policy: An assertion that makes a value judgment about the worth or righteousness of a policy, action or thing.
proposition of value: An assertion that advocates for a particular solution to a problem or for a specific course of action to be taken.
proverbs: Sayings that are passed down from one generation to the next that summarize many of the key values and beliefs of the culture.
provisional language: Language that expresses openness to alternative possibilities or exceptions.
quasilogical: A logical style that relies on objective evidence and linear reasoning to persuade.
quotation: Giving credit to and using the words of someone else to make a point, clarify an idea or support a position.
racist language: Discriminatory language based on race and ethnicity.
ratio: A manner of expressing a proportional relationship between two numbers.
receiver apprehension: A type of communication apprehension experienced by the receiver of the communication wherein the person fears misunderstanding or misinterpreting the messages of others.
receiver/listener/audience: The person who gets the message the sender is sending.
recency: The last, or most recently, received message in a communication.
reference collection: Research materials used frequently for general information, such as encyclopedias, dictionaries, indexes, and atlases.
reference desk: A desk usually located in or near the reference section of the library where you can find librarians to answer your research questions.
reference librarian: A librarian who specializes in the retrieval of information. They can be found at the reference desk of any library helping researchers (students, faculty, and the public) find the information they need.
relative language: Language that provides meaning by comparison.
renew: Extending the loan period of a book you have checked out.
repetition: The repeating of a word, phrase, or grammatical structure in a speech in order to create rhythm.
research guide: A document prepared by the librarian that highlights essential research materials on a specific subject.
reserves: Required books and other materials set aside by professors for students that may be borrowed for in-library use only.
resource: Anything that can be used to support or assist in writing.
rhetoric: The effective use of language in both speaking and writing; the study of persuasion and persuasive methods through speaking and writing.
rhetorical convention: The culture-specific manner in which messages are expected to be prepared and delivered in a particular context.
rhetorical Conventions: The culture-specific manner in which messages are expected to be prepared and delivered in a particular context.
rhetorical Situation: The elements (speaker, audience, topic, purpose and context) of a communication interaction that interact and influence each other and the interaction.
rhetorical Situation: The elements (speaker, audience, topic, purpose and context) of a communication interaction that interact and influence each other and the interaction.
rhetorical Structure: The manner in which a piece of rhetoric (writing or speech) is presented, developed, organized, and supported.
rhetorical Style: The manner in which a person builds and presents an argument.

rhythm: A somewhat predictable pattern created in a speech through a variety of linguistic tools that make a speech easier to follow and more interesting.
scaled questions: Survey questions that allow the interviewer to learn what respondents know and to what degree they agree or disagree.
search engine: A program found on the Internet that is designed to search for particular keywords on the net and provide links to the websites, pages, and documents that contain them.
secondary sources: Sources that are at least once removed from actual events or people but that interprets or analyzes the events or phenomena.
sender/speaker/source: The person who is sending a message to others whether intentionally or unintentionally.
sensitive language: Language choices that is not sexist, racist, homophobic or other wise hurtful or discriminatory.
serial/journal/magazine/periodical: A type of publication that is usually published weekly, monthly, quarterly, or annually in successive order.
sexist language: Discriminatory language based on sex and gender, usually discriminatory against women.
signaling connectives: (Also called *Signpost*) Words or phrases that highlight where in the speech or within a list a speaker is.
signposts: Single words or phrases that indicate in which section of the speech a speaker is or that emphasize key ideas.
simile: A comparison between two things using the terms *like* or *as*.
site: Short for web*site*—a group of interconnected web pages found on the Internet.
slang: Informal words, expressions and language used by people to replace more standard, formal or proper ones.
spatial organization: The organizational pattern that orders main points according to position or direction.
speaking outline: A brief outline of a speech that includes only a few key words and phrases that a speaker uses to deliver a speech.
specific purpose: A single infinitive phrase that identifies the audience and specific goal for a speech.
stacks: The bookshelves in the library where books, journals, and other printed material are kept.
static evaluations: A type of indiscriminate language that describes a person or thing in terms that indicate how the person or thing always is or a description that is unchanging.
statistics: Numerical values used to describe or characterize a defined grouping, population, or occurrence.
stereotypes: Oversimplified, standardized or formulaic image, idea or opinion about a group of people.
subdivide: The breaking down of an item, idea, or object into smaller parts.
subdivisions: The individual parts of a larger item that, when combined with the other individual parts, make up the whole.
subject headings: The formal and authoritative terms consistently used to describe the topics of library materials.
subject terms: See keywords
subjective evidence: Information that is based on personal experience, opinions, or feelings without regard to independent sources of information, such as facts and statistics.
sub-points (sub-sub-points): The subdivided and subordinate material used to support larger and primary points.
summaries: Statements that briefly review what has been discussed.
summary: A brief review of preceding information that includes only the most important aspects.
supporting material: Anything that clarifies, amplifies, proves, describes, explains, or makes more interesting a speech.
surfing the net: The act of searching a variety of web pages for information or entertainment.
sweeping generalizations: A type of indiscriminate language that claims a general truth about a large group or category that is based on limited inaccurate or incomplete evidence.
symbolization: The letters and numbers used to represent the various points and sub-points in an outline.
sympathetic audience: An audience that is both favorable to the speaker and to the topic or position of the speech.
terminology: A set of words and expressions used in a particular field or topic of study.
thesaurus: A type of dictionary that lists related words together, such as synonyms (words that have the same or similar meaning) and antonyms (words that have opposite meanings).
thesis: A single sentence that states the central idea and previews the main points of a speech or piece of writing.
topic: The general subject about on which the speech is focused.
topical organization: The organizational pattern that divides a topic into logical and consistent subdivisions.
transition: A connective sentence that leads out of one point into the next one.
trigger words: (Also called *Red Flag words*) Words that can shock, upset, startle, surprise, or otherwise activate a listener to have a strong emotional response.

uncertainty avoidance: The cultural taxonomy that distinguishes between cultures' relative comfort level with uncertainty and the unknown.

universal he: Using the singular third person, male pronoun as a generic reference to any person.

universal messages: Messages that convey common human emotions, experiences, and values regardless of culture or language.

values: A manner of expressing numbers in terms of their significance to a larger set of numbers.

- *Mean*: The average value of a set of numbers.
- *Median*: The value in a set of numbers that falls in the middle when the numbers have been arranged in ascending or descending order.
- *Mode*: The value that is found most frequently in a set of numbers.

verbal communication: Communication that uses language either spoken, written, or signed.

visualization: A technique for minimizing anxiety before a communication interaction wherein one imagines him or herself successfully performing the communication.

vulgarity: Crude, offensive or tasteless way of speaking or behaving.

WIIFM: (What's In It For Me) The idea that people will listen to and retain information that is relevant to them more than any other information.

word pairs: Two or more words that have similar meanings or pronunciations, but actually represent different meanings.

works cited: A page at the end of a document that provides all the source information used.

world wide web: The system that provides access to the Internet from personal computer.

Index

Credits

Page 1, © Richard Drew/AP Images; 5, 6, © Kobal Collection/Picture Desk; 24, © Themba Hadebe/AP Images; 26, © Dorling Kindersley Media Library; 28, 29, 31, © Grass Hemmert; 37, © DILBERT reprinted by permission of United Feature Syndicate, Inc.; 38, © Artville LLC/Getty Images; 41, AP Images; 42, © Kateland Photo; 46, © Bettmann/CORBIS, 54, Clay Bennett / © 1998 The Christian Science Monitor (www.csmonitor.com). All rights reserved; 66, AP Images; 68, 73, 75, 78, © Grass Hemmert; 88, AP Images; 95, © Tony Craddock/Photo Researchers; 100, © Grass Hemmert; 105, © J. Bucklan/Sygma/CORBIS; 108, Jeff Greenberg/PhotoEdit; 118, © Michael Nichols/National Geographic Image Collection; 122, © Comstock Royalty Free Division; 128, 130, © Grass Hemmert; 135, © Michael Newman/PhotoEdit; 136, © Grass Hemmert; 147, © AFP/Getty Images; 152, © Richard Price/Getty Images; 159, © Digital Vision/Getty Images; 169, © Micheline Pelletier/CORBIS; 171, © AP Images; 177, © Jon Lomberg/Photo Researchers; 179, © Robert Daly/Getty Images; 192, © AP Images; 205, © Ewing Galloway/Index Stock Imagery; 213, © Rick Kirkman & Jerry Scott/King Features Syndicate; 228, © Airedale Brothers/ Getty Images; 236, Leo Cullum © 1997 from The New Yorker Collection. All Rights Reserved; 242, © PhotoDisk/Getty Images; 246, © Michael Newman/PhotoEdit; 248, 255, © Hulton Archive/Getty Images; 261, © Dorling Kindersley Media Library; 266, © Frank Siteman; 267, © Dorling Kindersley Media Library; 275, © Jasper Juinen/AP Images; 276, © Bruce Gardner/Getty Images; 280, © Hulton Archive/Getty Images; 288, © Pearson Education/PH College; 290, © Grass Hemmert; 295, © Dwayne Newton/PhotoEdit; 296, © Dorling Kindersley Media Library; 300, © Alison Wright/CORBIS; 309, © Alan Evrard/Robert Harding World Imagery; 315, © Lee Celano/AFP/Getty Images; 317, © Grass Hemmert; 320, © Jacob Silberberg/Liaison/Getty Images; 327, © Hulton Archive/ Getty Images; 332, © AP Images; 342, American Cancer Society.